A LAWYER'S GUIDE TO

SECTION 337

INVESTIGATIONS

BEFORE THE

U.S. INTERNATIONAL

TRADE COMMISSION

SECOND EDITION

Tom M. Schaumberg, Editor

Cover design by Kelly Book/ABA Publishing.

The materials contained herein represent the opinions and views of the authors
and/or the editors, and should not be construed to be the views or opinions of
the law firms or companies with whom such persons are in partnership with,
associated with, or employed by, nor of the Section of Intellectual Property
Law of the American Bar Association unless adopted pursuant to the bylaws
of the Association.

Nothing contained in this book is to be considered as the rendering of legal
advice for specific cases, and readers are responsible for obtaining such advice
from their own legal counsel. This book and any forms and agreements herein
are intended for educational and informational purposes only.

17 16 15 14 13 6 5 4 3 2

Cataloging-in-Publication Data is on file with the Library of Congress

Section 337 Investigations Before the U.S. ITC/Tom M. Schaumberg, ed.

ISBN: 978-1-61438-769-5

Discounts are available for books ordered in bulk. Special consideration is
given to state bars, CLE programs, and other bar-related organizations. Inquire
at Book Publishing, ABA Publishing, American Bar Association, 321 North
Clark Street, Chicago, Illinois 60654.

www.ShopABA.org

Contents

Preface

This second edition of the guide reflects insights from more than 30 years of experience practicing under Section 337 by the editor and the firm of Adduci, Mastriani & Schaumberg, LLP. Source materials include numerous articles, speeches, legal memoranda, and briefs prepared over the years, which have been revised, edited, and updated for use here. In addition, newly written materials have been provided to fill in the gaps. Many new opinions and rules have been written by the Commission in the three years since the first edition and have been used in updating the materials.

The guide is intended to serve as an introduction to practice under Section 337 before the U.S. International Trade Commission (ITC) for those who are not familiar with it or those who want a quick update. The reader should not rely on the contents of the guide to provide legal advice but, rather, as a starting point for further inquiry. As practice under Section 337 has grown, so has interpretation of the law. Many precepts once taken for granted have been overruled, and others have arisen that will survive until challenged in the future.

The guide also provides analysis and explanation of the participants in Section 337 investigations and discusses the unique role played by the ITC. It also focuses on the procedural rules of a Section 337 investigation, including preparation of a complaint, the discovery process and other prehearing procedures, the hearing and post-hearing processes, and the remedies available to a successful complainant. Other elements addressed include enforcement of a violation ruling, parallel litigation, and appellate court review of an ITC decision. The guide will give the reader a clearer idea of what to expect when filing a complaint or in being named as a respondent in a Section 337 investigation.

Once a backwater of intellectual property practice, Section 337 has become mainstream as imports have come to play an ever more significant role in the U.S. economy. This has been particularly true over the last three years as the caseload has grown to 70 per year, practically double the 10-year average. We hope this guide will assist those who wish to learn more about the use of Section 337 and about practice before a little-known but active administrative agency entrusted with its administration.

Tom M. Schaumberg
Editor
September 2012

Acknowledgments

This second edition of the book would not have been possible without the tireless efforts of the entire firm of Adduci, Mastriani & Schaumberg, LLP and the support of Jim Adduci and Lou Mastriani. The undersigned specifically acknowledges the significant contributions of both partners and associates of the firm who added new information and updated the discussion of both law and procedure: Michael L. Doane, Sarah E. Hamblin, Deborah S. Strauss, Qian Sheng, Katherine R. Lahnstein, Daniel F. Smith, Asha Allam, Beau Jackson, Thomas R. Burns, Jr., Rowan E. Morris, Evan H. Langdon, Paul M. Bartkowski, Gregory F. Geary, Dana L. Watts, and Lauren E. Peterson. In addition, this edition benefited from the careful work performed by the firm's law clerks during the past year: Julia V. Svintsova, Aminata Sabally, Clare W. Adams, Dallin G. Glenn, and Sean J. Williams. Thanks also go to Marguerite G. Downey and Terri J. Barker, who provided a constant stream of new information for inclusion in this edition.

I wish to make special mention of the efforts of my partner, David H. Hollander, who helped edit and reorganize the manuscript, and Emi Ito, one of the firm's associates, who, in addition to her writing and editing responsibilities, maintained our procedural and organizational structure to get the job done.

Finally, I wish to thank Joseph Potenza and Denise DeFranco, leaders of the Intellectual Property Law Section of the ABA, for their encouragement in the initiation of the original project to create a guide for Section 337 practice.

Tom M. Schaumberg
Editor
September 2012

About the Editor

Tom M. Schaumberg has more than 30 years of experience before the U.S. International Trade Commission (ITC). He has handled more than 65 Section 337 investigations, has counseled and represented clients on licensing and trade policy issues, has conducted intellectual property litigation in the federal courts, and has engaged in international arbitration. Currently, Mr. Schaumberg is a partner with Adduci, Mastriani & Schaumberg, LLP, an international trade law firm based in Washington, D.C., with one of the largest and top-ranked Section 337 practices in the United States. He and his firm have received recognition from publications such as *Chambers USA: America's Leading Lawyers for Business, The Legal 500, IP Law & Business, Managing Intellectual Property,* and *SuperLawyers.*

A longtime advocate of the importance of Section 337 as an effective border enforcement mechanism against unfair import competition, Mr. Schaumberg has been a pioneer in various trade bar groups and associations with an interest in the statute. In 1984 he helped found the ITC Trial Lawyers Association, was its first president, and continues to participate on its executive committee. As an active member of the American Intellectual Property Law Association, he was asked to establish and chair the Committee on the International Trade Commission in 2007. Mr. Schaumberg also helped to establish and served on the ITC Committee of the Intellectual Property Owners Association and, from 2004 to 2006, served as the committee's first vice chair. He is a member of the Intellectual Property Law Sections of both the District of Columbia Bar and the American Bar Association, as well as a member of the Federal Circuit Bar Association.

Mr. Schaumberg has long been involved in shaping policies that have an impact on Section 337. Currently he is working on issues that have arisen under Section 337 with respect to non-practicing entities and standard-setting organizations. Mr. Schaumberg also spent time developing ideas with an ad hoc committee of interested corporations and organizations to address the 1988 General Agreement on Tariffs and Trade Panel

Report objecting to certain aspects of Section 337. These efforts contributed to the 1995 amendments to Section 337 establishing target dates, providing for district court stays, removing counterclaims to district court, and codifying commission practice with respect to general exclusion orders.

Mr. Schaumberg was born in Amsterdam, Holland. He studied for one year each at the University of Paris, France, and the University of Frankfurt, Germany, and he received his undergraduate degree from Yale University and his LLB from Harvard Law School. He is proficient in German, French, and Dutch. Mr. Schaumberg's international background, as well as his experience in antitrust, business, and administrative law, have enabled him to represent both domestic and foreign clients effectively in connection with international trade issues.

Mr. Schaumberg has lectured extensively before bar groups on international trade law and has published numerous articles on Section 337 practice. He was selected by the U.S. Trade Representative to serve on the bi-national panels convened under the United States–Canada Free-Trade Agreement to provide review of antidumping and countervailing duty decisions.

Prior to beginning his career as a Section 337 practitioner, Mr. Schaumberg was active as a business lawyer. He began his career as an attorney in the Merger Division, Bureau of Restraint of Trade, at the U.S. Federal Trade Commission. Mr. Schaumberg is admitted to the U.S. Supreme Court, where he had the privilege of arguing one of the first Freedom of Information Act cases; the U.S. Court of International Trade; and the U.S. Court of Appeals for the Federal Circuit.

List of Abbreviations

Administrative Law Judge	ALJ
Administrative Procedure Act	APA
Confidential Business Information	CBI
Initial Determination	ID
Intellectual Property	IP
Federal Circuit Advisory Council	FCAC
Fair, Reasonable, and Non-Discriminatory	FRAND
General Agreement on Tariffs and Trade	GATT
General Exclusion Order	GEO
Leahy-Smith America Invents Act	AIA
Limited Exclusion Order	LEO
Non-Practicing Entity	NPE
Office of the General Counsel	OGC
Office of the U.S. Trade Representative	USTR
Office of Unfair Import Investigations	OUII
Presidential Review Period	PRP
Recommended Determination	RD
Standard-Setting Organization	SSO
Temporary Exclusion Order	TEO
Uruguay Round Agreements Act	URAA
U.S. Court of Appeals for the Federal Circuit	CAFC
U.S. Court of International Trade	CIT
U.S. Customs and Border Protection	Customs
U.S. International Trade Commission	ITC or Commission
U.S. Patent and Trademark Office	PTO

CHAPTER 1

Introduction to
Section 337 Investigations

A primary concern for intellectual property (IP)[1] rights holders is protection from unfair foreign competition. Since the advent of the patent as a method of publicly disclosing novel inventions, it has been imperative that those inventions, and thus those patents, be protected during their period of exclusivity. This applies in the United States just as elsewhere in the world. Indeed, globalization of the marketplace has made IP protection and international trade inextricably linked. Enforcing U.S. patent and other IP rights is one way of protecting domestic industry from unfair competition emanating from outside the United States.[2]

Owners of U.S. IP, primarily patent owners, have used Section 337 of the Tariff Act of 1930 to protect their rights against infringing imported products. Although not widely used at its inception, Section 337 has become increasingly popular over the past 40 years as rights holders have learned how to take advantage of the protection the statute affords. The International Trade Commission (ITC or Commission) has sole authority to investigate alleged Section 337 violations. The ITC has become a popular forum for a multitude of reasons: the effective remedies it offers IP holders; its ability to conduct expedited hearings; its broad

---

1. Please refer to the "List of Abbreviations" at the beginning of this book for all abbreviations.

2. Section 337 can be used to address a variety of "unfair methods of competition and unfair acts," although the vast majority of cases involve claims regarding IP, the most frequent of which are allegations of patent infringement. *See* 19 U.S.C. § 1337(a)(1)(A) (2006). For that reason, this book speaks largely and generally about "infringement."

jurisdiction; and its specialized knowledge of patent law. The number of complaints instituted[3] increased from an annual average of 12 investigations during the years 1990 to 2000 to an annual average of 34 investigations for the years 2001 to 2011, with 2011 having set a record high of 69 new investigations and 2012 on a similar track.

Under the statute, the ITC has the power to exclude infringing products from entry into the United States. This exclusion is based on the existence of an unfair method of competition, which, in the case of patents, federal trademarks, and copyrights, is presumed or, for common law-based allegations, is proven to cause substantial injury to a domestic industry. Traditionally, the "domestic industry" criterion was satisfied by demonstrating that facilities, equipment, and labor in the United States were utilized to produce a protected item. However, in 1988, amendments to the law relaxed the domestic industry requirement in recognition of the fact that much actual production had moved off-shore. As the law stands now, importing articles that infringe a patent, federal trademark, or copyright is unlawful if "an industry in the United States" exists "relating to" articles protected by the patent, trademark, or copyright.[4] That industry is defined to "exist" if there is: (1) significant investment in plant and equipment; (2) significant employment of labor or capital; or (3) substantial investment in the exploitation of the patent, trademark, or copyright as evidenced by expenditures on engineering, research, development, or licensing.[5] The third portion of this definition, added as part of the 1988 amendments, means that, with respect to most cases brought under Section 337, it is no longer necessary for the complainant to have production facilities located in the United States. However, the meaning of "substantial" is not apparent from the statute itself or its legislative history and is being developed on a case-by-case basis, particularly in the context of "licensing."[6]

---

3. The filing of a complaint does not begin a formal ITC Section 337 investigation but, instead, results in a 30-day "presinstitution proceeding"; a Section 337 investigation on a complaint begins once the ITC "determine[s] whether the complaint is properly filed and whether an investigation should be instituted on the basis of the complaint" and provides official notice by publication in the Federal Register. *See* 19 C.F.R. §§ 210.8, 210.9, 210.10(a)-(b) (2012).

4. 19 U.S.C. § 1337(a)(2).

5. *Id.* at § 1337(a)(3).

6. The different industry requirements are discussed in Chapter 5, Section C, "Domestic Industry."

The 1988 amendments also eliminated the need to show injury to a domestic industry in patent, trademark, or copyright cases brought under Section 337. Seeking to make Section 337 "a more effective remedy for the protection of U.S. intellectual property rights," Congress determined that requiring proof of injury beyond that presumed by proof of the infringement itself was not necessary.[7] The elimination of this requirement has had an important practical effect: prior to the amendment, over half of the total expense litigating a Section 337 case was incurred in establishing injury, making such actions inaccessible to many prospective complainants. Without the burden of proving injury, many more IP owners can afford to bring a claim.[8]

A Section 337 investigation involves a number of players: the Commission itself, the administrative law judge,[9] an investigative attorney from the Office of Unfair Import Investigations (in most cases), the complainant(s), the respondent(s), possible third parties, the Office of the Secretary, and the Commission's General Counsel's office.[10] Nonetheless, the speed at which Section 337 investigations are conducted is remarkable—an important advantage for companies seeking immediate relief. The actual hearing generally occurs seven to nine months from the date of institution of the investigation, as opposed to the typical two to three years in federal district court. The majority of Section 337 investigations are targeted for completion in approximately 16 months, which is quicker than even the fastest dockets in the Eastern District of Virginia and the Eastern District of Texas.

---

7. H.R. Rep. No. 40-100, pt. 1, at 156 (1987).

8. *See* Andrew S. Newman, *The Amendments to Section 337: Increased Protection for Intellectual Property Rights*, 20 L. & Pol'y Int'l Bus. 571, 576 (1989).

9. Currently, there are six administrative law judges at the ITC.

10. The roles of these players are explained in Chapter 4, "Participants."

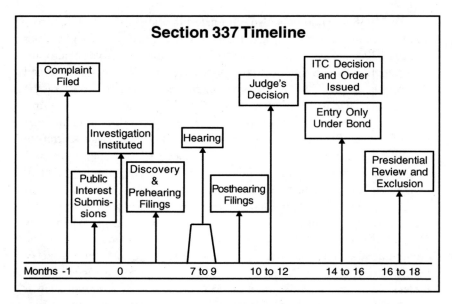

Although the ITC offers complainants a number of distinct advantages over a federal district court, there are a few drawbacks. First, a prospective complainant must make extensive preparations before filing a Section 337 complaint, as it requires more documentation than does notice pleading in federal district court. Second, there is a public interest aspect resulting from Section 337's origin as a trade statute. Third, and perhaps most important, a Section 337 investigation cannot result in a monetary award, whereas an infringement action in federal court can. However, a monetary award may not be critical to the IP owner, particularly when the infringing goods have just begun entering the market and protection of the market is the owner's paramount concern. Nevertheless, the options need not be mutually exclusive, as parallel litigation is possible: an IP owner may seek institution of a Section 337 investigation in conjunction with initiating an infringement action in federal court. However, 28 U.S.C. § 1659(a) gives the district court defendant a right to a stay the court action if it is also named as a respondent in a Section 337 investigation.

Between 2000 and 2011, almost 50 percent of investigations settled, 10 percent of complaints were withdrawn, and about 1 percent were terminated due to arbitration. Of the cases that received a final Commission determination, as might be expected in proceedings governed by due process, findings of violation and non-violation were virtually equal. There are four primary remedies available under the statute: a temporary exclusion order, a general exclusion order, a limited exclusion order, and a cease and desist order.[11] When an exclusion order becomes effective, U.S. Customs and Border Protection (Customs), which is part of the Department of Homeland Security, will bar the infringing products from entering the country. If there is evidence that infringing products are still entering the United States in violation of an exclusion order, an enforcement proceeding may take place at the ITC. Any party adversely affected by a Commission decision under Section 337 may appeal the decision to the U.S. Court of Appeals for the Federal Circuit.

A. HISTORICAL BACKGROUND

The ITC was established in 1916 as the U.S. Tariff Commission. Its primary function was to maintain and update the tariff schedules of the United States, a critical responsibility given the importance of tariffs on government revenue. It also acted as an independent, nonpartisan, quasi-judicial executive agency in charge of studying the economic effects of customs laws. When Section 337 of the Tariff Act of 1930 was enacted, it was not well understood and did not offer any defined procedures. Consequently, it was infrequently used.

That did not change until 1974, when the statute was significantly amended. These changes made Section 337 much more appealing to litigants seeking a quick remedy—namely, to stop the entry of infringing imports. First, all Section 337 investigations, at that time, were to be completed within 12 months, or, if deemed "more complicated," 18 months. Moreover, Section 337 investigations became subject to due process requirements under the Administrative Procedure Act,[12] thus mandating an adjudicative hearing.

Despite these changes, the revamped Section 337 did not immediately attract a substantial number of litigants. In 1975, only five investigations were launched, and, for the next decade, the Section 337 caseload remained extremely light. A few common denominators characterized Section 337 investigations from 1975 through 1984. Most of the articles involved were low-tech items, such as tools or basic consumer products.

---

11. The differences among these types of remedies can be found in Chapter 11, "Types of Relief."

12. The Administrative Procedure Act (APA) governs the manner in which federal administrative agencies create and enforce regulations in order to implement legislation. 5 U.S.C. §§ 551–559. Section 337 is unique among trade remedy laws in that it is the only such law subject to the APA.

In addition, individual patent holders and small companies were the most active in taking advantage of Section 337. Geographically, the majority of the allegedly infringing products, 62 percent, came from highly developed parts of the world: Western Europe, Canada, and Japan.

Between 1985 and 1994, two major developments stimulated great change in Section 337 litigation. The first development, and ultimately the most catalyzing event, was congressional passage of the Omnibus Trade and Competitiveness Act of 1988, a bill that included important reforms to Section 337. As mentioned above, these reforms removed the injury requirement for federally recognized IP violations and substantially relaxed the definition of domestic industry. The 1988 amendments made Section 337 claims much more attractive to IP owners. The second major development was the rapid rise of the electronics industry. By 1995, 16 percent of Section 337 cases involved a dispute over electronics articles. A corollary to this development was the geographic shift in Section 337 investigations—most respondents were now from the newly developing Asian economies of Taiwan, Hong Kong, Singapore, and South Korea. Soon thereafter, an increasing number of Chinese companies became respondents in Section 337 actions. Between 1995 and 2011, the trends of the previous 10 years continued. By 2004, 46 percent of all cases at the ITC involved high-tech articles, most of which were produced in Asia, a 30 percent increase over the previous decade. Today, articles from Asia represent approximately 85 percent of allegedly infringing products, with Taiwan and China leading the list of source countries.[13]

The volume of Section 337 cases has skyrocketed. In 2009, 31 cases were instituted. This figure grew to 56 cases in 2010 and 69 cases in 2011.[14] In recent years, the statute's popularity has also been fueled by the surge of foreign-based complainants owning U.S. IP who are quickly learning how to take advantage of reforms within the law to protect their position in the U.S. market against "foreign" infringers.

---

13. Data compiled from complaints of all cases filed at the ITC in 2010 and 2011. Note that this large percentage of products originating in Asia includes products contracted by or made for U.S.-based companies.

14. Number of Section 337 Investigations Instituted By Calendar Year, USITC, http://usitc.gov/intellectual_property/documents/cy_337_institutions.pdf (last visited July 6, 2012).

B. THE FUTURE OF SECTION 337

While the future cannot be predicted, there are signs that the Commission will provide more focus to the domestic industry and public interest aspects of the statute. Many articles are being published and legislation introduced seeking to provide a clearer definition of the word "licensing," which was added as part of the domestic industry amendments to the statute in 1988. At the same time, the Commission, as an expert administrative agency, is interpreting this term as cases come before it. Similarly, the public interest inquiry, required to be undertaken before the Commission imposes a remedy, is receiving new impetus in balancing the benefits of protecting IP against the effects of exclusion on the public. At the same time, a recent Federal Circuit case held that the traditional district court four-factor test for injunctive relief does not apply to the ITC, since the ITC provides different relief from that available in the federal courts.[15] As a result, Section 337's public interest considerations are not necessarily connected to the equitable principles applied in district court. These matters will be given in-depth treatment in Chapters 5 ("Elements of a Section 337 Investigation") and 12 ("Interlocutory Appeals of ALJ Decisions, Commission Review, Public Interest, and Presidential Review").

---

15. Spansion, Inc. v. U.S. Int'l Trade Comm'n, 629 F.3d 1331 (Fed. Cir. 2010).

CHAPTER 2

Uniqueness of the ITC

IP owners have various mechanisms available to them for the protection of their rights. Section 337, once a relatively unknown and under-utilized statute, has been transformed into one of the most important weapons companies can wield to protect their U.S. IP against infringing imports. Many companies seeking to protect their IP are turning to the ITC and its powers under Section 337 for redress. When deciding whether to pursue a Section 337 investigation, to file suit in U.S. district court, or both, there are several aspects of a Section 337 investigation that should be considered.

Section 337 provides a number of advantages over a district court, including expansive jurisdiction, expedited hearings, expert judges, and effective remedies. These advantages make Section 337 an important enforcement mechanism in today's economy. The Commission is a quasi-judicial administrative agency; however, it lacks some of the powers of a U.S. district court, such as the ability to award monetary damages. Moreover, the Commission's determinations as to infringement and validity of a patent have no preclusive effect. Because of these pros and cons, it is not uncommon for an IP owner to file complaints in both the ITC and U.S. district court. In any event, the value of including a Section 337 investigation as part of a comprehensive IP enforcement plan is plainly evident.

A. STATUTORY ELEMENTS

The first issue to address when considering whether to institute a Section 337 investigation is whether the statutory elements can be met. Pursuant to the statute, the Commission conducts adversarial investigations to address unfair acts and unfair methods of competition, including the infringement of IP, in the importation of goods into the United States, the sale of goods for importation into the United States, and/or the sale of goods in the United States after importation. The elements required to prove a Section 337 violation depend on the nature of the unfair act—for instance, whether the intellectual property right at issue is registered with the U.S. government. If the alleged unfair act is the infringement of a type of IP specified in the statute—for example, a U.S. patent or federally registered copyright, trademark, semiconductor mask work, or boat hull design—the complainant must establish only importation, infringement, and the existence of a domestic industry. If the alleged unfair act is not set forth by statute—for example, common-law trademark infringement, passing off, trade secret misappropriation, false designation of origin, etc.—the complainant must establish all of the foregoing elements and, in addition, show that the unfair act creates the threat or effect of destroying or substantially injuring the domestic industry, preventing the establishment of such an industry, or restraining or monopolizing trade and commerce in the United States.

While the infringement element of Section 337 is equivalent to its U.S. district court counterpart, the importation and domestic industry elements reflect the origins of Section 337 as a trade statute. The Commission has interpreted the importation element liberally. A single sample[1] or a contract for future sale for importation into the United States[2] has been deemed sufficient to establish importation. Similarly, the Commission's threshold for establishing the domestic industry element is relatively low. To prove domestic industry, a complainant must demonstrate that an industry relating to the IP exists in the United States or is in the process of being established. The proof required can be divided into an economic prong and a technical prong. To satisfy the economic prong,

---

1. *Certain Trolley Wheel Assemblies,* Inv. No. 337-TA-161, USITC Pub. 1605, Views of the Comm'n (Pub. Version), at 7 (Nov. 1984).

2. *Certain Variable Speed Wind Turbines & Components Thereof,* Inv. No. 337-TA-376, Initial Determination (Pub. Version), at 17–19 (June 20, 1996), *aff'd sub nom.* Enercon GmbH v. U.S. Int'l Trade Comm'n, 151 F.3d 1376, 1381 (Fed. Cir. 1998).

a complainant must show that, with respect to the IP at issue, it has made significant investment in plant and equipment, significant investment in labor or capital, and/or substantial investment in the exploitation of the IP, including engineering, research and development, or licensing (if a federally registered IP right is at issue). To meet the technical prong, a complainant must show that it practices/exploits the IP at issue in the United States. Although Section 337 was originally designed to protect U.S. industries against products from abroad, a foreign-based entity can establish a domestic industry as long as it is engaged, in the United States, in the requisite amount of activity related to the IP it seeks to enforce.

Another unique aspect of a Section 337 investigation, again reflecting its origin as a trade statute, is the mandated consideration of the public interest. If the Commission finds a violation of Section 337, before it issues a remedy it must consider the impact of any relief upon the public interest, which is defined to include (1) the public health and welfare; (2) competitive conditions in the United States; (3) the production of competitive articles in the United States; and (4) U.S. consumers.[3] Historically, these public interest factors have not played a prominent role in Commission determinations. Indeed, only three investigations out of more than 600 have resulted in a denial of relief due to negative effects on the public interest.[4]

Interest in the public interest factors has recently increased, however, partly as a result of the ITC's detailed treatment of these factors in its *Baseband Processor Chips* opinion.[5] In 2010, the Commission proposed amendments to its rules of practice and procedure to enable it "to gather more information on public interest issues arising from complaints filed" and "to aid the Commission in identifying investigations that require further development of public interest issues in the record, and to identify and develop information regarding the public interest at

---

3. 19 U.S.C. § 1337(d).

4. *See Certain Fluidized Supporting Apparatus & Components Thereof*, Inv. Nos. 337-TA-182/188, USITC Pub. 1667, Comm'n Det. (Pub. Version), at 2, 24 (Oct. 1984); *Certain Inclined-Field Acceleration Tubes & Components Thereof*, Inv. No. 337-TA-67, USITC Pub. 1119, Comm'n Op., at 29-31 (Dec. 1980); *Certain Automatic Crankpin Grinders*, Inv. No. 337-TA-60, USITC Pub. 1022, Comm'n Det. & Order (Pub. Version), at 17-21 (Dec. 1979).

5. *Certain Baseband Processor Chips & Chipsets, Transmitter & Receiver (Radio) Chips, Power Control Chips & Prods. Containing Same, Including Cellular Telephone Handsets*, Inv. No. 337-TA-543, Comm'n Op., at 136–54 (June 19, 2007).

each stage of the investigation."[6] The amendments became final on October 19, 2011, and require a complainant to file a statement regarding how the requested relief may impact the public interest, while concurrently inviting the public and proposed respondents similarly to submit such statements.[7] The Commission uses these submissions to determine whether to instruct the administrative law judge (ALJ) "to take evidence and to issue a recommended determination on the public interest."[8] It should be noted, however, that if the Commission instructs the ALJ to take evidence as to public interest, the ALJ must "limit public interest discovery appropriately, with particular consideration for third parties, and will ensure that such discovery will not delay the investigation or be used improperly."[9] Moreover, the amendments have no impact on whether the Commission institutes an investigation based on a properly filed complaint.

If the Commission determines a remedy is appropriate, the Commission's determination of violation and remedy is forwarded to the President, together with the record upon which it is based. The President has 60 days to disapprove, but not alter, the Commission's order "for policy reasons."[10] If the President does so, the Commission's action will have no force or effect. Much like the Commission basing a decision on the public interest, presidential disapproval of a Commission order is extremely rare and, in fact, has occurred only five times in the history of the statute.[11] Of those five instances, three resulted in a

---

6. *See* 75 Fed. Reg. 60,671 (Oct. 1, 2010).

7. *See* 19 C.F.R. § 210.8(b) (2012). *See also* Rules of General Application, Adjudication, and Enforcement (Proposed Rules), 77 Fed. Reg, 41,122 (proposing that a public version of every confidential submission on the public interest be filed simultaneously) (proposed July 11, 2012) (to be codified at 19 C.F.R. pt. 210).

8. *Id.* at § 210.10(b).

9. *Id.*

10. In 2005, the President delegated the authority to disapprove Commission exclusion orders to the U.S. Trade Representative. *See* Assignment of Certain Functions Under Section 337 of the Tariff Act of 1930, 70 Fed. Reg. 43,251 (July 26, 2005).

11. These include *Certain Dynamic Random Access Memories, Components Thereof & Prods. (DRAMs)*, Inv. No. 337-TA-242, USITC Pub. 2034 (Nov. 1987); *Certain Alkaline Batteries*, Inv. No. 337-TA-165, USITC Pub. 1616 (Nov. 1984); *Certain Molded-In Sandwich Panel Inserts & Methods for Their Installation (Sandwich Panel Inserts)*, Inv. No. 337-TA-99, USITC Pub. 1297 (Oct. 1982); *Certain Headboxes & Papermaking Mach. Forming Sections for the Continuous Prod. of Paper & Components Thereof (Headboxes)*,

revised remedy.[12] If the President approves the order or takes no action, the Commission's order becomes final. Any appeal of a final Commission determination may be taken to the U.S. Court of Appeals for the Federal Circuit by an adversely affected party within 60 days. The prevailing party may participate by intervening in such an action.

B. ADVANTAGES OF SECTION 337

If the statutory elements are met, the distinctive features of Section 337 afford several advantages to those seeking to enforce their IP against infringing imported goods. One of the unique characteristics of Section 337 is that the ITC exercises jurisdiction over the accused products rather than only over the parties. That is, in Section 337 investigations, the ITC exercises in rem, as well as in personam, jurisdiction.[13] As long as a respondent's products are being imported into the United States or are on their way there, the ITC may grant relief related to those products. This broad jurisdiction is advantageous when seeking to join multiple infringers in one proceeding, particularly if some or all of the infringers are foreign entities with limited contacts with the United States. By contrast, an entity wishing to enforce its IP in U.S. district court may have to bring several separate lawsuits in multiple locations in order to satisfy the jurisdictional and venue requirements for each infringer. This challenge is now compounded by the addition of 35 U.S.C. § 299, which limits joinder of ac-

---

Inv. No. 337-TA-82, USITC Pub. 1138 (Apr. 1981); *Certain Welded Stainless Steel Pipe & Tube*, Inv. No. 337-TA-29, USITC Pub. 863 (Feb. 1978). *See also* DONALD KNOX DUVALL ET AL., UNFAIR COMPETITION AND THE ITC 365–73 (2008).

12. The modified investigations include *DRAMs*, Inv. No. 337-TA-242, Comm'n Action & Order; *Sandwich Panel Inserts*, Inv. No. 337-TA-99, Comm'n Action & Order; *Headboxes*, Inv. No. 337-TA-82, Comm'n Action & Order.

13. The in rem nature of the ITC's jurisdiction is responsible for the sometimes unwieldy investigation titles. They are simply a description of the products over which the Commission has jurisdiction (e.g., *Certain Baseband Processor Chips & Chipsets, Transmitter & Receiver (Radio) Chips, Power Control Chips, & Prods. Containing Same, Including Cellular Tel. Handsets,* rather than Broadcom Corp. v. Qualcomm, Inc., 2005 WL 5925584 (C.D. Cal. 2005). *See generally* William P. Atkins, *Appreciating 337 Actions at the ITC: A Primer on Intellectual Property Issues and Procedures at the U.S. International Trade Commission,* 5 U. BALT. INTELL. PROP. L.J. 103, 113 (1997).

cused infringers to defendants whose liability arises out of the same accused products, or who share common questions of fact.[14]

The broad jurisdiction of the ITC is also advantageous in discovery.
Often, a great deal of the information the complainant needs to prove its
case is located in foreign countries. This information may be difficult to
obtain, not only because of the volume of material and geographical
distance, but also because foreign governments may burden complainants by placing restrictions on discovery procedures. By virtue of the
Commission's in rem jurisdiction, and pursuant to the Hague Convention, a complainant does not have to wait to perfect service on foreign
parties as it would in a U.S. district court matter.[15] Instead, discovery can
begin as soon as the notice of investigation is published in the *Federal
Register*. The Commission cannot issue subpoenas to compel foreign companies to divulge information or documents in the same way it can force
U.S. companies or persons to do so. However, the Commission can impose sanctions similar to those set forth in Rule 37 of the Federal Rules
of Civil Procedure for a party's failure to comply with discovery requests generated in an ITC investigation. Because these sanctions may
include a finding that the withheld information would have been unfavorable to the respondent's position or, in extreme cases, result in a final
ruling in favor of the complainant, foreign respondents have an incentive
to participate in these investigations.[16] Moreover, the ITC has nationwide
subpoena power. Third-party subpoenas are obtained through an application to the ALJ. If a third party is noncompliant, the Commission can
pursue enforcement through the U.S. district courts.[17]

---

14. *See* Leahy-Smith America Invents Act, Pub. L. No. 112-29, § 19, 125
Stat. 332-333 (2011). This provision may well lead to additional filings
under Section 337 where importation is involved. *See infra* Chapter 16,
Section E for a discussion of the America Invents Act patent reforms and their
possible effect on ITC litigation.

15. *Hague Convention on the Service Abroad of Judicial and Extra-
Judicial Documents in Civil or Commercial Matters*, Nov. 15, 1965, 20 U.S.T.
361; 658 U.N.T.S. 163; Appendix C4-6 following Fed. R. Civ. P. 4.

16. Sanctions may similarly be imposed against a complainant who fails
to cooperate in discovery.

17. The sole disadvantage of the ITC's subpoena power is that the mechanism for enforcing the subpoena can be cumbersome and time-consuming. If it
becomes necessary for the ITC to enforce its subpoena in U.S. district court,
this effort might not be effective until after the Section 337 investigation is
completed. For example, the enforcement of a subpoena caused the target date
for completion of one investigation to be extended multiple times while the

All parties to a Section 337 investigation have the advantage of litigating before ALJs who have particular expertise in IP disputes. Unlike U.S. district court judges whose dockets cover a wide range of topics, the ALJs at the ITC handle primarily IP issues. Thus, little time is spent educating the bench, other than in a case-specific tutorial on the technology at issue. The expertise of the ALJs is reflected in the high number of determinations that are affirmed at the Commission level and on appeal before the Federal Circuit. For example, a recent examination of the rate of review of ALJ determinations, by issue, over a two-year dataset found that "[t]he Commission determined to review only about a third of issues petitioned (37%), and, on review, it affirmed the ALJ (either outright or with additional clarification or explanation) 66% of the time."[18] Likewise, on appeal of Commission final determinations by issue over the same two years, on average, "the Federal Circuit reversed the Commission on 27% of the issues captured in the dataset."[19] By contrast, studies show a higher rate of reversal by the Federal Circuit of district court or U.S. Patent and Trademark Office (PTO) judgments on at least one issue.[20]

Another advantage of pursuing a Section 337 investigation is the speed at which the ITC will resolve the matter. Although the statute no longer mandates a specific timetable,[21] it nonetheless requires that each Section 337 investigation be resolved "at the earliest practicable time."[22] The Commission adheres strictly to this requirement. A typical ITC investigation is completed in 14 to 16 months, whereas a similar district

---

Commission held the record open until the subpoenaed information could be produced and considered by the Commission. *See Certain Encapsulated Integrated Circuit Devices & Prods. Containing Same*, Inv. No. 337-TA-501, Comm'n Order (July 1, 2009).

18. Michael Diehl, *Does ITC Review of Administrative Law Judge Determinations Add Value in Section 337 Investigations?*, 21 FED. CIR. B.J. 119, 138 (2011).

19. *Id.* at 148.

20. *Id.* at 145 & n.101, 149 n.117 (citing a 2001 study by Kimberly A. Moore, which concluded that the Federal Circuit "reversed the lower tribunal on claim construction on 28% of the issues and 33% of cases;" another 2001 study by Christian A. Chu "found that the Federal Circuit reversed at least one aspect of the judgment below in 47.3% when all issues were considered and 44% of cases when only claim construction was considered").

21. *See* Uruguay Round Agreements Act, Pub. L. No. 103-465, § 321, 108 Stat. 4809, 4943 (1994).

22. 19 U.S.C. § 1337(b)(1).

court action would usually take at least two to three years.[23] The likelihood that an ITC investigation will be completed within one and a half years allows complainants to predict better the capital outlay needed and the commercial risk involved. The speed of Section 337 investigations is especially important for high-tech products with a short life span.

Assuming the complainant plans accordingly, the swift pace of a Section 337 investigation can place it in an excellent tactical position. Because the complainant chooses when to file its complaint, it has the opportunity to make substantial preparations for discovery before the rigorous investigation schedule begins to run. A respondent, on the other hand, necessarily enters the investigation well behind. It must grapple with a barrage of tasks immediately, including responding to the complaint within 20 days[24] and, if the complainant is on its toes, discovery requests within 10 days of publication of the notice of institution in the *Federal Register*. For a respondent to get on equal strategic footing, it is critical to retain counsel that is well versed in Section 337 practice at the earliest opportunity.

Within this already fast-moving forum, a complainant may be able to obtain expedited relief in the form of a temporary exclusion order (TEO). If a complainant is facing substantial, immediate, and irreparable harm from infringing imports, it may file a request that the ITC exclude the accused goods from entry on a preliminary basis during the pendency of an investigation. The criteria for a TEO are the same as those for a preliminary injunction in federal court and are thus difficult to meet. Not surprisingly, then, such requests are infrequent. By statute, the determination on entry of a TEO must be issued within 90 days after initiation of the investigation. The Commission can grant a 60-day extension in more complicated cases, but it must publish its reasons in the *Federal Register*.

Arguably, the most valuable advantage Section 337 provides to IP owners is the effective nature of the remedies available. The most common type of relief granted under the statute is an exclusion order. That order can take one of two forms. A limited exclusion order (LEO) directs Customs to bar infringing articles originating from a specific source. Usually the source identified is the respondent itself. The far more pow-

---

23. *See* V. James Adduci II & William C. Sjoberg, *Everybody Comes to the ITC,* LEGAL TIMES, July 11, 2005, *available at* http://www.adduci.com/sites/default/files/EverybodyComesToTheITC.pdf.

24. If the respondent is located in a foreign country, it is given additional time to account for delays in service. *See* 19 C.F.R. § 201.16(d).

erful alternative is a general exclusion order (GEO), which applies to all infringing goods, regardless of source. That is, the order is enforceable against infringing products imported by or from entities that were not parties to the investigation. Thus, such an order protects a complainant's market against all known and unknown infringers, both at the time of the order's issuance and in the future. There is simply no equivalent in U.S. district court, as an injunction in that forum cannot extend to non-parties. Because a general exclusion order has sweeping application, the ITC imposes a high burden of proof. A complainant must demonstrate that such a remedy "is necessary to prevent circumvention of an exclusion order limited to products of named persons," and "there is a pattern of statutory violation of . . . [Section 337] and it is difficult to identify the source of infringing products."[25] Both types of exclusion orders are enforced by Customs.

If an entity attempts to import infringing goods in violation of an exclusion order, Customs will prevent the entry of the goods, with further attempts potentially subject to seizure and forfeiture of the goods. If infringing products covered by the order are entering the United States in spite of Customs' efforts, the complainant can also request that the ITC institute an enforcement proceeding. On the other end of the spectrum, if an importer believes it is not in violation of the order, it can request an advisory opinion from the Commission or from Customs. The former is more effective, because a Customs opinion is not binding on the ITC.[26] Thus, a Customs opinion in favor of an importer would not prevent a complainant from bringing an ITC enforcement action that could result in sanctions to that importer.[27]

Another type of remedy available from the Commission is a "cease and desist order" (CDO), which can be issued in lieu of, or in addition to, an exclusion order. Such orders apply only within the United States, and personal jurisdiction is required. Although cease and desist orders can prohibit a wide range of activities, including importation, sale, market-

---

25. This test comes from the ITC's 1981 determination in *Certain Airless Paint Spray Pumps & Components Thereof*, Inv. No. 337-TA-90, USITC Pub. 1199, Comm'n Op. (Pub. Version), at 18 (Nov. 1981), and is codified at 19 U.S.C. § 1337(d)(2) pursuant to Section 321(a) of the Uruguay Round Agreements Act of 1994, *supra* note 21.

26. *See* Tom M. Schaumberg et al., *Advantages of a Section* 337 *Investigation at the U.S. International Trade Commission,* IP Litigator, May/June 2006, at 37.

27. *Id.*

ing, distribution, and advertising of infringing products in the United States, they are most often issued to prevent a respondent from selling a "commercially significant" inventory of infringing goods that has already been imported into the United States in an attempt to elude the effects of Section 337.[28] To enforce these orders, the Commission has the authority to bring a civil action seeking a monetary penalty. The maximum of such a penalty is the greater of either $100,000 for each day the proscribed activities or imports occur or twice the domestic value of the imported items.

Finally, the Commission has the authority to issue "consent orders." A consent order is used when a respondent desires to withdraw from an investigation without admitting liability. In essence, it is an agreement between the respondent and the Commission in which the respondent stipulates to certain jurisdictional facts and agrees to refrain from importing products that encompass the allegedly infringing activity. The Commission maintains authority to enforce the agreement and can do so in much the same way it enforces cease and desist orders.

As referenced above, it is also important to note that a Section 337 investigation and a U.S. district court action may be pursued simultaneously. The ability to utilize the best of each forum can maximize a party's opportunity for relief and/or give a party a strategic edge. For example, a complainant may wish to file a parallel action in U.S. district court in order to obtain monetary damages, which are not available at the ITC, while at the same time pursuing a general exclusion order before the Commission. The complainant may also choose to file a parallel U.S. district court case to prevent the alleged infringer from bringing a declaratory judgment suit in an unfavorable jurisdiction.

Respondents have a tactical tool at their disposal with regard to parallel proceedings—the stay. A district court must grant any timely request to stay claims in a parallel proceeding as long as (1) the district court claims involve the same issues being adjudicated before the Commission, and (2) the moving party is also a respondent in the ITC investigation.[29] Such a stay cannot be dissolved until the ITC investigation is no longer subject to appellate review.[30] On the other hand, a complainant that is not faring well or whose case is being delayed in a parallel U.S. district court case over a disputed trademark, for example, may wish to

---

28. *Id.*
29. 28 U.S.C. § 1659 (2007).
30. *See In re* Princo Corp., 478 F.3d 1345, 1355 (Fed. Cir. 2007).

file a Section 337 action in the hope that the ITC investigation will result in a better outcome and even attain res judicata effect. The same strategy could not be employed in a patent dispute. Although a parallel Section 337 action could be initiated, Commission determinations involving patents do not result in res judicata in district court.[31] However, if a stay is entered by the U.S. district court, the Commission's record may be used in subsequent district court proceedings.[32] U.S. district court judges have shown deference to Section 337 determinations in the patent arena.

The ruling by the U.S. Supreme Court in *eBay v. MercExchange*[33] created yet another advantage for Section 337 investigations. In *eBay*, the Supreme Court held there is no "general rule" that permanent injunctions will be issued automatically upon a finding of infringement in U.S. district court cases. Instead, a plaintiff must satisfy the standard four-factor test requiring that: (1) it has a likelihood of success on the merits; (2) harm is irreparable because remedies available at law are inadequate to compensate for the injury; (3) a remedy in equity is warranted after considering the balance of hardships between the parties; and (4) the public interest would not be disserved.[34] Because the *eBay* decision has made it much more difficult to obtain a permanent injunction against infringers in district court, many commentators suggest this will induce larger numbers of patent owners, particularly so-called non-practicing entities, to seek ITC exclusion orders, which can have the same effect as U.S. district court injunctions.[35]

Section 337 investigations can serve as the basis for a highly effective global strategy for protecting domestic IP against infringing im-

---

31. The rationale behind this difference in treatment is that Congress has given district courts original jurisdiction over patent disputes. *See* 28 U.S.C. § 1338; *see, e.g.,* EyeTicket Corp. v. Unisys Corp., 155 F. Supp. 2d 527, 534 (E.D.Va. 2001) (citing 28 U.S.C. § 1338(a); "As a case involving a claim for patent infringement, this Court has original jurisdiction of this matter.").

32. 28 U.S.C. § 1659(b).

33. *See* eBay Inc. v. Mercexchange, L.L.C., 547 U.S. 388 (2006).

34. *See id.* at 391.

35. The Commission rejected the argument that it is required to follow the *eBay* test for granting injunctive relief in *Baseband Processor Chips, Power Control Chips & Prods. Containing Same, Including Cellular Telephone Handsets,* Inv. No. 337-TA-543, Comm'n Op., at 62 n.230 (June 19, 2007). The Federal Circuit agreed, holding that the ITC's exclusion orders have "different statutory underpinnings" from relief available in district court and are therefore not subject to the four-factor *eBay* test. *See* Spansion, Inc. v. U.S. Int'l Trade Comm'n, 629 F.3d 1331, 1359 (Fed. Cir. 2010).

ports. The statute offers significant advantages that are not available in U.S. district court, such as broader jurisdiction, faster resolution of disputes, judges with IP expertise, and sweeping remedial relief. While these features are particularly suited to combat infringement in the internationalized U.S. marketplace, a successful approach to enforcement will likely utilize both ITC and U.S. district court mechanisms to obtain the maximum protection the law provides.

CHAPTER 3

Types of Investigations

Section 337 investigations conducted by the International Trade Commission most often involve claims regarding IP rights, including allegations of patent, trademark, and copyright infringement by imported goods. Utility and design patents, as well as process patents and registered and common-law trademarks, may be asserted in these investigations. Other forms of unfair competition involving imported products, such as misappropriation of trade secrets or trade dress, passing off, and false advertising, may also be asserted.

In 1988, Section 337 was significantly amended by the Omnibus Trade and Competitiveness Act. These amendments removed the requirement from all investigations that the domestic industry be efficiently and economically operated and, in cases involving statutory intellectual property rights, such as patents, copyrights, and registered trademarks, removed the injury requirement, as well.[1] The amendments also expanded the bases upon which complainants may demonstrate the existence of a domestic industry related to statutory IP, adding investment in the statutory IP's exploitation, including engineering, research and development, or licensing.[2] This special status under the statute given to patents, copyrights, and registered trademarks extends also to mask works and boat hull designs, which will not receive significant discussion here, due to the limited number of cases addressing those types of IP.

---

1. *See* 19 U.S.C. § 1337(a)(1) (2006).
2. *See id.* § 1337(a)(3)(C).

A. PATENT

Although Section 337 has always proscribed unfair methods of competition and unfair acts, its impact has been focused on the area of patent infringement by imported products.[3] The ITC has held that "Section 337 prohibits unfair methods of competition and unfair acts, not patent infringement per se,"[4] and the Federal Circuit pointed out, prior to the 1988 amendments to the statute, that "[S]ection 337 does not function merely as an international extension of private rights under the patent statute."[5] While the statute did not explicitly mention patent infringement prior to the 1988 amendments, it was nonetheless used to address patent infringement as one of the "unfair methods of competition and unfair acts" that were "declared unlawful" by the statute and "dealt with" by the Commission.[6] Since the 1988 amendments, patent infringement is directly referenced in the text of the statute.[7]

Until 1988, Section 337 provided the only means by which the owner of a U.S. process patent could obtain any relief as a result of the unauthorized practice of process claims abroad. The 1988 amendments to Sec-

---

3. From Oct. 1, 2010 through Sept. 30, 2011, for example, patent infringement was asserted as an unfair act in 68 of the 70 Section 337 investigations instituted by the Commission. Ashley Miller, The Donald K. Duvall Annual Year in Review, Developments in Section 337 Law and Practice Address, 2011 ITC Trial Lawyers' Association Annual Meeting (Nov. 9, 2011).

4. *Certain Apparatus for the Continuous Prod. of Copper Rod*, Inv. No. 337-TA-89, USITC Pub. 1132, Comm'n Op., at 6 (Apr. 1981); *see also Certain Cold Cathode Fluorescent Lamp (CCFL) Inverter Circuits & Prods. Containing the Same*, Inv. No. 337-TA-666, Order No. 31 (Initial Determination), at 3 (Sept. 24, 2009) (unreviewed).

5. Corning Glass Works v. U.S. Int'l Trade Comm'n, 799 F.2d 1559, 1567 (Fed. Cir. 1985); Textron, Inc. v. U.S. Int'l Trade Comm'n, 753 F.2d 1019 (Fed. Cir. 1986).

6. The pre-1988 text of subsection (a) reads as follows:

> Unfair methods of competition and unfair acts in the importation of articles into the United States, or in their sale by the owner, importer, consignee, or agent of either, the effect or tendency of which is to destroy or substantially injure an industry, efficiently and economically operated, in the United States, or to prevent the establishment of such an industry, or to restrain or monopolize trade and commerce in the United States, are declared unlawful, and when found by the Commission to exist shall be dealt with, in addition to any other provisions of law, as provided in this section.

7. *See* 19 U.S.C. §§ 1337(a)(1)(B)(i), (ii).

tion 337 maintained this aspect of Section 337 by eliminating Section 337a but specifying that owners of U.S. process patents could seek an exclusion order from the ITC barring imports of articles made with a process that infringes their valid patents.[8] Also to the benefit of process patent holders, Title IX of the 1988 Trade Act amended U.S. patent law to extend the protection of process patents to imports produced by a process without authorization from the U.S. process patent holder.[9]

The ITC may be the preferred forum for holders of process patents in some circumstances due to the rapid resolution of cases and the prospect of an exclusion order. An additional advantage for process patent holders at the ITC is the possibility of global discovery that is unavailable in federal court and that can be useful for purposes such as inspection of the alleged infringer's foreign manufacturing facilities.[10]

Under the current version of Section 337, the substantive showing necessary to establish a prima facie violation of the statute in a patent case may be parsed into three separate elements:

(1) Importation into the United States, the sale for importation, or the sale within the United States after importation by the owner, importer, or consignee of articles;

(2) Infringement by the articles of one or more claims of a valid and enforceable U.S. patent; and

(3) An industry in the United States relating to the articles protected by the patent exists or is in the process of being established.

B. TRADEMARK

Section 337 has also been successfully employed by trademark owners to exclude foreign-made products that infringe U.S. trademarks. To be entitled to a remedy under Section 337, the trademark owner must establish that there is (1) importation, sale, or sale for importation of a product that (2) infringes a valid and enforceable U.S. trademark, and (3) that there is a "domestic industry" relating to the product protected by the trademark.[11]

---

8. *See id.* at § 1337(a)(1)(B)(ii).

9. *See* 1988 Trade Act, § 9002, 35 U.S.C. § 271(g) (2006).

10. *See, e.g., Certain Acesulfame Potassium & Blends & Prods. Containing Same,* Inv. No. 337-TA-403, Order No. 4, at 2 (Feb. 6, 1998) (unreviewed) (compelling, inter alia, inspection of production facilities in China).

11. 19 U.S.C. §§ 1337(a)(1)(c), (a)(2).

Section 337's trademark protection also extends to importation of "gray market goods."[12] Gray market goods are genuine goods that "are of foreign manufacture, bearing a legally affixed foreign trademark that is the same mark as is registered in the United States; gray [market] goods are legally acquired abroad and then imported without the consent of the U.S. trademark holder."[13] In order to prevent the importation and sale of gray market goods, a complainant must show that the gray market goods are materially different from the authorized goods.[14] "A material difference is a difference that consumers are likely to find significant when purchasing the [goods] because such differences would suffice to erode the goodwill of the domestic source."[15] "The purpose of the material differences inquiry in gray market cases is to assess whether consumer confusion is likely to occur."[16] The CAFC has held that, although the threshold for this standard of materiality is low,[17] "a plaintiff in a gray market trademark infringement case must establish that *all or substantially all* of its sales are accompanied by the asserted material difference in order to show that its goods are materially different."[18] In other words, a complainant cannot seek gray market protection from goods it sells itself.[19] Otherwise, the complainant would be able to contribute to the very market confusion for which it seeks redress.[20] The Commission also rejected the notion that *physical* material differences are required to show

---

12. *See, e.g.*, *Certain Cigarettes & Packaging Thereof (Cigarettes)*, Inv. No. 337-TA-643, Comm'n Op. (Oct. 1, 2009), *aff'd sub nom.* Alcesia SRL v. ITC, No. 2010-1156, (Fed. Cir. Jan. 24, 2011); *Certain Bearings & Packaging Thereof (Bearings)*, Inv. No. 337-TA-469, Comm'n Op. (June 30, 2004).

13. *Bearings,* Inv. No. 337-TA-469, Comm'n Op., at 9 (quoting Gamut Trading Co. v. U.S. Int'l Trade Comm'n, 200 F.3d 775, 778 (Fed. Cir. 1999)).

14. *Cigarettes*, Comm'n Op., at 5–6; *Bearings*, Comm'n Op., at 10.

15. *Bearings*, Comm'n Op., at 10–11.

16. *Cigarettes,* Comm'n Op., at 6.

17. Bourdeau Bros. v. U.S. Int'l Trade Comm'n, 444 F.3d 1317, 1321 (Fed. Cir. 2006).

18. *Id.* (emphasis in original) (citing SKF USA, Inc. v. U.S. Int'l Trade Comm'n, 423 F.3d 1307, 1315 (Fed. Cir. 2005) (affirming Commission determination that even though 87.4% of complainant's products bore a material difference from the gray market goods, that percentage was not sufficient to satisfy the "all or substantially all" standard)).

19. *See id.*

20. *Id.*

gray market infringement, even when the foreign manufacturer and the U.S. trademark owner are under common control.[21]

Trademark dilution has been alleged as an unfair act in several Section 337 investigations,[22] but the Commission has never reached the issue. In *Certain Cigarettes and Packaging Thereof*, Inv. No. 337-TA-424, a case involving gray market sales, the ALJ found that the less rigorous post-manufacturing quality control of the gray market goods increased the like-lihood that they might be damaged or stale, which could "injure the goodwill associated with the asserted trademarks," thereby violating the anti-dilution provisions of the Lanham Act. The Commission declined review.[23]

The value of Section 337 for trademark holders is enhanced because courts give ITC determinations on trademark issues preclusive effect. Although the CAFC has held that ITC decisions on patent issues are not res judicata,[24] courts have recognized that the Commission's trademark determinations do have preclusive effect in subsequent cases.[25] As such, ITC determinations in trademark cases can be useful for subsequent actions seeking damages in U.S. district court.

C. COPYRIGHT

To sustain a claim of copyright infringement, a complainant must establish (1) *ownership* by complainant of the copyright in question and (2) *copying* by respondent.[26] Copyright ownership can, in turn, be broken down into the following elements:

(1)   originality in the author;
(2)   copyrightability of the subject matter;

---

21. *Id.*

22. *See, e.g., Certain Agric. Vehicles & Components Thereof*, Inv. No. 337-TA-487, USITC Pub. 3735 (Dec. 2004); *Certain Bearings & Packaging Thereof*, Inv. No. 337-TA-469, USITC Pub. 3736 (Dec. 2004); *Certain Aerospace Rivets & Prods. Containing Same*, Inv. No. 337-TA-447 (2001).

23. *Certain Cigarettes & Packaging Thereof*, Inv. No. 337-TA-424, Comm'n Op., at 1 (Nov. 3, 2000).

24. Texas Instruments, Inc. v. Cypress Semiconductor, 90 F.3d 1558 (Fed. Cir. 1996).

25. *See, e.g.,* Union Mfg. Co. v. Han Baek Trading Co., 763 F.2d 42, 45–46 (2d Cir. 1985).

26. *Certain Prods. with Gremlins Character Depictions*, Inv. No. 337-TA-201, Initial Determination, at 10 (Dec. 10, 1984) (unreviewed) (emphasis added); Gaylord v. United States, 595 F.3d 1364, 1372 (Fed. Cir. 2010).

(3) citizenship status of the author such as to permit a claim of copyright;

(4) compliance with applicable statutory formalities; and, if the complainant is not the author;

(5) a transfer of rights or other relationship between the author and the complainant so as to constitute in complainant the valid copyright claimant.[27]

A copyright registration certificate constitutes prima facie evidence in favor of complainant of most of the above elements of ownership.

Because direct evidence of copyright infringement is rarely available to a complainant, copying is ordinarily established indirectly by showing that the accused copyright infringer had *access* to the copyrighted work and that the accused work is *substantially similar* to the copyrighted work.[28] Access is usually defined to be merely the opportunity to copy.[29] The determination of whether one work is "substantially similar" to another is one of the most vexing questions in copyright law and one that is not susceptible to generalization. The problem is essentially one of drawing lines, and, as Judge Learned Hand has said, the lines "wherever [they are] drawn will seem arbitrary" and "the test for infringement of a copyright is of necessity vague."[30]

Claims of copyright infringement have not arisen frequently in Section 337 investigations. One notable case, however, is *Products with Gremlins Character Depictions*, which provided part of the impetus for the 1988 amendments to Section 337.[31] In that investigation, the Commis-

---

27. *Certain Coin Operated Audio-Visual Game & Components Thereof*, Inv. No. 337-TA-87, Comm'n Op., at 13 (June 1981); MELVILLE NIMMER, NIMMER ON COPYRIGHT, § 1301[A] (2012).

28. *See, e.g.*, Oravec v. Sunny Isles Luxury Ventures, L.C., 527 F.3d 1218, 1223 (11th Cir. 2008) ("If the plaintiff does not have direct proof of copying, the plaintiff may show copying by demonstrating that the defendants had access to the copyrighted work and that the works are 'substantially similar.'"); *see also* Beal v. Paramount Pictures Corp., 20 F.3d 454, 459 (11th Cir. 1994).

29. Grubb v. KMS Patriots, L.P., 88 F.3d 1, 3 (1st Cir. 1996).

30. Nichols v. Universal Pictures Co., 45 F.2d 119, 122 (2d Cir. 1930); Peter Pan Fabrics, Inc. v. Martin Weiner Corp., 274 F.2d 487, 489 (2d Cir. 1960) (quoted in MELVILLE NIMMER, NIMMER ON COPYRIGHT, § 13.03[A]).

31. *Certain Prods. with Gremlins Character Depictions*, Inv. No. 337-TA-201, USITC Pub. 1815 (Mar. 1986).

sion found no violation of Section 337, in part because it determined that, without production-related activities in the United States, even the extensive domestic copyright licensing activities of the complainant did not satisfy the statutory domestic industry requirements of Section 337. The 1988 amendments included Section 337(a)(3), which provides that a domestic industry may be established through substantial investment in the "exploitation, including engineering, research and development, or licensing" of the "patent, copyright, trademark, or mask work concerned"; actual production of articles in the United States is not required.[32]

Other Commission copyright cases have involved allegations that a respondent had illegally copied an owner's manual or advertising brochure prepared by the complainant to accompany its domestic products and that the respondent was using the copied material in conjunction with its imported products.[33] Copyright claims were also present in two ITC investigations involving coin-operated audiovisual games.[34] In those cases, however, the principal copyright issue was not infringement (the imported games were almost identical to complainant's games), but rather whether the audiovisual games were copyrightable.

D. TRADE DRESS

A less common claim under Section 337 is to seek exclusion of products or packaging that misappropriate trade dress. Complainants have won relief in investigations concerning coin-operated video games,[35] novelty glasses,[36] ink markers,[37] and, more recently, digital multimeters.[38] The law defines

---

32. 19 U.S.C. § 1337(a)(3).

33. *See, e.g., Certain Radar Detectors & Accompanying Owner's Manuals,* Inv. No. 337-TA-149, Complaint at ¶¶ 26–32 (May 28, 1983).

34. *Coin-Operated Audio-Visual Games & Components Thereof,* Inv. No. 337-TA-87 USITC Pub. 1160, (June 1981); *Certain Coin-Operated Audiovisual Games & Components Thereof,* Inv. No. 337-TA-105, USITC Pub. 1267 (July 1982).

35. *Certain Coin-Operated Audio-Visual Games & Components Thereof,* Inv. No. 337-TA-87, USITC Pub. 1160, Comm'n Action & Order, at 6 (June 1981).

36. *Certain Novelty Glasses,* Inv. No. 337-TA-55, USITC Pub. 991, Comm'n Determination & Order, at 3 (July 1979).

37. *Certain Ink Markers & Packaging Thereof,* Inv. No. 337-TA-522, USITC Pub. 3971, Comm'n Op. (Dec. 2007).

38. *Certain Digital Multimeters, & Prods. with Multimeter Functionality,* Inv. No. 337-TA-588, Comm'n Op. (Dec. 3, 2007).

"trade dress" as the "total image and overall appearance" of a product, which may involve aspects such as shape, size, color, text, and graphics.[39] Although this interpretation fits within the Lanham Act definition of a trademark,[40] trade dress claims are typically used to protect elements of product or packaging design that do not qualify for trademark registration.

To establish a cognizable trade dress claim at the ITC, a complainant must show that the elements in question are both non-functional and distinctive.[41] Design elements are deemed functional if they are "essential to the use or purpose of the device" or "affect the cost and quality of the device," or if a monopoly on the use of the feature "would put competitors at a significant non-reputation-related disadvantage."[42] In evaluating non-functionality, the ITC has considered utilitarian advantage, availability of alternative designs, costs of alternatives, and whether the trade dress elements have been advertised as functional. Notably, the ITC has indicated that no single factor is dispositive of the issue.[43]

Distinctiveness in trade dress may be either inherent or acquired through secondary meaning. Inherent distinctiveness can be shown in three ways: (1) if the design has no relevance to the product other than identification of the manufacturer; (2) if the design is arbitrary, fanciful, or suggestive; or (3) if the design suggests a link between the elements of a particular product and its producer.[44] The Supreme Court has held that only packaging can be inherently distinctive, and, therefore, a trade dress claim based upon elements of product design must be supported by a showing of acquired distinctiveness through secondary meaning.[45] A showing of secondary meaning requires that a complainant establish that, in the minds of the public, the essential significance of the element at issue is not to identify the product itself, but rather to identify the *source* of the product.[46]

---

39. Two Pesos, Inc. v. Taco Cabana, Inc., 505 U.S. 763, 764 n.1 (1992); *see also* Hartco Eng'g, Inc. v. Wang's Int'l, Inc., 142 Fed. Appx. 455, 460 (Fed Cir. 2005).

40. 15 U.S.C. § 1127 (2006) ("Any word, name, symbol, or device, or any combination thereof" used to identify goods).

41. Wal-Mart Stores, Inc. v. Samara Bros., 529 U.S. 205, 210 (2000).

42. TrafFix Devices v. Mktg. Displays, 532 U.S. 23, 32 (2001).

43. *Certain Digital Multimeters, & Prods. with Multimeter Functionality*, Inv. No. 337-TA-588, Order No. 22, at 7 (Jan. 14, 2008) (unreviewed) (quoting *Certain Woodworking Machines*, USITC Pub. 1979, Inv. No. 337-TA-174, Comm'n Op., at 7–8 (Oct. 1985)).

44. *Wal-Mart Stores, Inc.*, 529 U.S. at 210.

45. *Id.*

46. *Id.* at 211.

To prevail in an investigation premised on trade dress claims, a complainant must establish—in addition to the statutory elements of importation and domestic industry—that there is a likelihood of confusion in a significant portion of the consumer market as to the source or sponsorship of the product,[47] and that there is an actual or threatened injury to the domestic industry.[48]

E. TRADE SECRET

Trade secret misappropriation has been alleged in a number of Section 337 investigations.[49] In order to prevail on a claim of trade secret misappropriation before the Commission, a complainant must demonstrate (1) the existence and ownership of the alleged trade secret,[50] (2) that the trade secret is generally not known to others,[51] (3) that respondent had access to the trade secret as a result of a confidential relationship with complainant or that it obtained the trade secret through wrongful or unfair means,[52] and (4) that the respondent's use of the misappropriated trade secret has injured the complainant.[53] The Commission's authority to issue exclusion orders in trade secret cases has been characterized as "formidable" and "powerful" by one of the leading commentators on trade secret law.[54]

Trade secret misappropriation constitutes an "unfair act" justiciable under Section 337.[55] The ITC can adjudicate those unfair acts occurring "in the importation of articles into the United States, or in their sale by

---

47. *Certain Chemiluminescent Compositions*, Inv. No. 337-TA-285, USITC Pub. 2370, Comm'n Op., at 5 (Mar. 1991).

48. 19 U.S.C. § 1337(a)(1)(A)(i).

49. *See* Gary Hnath & James Gould, *Litigating Trade Secret Cases at the International Trade Commission*, 19 AIPLA Q.J. 87 (1991).

50. *Certain Cast Steel Railway Wheels, Processes for Manufacturing or Relating to Same & Certain Prods. Containing Same*, Inv. No. 337-TA-655, Initial Determination, at 21 (Nov. 23, 2009), *aff'd*, TianRui Group Co. Ltd. v. U.S. Int'l Trade Comm'n, 661 F.3d 1322, 1328 (Fed. Cir. 2011).

51. *Id.*

52. *Id.*

53. *Id.* at 81.

54. ROGER M. MILGRIM, TRADE SECRETS §§ 6.02[6] and 7.03[3] at 6-46.2 and 7-56.

55. *See, e.g., Certain Nut Jewelry & Parts Thereof*, Inv. No. 337-TA-229, USITC Pub. 1929 (Nov.1986).

the owner, importer, or consignee."[56] The Commission's jurisdiction, accordingly, depends on the existence of a nexus between the claimed unfair acts and importation.[57]

The Court of Appeals for the Federal Circuit recently held that the requisite nexus exists even where the trade secret misappropriation occurs entirely abroad. In *TianRui Group Co. Ltd. v. U.S. International Trade Commission*,[58] the court upheld the Commission's finding of violation of Section 337 where the complainant proved that the accused imported products had been produced abroad through a trade secret-protected process that was misappropriated entirely in China by one of the respondents. In reaching this conclusion, the CAFC held that the Commission erred in applying Illinois trade secret law; instead, a "single federal standard, rather than the law of a particular state, should determine what constitutes a misappropriation of trade secrets sufficient to establish an 'unfair method of competition' under [S]ection 337."[59] The court noted that "the federal criminal statute governing theft of trade secrets bases its definition of trade secrets on the Uniform Trade Secrets Act, so there is no indication of congressional intent to depart from the general law in that regard.[60] But, because the court found that "trade secret law varies little from state to state and is generally governed by widely recognized authorities," the application of Illinois law did not affect the outcome of the case.[61]

---

56. 19 U.S.C § 1337(a)(1)(A).

57. A contract for sale may be sufficient if the contract is valid and importation is imminent. *See, e.g., Certain Variable Speed Wind Turbines and Components Thereof,* Inv. No. 337-TA-376, Initial Determination, at 11–12 (June 20, 1996); *Certain Steel Rod Treating Apparatus & Components Thereof,* Inv. No. 337-TA-97, 215 U.S.P.Q. (BNA) 237 (1981); *Certain Apparatus for the Continuous Prod. of Copper Rod,* Inv. No. 337-TA-52, 206 U.S.P.Q. (BNA) 138, 150 (1979); *Certain Minutiae-Based Automated Fingerprint Identification Sys.,* Inv. No. 337-TA-156, Initial Determination, at 82–83 (Dec. 5, 1983), *cf. Certain Ceramic Drainage Foils,* Inv. No. 337-TA-216, Order No. 3 (Apr. 16, 1985) (jurisdiction absent where contract cancelled before exportation); *see also* DONALD KNOX DUVALL, FEDERAL UNFAIR COMPETITION ACTIONS: PRACTICE AND PROCEDURE UNDER SECTION 337 OF THE TARIFF ACT OF 1930 59–64 (1990).

58. TianRui Group Co. Ltd. v. U.S. Int'l Trade Comm'n, 661 F.3d 1322 (Fed. Cir. 2011).

59. 661 F.3d at 1327. The court reasoned that "[i]n light of the fact that [S]ection 337 deals with international commerce, a field of special federal concern, the case for applying a federal rule of decision is particularly strong."

60. 661 F.3d at 1328.

61. *Id.* The Court noted that while the choice of law issue was not determinative in the TianRui investigation, it "could be important in other cases."

In affirming that there was a violation of Section 337, the *TianRui* majority held, over a strong dissent, that the Commission had not applied Section 337 to purely extraterritorial conduct because the "the foreign 'unfair' activity at issue in this case is relevant only to the extent that it results in the importation of goods into this country causing domestic injury. In light of [Section 337's] focus on the act of importation and the resulting domestic injury, the Commission's [limited exclusion order] does not purport to regulate purely foreign conduct."[62]

In an earlier investigation, *Garment Hangers*, the complainant was unable to show the requisite nexus between importation and the unfair acts giving rise to complainant's claim of injury.[63] Respondents were importers of the accused garment hangers, as well as producers of the garment hangers in the United States. There was evidence that respondents had access to the trade secrets but no evidence that any particular trade secrets had actually been used. The ALJ held that the complainant failed to sustain its burden of showing a nexus between the alleged unfair acts and the respondents' importation of the accused article.[64]

F. OTHER UNFAIR ACTS

The terms "unfair methods of competition" and "unfair acts" are not defined in the statute.[65] However, the legislative history and the generality of the terms themselves indicate they are to be construed broadly.[66] Indeed, the unfair method or act provision of Section 337 reflects the

---

62. 661 F.3d at 1329 (citing Morrison v. Nat'l Austl. Bank Ltd., 130 S. Ct. 2869, 2884 (2010)).

63. *Certain Garment Hangers*, Inv. No. 337-TA-255, Initial Determination, at 107–11 (June 17, 1987).

64. *Id.*

65. Tom M. Schaumberg, *Section 337 of the Tariff Act of 1930 as an Antitrust Remedy*, 27 J. Am. & Foreign Antitrust & Trade Reg. 51, 54 (1982) (as reprinted in Antitrust Bull.).

66. In discussing Section 316 of the Tariff Act of 1922 (the predecessor to Section 337), the Senate Finance Committee stated that:

> [t]he provision relating to unfair methods of competition in the importation of goods is broad enough to prevent every type and form of unfair practice and is, therefore, a more adequate protection to American industry than any antidumping statute the country has ever had.

H.R. 7456, Report No. 595, 67th Cong., 2d Sess., at p.3 (1992).

statute's history as part of the Tariff Act of 1922. The aim of that act was to prohibit an array of unfair acts not then covered by other import laws. The provision was even used in antitrust and false advertising cases.[67]

Theoretically, any practice or course of conduct the ITC deems unfair is cognizable under Section 337. As a practical matter, however, the ITC will not deviate too far from what the courts have found actionable under statutory or common law because of the risk of placing the United States in violation of its obligations under Article III of the General Agreement on Tariffs and Trade. Article III requires that imported products be treated under U.S. law no less favorably than domestic products. Were the ITC to find a practice unfair that is not regarded as unfair by the courts and order exclusion of the offending goods, such action could violate Article III. Although there may potentially be many types of unfair acts cognizable under Section 337, only a handful of these have accounted for the bulk of litigation under Section 337.

Common law trademark infringement is a form of unfair competition under 19 U.S.C. § 1337(a)(1)(A).[68] In order to assert common law trademark rights, a party must show that: (1) it has the right to use the alleged mark; (2) the mark is either inherently distinctive or has acquired secondary meaning; (3) the mark has not become generic; and (4) the mark is not primarily functional.[69] Once a complainant establishes common law trademark rights, the markholder, in order to demonstrate infringement, must show that the allegedly infringing mark is likely to cause confusion.[70] The right to a trademark does not depend upon the statutory enactment of the Lanham Act. Rather, the "first to use a mark in the sale of goods or services . . . gains common law rights to the mark."[71] Thus, in order to establish existence of a trademark under both the Lanham Act and common law, a complainant must prove that: (a) the complainant has the right to use the mark, and (b) the mark is inherently distinctive or has acquired a secondary meaning. After establishing that the mark functions to identify the goods or services of a particular seller, the complainant must prove that the alleged unauthorized use of the mark by

---

67. RAJ BHALA, INTERNATIONAL TRADE LAW: INTERDISCIPLINARY THEORY AND PRACTICE 1647 (3d ed. 2008).

68. *See Certain Endoscopic Probes for Use in Argon Plasma Coagulation Systems*, Inv. No. 337-TA-569, Order No. 20 (May 21, 2007).

69. *Id.* at 3.

70. *Id.*

71. *Certain Vacuum Bottles & Components Thereof*, Inv. No. 337-TA-108, USITC Pub. 1305, Comm'n Op., at 6 (Nov. 1982).

another causes "likelihood of confusion." The established rule is that "likelihood of confusion" is the basic test for common law trademark infringement.[72] The essence of likelihood of confusion is that purchasers will likely buy respondent's product thinking they are getting complainant's product.

"Passing off" and its synonym, "palming off," are also considered unfair acts and have been subjected to a variety of interpretations. Passing off has been used to cover several situations: (1) trademark infringement where the infringer intends to defraud and confuse the buyer; (2) trademark infringement where there is no proof of fraudulent intent, but there is likelihood of confusion; and (3) substitution of one brand of goods when another is ordered.[73]

Passing off developed at common law to deal with intentional or fraudulent acts aimed at confusing the public into believing that the respondent's product was actually the complainant's product.[74] The focus of a passing off inquiry was typically on respondent's *intent* rather than the confusion that may have been caused among purchasers. The ITC, however, has taken a different position. In several cases, it seems to have equated passing off with trademark infringement and simulation of trade dress.[75] *Steel Toy Vehicles, Surveying Devices,* and *Plug-In Blade Fuses* are investigations that indicate that the same elements required to prove trademark infringement (non-functionality, secondary meaning, and likelihood of confusion), as well as intent to deceive, must be shown in order to prove passing off. The rationale for this view is that, in order for passing off to occur, the buyer must have something in mind with which to confuse the respondent's product; therefore, secondary meaning and non-functionality are necessary.

This view of passing off is supported by some case law; however, the holdings of most recent ITC and court decisions indicate that one need not establish the elements of trademark infringement as a prerequisite to proving passing off. Specifically, ITC decisions have viewed passing off as directed at *intentional* acts of deception that are aimed at confusing the

---

72. MCCARTHY, TRADEMARKS AND UNFAIR COMPETITION § 23:1, at 34 (2008).

73. *Id.* § 25:1, at 169.

74. *Id.* at 172.

75. *See, e.g., Certain Steel Toy Vehicles,* Inv. No. 337-TA-31, USITC Pub. 800, Comm'n Op. (Apr. 1978); *Certain Surveying Devices,* Inv. No. 337-TA-68, USITC Pub. 1085, Comm'n Op. (July 1980); *Certain Miniature Plug-In Blade Fuses,* Inv. No. 337-TA-114, USITC Pub. 1337, Comm'n Op. (Nov. 1982).

public into believing that respondent's product is the complainant's product. In *Vacuum Bottles*, the ITC stated that "[t]he essential component in a case of passing off lies in an act of deception, beyond mere copying . . . ."[76] In that case, the ITC did not indicate that its analysis of passing off was contingent on its finding regarding trademark infringement.

False advertising under Section 43(a) of the Lanham Act is also an unfair act or method of competition within the meaning of Section 337.[77] The falsity of the advertising must relate to the respondent's own product.[78] For purposes of Section 337, the complainant is not required to plead and prove actual deception; rather, a mere tendency to deceive is sufficient.[79] In addition to the specifically enumerated claims of false designation of origin and false designation/representation, Section 43(a) has been interpreted to allow traditional common law unfair competition claims, such as trademark infringement, simulation of trade dress, and passing off.[80] In effect, Section 43(a) grants federal jurisdiction to most common law unfair competition actions. The common element in all Section 43(a) violations is that goods or services have been deceptively represented to the purchaser, who is likely to be confused as to the source or nature of the product.

False designation of origin and false description or representation are expressly proscribed by Section 43(a) of the Lanham Act.[81] The ITC has indicated that the term "false designation of origin" should be reserved for false designation of a *geographic* origin, whereas the term "false representation" should be used to refer to false designation of a *manufacturer*.[82] The Commission's interpretation is supported by author-

---

76. *Certain Vacuum Bottles & Components Thereof,* Inv. No. 337-TA-108, USITC Pub. 1305, Comm'n Op., at 28 (Nov. 1982).

77. *Certain Plastic Food Storage Containers*, Inv. No. 337-TA-152, Initial Determination at 66, 86, Notice of Comm'n Determination Not to Review, 49 Fed. Reg. 21,807 (May 23, 1984).

78. *Certain Insulated Security Chests,* Inv. No. 337-TA-244, Order No. 7, at 2 (June 17, 1986).

79. *Certain Vertical Milling Machines & Parts, Attachments & Accessories Thereto*, Inv. No. 337-TA-133, Views of the Commission, at 41 (1984), *aff'd sub nom.* Textron v. U.S. Int'l Trade Comm'n, 753 F.2d 1019 (Fed. Cir. 1985); *Certain Miniature Plug-In Blade Fuses*, Inv. No. 337-TA-114, Comm'n Op., at 32 (1983).

80. J. THOMAS MCCARTHY, MCCARTHY ON TRADEMARKS, § 27:8, at 256.

81. *Id.* at § 27:3, at 247.

82. *See Certain Log-Splitting Pivoted Lever Axes*, Inv. No. 337-TA-113, Comm'n Op. (July 2, 1982).

ity that treats misrepresentation of the source of manufacture as one of many types of claims included under the umbrella of false representation.[83] The Commission's distinction between false designation of origin and false representation is logical in the context of Section 337, where the geographic location of the manufacturer may be significant in determining the appropriate remedy when a violation of the statute is found.

---

83. McCarthy treats false representation of manufacturer as one subcategory of false description/representation. MCCARTHY, § 27:7, at 254. Such treatment is supported by *Federal-Mogul-Bower Bearings, Inc. v. Azoff,* 313 F.2d 405 (6th Cir. 1963); *Franklin Mint, Inc. v. Franklin Mint, Ltd.,* 331 F. Supp. 827 (E.D. Pa. 1971); *Eastman Kodak Co. v. Royal-Paper Box Mfg. Co.,* 197 F. Supp. 132 (D.C. Pa. 1961); and *Geisel v. Poynter Prods.,* 283 F. Supp. 261 (S.D.N.Y. 1968).

CHAPTER 4

Participants

One of the distinct characteristics of Section 337 investigations is the array of participants in addition to the Commission itself. Unlike most actions in U.S. district court, Section 337 investigations involve more players than just the IP owner and the foreign manufacturer alleged to be infringing. While those parties are often involved as the complainant and only respondent, respectively, the Commission's Office of Unfair Import Investigations (OUII) also plays an active role in many investigations. In addition, many investigations involve other parties, such as importers of the articles in question or customers, who may also be named as respondents. The two-tier interplay between the administrative law judge (ALJ) and the Commission is yet another feature of Section 337 investigations that is not present in district court proceedings. This chapter provides an introduction to the typical participants in a Section 337 investigation and the role that each plays throughout an ITC investigation.

A. COMMISSION

The Commission is comprised of six commissioners, no more than three of whom can be from the same political party, and a chairmanship that alternates partisanship every two years. Each commissioner is appointed by the President and confirmed by the U.S. Senate for a nine-year term.[1] While an ALJ handles most of the day-to-day aspects of an investigation,

---

1. 19 U.S.C. § 1330(a) (2006).

the Commission is nonetheless a crucial player from the beginning to the end of any Section 337 proceeding.

At the outset, the Commission decides whether to institute an investigation. When a complaint is filed, the Commission has 30 days to make its determination regarding institution of an investigation. Absent exceptional circumstances, for example, where the Commission requires additional time in connection with a request for temporary relief, or a complainant requests the Commission to postpone institution or withdraws the complaint,[2] the Commission's statutory mandate[3] requires institution of the investigation if a complaint is in compliance with Commission Rule § 210.12.[4] An investigation is instituted by public notice in the *Federal Register* setting the scope of the investigation.[5] If the Commission decides not to institute an investigation, it will dismiss the complaint and provide the complainant and all proposed respondents with written notice of the reasons for its rejection.[6] However, in the history of Section 337, the Commission has rarely determined not to institute an investigation after reviewing a complaint.[7] Because the Commission must institute an investigation if the complaint complies with Commission rules, institution does not reflect any determination by the Commission on the merits of the complainant's allegations.

Once the investigation has been instituted, it is assigned to an ALJ, who presides over discovery, pretrial issues, and the hearing. The pro-

---

2. 19 C.F.R. § 210.10(a) (2012).

3. 19 U.S.C. § 1337(b)(1) provides, "The Commission shall investigate any alleged violation of this section on complaint under oath or upon its initiative."

4. A complainant is well advised to preview its complaint with OUII to increase the likelihood that it meets the requirements of the Commission's detailed rules. *See. e.g.,* Rules of General Application, Adjudication, and Enforcement (Proposed Rules), 77 Fed. Reg. 41,122 (proposing, among other things, that the complaint make clear whether complainant alleges the presence of an existing domestic industry or whether a domestic industry is in the process of being established) (proposed July 11, 2012) (to be codified at 19 C.F.R. pt. 210).

5. 19 U.S.C. § 1337(b)(1) (2006); 19 C.F.R. § 210.10(b).

6. 19 C.F.R. § 210.10(c).

7. There have been only two cases where the Commission has determined not to instituted an investigation: Complaint Concerning Certain Grain Oriented Silicon Steel, USITC Docket No. 1479 (1989) and Complaint concerning Certain Fruit Preserves in Containers Having Lids with Gingham Cloth Design, USITC Docket No. 1056 (1984).

ceedings before the ALJ ultimately culminate in the issuance of a final initial determination (ID) as to whether there is a Section 337 violation.[8] During the early phases of an investigation, the Commission's participation is limited to reviewing any interim IDs issued by the ALJ. These interim determination and review procedures occur as set forth in the Commission Rules of Practice and Procedure. Unlike a final ID, interim IDs are not dispositive of the ultimate issue of a Section 337 violation and are issued, for example, when a motion to amend the complaint and notice of investigation under 19 C.F.R. § 210.14 is granted, after a respondent has failed to show cause why it should not be found in default under 19 C.F.R. § 210.16, or the ALJ issues an order of summary determination under 19 C.F.R. § 210.18.[9]

Once a final ID has been certified to the Commission by the ALJ, any further submissions by the parties regarding the matter must be directed to the Commission. The Commission may determine to review the ID, in whole or in part, sua sponte, or the parties may petition the Commission to review all or part of the ID. The Commission's decision regarding an ID is final and ripe for appeal to the Federal Circuit, however, it must inform the public of its determination. If the Commission notice indicates that the Commission will not review an ID, it automatically becomes the determination of the Commission after 60 days for an ID on violation and after 30 days for an ID pertaining to most other issues.[10]

Once the ALJ issues the final ID on violation and recommended determination on remedy, the Commission can request further briefing by the parties and/or (1) adopt the ALJ's ID, (2) affirm the ALJ's finding but issue its own opinion to clarify its reasoning, or (3) review and reverse all or part of the ALJ's ID. Should the Commission find a violation, it will then issue a remedy in the form of a limited or general exclusion order and/or a cease and desist order(s) and terminate the investigation. Should the Commission find no violation, it will terminate the investigation based on that finding and not issue any remedy. In ei-

---

8. For more on ALJs, *see infra,* Section B.

9. *See also* 19 C.F.R. § 210.42(c). *See also* Proposed Rules, 77 Fed. Reg. 41,124 (clarifying motions which may be granted or denied by initial determination, including decisions by an ALJ on motions for forfeiture or return of respondents' bond) (proposed July 11, 2012) (to be codified at 19 C.F.R. pt. 210).

10. *Id.* at § 210.42(h).

ther event, any party adversely affected by a final determination of the
Commission may, within 60 days, appeal to the CAFC.[11]

B. ADMINISTRATIVE LAW JUDGE

Once an investigation is instituted, it is assigned by the Chief Administrative Law Judge to one of the administrative law judges, of whom there
are presently six. ALJs manage the day-to-day business of Section 337
investigations and serve as the initial trier of fact. ALJs preside over
investigations under the Commission Rules of Practice and Procedure[12]
and the Administrative Procedure Act.[13] While the Federal Rules of Civil
Procedure and the Federal Rules of Evidence are not specifically applicable to Section 337 proceedings, the ALJs may look to them, particularly where there is a gap in the Commission's own rules, for guidance in
overseeing discovery and conducting hearings.

Once assigned a case, an ALJ will typically begin by issuing a standard
Commission Protective Order to govern the disclosure of confidential information over the course of the investigation. This routine act by the ALJ
replaces the (often) months of wrangling over the terms of the equivalent
order in federal court litigation. Disclosure of protected information is
usually limited to Commission personnel, outside counsel, and qualified
experts. Early in each investigation, the ALJ will also issue an order setting
forth his ground rules. These rules set forth a detailed procedural schedule
and guidelines that govern the conduct of the investigation and supplement
the Commission Rules as set forth in 19 C.F.R. Part 210.[14] The ground
rules inform the parties of the required formalities for discovery and motions and the filing of documents, pre- and post-hearing statements, and
exhibits, among other issues, and the timing of each.

Within 45 days after institution of the investigation, the ALJ must
issue an order setting a target date for completion of the investigation.[15]
This is one of the mechanisms that encourage speedy decision-making

---

11. 19 U.S.C. § 1337(c).
12. 19 C.F.R. Part 210. *See generally* Proposed Rules, 77 Fed. Reg.
134,41121 (proposed July 11, 2012) (to be codified at 19 C.F.R. pt. 210).
13. 5 U.S.C. §§ 551–559.
14. *See, e.g., Certain Mobile Tels. & Wireless Commc'ns Devices Featuring Digital Cameras, & Components Thereof,* Inv. No. 337-TA-663, Order
No. 3 (Jan. 6, 2009).
15. 19 C.F.R. § 210.51(a).

under Section 337. If the ALJ sets this date within 16 months from the date of institution (the date the notice of institution is published in the *Federal Register*), his order is final and not subject to interlocutory review. If this date is set beyond 16 months, however, the order setting the target date constitutes an ID, which can be reviewed by the Commission.[16]

While the Commission has the ultimate decision-making authority in Section 337 investigations, ALJs possess decisional independence under the Administrative Procedure Act.[17] ALJs largely function like federal district court judges in civil cases without juries. They rule on motions, preside over trial-like hearings, and set the procedural schedule within the target date for the investigation. Their jurisdiction ends, however, once they certify an ID to the Commission.[18] At that time, any further communication regarding that particular matter must be addressed to the Commission.

No later than four months prior to the target date set by the Commission, the ALJ must issue an ID on violation.[19] Within 14 days of certifying his determination, the ALJ must also issue a recommended determination on remedy and bonding unless the Commission orders otherwise.[20] Under normal circumstances, this ID on violation will become the final determination of the Commission 60 days after the date of service of the ID, unless the Commission determines to review the ID.[21] If the Commission determines to review all or part of the ID on violation, one of three scenarios will occur. If the Commission issues a notice and/or opinion affirming the portions of the ID that were under review, those portions will become the binding final determination of the Commission (as modified by any opinion the Commission may have issued with such notice). If the Commission disagrees with any

---

16. *Id. But see* Proposed Revisions to § 210.51, 77 Fed. Reg. 134,41125 (providing that a target date greater than 12 months in a formal enforcement proceeding will require an initial determination, while a target date of 12 months or less may be set by an order) (proposed July 11, 2012) (to be codified at 19 C.F.R. pt. 210).

175 U.S.C. § 557(b).

18. *Id.* at § 557(d)(1).

19. 19 C.F.R. § 210.42(a)(1)(i). *See also* Proposed Rules, 77 Fed. Reg. 41,124 (proposed July 11, 2012) (to be codified at 19 C.F.R. pt. 210).

20. *Id.* at § 210.42(a)(1)(ii).

21. *Id.* at § 210.42(h).

portion or all of the ID, it will issue its own opinion, which will supersede that of the ALJ. If the Commission determines to take no position on any issue it reviewed in the ID, then that portion of the ID is not reversed, but also is not binding precedent on future proceedings.[22] After making its final determination on violation, the Commission then considers the ALJ's recommended determination in issuing an appropriate remedy (if any) in the investigation.

ALJs at the Commission are Article I judges and must qualify under the requirements of the Administrative Procedure Act. ALJs have career tenure. Historically, there were usually three or four ALJs at any given time. Due to the spike in Section 337 investigations in recent years, this number has increased. As of August 2012, there were six ALJs, one of whom and the longest tenured, Judge Charles E. Bullock, was designated Chief ALJ on October 20, 2011.[23] The Chief ALJ provides "administrative guidance and leadership to assure a thorough, yet expeditious, processing of the agency's section 337 investigation caseload."[24] However, like his predecessor, Chief Administrative Law Judge Paul J. Luckern, Judge Bullock shows respect for the independence of each ALJ.

---

22. Recently, the Court of Appeals for the Federal Circuit considered a circumstance in which the Commission "noticed" certain issues in an initial determination but took no position on those issues in their opinion. The effect of this "noticing" was that those issues were not immediately appealable, and the effect of the Commission's taking no position on those same issues was that they were never to be appealable by the losing party. The CAFC originally held that issues "noticed" for review by the Commission and subsequently not reviewed were still appealable to the CAFC. General Elec. v. U.S. Int'l Trade Comm'n, 670 F.3d 1206, 1220 (Fed. Cir. 2012). On rehearing, the CAFC withdrew this portion of its opinion. General Electric v. U.S. Int'l Trade Comm'n, 2012 WL 2626902 (July 6, 2012); *see also* Order No. 2010-1233 (Fed. Cir. July 6, 2012) (order released at the same time as the rehearing decision withdrawing a portion of its earlier opinion). Thus, the question of whether issues "noticed" for review by the Commission and subsequently not reviewed are appealable remains unanswered. *See infra* Chapter 12, Section B for a discussion of Commission Review and the *General Electric* case.

23. News Release, Bullock Named Chief Administrative Law Judge at U.S. International Trade Commission (Oct. 20, 2011) (*available at* http://www.usitc.gov/press_room/news_release/er1020jj1.htm).

24. *Id.*

C. OFFICE OF UNFAIR IMPORT INVESTIGATIONS

Attorneys in the Office of Unfair Import Investigations (OUII) play a vital role in both the pre- and post-initiation stages of a Section 337 proceeding. Before a complaint is filed with the Commission, it is typical for the prospective complainant to confer with OUII to ensure that the complaint will be properly filed under 19 C.F.R. § 210.12, both as to form and content required by the Commission rules. Any information obtained during this pre-filing process is treated as confidential and protected from disclosure. The reviewing OUII attorney will not necessarily be assigned to the case after institution.

Once a complaint has been filed with the Commission, OUII conducts an informal investigation of the allegations within the complaint. During this time, OUII may consult informally with both complainants and respondents on various issues raised in the complaint. Based upon this investigation, OUII will make a recommendation to the Commission as to whether or not it should institute a formal Section 337 investigation.

Once an investigation has been instituted, an OUII staff attorney may participate in the investigation as a neutral party whose primary purpose is to protect the public interest throughout the proceedings. Because the decision-maker is explicitly required by statute and Commission rules to consider whether issuing a particular remedy or terminating the investigation is in the public interest, the staff attorney is there to assist in ensuring that the public interest is kept at the forefront of decision-making on all issues.

Traditionally, an OUII staff attorney participated in every investigation at the Commission. That is no longer the case. In May 2011, the Commission adopted a rule amendment focusing the role of OUII in Section 337 investigations to implement a resource allocation proposal from the Commission's January 2011 Supplement to the Strategic Human Capital Plan 2009-2013.[25] The rule amendment does not affect the role of OUII in reviewing draft complaints prior to filing and advising the Commission

---

25. The Strategic Human Capital Plan proposes staffing and budgetary allocation solutions to utilize effectively the Commission's limited resources to handle the increased size and complexity of Section 337 investigations, which are increasing in number every year. *See* Supplement to the Strategic Human Capital Plan 2009-2013 (Jan. 2011), *available at* http://www.usitc.gov/intellectual_property/documents/2009_13_SHCP.pdf; 76 Fed. Reg. 24363 (May 2, 2011) (to be codified at 19 C.F.R. pt. 210).

on whether to institute an investigation. Rather, it eliminates the mandatory participation of OUII in each investigation and permits OUII to assign a staff attorney to an investigation on an issue-by-issue basis, including assignment for limited participation on specific issues after an investigation is instituted. The rule amendment permits such selective and focused participation to promote efficiency and fiscal responsibility.

The rule amendment has been implemented through three models of OUII's participation in Section 337 investigations. The model selected for an investigation depends on the nature of the issues involved, and selection is made on a case-by-case basis. The first model retains OUII's traditional role of participating as a party and addressing all or nearly all of the issues. The staff attorney can initiate discovery, file motions, respond to motions by the other parties, and examine witnesses at depositions and the hearing. While the staff attorney generally takes a position on all issues to be adjudicated at the hearing, the ALJ and the Commission are generally believed to give the staff attorney's positions particular weight on issues affecting the public interest or that have policy implications beyond the concerns of the private parties. Staff attorneys are also typically involved in conferences between the parties. Because OUII itself is a party, such communications between counsel for the parties and the staff attorney do not fall under the general prohibition against ex parte communications between parties to a proceeding before the Commission and employees of the Commission.[26]

In the second model, OUII will assign a staff attorney to participate and concentrate "on those issues on which it is able to provide the greatest added value and expertise."[27] In these cases, OUII will issue a "Notice of Commission Investigative Staff's Partial Participation" and identify the issues to which OUII's participation is limited. Such issues typically include domestic industry, remedy, the public interest, and bonding, but may include infringement and invalidity.[28]

---

26. For the general prohibition on ex parte communications with Commission employees, see 5 U.S.C. § 557(d)(1)(A).

27. Supplement to the Strategic Human Capital Plan 2009-2013, at 3.

28. *See, e.g., Certain Flip-top Vials & Prods. Using the Same*, Inv. No. 337-TA-779, Notice of Comm'n Investigative Staff's Partial Participation (June 20, 2011) (limiting participation to issues relating to the economic prong of domestic industry, remedy, the public interest, and bonding); *but see Certain Digital Televisions & Components Thereof, & Certain Elec. Devices Having a Blu-Ray Player & Components Thereof*, Inv. No. 337-TA-764, Notice of Comm'n Investigative Staff's Partial Participation (May 16, 2011) (limiting participation to "issues relating to" the patents at issue).

In the third model, OUII will cease to be a party altogether in Section 337 cases "which are less likely to draw upon its expertise."[29] In these cases, OUII will issue a "Commission Investigative Staff's Notice of Non-Participation" and affirmatively state that "OUII will not participate at any stage of the investigation, including discovery, motions practice, and the evidentiary hearing."[30]

D. OTHER OFFICES WITHIN THE COMMISSION

The Commission's Annual Report discloses the internal organization of its various offices, including the offices most closely involved in Section 337 investigations, such as the ALJs, OUII, Office of the Secretary, and Office of the General Counsel.[31]

---

29. Supplement to the Strategic Human Capital Plan 2009-2013, at 3.

30. *See, e.g., Certain Elec. Devices Having a Digital Television Receiver & Components Thereof,* Inv. No. 337-TA-774, Comm'n Investigative Staff's Notice of Nonparticipation (July 5, 2011); *Certain Mobile Tels. & Modems,* Inv. No. 337-TA-758, Comm'n Investigative Staff's Notice of Nonparticipation (July 22, 2011).

31. Budget Justification Fiscal Year 2013, at 62 (2012), *available at* http://www.usitc.gov/press_room/documents/budget_2013.pdf.

Fiscal Year 2012 U.S. International Trade Commission Office-Level Organization Chart

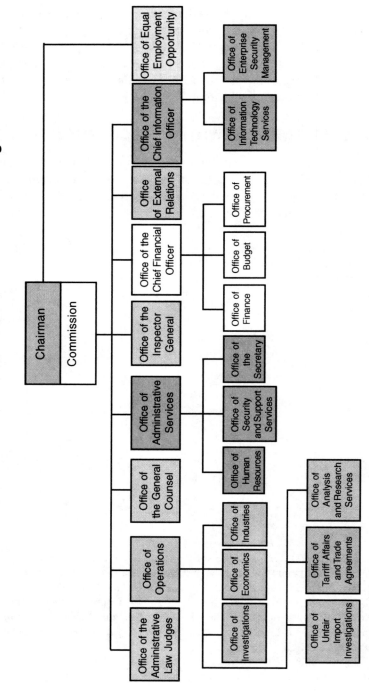

In addition to the Commission, ALJs, and OUII, the Office of the Secretary and Office of the General Counsel perform particularly important roles in the course of a Section 337 investigation.

The Office of the Secretary's formal mission is "to maintain the official records and documents" of the Commission.[32] Parties before the Commission frequently interact with this office over the course of an investigation. The Office of the Secretary's Docket Services is responsible for receiving all filings at the Commission and maintaining the Electronic Documents Information System (EDIS). Importantly, on November 7, 2011, new e-filing rules went into effect at the ITC, mandating e-filing[33] for most documents, public or confidential, under the general rules set out in 201.8 and 210.4.[34] In addition, the Office of the Secretary is responsible for issuing Commission notices, reports and orders, scheduling and participating in all Commission meetings and hearings, and making determinations regarding the treatment and release of confidential information received by the Commission under a protective order.[35]

The Office of the General Counsel (OGC) serves as the Commission's chief legal advisor, providing advice on legal issues including those that arise in Section 337 investigations, as well as on general administrative matters germane to the agency such as personnel and contracts.[36] While OGC manages a wide range of issues, with respect to Section 337 investigations its two most important functions are advising the Commission

---

32. Office of the Secretary, USITC, *available at* http://www.usitc.gov/secretary/ (last visited Apr. 13, 2012).

33. It is important to note that specific types of documents may require a paper submission in addition to an e-filing submission. Such documents generally require that the paper copies (2 for the ALJ, 8 for the Commission) be submitted by noon the next business day.

34. Exceptions are outlined in the Commission rules and the Handbook on Filing Procedures. Further exceptions may be granted with permission from the Secretary, which may be petitioned for via a waiver request. *See* Handbook on Filing Procedures, USITC (Nov. 7, 2011), *available at* http://www.usitc.gov/secretary/documents/handbook_on_filing_procedures.pdf. *See also* Proposed Rules, 77 Fed. Reg. 41,121 (expanding the list of submissions which must be filed electronically to include filings under §§ 210.38, 210.66, and 210.70) (proposed July 11, 2012) (to be codified at 19 C.F.R. pt. 210).

35. *See e.g.*, Office of the Secretary, http://www.usitc.gov/secretary/ (last visited Apr. 13, 2012).

36. Annual Performance Report, at 50 (2012), *available at* http://www.usitc.gov/press_room/documents/USITCFY2011APR.pdf.

during the review process and defending final determinations of the Commission in appellate litigation before the U.S. Court of Appeals for the Federal Circuit.[37]

E. THE PRIVATE PARTIES

In addition to the offices that participate in a Section 337 investigation on behalf of the Commission and the public, there are a number of private interests implicated, such as the complainant that files a complaint, the respondent(s) named in the investigation, and any third parties whose involvement with the complainant or a respondent bears on issues to be resolved in the investigation.

1. Complainant

The complainant in a Section 337 investigation is the party that files the complaint with the Commission alleging infringement of one or more of its intellectual property rights or another unfair act as delineated by 19 U.S.C. § 1337. A complaint can be filed by one or more entities that have standing to bring a Section 337 action. In many ways, the complainant in a Section 337 proceeding is similar to the plaintiff in a U.S. district court patent, trademark, or copyright infringement action. However, there are a number of significant differences. Primary among these is the requirement that the complainant ultimately prove that it, or at least one of its licensees,[38] has an established industry in the United States for the patent, copyright, trademark, mask work, boat hull design, or more general right concerned, or that such an industry is in the process of being established.[39] Thus, not all intellectual property holders can successfully bring a Section 337 action. Domestic industry can be shown through significant investment in plant and equipment, significant em-

---

37. Budget Justification Fiscal Year 2013, at 20, *available at* http://www.usitc.gov/press_room/documents/budget_2013.pdf.

38. *See, e.g., Certain Electronic Imaging Devices,* Inv. No. 337-TA-726, Order No. 18 (Initial Determination) (Feb. 7, 2011) (unreviewed); *Certain Electronic Devices,* 337-TA-673/667, Order No. 49C (Initial Determination) (Oct. 15, 2009) (unreviewed).

39. For IP-based investigations, the domestic industry requirement is set forth in 19 U.S.C. § 1337(a)(2)-(3). For other investigations, such as those based on trade secrets or other "unfair acts," this requirement is set forth in 19 U.S.C. § 1337(a)(1)(A)(i)–(iii) and further explained in applicable precedent.

ployment of labor or capital, or, in the case of patents, copyrights, and registered trademarks, substantial investment in the exploitation of the intellectual property right, including engineering, research and development, or licensing.[40]

A complainant does not have to be based in the United States to satisfy the domestic industry requirement. As long as the complainant can show that it has a valid U.S. intellectual property interest and that it has a sufficient level of business activity in the United States, it can proceed with its case. A growing number of foreign-based complainants are filing Section 337 actions and satisfying the domestic industry requirement.[41] In fact, in 2007, nearly one-third of complainants were foreign-based entities.[42] By 2011, nearly 40 percent of complainants were foreign-based entities.[43]

2. Respondent

The respondents in a Section 337 investigation are the parties named in the complaint (and subsequently in the notice of investigation issued by the Commission) against whom the complainant alleges a violation of Section 337. Respondents in Section 337 investigations are in many ways like the defendants in a U.S. district court infringement action. For instance, they have the burden of proving any affirmative defenses they wish to raise. One primary difference, however, is that, while any legal or equitable defense can be raised before the Commission, any counterclaims brought by the respondents must be removed to U.S. district court.[44] Additionally, discovery from foreign respondents before the Commission is often easier to obtain than that available to parties in U.S. district court, making the Commission an attractive forum for parties seeking a remedy against foreign entities.[45]

---

40. 19 U.S.C. § 1337(a)(3); *see also infra* Chapter 5, Section C.

41. *See* Gary Hnath & Mit Winter, *Protecting Your American Intellectual Property Rights: How Foreign Companies Can Utilize the U.S. International Trade Commission and Section 337 Investigations*, 4 NCCU INTELL. PROP. REV. 143 (2006).

42. Tom M. Schaumberg, *Section 337: A Thoroughly International IP Statute* (May 16, 2008), *available at* http://www.law360.com (can be accessed via http://www.adduci.com).

43. Data compiled from the website of the U.S. Int'l Trade Comm'n, http://www.usitc.gov (last visited Mar. 20, 2012).

44. 19 U.S.C. § 1337(c); 19 C.F.R. § 210.14(e).

45. For more information on discovery against foreign respondents, *see infra* Chapter 7.

Complainants have a choice of whom to name as respondents in an investigation, and they employ different strategies in making that choice. Generally, a complainant will name all foreign manufacturers and importers known to import the allegedly infringing articles. The significance of deciding whom to name as a respondent was heightened by the Federal Circuit's decision in *Kyocera Wireless Corp. v. U.S. International Trade Commission*.[46] Under that ruling, complainants may only obtain downstream relief—exclusion of finished products that incorporate the infringing product at issue in the investigation—via a limited exclusion order against the goods of parties that were named as respondents in the investigation. In other words, if a complainant is seeking a limited exclusion order and wishes to obtain downstream relief, it must name as respondents all downstream parties against whom the complainant wants relief.

If a complainant wishes to add a respondent after the investigation has been instituted, it may do so only by moving to amend the complaint and notice of investigation.[47] The ALJ's decision on this motion must be certified to the Commission as an ID. If an investigation is at a point where allowing the additional party into the investigation would be unfair or significantly inefficient, the ALJ or Commission may not allow it.[48]

When an entity has been named as a respondent to an investigation, it may proceed as an active participant, a limited participant for purpose of agreeing to discontinue its accused activities and obtaining a consent order,[49] or not participate at all. If it chooses not to participate, it runs the likely risk of being found in default and having a remedy imposed against it.[50] Many times, where multiple respondents are named in an investigation, the respondents will pool resources and work together on common issues to save costs and make defending their case more feasible.

Section 337 investigations have been brought against a wide variety of respondents over the years, spanning various regions across the world.

---

46. Kyocera Wireless Corp. v. U.S. Int'l Trade Comm'n, 545 F.3d 1340 (Fed. Cir. 2008).

47. 19 C.F.R. § 210.14(b). *See also* Proposed Rules, 77 Fed. Reg. 41,123 (moving the requirement for service on proposed respondents from § 210.15(a)(2) to § 210.14(b)(1)) (proposed July 11, 2012) (to be codified at 19 C.F.R. pt. 210).

48. *See, e.g., Certain Digital Televisions & Components Thereof*, Inv. No. 337-TA-789, Order No. 22 (Nov. 23, 2011).

49. *See* 19 U.S.C. § 1337(c); 19 C.F.R. § 210.21(c); *see also infra* Chapter 8, Section C for a discussion of consent orders.

50. For more on the procedures and effects of being found in default, *see infra* Chapter 8, Section D.

Between 2005 and 2011,[51] approximately 54 percent of respondents were U.S. companies, with the remaining respondents from foreign[52] countries:

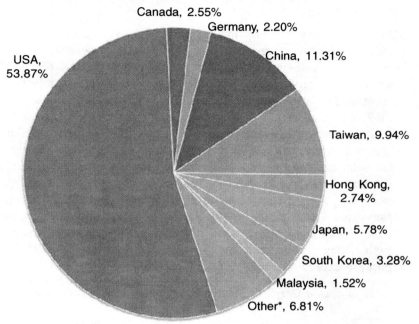

Respondents by Country, 2005-2011

Canada, 2.55%
Germany, 2.20%
USA, 53.87%
China, 11.31%
Taiwan, 9.94%
Hong Kong, 2.74%
Japan, 5.78%
South Korea, 3.28%
Malaysia, 1.52%
Other*, 6.81%

*   Other denotes countries with less than 1% representation at the ITC (each): Australia, Austria, Belgium, Belize, British Virgin Islands, Cayman Islands, Costa Rica, Denmark, Finland, France, Gibraltar, Haiti, India, Indonesia, Ireland, Israel, Italy, Kyrgyzstan, Macao, Mauritius, Mexico, Moldova, Netherlands, Nicaragua, Norway, Pakistan, Panama, Philippines, Portugal, Singapore, Spain, Sweden, Switzerland, Thailand, Turkey, United Arab Emirates, United Kingdom, Ukraine, and Vietnam.

51. Data compiled from the Web site of the U.S. Int'l Trade Comm'n, http://www.usitc.gov (last visited Mar. 20, 2012).

52. Between 2005 and 2011, approximately 33% of respondents were Asia-based respondents, of which approximately 32% were Chinese, 28% were Taiwanese, 16% were Japanese, 9% were South Korean, 8% were from Hong Kong, 1% were from Singapore, and the rest, with less than 1% each, were from India, Indonesia, Kyrgyzstan, Macao, Malaysia, Pakistan, the Philippines, or Thailand.

Compared to historical data, this breakdown shows an increasing number of named respondents being United States-based companies, reflecting increased offshore production by American companies.[53]

3. Third Parties

Due to the potentially vast implications of Section 337 relief, the interests of non-parties often come into play. This is particularly true with regard to the customers and importers of the named respondents' goods. When a third party's interests are affected or are likely to be affected by a Section 337 investigation, that party may seek to intervene under 19 C.F.R. § 210.19.[54]

If a party wishes to intervene in a Section 337 investigation, it must do so via written motion.[55] It may seek to intervene with full participation rights or it may move to intervene in a limited capacity.[56] Additionally, when moving to intervene, a third party must specify if it wishes to intervene on the side of complainants or respondents.[57] If a potential intervenor chooses to intervene on the side of respondents, it may request either "intervenor" or "respondent" status.[58] If "respondent" status is granted, then the intervenor may have the power to stay parallel district court proceedings under 28 U.S.C. § 1659.[59]

---

53. *See supra* Chapter 1, Section A, discussing origins of accused products.

54. *See, e.g., Certain GPS Devices & Prods. Containing Same*, Inv. No. 337-TA-602, Garmin Int'l's Submission on Remedy, the Public Interest and Bonding (Nov. 13, 2008).

55. 19 C.F.R. § 210.19.

56. *See, e.g., Certain Rare-Earth Magnets & Magnetic Materials & Articles Containing the Same*, Inv. No. 337-TA-413, Order No. 15 (Nov. 30, 1998) (potential intervenor moved for the limited purpose of submitting arguments to oppose complainants' motion to amend the Complaint); *Certain Baseband Processor Chips & Chipsets, Transmitter & Receiver (Radio) Chips, Power Control Chips, & Prods. Containing Same*, Inv. No. 337-TA-543, Order No. 27 (Feb. 15, 2006) (potential intervenors moved to intervene only as to the remedy phase of the investigation).

57. John Downing, Kati Hong & David Saunders, *Third-Party Intervention in Section 337 Investigations*, 22 ITCTLA 337 REP. 53, 57–58 (Summer Associate Ed., 2006).

58. *Id.* at 57.

59. *Id.; see also Certain Network Interface Cards & Access Points for Use in Direct Sequence Spread Spectrum Wireless Local Area Networks & Prods. Containing Same*, Inv. No. 337-TA-455, Comm'n Op. (Pub. Version), at 9 (July 17, 2001).

ALJs have discretion to grant a motion to intervene "to the extent and upon such terms as may be proper under the circumstances."[60] Generally, however, ALJs will look to the four-part test set forth in Federal Rule of Civil Procedure 24(a) for guidance.[61] If the ALJ decides to allow a party to intervene and the potential intervenor is seeking full participation rights, the ALJ must decide whether to limit the scope of intervention in any way.[62] The decision by an ALJ regarding a motion to intervene is an ID reviewable by the Commission.[63]

Before the Commission issues any remedial order in the investigation, it solicits briefing on remedy, the public interest, and bonding from the parties, interested agencies, and other interested parties.[64] Thus, even if a third party potentially implicated by an exclusion order chooses not to intervene, it may still seek to protect its interests by submitting a remedy or public interest brief. This might be particularly important where a general exclusion order could issue, which could prohibit importation of the third party's goods.

Additionally, third parties may be involved in Section 337 investigations during discovery. It is well established that parties to a Section 337 investigation may seek discovery from non-parties.[65] The primary mecha-

---

60. *Id.*; *see also Certain Garage Door Operators Including Components Thereof*, Inv. No. 337-TA-459, Order No. 7 (Nov. 20, 2001).

61. Downing et al., *supra* note 57, at 54 (2006); *see also Certain Recombinant Erythropoietin*, Inv. No. 337-TA-281, Order No. 6 (Mar. 31, 1988).

62. Downing et al., *supra* note 57, at 55.

63. 19 C.F.R. § 210.42(c). *But see* Proposed Rules, 77 Fed. Reg. 134,41124 (altering the kinds of motions that may be granted or denied by initial determination) (proposed July 11, 2012) (to be codified at 19 C.F.R. pt. 210).

64. *Id.* at § 210.50(a)(4). *See also* Proposed Rules, 77 Fed. Reg. 41,124 (clarifying that the 5-page limit applies only to submissions under § 210.50, in response to a recommended determination) (proposed July 11, 2012) (to be codified at 19 C.F.R. pt. 210).

65. However, the ALJ rejected complainant's requests to obtain public interest discovery from third party Google and significantly limited discovery from third party Broadcom because the companies were responding to the Commission's invitation to provide commentary on the impact on the public interest of the investigation, which did not provide the complainant with any basis for obtaining discovery from them. *See Certain Commc'ns Equip., Components Thereof, & Prods. Containing the Same, Including Power Over Ethernet Tels., Switches, Wireless Access Points, Routers & Other Devices Used in LANs, & Cameras*, Inv. No. 337-TA-817, Order No. 12 (May 29, 2012) and Order No. 13 (May 29, 2012). For more on third-party discovery, *see infra* Chapter 7, Section L.

nism for doing so against domestically based third parties is by a sub-poena.[66] To obtain discovery from foreign third parties, a party to a Section 337 investigation either may try to pursue that company's domestic affiliates (if any exist) or may attempt to obtain discovery through international procedures such as those set forth in the Hague Convention. Additionally, if third-party information is discoverable and in the possession of a party to the investigation, production of it may be required.

---

66. *See* 19 U.S.C. § 1333(a) regarding the Commission's subpoena power; *see also infra* Chapter 7.

CHAPTER 5

Elements of a Section 337 Investigation

A. IMPORTATION

Not surprisingly, given that the statute is titled Unfair Practices in Import Trade, importation is an essential element of a Section 337 investigation. Though importation is sometimes viewed as a jurisdictional issue, it is also a substantive one. For instance, the CAFC indicated in *Amgen v. International Trade Commission* that the ITC should not dismiss an investigation for lack of jurisdiction if a mixed issue of jurisdiction and substance, such as importation, is alleged to be absent.[1] Rather, the ITC should assume jurisdiction and decide the case on the merits.[2] Still, in many cases, importation is not a heavily contested issue; indeed, it is frequently the subject of a stipulation.[3] Some investigations, however, have tested the limits of the importation requirement.

The Commission generally interprets the term "importation" consistently with the definition applied by U.S. Customs and Border Protec-

---

1. Amgen Inc. v. U.S. Int'l Trade Comm'n, 902 F.2d 1532, 1536 (Fed. Cir. 1990); *see also Certain Elec. Devices with Image Processing Systems, Components Thereof, & Associated Software*, Inv. No. 337-TA-724, Comm'n Op., at 9-10 (Dec. 21, 2011).

2. *Id.*

3. *See, e.g., Certain Integrated Circuits, Chipsets, & Prods. Containing Same Including Televisions, Media Players, & Cameras*, Inv. No. 337-TA-709, Order No. 43 (Feb. 4, 2011); *Certain Mobile Tel. & Wireless Commc'n Devices Featuring Digital Cameras, & Components Thereof*, Inv. No. 337-TA-703, Order No. 10 (Apr. 16, 2010); *Certain Digital Cameras*, Inv. No. 337-TA-671, Order No. 12 (Aug. 13, 2009).

tion (Customs)—namely, "the bringing of goods within the jurisdictional limits of the United States with the intention to unlade them."[4] The "United States" for purposes of Section 337 includes Puerto Rico, but no other U.S. territories.[5] The entry of foreign goods into a foreign trade zone or a bonded warehouse is not considered importation unless the goods leave the foreign trade zone or bonded warehouse for consumption in the United States.[6] But almost any other type of importation can satisfy the statutory requirement. For example, reimportation of a product originally manufactured in the United States and shipped abroad—perhaps for further manufacturing steps or incorporation into downstream products—qualifies as importation under Section 337.[7] The Commission has also asserted authority over importations in the form of electronic transmissions of infringing software.[8] In light of the fact that Customs does not regulate electronic transmissions, however, the Commission has not included electronic "importations" within the scope of its exclusion orders.[9] The Commission has, however, barred such electronic importations of software in a cease and desist order.[10]

Investigations based on allegations of infringement of a statutory intellectual property right require "the importation into the United States, the sale for importation, or the sale within the United States after importation" of an infringing article[11] by an "owner, importer, or consignee," including agents thereof.[12] The statutory language with respect to inves-

---

4. Headquarters Ruling 115311 (May 10, 2001) (quoting Hollander Co. v. United States, 22 C.C.P.A. 645, 648 (1935), and United States v. Field & Co., 14 Ct. Cust. App. 406 (1927)).

5. *See* 19 C.F.R. § 101.1 (2012) ("Customs territory of the United States' includes only the States, the District of Columbia, and Puerto Rico.").

6. Bonded warehouses and foreign trade zones are designed to allow domestic activity involving foreign items to take place as if it were outside U.S. Customs territory. *See* 15 C.F.R. § 400 (2012).

7. *See Certain Sputtered Carbon Coated Computer Disks*, Inv. No. 337-TA-350, USITC Pub. 2701, Comm'n Op., at 9 (Nov. 1993) (reversing the ALJ's Initial Determination).

8. *Certain Hardware Logic Emulations Sys.*, Inv. No. 337-TA-383, USITC Pub. 3089, Comm'n Op. (Pub. Version), at 20 (Mar. 31, 1998).

9. *See id.*

10. *See id.* at 28–29.

11. In the case of a process patent, a violation can be based on the importation into the United States, the sale for importation, or the sale within the United States after importation of an article made by the patented process. 19 U.S.C. § 1337(a)(1)(B)(ii) (2006).

12. *See id.* at §§ 1337(a)(1)(B)–(E), (a)(4).

tigations based on unfair acts other than infringement of IP is somewhat different, but nonetheless requires importation or sale.[13] Thus, the statute reaches beyond importers of infringing articles to affect both pre- and post-importation sellers.

The "sale for importation" provision allows the statute to reach foreign manufacturers of infringing products, even if the foreign manufacturer has no direct involvement in the act of importation. Conceivably, any foreign sale of an infringing article later imported into the United States could constitute a "sale for importation." However, the Commission would likely be reluctant to find a violation based solely on such a sale absent evidence that the seller intended, or at least had knowledge, that the article in question was destined for importation into the United States. A "sale for importation" has been found even absent a subsequent importation. In *Variable Speed Wind Turbines*, the Commission determined that the existence of a contract for sale of infringing wind turbines intended for importation into the United States was sufficient to confer jurisdiction, even without performance of the contract or an actual importation of the articles in question.[14] A mere offer to sell, however, would not be sufficient to satisfy the importation requirement.[15]

Under the "sale in the United States after importation" provision, U.S. wholesalers and retailers with no direct involvement in the act of importation can be found in violation of the statute. The ability to obtain cease and desist orders against such entities, particularly where they maintain a substantial inventory of infringing products in the United States, can make it worthwhile to include such entities as respondents in Section 337 investigations.

Unlike the prohibitions against "sale for importation" and "sale in the United States after importation" requirements, "importation into the United States" does not require that an imported article be involved in a commercial sale. For example, importation of an infringing article for

---

13. *See id.* at § 1337(a)(1)(A).

14. *See Certain Variable Speed Wind Turbines*, Inv. No. 337-TA-376, Initial Determination, at 7–19 (June 20, 1996), *aff'd on appeal*, Enercon GmbH v. U.S. Int'l Trade Comm'n, 151 F.3d 1376, 1383 (Fed. Cir. 1998).

15. *See Certain Tool Handles, Tool Holders, Tool Sets & Components Therefor*, Inv. No. 337-TA-483, Order No. 13, at 3 (May 29, 2003) ("A mere offer for sale, which could have been rejected for an unlimited number of reasons and unconnected with any channels of trade, is no assurance that the accused product traveled any channel of trade.").

use as a promotional sample,[16] or importation for the purpose of clinical trials or basic research, satisfies the importation requirement.[17] Even importation of a single accused product suffices; there is no de minimis exception.[18] However, it is unclear whether an "imminent importation" alone is sufficient to satisfy the requirement.[19]

In a case based on utility patent infringement, the article must meet every limitation of the asserted claim as it is sold for importation, imported, or sold after importation.[20] Articles capable of performing a patented method may be analyzed under the statutory rubrics of indirect infringement.[21] Indirect infringement requires a showing of direct infringement by a third party, which cannot be established until the patented claim is used. While "use" may constitute infringement under 35

---

16. *See Certain Abrasive Prods. Made Using a Process for Making Powder Performs & Prods. Containing Same*, Inv. No. 337-TA-449, Initial Determination on Violation (Pub. Version), at 61 (Feb. 8, 2002) (unreviewed) (finding it irrelevant that respondent's had not sold accused product in the United States. The fact that the accused products had been imported was sufficient to satisfy the importation standard.)

17. *See Certain Recombinantly Produced Human Growth Hormones*, Inv. No. 337-TA-358, Order No. 64 (Jan. 26, 1994); *see also Certain Modified Vaccinia Ankara (MVA) Viruses & Vaccines & Pharmaceutical Compositions Based Thereon*, Inv. No. 337-TA-550, Initial & Recommended Determinations (Pub. Version) (Sept. 6, 2006) (unreviewed on this issue).

18. *Certain Digital Set-Top Boxes & Components Thereof*, Inv. No. 337-TA-712, Order No. 30, at 5 (Jan. 4, 2011) (quoting *Certain Purple Protective Gloves*, Inv. No. 337-TA-500, Order No. 17, at 5 (Sept. 23, 2004) ("[a] complainant need only prove importation of a single accused product."))

19. *See* Amgen, Inc. v. U.S. Int'l Trade Comm'n, 565 F.3d 846, 853 (Fed. Cir. 2009) (finding it unnecessary to decide whether the ITC has authority under Section 337 to address "imminent" importations because an actual importation occurred), revising earlier decision that the ITC had authority, 519 F.3d 1343, 1350–52 (Fed. Cir. 2008); *but see Certain GPS Chips, Associated Software & Sys., & Prods. Containing Same*, Inv. No. 337-TA-596, Final Initial & Recommended Determinations (Pub. Version), at 54 (June 13, 2008) (unreviewed) (finding that the Commission has authority to address imminent importations, but there was no such imminent importation because the product was still under development).

20. *Certain Elec. Devices with Image Processing Sys., Components Thereof, & Associated Software*, Inv. No. 337-TA-724, Comm'n Op., at 13–15 (Dec. 21, 2011).

21. *Id.* at 18.

U.S.C. § 271, wholly domestic "use," with no connection to the "importation" or "sale" of infringing articles, will not violate Section 337.[22]

Proof of importation is typically as simple as showing that an infringing product can be purchased in the United States and that the product bears markings of foreign origin—e.g., "Made in Japan." Complainants normally submit evidence of such a purchase with their initial complaint. For purposes of institution of the case, even a purchase through a website can be sufficient. However, evidence of additional importations should be sought in discovery. The Commission may be reluctant to find a Section 337 violation, or to issue a remedial order, if the only evidence of importation was a single sale, particularly if that sale was initiated by the complainant.

The importation of an infringing article can give rise to a Section 337 violation even if such imports ceased subsequent to, or even prior to, the filing of the complaint. In an early Section 337 case, the Commission held that "cessation of the importation alone does not obviate the possibility of finding a violation of § 337."[23] Similarly, in *Apparatus for the Continuous Production of Copper Rod*, the Commission upheld the ALJ's determination that

> [even if] all the practices of [the respondent] occurred before the notice of investigation was issued, the practices are still under the Commission's jurisdiction because they may show whether Section 337 violations are likely to occur in the future.[24]

Although the statute requires a determination to be made as to whether an unfair act "exists," it is not read so narrowly that the importation must occur on the precise day that the Commission makes this determination. Recent importations can be used to show whether future importations are likely. If past importations constituted unfair acts, it may be reasonable to expect that future importations will be, as well.[25]

---

22. *Id.* at 18–19.

23. *Certain Steel Toy Vehicles*, Inv. No. 337-TA-31, USITC Pub. 880, Comm'n Op., at 4 (Apr. 1978).

24. *Certain Apparatus for the Continuous Prod. of Copper Rod*, Inv. No. 337-TA-52, USITC Pub. 1017, Comm'n Op. (Nov. 1979).

25. *Id.*

B. UNFAIR ACT

As set forth in Chapter III, Section 337 actions can be based on infringement of statutory IP as well as other types of "unfair methods of competition."[26] Regardless of the asserted cause of action, establishing an "unfair act" generally requires the complainant to prove the same elements, and overcome the same affirmative defenses, as would be required to prevail in district court litigation involving that cause of action. However, Section 337 investigations based on patent infringement—by far the most commonly asserted "unfair act"—differ from district court litigation in several important, substantive aspects.

In an investigation based on patent infringement, demonstrating an "unfair act" requires proof that the imported articles in question infringe or are made through a process covered by a U.S. patent.[27] Just as in U.S. district court, an asserted patent is presumed to be valid and enforceable, and respondents can raise invalidity and unenforceability as defenses. Most other affirmative defenses that could be raised in a district court infringement action are also available at the Commission. While respondents may raise counterclaims, these are not decided by the Commission but are instead immediately removed to U.S. district court.[28]

Unlike a district court, the Commission lacks the general authority to declare patents invalid or unenforceable. But this distinction is typically of little consequence (except with respect to the res judicata effect of a Commission decision), because the Commission is empowered to consider invalidity and unenforceability defenses when determining whether Section 337 has been violated.[29] The Commission also lacks the authority to correct inventorship flaws in the patents asserted before it.[30] If an asserted patent fails to name one of the true inventors (nonjoinder),

---

26. 19 U.S.C. § 1377 (a)(1).

27. *See id.* at § 1337(a)(1)(B)(i)–(ii).

28. *See id.* at § 1337(c) ("A respondent may raise any counterclaim in a manner prescribed by the Commission. Immediately after a counterclaim is received by the Commission, the respondent raising such counterclaim shall file a notice of removal with a United States district court in which venue for any of the counterclaims raised by the party would exist under section 1391 of title 28. . . . Action on such counterclaim shall not delay or affect the proceeding under this section, including the legal and equitable defenses that may be raised under this subsection."); 19 C.F.R. § 210.14(e).

29. *See, e.g.,* Corning Glass Works v. U.S. Int'l Trade Comm'n, 799 F.2d 1559, 1566 (Fed. Cir. 1986) (citing S. REP. No. 1298, at 196 (1974)).

30. *Cf.* 35 U.S.C. § 256 (2006).

the patent is unenforceable at the Commission, unless or until the inventorship flaw is cured at the PTO.[31]

One important exception to the general rule that all defenses are available in a Section 337 investigation concerns the defense of laches. In a district court patent infringement case, laches—i.e., an unreasonable delay in asserting the claim—can preclude the recovery of prefiling damages, but the defense does not preclude prospective relief.[32] Because Commission relief is prospective only, the defense of laches is not available in a Section 337 investigation.[33] Equitable estoppel is available as a defense, however.[34]

Another important distinction between Section 337 practice and U.S. district court patent litigation concerns articles made abroad using a patented process. Such articles have historically been covered by Section 337, but only became the subject of district court infringement actions with the 1988 enactment of 35 U.S.C. § 271(g), which established that the import, sale, or use of a product made by a patented process constitutes infringement.[35] Section 271(g) has two exceptions: it does not ap-

---

31. *See Certain Home Vacuum Packaging Prods.,* Inv. No. 337-TA-496, USITC, Pub. 3681 (Temporary Relief Proceeding), Order No. 36 (Initial Determination), at 67 (Dec. 16, 2004) (*aff'd in relevant part* on Comm'n review); *Certain EPROM, EEPROM, Flash Memory, & Flash Microcontroller Semiconductor Devices & Prods. Containing Same,* Inv. No. 337-TA-395, Final Initial & Recommended Determinations, at 95–96 (Mar. 19, 1998) (unreviewed on this issue).

32. *See* A.C. Aukerman Co. v. R.L. Chaides Constr. Co., 960 F.2d 1020, 1040–41 (Fed. Cir. 1992) (en banc) ("laches bars relief on a patentee's claim only with respect to damages accrued prior to suit").

33. *See, e.g., Certain Coaxial Cable Connectors & Components Thereof,* Inv. No. 337-TA-650, Order No. 19 (Pub. Version), at 7 (Apr. 10, 2009) ("laches does not provide a respondent accused of patent infringement with any meaningful defense in a Section 337 investigation"); *Certain Bearing &Packaging Thereof,* Inv. No. 337-TA-469, Initial Determination Concerning Violation of Section 337, at 27 (Apr. 10, 2003) ("[L]aches is never a valid defense to patent infringement claims brought before the Commission."); *Certain Methods of Making Carbonated Candy Prods.,* Inv. No. 337-TA-292, USITC Pub. 2390, Initial Determination (Pub. Version), at 116–17 (June 1991) ("[C]lear, controlling Federal Circuit precedent compels the result that laches in patent-based litigation applies only to recovery of pre-filing monetary damages, and does not apply to prospective relief.").

34. *See, e.g., id.* at 118; *Certain Notebook Computer Prods. & Components Thereof,* Inv. No. 337-TA-705, Order No. 22 (Initial Determination), at 15 (Sept. 28, 2010) (unreviewed).

35. 35 U.S.C. § 271(g).

ply if the product made by the patented process "is materially changed by subsequent processes,"[36] or if the product made by the patented process "becomes a trivial and nonessential component of another product."[37] Significantly, neither of these exceptions applies at the ITC.[38] Thus, an unfair act under Section 337(a)(1)(B)(ii), which covers articles made by a patented process, can be established even under circumstances where relief would be unavailable in district court.

In contrast, the "safe harbor" provision of 35 U.S.C. § 271(e)(1), which exempts from infringement the use or sale of patented drug products for the purpose of development and submission of information pursuant to federal drug regulations, does apply at the ITC.[39]

C. DOMESTIC INDUSTRY

The nature of Section 337 as a trade statute, as opposed to an enforcement statute for IP, explains the importance attached to the requirement that the relief provided by the statute be available only to entities maintaining an industry in the United States.[40] The domestic industry requirement is imposed "to prevent the ITC from becoming a forum for resolving disputes brought by foreign complainants whose only connection with the United States is ownership of a U.S. patent."[41] Similar sentiments are

---

36. *See id.* at § 271(g)(1).

37. *See id.* at § 271(g)(2).

38. *See Certain Sucralose, Sweeteners Containing Sucralose, & Related Intermediate Compounds Thereof,* Inv. No. 337-TA-604, Comm'n Op., at 13–16 (Apr. 28, 2009); Kinik Co. v. U.S. Int'l Trade Comm'n, 362 F.3d 1359, 1363 (Fed. Cir. 2004) (determining that Congress did not intend to alter the scope of Section 337 in enacting 35 U.S.C. § 271).

39. *See* Amgen, Inc. v. U.S. Int'l Trade Comm'n, 565 F.3d 846, 851–52 (Fed. Cir. 2009) (determining that the Congressional purpose of removing all patent-based barriers to proceeding with federal regulatory approval of medical products weighs heavily against selectively withholding the § 271(e)(1) exemption depending on whether infringement action is in the district court or the ITC).

40. *See Certain Stringed Musical Instruments & Components Thereof,* Inv. No. 337-TA-586, Initial & Recommended Determinations, at 25 (Dec. 3, 2007) (aff'd on Comm'n review) ("The domestic industry requirement [serves] as a gatekeeper to prevent the excessive use of the ITC under Section 337.") (citation omitted).

41. *Certain Battery-Powered Ride-On Toy Vehicles & Components Thereof,* Inv. No. 337-TA-314, USITC Pub. 2420, Comm'n Op., at 21 (Aug. 1991).

expressed in the legislative history of the 1988 Amendments to Section 337. Despite abolishing the injury requirement for certain statutory IP— e.g., patents, trademarks, copyrights, etc.—the House commented and the Senate confirmed (almost verbatim) that:

> [T]his [domestic industry] requirement was maintained in order to preclude holders of U.S. intellectual property rights who have no contact with the United States other than owning such intellectual property rights from utilizing Section 337. The purpose of the Commission is to adjudicate trade disputes between U.S. industries and those who seek to import goods from abroad. Retention of the requirement that the statute be utilized on behalf of an industry in the United States retains that essential nexus.[42]

Thus, in order to obtain relief under Section 337, a complainant bears the burden of establishing the existence of a domestic industry.

In cases based on statutory IP, which constitute the vast majority of Section 337 investigations, the Commission typically divides the domestic industry analysis into an "economic prong" (the existence of significant operations within the United States consisting of more than mere sales activity) and a "technical prong" (a showing that the complainant's economic activities are linked to its utilization of the asserted IP—generally by demonstrating that the complainant's products practice the IP in question).[43] This method of analysis is not always used, however. In investigations based on non-statutory IP, it is necessary to show that the unfair act threatens to destroy or substantially injure a domestic industry, without an express requirement that the threatened industry be based on the IP at issue.[44] In non-IP investigations, the scope of the domestic industry is defined based on the industry that is "the target of the unfair

---

42. H.R. Rep. No. 100-40, at 156-157 (1987); *see also* S. Rep. No. 100-71, at 129 (1987); 19 U.S.C. § 1337(a)(1)(A)(i)–(iii), (a)(2).

43. *See Certain Video Graphics Display Controllers*, Inv. No. 337-TA-412, USITC Pub. No. 3224, Initial Determination (Pub. Version), at 9 (Aug. 1999) (unreviewed); *Certain Hybrid Elec. Vehicles & Components Thereof*, Inv. No. 337-TA-688, Order No. 5, at 3–6 (Feb. 26, 2010); *Certain Semiconductor Integrated Circuits & Prods. Containing Same*, Inv. No. 337-TA-665, Initial Determination on Violation, at 153–55 (Oct. 14, 2009) (unreviewed in relevant part)

44. *See* TianRui Group Co. Ltd. v. U.S. Int'l Trade Comm'n, 661 F.3d. 1322, 1335–37 (Fed. Cir. 2011).

acts and practices."[45] Finally, as explained below, even in investigations based on statutory IP, if the domestic industry is based on licensing, the Commission typically does not conduct a technical prong analysis.[46]

1. Economic Prong

For statutory IP–based investigations, Section 337 provides that a domestic industry will be deemed to exist:

> if there is in the United States, with respect to the articles protected by the patent, copyright, [registered] trademark, or mask work concerned—
> (A) significant investment in plant and equipment;
> (B) significant employment of labor or capital; or
> (C) substantial investment in its exploitation, including engineering, research and development, or licensing.[47]

The complainant need only satisfy one of these criteria to meet the economic prong of the domestic industry requirement.[48] The burden of

---

45. *See Certain Nut Jewelry & Parts Thereof*, Inv. No. 337-TA-229, USITC Pub. No. 1929, Comm' Op., at 8 (Nov. 1986); *Certain Cast Steel Railway Wheels, Certain Processes for Mfg. or Relating to Same & Certain Prods. Containing Same (Cast Steel Railway Wheels)*, Inv. No. 337-TA-655, Initial Determination, at 76 (Oct. 16, 2009) (unreviewed) (citing *Certain Processes for the Manufacture of Skinless Sausage Casings & Resulting Prod.*, Inv. No. 337-TA-148/169, Initial Determination, at 341–43 (Dec. 1984) (unreviewed)).

46. *See Certain Semiconductor Chips with Minimized Chip Package Size & Prods. Containing Same*, Inv. No. 337-TA-432, Initial Determination (Pub. Version), at 11 (Jan. 24, 2001) ("[A] complainant is not required to show that it or one of its licensees practices a patent-in-suit in order to find that a domestic industry exists pursuant to 19 U.S.C. § 1337(a)(3)(C), which pertains to licensing."); *Certain Short-Wavelength Light Emitting Diodes, Laser Diodes & Prods. Containing Same*, Inv. No. 337-TA-640, Order No. 72 (Initial Determination), at 5 (May 8, 2009) (unreviewed on this issue) ("[D]omestic industry analysis under subsection (C) 'subsumes within it the technical-prong aspect' and, thus, only the economic prong needs to be proven") (citation omitted).

47. 19 U.S.C. § 1337(a)(3).

48. *Certain Variable Speed Wind Turbines & Components Thereof*, Inv. No. 337-TA-376, USITC Pub. 3003, Comm'n Op. (Pub. Version), at 15 (Nov. 1996); *Certain Static Random Access Memories & Prods. Containing the Same*, Inv. No. 337-TA-792, Order No. 37 (Initial Determination), at 3 (Feb. 14,

showing a "significant" or "substantial" investment is not particularly high, but de minimis investments have been held insufficient.[49] Importantly, the evaluation is not made according to a rigid mathematical formula. Rather, it is a fact-based inquiry taking into account the articles of commerce, the industry in question, and the complainant's relative size.[50]

The statutory language quoted above applies only to investigations based on statutory IP. For investigations based on other types of "unfair acts," the statute does not define "industry," but Commission precedent as well as legislative history indicates that an industry can be based on criteria (A) and (B)—significant investment in plant and equipment or significant employment of labor or capital—but not on (C)—substantial investment in exploitation, including engineering, research and development, or licensing.[51] In addition, such investigations require a showing of injury, as discussed later in this chapter.[52]

a. Manufacturing-Based Domestic Industry Analysis

Domestic manufacturing activity has traditionally served as the basis for satisfying the domestic industry requirement.[53] In Commission deci-

---

2012) (unreviewed) ("Given that [the] criteria are listed in the disjunctive, satisfaction of any one of them will be sufficient to meet the economic prong of the domestic industry requirement.").

49. *See Certain Stringed Musical Instruments & Components Thereof (Stringed Musical Instruments)*, Inv. No. 337-TA-586, Comm'n Op., at 26–27 (May 16, 2008) (finding the economic prong was not satisfied where complainant's investments totaled $8,500 over a 17-year period plus unquantified "sweat equity").

50. *See Certain Printing & Imaging Devices & Components Thereof*, Inv. No. 337-TA-690, Comm'n Op., at 27 (Feb. 17, 2011); *Stringed Musical Instruments*, Inv. No. 337-TA-586, Comm'n Op., at 26 (May 16, 2008).

51. *See* 19 U.S.C. § 1337(a)(3); H.R. Rep. No. 100-40, at 157 (1987) (concerning § 1337(a)(3)(A)–(C), "[t]he first two factors in this definition [significant employment of labor and capital, and significant investment in plant and equipment] have been relied on in some Commission decisions finding that an industry does exist in the United States. The third factor [substantial investment in exploitation, including engineering, research and development, and licensing], however, goes beyond ITC's recent decisions in this area.").

52. *See* 19 U.S.C. § 1337(a)(1)(A).

53. *See Certain Products with Gremlins Character Depictions*, Inv. No. 337-TA-201, USITC Pub. 1815, Comm'n Op., at 5 (Mar. 1986), ("In accordance with [Section 337's legislative history], the commission has consistently defined the industry in Section 337 cases to be the domestic production of the products covered by the intellectual property rights in question."); *see*

sions finding a significant investment in plant, equipment, labor, or capital pursuant to subsections (A) and (B), complainants have typically demonstrated multimillion-dollar expenditures on items such as manufacturing facilities and employee salaries.

Importation and sales activities alone have been deemed insufficient to establish domestic industry. For example, in *Miniature Battery-Operated, All-Terrain, Wheeled Vehicles*,[54] the CAFC, in affirming the Commission's determination of no domestic industry, explained that:

> [T]he entire manufacturing of the toy vehicles occurs in Hong Kong, as does most of the packaging and quality control. [Complainant] Schaper purchases from Kader the toy vehicles, the great bulk of which are already packaged for sale in blister packs, and imports them into the United States. . . . Schaper's inspection activities upon receipt in this country appear to involve ordinary sampling techniques. . . . Also, Schaper's very large expenditures for advertising and promotion cannot be considered part of the production process. Were we to hold otherwise, few importers would fail the test of constituting a domestic industry.[55]

Nevertheless, the Commission has recognized that, in appropriate circumstances, a complainant may satisfy the economic prong by demonstrating that its service and repair activities and investments are significant with respect to the articles protected by its intellectual property rights.[56] For example, complainants have established domestic industries

---

also Certain Male Prophylactic Devices, Inv. No. 337-TA-546, Comm'n Op. (Pub. Version), at 39 (Aug. 1, 2007) ("The economic prong requirement exists to assure that domestic production-related activities, as opposed to those of a mere importer, are protected by the statute.").

54. *Certain Miniature Battery-Operated, All-Terrain Wheeled Vehicles* (Pub. Version), Inv. No. 337-TA-122, USITC Pub. 1300, Comm'n Op. (Oct. 1982).

55. Schaper Mfg. Co. v. U.S. Int'l Trade Comm'n, 717 F.2d 1368, 1372–73 (Fed. Cir. 1983).

56. *Certain Printing & Imaging Devices & Components Thereof*, Inv. No. 337-TA-690, Comm'n Op. (Pub. Version), at 29–30 (Feb. 17, 2011) (citing *Certain Battery-Powered Ride-on Toy Vehicles & Components Thereof*, Inv. No. 337-TA-314, USITC Pub. 2420, Initial Determination, at 20–21 (Aug. 1991) (unreviewed); *Certain Airtight Cast-Iron Stoves*, Inv. No. 337-TA-69, USITC Pub. 1126, Comm'n Op., at 10–11 (Jan. 1981); *Certain Airless Spray Pumps &*

based on operation of U.S. call centers that provide customer support and assist with technical service of products.[57]

A domestic industry can exist even if only a portion of the manufacturing activity takes place in the United States. For example, one ALJ noted that "[t]raditionally, the Commission has not required that raw materials or any specific production step be of U.S. origin, but rather has employed a value-added analysis to arrive at its definition of a particular domestic industry when a complainant's manufacturing process involves offshore activity."[58] In one investigation, a domestic industry was found to exist because, "[although] a portion of [complainant's product] [was] manufactured in Brazil, between 30 and 40 percent of the dollar value of the machine [was] produced in the United States."[59]

A domestic industry must exist or be "in the process of being established."[60] In most cases, the appropriate date for determining whether a domestic industry exists or is in the process of being established is the date the complaint is filed.[61] In a limited number of cases, however, the Commission will evaluate whether a domestic industry exists based on a time

---

Components Thereof, Inv. No. 337-TA-90, USITC Pub. 1199, Comm'n Op., at 10-11 (Nov. 1981); *Certain Male Prophylactic Devices,* Inv. No. 337-TA-546, Comm'n Op., at 41–45 (Aug. 1, 2007); *Certain Video Displays, Components Thereof, & Prods. Containing Same,* Inv. No. 337-TA-687, Order No. 20 (Initial Determination) (May 20, 2010) (unreviewed)).

57. *See, e.g., Certain Video Displays, Components Thereof, & Prods. Containing Same,* Inv. No. 337-TA-687, Order No. 20 (Initial Determination), at 11 (May 20, 2010) (unreviewed); *Certain Liquid Crystal Display Devices & Prods. Containing Same,* Inv. No. 337-TA-631, Order No. 18 (Initial Determination), at 8 (Sept. 23, 2008) (unreviewed).

58. *Certain Nut Jewelry & Parts Thereof,* Inv. No. 337-TA-229, USITC Pub. 1929, Initial Determination (Pub. Version), at 28 (Nov. 1986).

59. *Certain Woodworking Machs.,* Inv. No. 337-TA-174, USITC Pub. 1979, Initial Determination (Pub. Version), at 30 (May 1987). *See also Certain Microlithographic Machs. & Components Thereof (Microlithographic Machines),* Inv. No. 337-TA-468, Initial & Recommended Determinations, at 341–61 (Jan. 29, 2003) (unreviewed) (comparing the complainant's domestic activities to its foreign activities and finding that, because the complainant's U.S. expenditures constituted a minor part of its overall investments with respect to the products at-issue, there had not been a "significant" U.S. investment in equipment or employment of labor).

60. 19 U.S.C. § 1337(a)(2).

61. *See Certain Video Game Sys. & Controllers,* Inv. No. 337-TA-743, Comm'n Op., at 5 (Jan. 20, 2012); *Certain Coaxial Cable Connectors & Components Thereof & Products Containing Same,* Inv. No. 337-TA-743-650, Comm'n Op. at 51 n.17.

other than the date the complaint is filed, such as when a "significant and unusual development has occurred."[62] For example, in several investigations, the Commission has considered significant developments that occurred after the complaint was filed. This may well be explained by the waning health of the complainant as a result of the alleged unfair acts.[63]

Prefiling expenditures and investments can also be considered by the Commission because "the domestic industry determination is not made by application of a rigid formula."[64] For example, in *Ride-On Toy Vehicles*, the respondents argued with respect to one of the asserted patents that there was no domestic industry because, as of the date of the complaint, the complainant no longer manufactured toys using technology covered by that patent.[65] The ALJ found that a domestic industry for the products covered by that patent still existed, explaining:

---

62. *Certain Concealed Cabinet Hinges & Mounting Plates*, Inv. No. 337-TA-289, Comm'n Op. (Pub. Version), 1990 WL 10608981, at *11 (Jan. 8, 1990) (evaluating the exisatence of the domestic industry "as of the discocery cutoff date prior to the evidentiary hearing").

63. *Certain Semiconductor Integrated Circuits & Prods. Containing the Same*, Inv. No. 337-TA-665, Initial Determination, at 229-30 (Oct. 19, 2009) (examining a complainant's domestic industry where the complainant filed for bankruptcy after filing a complaint with the Commission) (unreviewed in relevant part); *Certain Variable Speed Wind Turbines & Components Thereof (Variable Speed Wind Turbines)*, Inv. No. 337-TA-376, Comm'n Op., at 22-26 (Sep. 23, 1996) (same); *Certain Laser Imageable Lithographic Printing Plates*, Inv. No. 337-TA-636, Initial Determination, at 93-94 (July 24, 2009) (examining technical evidence prepared after the filing of the complaint when evaluating domestic industry) (unreviewed in relevant part).

64. *Certain Video Graphics Display Controllers & Prods. Containing Same*, Inv. No. 337-TA-412, Initial Determination (Pub. Version), at 13 (May 14, 1999) (unreviewed in relevant part) (finding that though the complainant was not currently manufacturing, past substantial investments and the maintenance of existing inventory sufficiently established the economic prong of domestic industry); *Variable Speed Wind Turbines*, Comm'n Op. at 25 ("[W]hile there have been circumstances where not practicing the patent claim in issue for a significant time has defeated a section 337 investigation, we note that in this case it has only been a matter of several months, at most, since the ALJ found that complainant was, in fact, exploiting the patent.").

65. *Certain Battery Powered Ride-on Toy Vehicles & Components Thereof*, Inv. No. 337-TA-314, USITC Pub. 2420, Initial Determination (Pub. Version) (Aug. 1991). In fact, complainant admitted that it stopped manufacturing the product covered by the patent in February 1989. The complaint was filed on May 15, 1990.

The case raises an issue of timing. The domestic industry issue in this case is whether there must be significant activities taking place in the United States at the time of infringement, or whether the patent is entitled to protection based on substantial past expenditures in the United States relating to the development and exploitation of the patent. . . . The issue here is whether a patent owner who clearly had a domestic industry when the invention was developed and the patent was obtained should lose his patent protection against foreign imports under Section 337 merely because his sales of the patented product have declined or even stopped. . . . I do not think that it was the intention of Congress to require that all of the costs that make up a domestic industry be incurred at the exact moment that the patent is infringed.[66]

Similarly, in *Rotary Wheel Printing Systems*, the ALJ considered manufacturing activities that occurred approximately nine months before the complaint was filed. Interpreting the *Bally v. ITC* decision liberally, the ALJ stated:

The [*Bally v. ITC*] Court also indicated that the focus of this inquiry is based on the actual business operations that the Commission is concerned to protect from unfair competition in the application of Section 337. From this context, it does not appear that the Court saw any magic in the date of filing the complaint from which all analysis must flow, but rather that the industry must be defined in accordance with market realities. The circumstances of the present case compel the conclusion that the date of filing the complaint has less significance than in most Section 337 investigations.[67]

In *Variable Speed Wind Turbines*, the ALJ concluded in an initial determination that the complainant had made sufficient investments in domestic manufacturing to support the existence of a domestic indus-

---

66. See *id.* at 19–20. The ALJ also found that a domestic industry existed even without using past expenditures on labor and capital because the complainant continued to do warranty and repair work on the older toys. *See id.* at 20–21.

67. *See Certain Rotary Wheel Printing Sys.*, Inv. No. 337-TA-185, USITC Pub. 1857, Initial Determination (Pub. Version), at 243 (May 1986).

try.[68] However, the complainant subsequently filed for bankruptcy and ceased its manufacturing activities, though it had continued its maintenance and operation services for previously sold products. The Commission determined that, based on its previous manufacturing investments and its continued operation and maintenance activities, the complainant had proven the existence of a domestic industry.[69]

The Commission has also found that the statutory language is broad enough to cover investments made not only before the complaint was filed but before issuance of the patent.[70]

b. Non-Manufacturing-Based Domestic Industry Analysis

In 1988, Congress amended Section 337 to permit the Commission to consider engineering, research and development, or licensing activities as a domestic industry under 19 U.S.C. § 1337(a)(3)(C). This amendment, which applies only to investigations based on statutory IP, relaxed the requirement that a domestic industry be based on manufacturing activities.[71] The change was, in part, intended to grant protection under Section 337 to entities like universities and small businesses that make substantial domestic investments but do not manufacture products in the United States.[72] "The 1988 amendment to the domestic industry statutory language of Section 337 and its legislative history support a liberal and flexible interpretation of the requirement."[73] Nevertheless, it remains the

---

68. *Certain Variable Speed Wind Turbines & Components Thereof*, Inv. No. 337-TA-376, Initial Determination, at 72–73 (May 30, 1996) (unreviewed on this issue).

69. *Id.* at Comm'n Op. (Pub. Version), at 24–25 (Sept. 6, 1996).

70. *Certain Video Game Sys. & Controllers*, Inv. No. 337-TA-743, Comm'n Op. (Pub. Version), at 6 (Apr. 14, 2011).

71. Prong (C) investments do not necessarily require "actual production of the article in the United States if it can be demonstrated that substantial investment and activities of the type enumerated are taking place in the United States." *Certain Microlithographic Machs. & Components Thereof (Microlithographic Machines)*, Inv. No. 337-TA-468, Initial & Recommended Determinations (Pub. Version), at 345 (Jan. 29, 2003) (unreviewed) (quoting H.R. REP. NO. 100-40, pt. 1, at 157 (1987)).

72. *See* H.R. REP. NO. 100-40, at 155–59 (1987); S. REP. NO. 100-71, at 127–30 (1987).

73. *Certain Video Graphics Display Controllers & Prods. Containing Same*, Inv. No. 337-TA-412, USITC Pub. 3224, Initial Determination (Pub. Version), at 13 (Aug. 1999) (unreviewed).

case that activities that would be typical of any importer or seller do not constitute a domestic industry.[74]

In non-manufacturing based domestic industry cases, the Commission requires that the facts relating to domestic industry be weighed in a context-based analysis.[75] In this analysis, whether the complainant's investment and/or employment activities are "substantial" is not measured in the abstract or in an absolute sense, but rather is assessed with respect to the nature of the activities and how they are "substantial" in relation to the articles protected by the intellectual property right. The Commission has explained that "the magnitude of the investment cannot be assessed without consideration of the nature and importance of the complainant's activities to the patented products in the context of the marketplace or industry in question."[76]

1) Engineering and Research & Development

Engineering and research and development activities under subsection 337(a)(3)(C) have often been considered in addition to the domestic investment and employment activities of subsection 337(a)(3)(A) and (B). In *Audio Digital-to-Analog Converters*, for example, the complainant did not manufacture the product practicing the asserted patents, but the ALJ concluded that the complainant's investment in pre- and post-manufacturing activities in the United States, such as conceptualizing product requirements and specifications, engineering, research and development, performing circuit designs, simulating designs, and testing, was sufficient to prove the existence of a domestic industry.[77]

Similarly, in *Encapsulated Integrated Circuit Devices*, the complainant had no manufacturing activity in the United States but did maintain a facility focused on engineering and research and development.[78] The ALJ

---

74. *See Microlithographic Machines,* Initial & Recommended Determinations, at 345 (Congress made it clear that "[m]arketing and sales in the United States alone would not . . . be sufficient to [satisfy prong (C)].") (citation omitted).

75. *Certain Printing & Imaging Devices & Components Thereof,* Inv. No. 337-TA-690, Comm'n Op. (Pub. Version), at 27–31 (Feb. 17, 2011).

76. *Id.* at 31.

77. *Certain Audio Digital-to-Analog Converters & Prods. Containing Same,* Inv. No. 337-TA-499, Final Initial & Recommended Determinations (Pub. Version), at 113–19 (Nov. 15, 2004) (unreviewed in relevant part).

78. *Certain Encapsulated Integrated Circuit Devices & Prods. Containing Same,* Inv. No. 337-TA-501, Final Initial & Recommended Determinations (Pub. Version), at 136–38 (Nov. 18, 2004). Finding of violation was

found that these activities in the United States were crucial to its operations, noting there is no requirement that a complainant's investment in the United States in "plants and equipment" be of any particular kind or devoted to any particular function, such as manufacturing facilities or manufacturing equipment.[79] Therefore, investment in facilities for the purposes of research and development, engineering, and sales can be sufficient to meet the domestic industry requirement.

In *Microcomputer Memory Controllers*, the complainant moved for summary determination that a domestic industry existed under subsection (C) based on engineering and research and development activities.[80] The respondent contended the complainant's proffered evidence fell short because some of the expenditures related to product marketing, and because the complainant did not allocate expenditures to each patent claim at issue. The judge rejected those arguments. Specifically, the judge concluded that (1) "customer participation in [research and development] and engineering support . . . can be included in a broad definition of research and development under subsection (C)"; and (2) "it is not necessary to allocate specific expenditures to each separate patent claim in issue."[81] The judge also stated that "[w]here the patented products are manufactured is not relevant to the subsection (C) issue."[82]

Research and development activities alone formed the basis of the alleged domestic industry in *NOR and NAND Flash Memory Devices*.[83] There, the complainant demonstrated expenditures of over $200 million in domestic research and development related to products that practiced the asserted patent. The complainant also showed that at least 160 U.S. employees conducted said research and development and that two facilities totaling over 349,000 square feet were used for such activities.

The complainant in *Optical Disk Controller Chips* also established a domestic industry through engineering and research and development

---

eventually reversed by Commission on the issue of prior art. *See id.* Comm'n Op. (Aug. 26, 2010).

79. *Id.* at 138.

80. *Certain Microcomputer Memory Controllers, Components Thereof & Prods. Containing Same*, Inv. No. 337-TA-331, Order No. 6 (Jan. 8, 1992).

81. *Id.* at 4.

82. *Id.* at 6.

83. *Certain NOR & NAND Flash Memory Devices & Prods. Containing Same*, Inv. No. 337-TA-560, Order No. 37, at 6–7 (Nov. 17, 2006).

investments.[84] But, such investments were not actually its own. The complainant relied on the activities of a wholly owned subsidiary of one of its licensee's wholly owned subsidiaries. Thus, the relationship between the complainant and the entity performing the subsection (C) activities was quite attenuated. Nevertheless, it was sufficient. The complainant demonstrated that the domestic entity "performed research and development and commercialization on the next generation . . . optical disk controller chip," employing many full-time individuals (including software engineers) and using substantial office space.[85]

In *Electronic Devices*, the complainant satisfied the economic prong based on the research and development activities of its licensee, Motorola.[86] The complainant proved that Motorola had expended millions of dollars at two U.S. facilities on, inter alia, engineering salaries for employees who designed and tested handsets that practiced the asserted patents. The respondents contended the complainant "failed to demonstrate the requisite nexus between the Motorola engineering activities and the patented technology," arguing the complainant must show that those activities were "directly related" to the inventions claimed in the asserted patents.[87] The judge disagreed. Specifically, the judge stated that "[t]he relevant inquiry is whether Motorola has made a substantial investment with respect to the articles protected by the patent, and not whether the investment relates to the specific features of the articles that contain the patented technology."[88] The judge concluded that the respondents had "confused the issue and [were] effectively argu[ing] that in order to meet the requirement of the economic prong, [the complainant] must also meet the . . . technical prong."[89] He did state, however, that "it is clear that both prongs must be met in order to establish" a domestic industry.[90]

---

84. *Certain Optical Disk Controller Chips & Chipsets & Prods. Containing Same, Including DVD Players & PC Optical Storage Devices*, Inv. No. 337-TA-506, USITC Pub. 3935, Comm'n Op., at 52–54 (Sept. 28, 2005).

85. *Id.* at 52.

86. *Certain Elec. Devices, Including Handheld Wireless Commc'ns Devices*, Inv. No. 337-TA-673, Order No. 49C (Initial Determination), at 5–7 (Oct. 15, 2009) (unreviewed).

87. *Id.* at 10.

88. *Id.*

89. *Id.* at 11.

90. *Id.*

2) Licensing

Section 337(a)(3)(C) allows for a domestic industry to be based on "substantial investment" in exploitation of the asserted IP, including the licensing of patents.[91] Simply owning a patent or patents will not satisfy the domestic industry requirement, but complainants that are actively engaged in licensing their patents in the United States can satisfy the economic prong.[92]

Complainants seeking to satisfy the domestic industry requirement with investments in patent licensing must establish that their investment activities satisfy three requirements of Section 337(a)(3)(C):

> First, the statute requires that the investment in licensing relate to "its exploitation," meaning an investment in the exploitation of the asserted patent. Second, the statute requires that the investment relate to "licensing." Third, any alleged investment must be domestic, *i.e.,* it must occur in the United States.[93]

In evaluating these investments, the Commission will determine first whether they fit within these statutory parameters and then whether they are "substantial" as required by the statute.[94]

Licensing activities have been found to constitute a domestic industry where, for example, a complainant had "developed a system of enforcing its patent rights through the solicitation and negotiation of license agreements . . . [and had] spent substantial sums on identification of prospective licensees and negotiation of licenses."[95] In analyzing whether a complainant's licensing investments are substantial, ALJs have also con-

---

91. *Certain Digital Processors & Digital Processing Sys., Components Thereof, & Prods. Containing Same*, Inv. No. 337-TA-559, Initial Determination (Pub. Version), at 88 (May 11, 2007) (unreviewed in relevant part).

92. *Id.* at 93 ("It is clear that the intent of Congress was to allow entities that were actively licensing their patents in the United States to be able to meet the domestic industry requirement under the statute.").

93. *Certain Multimedia Display & Navigation Devices & Sys., Components Thereof, & Prods. Containing Same (Navigation Devices)*, Inv. No. 337-TA-694, Comm'n Op., at 7–8 (July 22, 2008) (citations omitted).

94. *Id.* (citing 19 U.S.C. § 1337(a)(3)(C)).

95. *Certain Integrated Circuit Telecomms. Chips & Prods. Containing Same, Including Dialing Apparatus (Integrated Circuit Telecommunications Chips)*, Inv. No. 337-TA-337, USITC Pub. 2670, Initial Determination (Pub. Version), at 98 (Aug. 1993).

sidered, inter alia, the revenue generated by the complainant's licensing program.[96]

In the past, the Commission has not required complainants to allocate their licensing investments specifically to the individual patents-in-suit, based on a recognition that "the realities of the marketplace" often result in portfolio rather than individual patent licenses. For example, in *Semiconductor Chips*, the Commission found that, because of the complainant's large scale investments in licensing and the large number of licensees, a specific allocation of expenditures to the patents in suit was not necessary.[97] However, the Commission has since taken a more targeted approach toward alleged domestic industries based on licensing of patent portfolios and is likely to continue to do so as various fact patterns come before it.

In *Multimedia Display and Navigation Devices*, the Commission found that Pioneer's portfolio-based licensing activities did not constitute a substantial exploitation in the licensing of the patent.[98] The Commission evaluated "the strength of the nexus between the licensing activity and the asserted patent" using various factors, including: "(1) the number of patents in the portfolio, (2) the relative value contributed by the asserted patent to the

---

96. *See, e.g., Certain Digital Processors & Digital Processing Sys., Components Thereof, & Prods. Containing Same*, Inv. No. 337-TA-559, Initial Determination (Pub. Version), at 93–94, 98 (May 11, 2007) (unreviewed in relevant part) (noting that complainant had "received millions of dollars in royalties due to the successful licensing of its patent portfolio," including the patent at issue); *Certain Semiconductor Chips with Minimized Chip Package Size & Prods. Containing Same (Semiconductor Chips)*, Inv, No. 337-TA-432, Order No. 13 (Initial Determination) (Pub. Version), at 6 (Jan. 24, 2001) (unreviewed) (noting that complainant had received "substantial royalties" as a result of its licensing activities); *Integrated Circuit Telecommunications Chips*, Initial Determination, at 98 (noting "that complainant has realized substantial revenues from licensing the . . . patent [at issue]").

97. *Semiconductor Chips*, Order No. 13 (Initial Determination), at 14 n.9 (Jan. 24, 2002) (unreviewed); *see also Certain Semiconductor Chips with Minimized Chip Package Size & Prods. Containing Same (III)*, Inv. No. 337-TA-630, Order No. 31, (Initial Determination) (Pub. Version), at 7–8 (Sept. 16, 2008) (unreviewed) (rejecting the argument that the complainant "must segregate the amount of licensing activities and revenues attributable to the patents in suit," and holding that the complainants had shown a sufficient nexus between its licensing activities and the patents-in-suit by demonstrating that its licensing activities and revenues related to a field of technology of which the patents-in-suit constituted part of the complainant's license portfolio).

98. *Navigation Devices*, Comm'n Op., at 25.

portfolio, [and] (3) the prominence of the asserted patent in licensing discussions, negotiations, and any resulting license agreement."[99] These factors allow the Commission to evaluate the investments in exploiting the asserted patent as opposed to general investments relating to the entire portfolio. The Commission also considered whether the licensing efforts related to "an article protected by the asserted patent."[100] Next, the Commission evaluated whether the investments were "substantial" and considered "(1) the existence of other types of 'exploitation' of the asserted patent such as research, development, or engineering, (2) the existence of license-related ancillary activities such as ensuring compliance with license agreements and providing training or technical support to its licensees, (3) whether the complainant's licensing activities are continuing, and (4) whether complainant's licensing activities are those that are referenced favorably in the legislative history"[101] of the statute, noting that "industry-creating, production-driven licensing" is more favorable than "revenue-driven" licensing.[102] Using this framework as a guide, the Commission determined that Pioneer did not establish a strong nexus between its investments in licensing activities and the patents at issue, nor did it show that the relevant investments were substantial.[103] The Commission will likely employ a similar analysis in future portfolio-based licensing situations. However, the Commission has not applied this type of "nexus" analysis to domestic industries not based on licensing.[104]

In *Liquid Crystal Display Devices*, the ALJ found that "[the complainant's] investments in expenditures related to licensing the asserted patents represent a substantial investment in the exploitation of those patents."[105] The ALJ explained that the licensing expenditures relat-

---

99. *Id.* at 9–10.

100. *Id.*

101. *Id.* at 16.

102. *Id.* at 25.

103. *Id. See also* Louis S. Mastriani & Beau A. Jackson, *ITC's Domestic Industry Requirement Evolves Again*, LAW360 (July 26, 2011), http://www.law360.com/internationaltrade/archive/2011/07.

104. *See, e.g., Certain Ground Fault Circuit Interrupters & Prods. Containing Same*, Inv. No. 337-TA-739, Comm'n Op. at 74–81 (June 8, 2012) (reversing the ALJ's determination that the economic prong was not satisfied because the complainant failed to allocate its expenses in labor and capital, plants and equipment, and research and development to specific patents; finding significant investment in plant facilities and a significant employment of labor, and finding a violation of Section 337).

105. *Certain Liquid Crystal Display Devices, Including Monitors, Televisions, Modules, & Components Thereof (LCD Devices)*, 337-TA-741/749, Ini-

ing to the asserted patents represented a substantial portion of complainant's total U.S. and global licensing expenditures in light of the size of the licensing program encompassing the asserted patents relative to its total patent holdings.[106] The ALJ further found that the complainant had also demonstrated the substantial nature of its investment in licensing the asserted patents through its continued licensing activities, its investment in ancillary license-related activities, and its return on investment.[107] Finally, the ALJ noted that complainant's licensing investment had resulted in the collection of significant revenue from its licenses covering the patents-in-suit and found that this return on investment was strong evidence that complainant's investment was substantial.[108] Several of the respondents in the investigation filed petitions for review, and the Commission determined to review numerous aspects of the initial determination, including the economic prong of domestic industry.[109]

In noticing its determination to review, the Commission advised the parties of its particular interest in six questions relating to domestic industry.[110] These questions encompassed issues including allocation of expenses concerning a patent portfolio to asserted patents within the portfolio, factors going to the substantiality of investments in licensing the asserted patents, relevant comparisons in evaluating the substantiality of the investments, whether acquisition costs of a patent should be considered an exploitation of that patent under the statute, whether litigation costs for the investigation at issue and parallel district court actions should be considered,[111] and whether patent reexamination ex-

---

tial Determination (Pub. Version), at 430 (Jan. 12, 2012) *(aff'd in relevant part* on Comm'n review).

106. *Id.*

107. *Id.*

108. *Id.* at 431.

109. *Id.,* Notice of Comm'n Determination to Review-in-Part, at 2 (Mar. 26, 2012).

110. *Id.* at 3–6.

111. Patent litigation expenses may be used to support a domestic industry allegation, but "expenditures on patent litigation do not automatically constitute evidence of the existence of an industry." John Mezzalingua Associates, Inc. v. U.S. Int'l Trade Comm'n, 660 F.3d 1322, 1328 (Fed. Cir. 2011). The Federal Circuit has agreed with the Commission that "[a]llowing patent infringement litigation activities alone to constitute a domestic industry would place the bar for establishing a domestic industry so low as to effectively render it meaningless." *Id.* (quoting from the Commission Opinion under review.)

penses should be considered.[112] The Commission sustained the ALJ's determination that the complainant's licensing activities satisfied the domestic industry requirement. Notably, however, the Commission found that expenses associated with patent acquisition, litigation of the underlying investigation and parallel district court actions, and patent reexamination were not attributable to the domestic industry because they were not related to licensing. Thus, only activities pertaining to the actual licensing program—including employee time, facility use, travel, and acquisition of products for examination—constituted "exploitation" of the asserted patents and could be considered in determining the level of investments made.[113]

In finding such investments substantial, the Commission noted that "it may be challenging, if not impossible, to allocate a particular dollar amount to each asserted patent. This does not preclude a complainant from establishing a domestic industry."[114] The Commission found that, despite the complainant's portfolio-based licensing model, the asserted patents had been shown to play a particularly important role in the licensing activities and the complainant had invested "more heavily" in the asserted patents than in others.[115] Moreover, the substantiality of the complainant's investment was "bolstered by the fact that [it] invests in license-related ancillary activities and the fact that its licensing activities are ongoing."[116] Significantly, even though the complainant's "licensing activities are revenue-driven and target existing production," entitling the investments to "less weight," the complainant successfully established a domestic industry through licensing investments alone.[117]

An increasing number of Section 337 complaints have been filed by non-practicing entities (NPEs) that own and license patents but do not themselves engage in production of patent-protected articles. NPEs typically seek to establish the requisite domestic industry based on their licensing activities.[118] In 2006, only two NPEs filed ITC ac-

---

112. *Id.* at 5–6.
113. *Certain Liquid Crystal Display Devices, Including Monitors, Televisions, Modules, & Components Thereof (LCD Devices)*, Inv. No. 337-TA-741/749, Comm'n Op. (Pub. Version), at 115 (July 6, 2012).
114. *Id.* at 115.
115. *Id.* at 123.
116. *Id.* at 123.
117. *Id.* at 124.
118. *See NPEs Increasingly Opt for ITC Action*, RPX CORP. (Mar. 23, 2012), http://www.rpxcorp.com/index.cfm?pageid=14&itemid=20.

tions, naming only eight respondents, and the number of such filings remained relatively stable until 2011, when 16 NPEs pursued investigations against 235 respondents.[119]

The spike in filings followed a decision in 2010 that may have inspired increased interest in Section 337 from NPEs. In *Coaxial Cable Connectors,*[120] a case described by commentators as a "seminal licensing case" that "provides key insight into the future of the domestic industry requirement," the complainant sought to establish a domestic industry by relying only upon its licensing activities—and also argued that its patent litigation expenses should be considered in the analysis.[121] Although the complainant in *Coaxial Cable Connectors* was not entirely successful (the domestic industry requirement was ultimately found not to have been satisfied as to certain of its asserted IP), the Commission's analysis was generally viewed as favorable to licensing-based domestic industries.

The appearance of NPEs as Section 337 complainants has created considerable controversy, with some calling for the banishment of NPEs from the ITC[122] while others point out that most of the United States' greatest inventors—including Thomas Edison—were NPEs.[123]

2. Technical Prong

Outside of the licensing context, a complainant must generally establish the "technical prong."[124] Typically, the technical prong analysis

---

119. *Id.*

120. *Certain Coaxial Cable Connectors & Components Thereof & Prods. Containing Same,* Inv. No. 337-TA-650, Comm'n Op. (Apr. 14, 2010).

121. Louis S. Mastriani & Beau A. Jackson, *Section 337 Investigations before the International Trade Commission: The Evolving Domestic Industry Requirement and its Implications for Global Intellectual Property Litigation,* INT'L TRADE L. & REG., Issue 2, SWEET & MAXWELL (2011).

122. Jan Wolfe, *Tech-Sector Lobbying Group Wants "Patent Trolls" Out of the ITC,* LAW.COM (Mar. 22, 2012), http://www.law.com/jsp/cc/PubArticleCC.jsp?id=1202546503103.

123. Bernard J. Cassidy, *Follow the Money—Will the ITC Lose Its Patent Jurisdiction?,* IP WATCHDOG (Feb. 27, 2012), http://www.ipwatchdog.com/2012/02/27/follow-the-money-will-the-itc-lose-its-patent-jurisdiction/id=22470/.

124. *See Certain Microlithographic Machs. & Components Thereof (Microlithographic Machines),* Inv. No. 337-TA-468, Initial & Recommended Determinations, at 341–61 (Jan. 29, 2003) (unreviewed); *Certain Video Graphic Display Controllers,* Inv. No. 337-TA-412, USITC Pub. 3224, Initial Determination (Pub. Version), at 14–15 (Aug. 1999) (unreviewed) (finding

employs the same analysis as is used to determine infringement: the claims asserted to be practiced by the complainant's products are construed and compared to the products allegedly covered by those claims.[125] The patent claim used to satisfy the technical prong can be distinct from those allegedly infringed by the respondent(s).[126] Somewhat surprisingly, the Commission has even indicated that the claim used to satisfy the technical prong need not be valid.[127] In a recent decision, however, that rule appears to have been reversed. In *Ground Fault Circuit Interrupters*, the Commission stated that, to prevail on the technical prong, a complainant must "establish by a preponderance of the evidence that the domestic product practices one or more *valid* claims of the patent, either literally or under the doctrine of equivalents."[128]

A similar procedure is followed in investigations based on other IP, such as trademarks.[129]

D. INJURY

Section 337(a)(1)(A) defines the following as unlawful:

> Unfair methods of competition and unfair acts in the importation of articles . . . into the United States, or in the sale of such

---

that the complainant failed to satisfy the technical prong of the "domestic industry" requirement because it intended to discontinue use of the technology in question).

125. *See Certain Excimer Laser Sys. for Vision Corr. Surgery & Components Thereof & Methods for Performing Such Surgery,* Inv. No. 337-TA-419, USITC Pub. No. 3299, Initial Determination (Pub. Version), at 133–46 (May 2000).

126. *See Certain Semiconductor Chips with Minimized Chip Package Size & Prods. Containing Same,* Inv. No. 337-TA-432, Initial Determination (Pub. Version), at 11 (Jan. 24, 2001)).

127. *See Certain Silicone Microphone Packages & Prods. Containing the Same,* Inv. No. 337-TA-695, Comm'n Notice to Review in Part an Initial Determination, at 3 (Jan. 21, 2011). It is Commission practice not to couple an analysis of domestic industry with a validity analysis.

128. *Certain Ground Fault Circuit Interrupters & Prods. Containing Same,* Inv. No. 337-TA-739, Comm'n Op., at 71 (June 8, 2012) (emphasis added) (citing Bayer AG v. Elan Pharm. Research Corp., 212 F.3d 1241, 1247 (Fed. Cir. 2000)).

129. *See Certain Agric. Tractors Under 50 Power Take-Off Horsepower,* Inv. No. 337-TA-380, Order No. 39 (Pub. Version), at 5 (Aug. 8, 1996) (holding that a domestic industry must be proven for each trademark in question).

articles by the owner, importer, or consignee, the threat or effect of which is—(i) to destroy or substantially injure an industry in the United States . . . .[130]

The *Omnibus Trade & Competitiveness Act of 1988*[131] amended Section 337 to eliminate the injury requirement in statutory intellectual property-based cases—i.e., cases involving registered patents, registered trademarks, registered copyrights, registered mask works, or registered vessel hull designs.[132] Economic injury must still be proven in Section 337 investigations involving alleged unfair acts that consist of non-statutory intellectual property or other unfair competition causes of action—e.g., common-law trademark, misappropriation of trade secrets, false advertising, and passing off.

As the Commission stated recently in *Digital Multimeters*,[133] where an injury requirement exists, the complainant bears the burden of proving that the respondent's unfair act or acts have "caused substantial injury to the domestic industry or that the presence of the accused imported

---

130. 19 U.S.C. § 1337(a)(1)(A).

131. *Id.* at § 2191.

132. The Report of the House Committee on Ways and Means commented on H.R.3:

> Unlike dumping or countervailing duties, or even other unfair trade practices such as false advertising or other business torts, the owner of intellectual property has been granted a temporary statutory right to exclude others from making, using, or selling the protected property . . . . In return for temporary protection [e.g., patent, trademark, or copyright], the owner agrees to make public the intellectual property in question. It is this trade-off which creates a public interest in the enforcement of protected intellectual property rights. Any sale in the United States of an infringing product is a sale that rightfully belongs only to the holder or licensee of that property. The importation of any infringing merchandise derogates from the statutory right, diminishes the value of the intellectual property, and thus indirectly harms the public interest. Under such circumstances, the Committee believes that requiring proof of injury, beyond that shown by proof of the infringement of a valid intellectual property right, should not be necessary. H.R. REP. NO. 100-40, at 156 (1987).

133. *Certain Digital Multimeters, & Prods. with Multimeter Functionality* (*Digital Multimeters*), Inv. No. 337-TA-588, Order No. 22 (Initial Determination) (Pub. Version), at 8–9 (Jan. 14, 2008) (unreviewed) (finding that the defaulting respondent caused and/or threatened to cause injury to complainant's domestic industry).

products demonstrate relevant conditions or 'circumstances from which probable future injury can be inferred.'"[134] Moreover, the complainant bears the burden of showing a causal nexus between the unfair act and the injury to the domestic industry.[135]

1. *Factors Considered in an Injury Analysis*

In making an injury determination the Commission does not adhere to a standard formula. Rather, it takes a case-by-case approach in examining evidence of injury, deciding the weight to be assigned to each factor based on the industry at issue in the investigation.[136] The Commission has generally considered a number of factors in its analysis, including:

(1) significant direct displacement of the complainant's customers by the infringing imports (lost sales);[137]

(2) increasing importation of infringing articles and increasing sales of such articles;[138]

(3) declining production of the patented article resulting from sales lost to the imported article;[139]

(4) declining profits of the complainant resulting from the imported infringing article;[140]

---

134. *Id.* at 8 (citation omitted).

135. *Id.*

136. *See, e.g., Certain Surveying Devices,* Inv. No. 337-TA-68, USITC Pub. 1085, Comm'n Op., at 34 (July 1980); Corning Glass Works v. U.S. Int'l Trade Comm'n, 799 F.2d 1559, 1568 (Fed. Cir. 1986) ("[T]he determination of injury necessarily must be based upon the particular facts of each case.").

137. *See Certain Inclined-Field Acceleration Tubes & Components Thereof,* Inv. No. 337-TA-67, USITC Pub. 1119, Comm'n Op., at 20 (Dec. 1980).

138. *See Certain Multicellular Plastic Film,* Inv. No. 337-TA-54, USITC Pub. 987, Comm'n Op., at 21–22 (June 1979); *Certain Reclosable Plastic Bags,* Inv. No. 337-TA-22, USITC Pub. 801, Comm'n Op. at 14 (Jan. 1977); *Certain Stabilized Hull Units & Components Thereof & Sonar Units Utilizing Said Stabilized Hull Units (Stabilized Hull Units),* Inv. No. 337-TA-103, USITC Pub. 1260, Comm'n Op., at 39–40 (June 1982).

139. *See Certain Roller Units (Roller Units),* Inv. No. 337-TA-44, USITC Pub. 944, Comm'n Op., at 10 (Feb. 1978); *Certain Vacuum Bottles & Components Thereof,* Inv. No. 337-TA-108, USITC Pub. 1305, Comm'n Op., at 29–30 (Nov. 1982).

140. *See Certain Thermometer Sheath Packages,* Inv. No. 337-TA-56, USITC Pub. 992, Comm'n Op., at 25–27 (July 1979); *Stabilized Hull Units,* Comm'n Op., at 39–40.

(5) sales of the infringing article at prices lower than the complainant's prices;[141]

(6) declining employment and declining productivity in the domestic industry;[142]

(7) declining prices obtained by the complainant resulting from its efforts to compete with the infringing imported article;[143]

(8) lost potential sales to customers that the complainant might have obtained if the infringing imported article were not being sold to these customers;[144]

(9) loss of royalties or potential income from licensees caused by either reduced sales of the articles made by the domestic industry due to the sale of the imported infringing article or the lack or reduction of licensees due to such sales;[145]

(10) foreign capacity to produce significant quantities of the infringing article, including a showing of intent by foreign manufacturer to further penetrate the U.S. market;[146]

(11) significant market penetration by the imported infringing article; and[147]

(12) presence of direct competition between the complainant's article and the imported infringing article without the presence of similar non-patented articles produced by other competition.[148]

The *Digital Multimeters* investigation, in which the complainant alleged infringement of a registered trademark and copying of trade dress, the threat or effect of which was both claimed to destroy or substantially

---

141. *See Certain Molded-In Sandwich Panel Inserts & Methods for Their Installation (Sandwich Panel Inserts)*, Inv. No. 337-TA-99, USITC Pub. 1246, Comm'n Op., at 9–10 (May 1982).

142. *See Certain Vacuum Bottles & Components Thereof*, Inv. No. 337-TA-108, USITC Pub. 1305, Comm'n Op., at 29–30 (1982).

143. *See id.*; *Stabilized Hull Units*, Comm'n Op., at 39–40.

144. *See Roller Units*, Comm'n Op., at 9–10.

145. *See Certain Limited-Charge Cell Culture Microcarriers*, Inv. No. 337-TA-129, Initial Determination, at 264 (June 6, 1983) (finding no injury by loss of royalties).

146. *See Certain Reclosable Plastic Bags*, Inv. No. 337-TA-22, USITC Pub. 801, Comm'n Op., at 13–14 (Jan. 1977).

147. *See Certain Combination Locks*, Inv. No. 337-TA-45, USITC Pub. 945, Comm'n Op., at 9–12 (Feb. 1979) (finding no tendency to substantially injure on basis of increasing sales trend and lack of market penetration).

148. *See Sandwich Panel Inserts*, Comm'n Op., at 9–10.

injure an industry in the United States, clarified these factors.[149] There, the ALJ asserted that the Commission will consider a "broad range of indicia" consisting of five primary factors when determining injury:

(1) the respondent's volume of imports and penetration into the market;

(2) the complainant's lost sales;

(3) underselling by the respondent;

(4) the complainant's declining production, profitability, and sales; and

(5) harm to goodwill and reputation.[150]

2. Threat of Substantial Injury

Injury may also be shown where "an assessment of the market in the presence of the accused imported products demonstrates relevant conditions or circumstances from which probable future injury can be inferred."[151] An inference of probable future injury, via the threat or tendency[152] to substantially injure the domestic industry, will be made on

---

149. *Certain Digital Multimeters & Prods. with Multimeter Functionality,* Inv. No. 337-TA-588 Order No. 22 (Initial Determination), at 8 (Jan. 14, 2008) (unreviewed).

150. *Id.* (citation omitted); *see also Certain Cast Steel Railway Wheels, Processes for Mfg. or Relating to Same & Certain Prods. Containing the Same (Cast Steel Railway Wheels),* Inv. No. 337-TA-655, Initial Determination (Pub. Version), at 26 (Oct. 16, 2009) (unreviewed) (citing *Certain Elec. Power Tools, Battery Cartridges &Battery Chargers,* Inv. No. 337-TA-284, Initial Determination at 246, USITC Pub. No. 2389 (1991))

151. *Cast Steel Railway Wheels,* Initial Determination, at 26 (internal quotation omitted) (finding that the complainant's domestic industry faced a continued threat of substantial injury as a result of the respondents' misappropriation); *see also Certain Ink Markers & Packaging Thereof,* Inv. No. 337-TA-522, Order No. 30 (Initial Determination) (Pub. Version), at 57 (July 25, 2005) (unreviewed) (finding injury based on direct displacement, poor product quality, and other adverse inferences against a defaulting respondent).

152. The 1988 Act also amended Section 337 to substitute the word "threat" for "tendency" with respect to the injury requirement set forth in § 1337(a)(1)(A). This does not appear to have been intended as a substantive change to the scope of the injury requirement. *See Certain Elec. Power Tools, Battery Cartridges, & Battery Chargers (Electric Power Tools),* Inv. No. 337-TA-284, USITC Pub. 2389, Initial Determination (Pub. Version), at 246 n.38 (June 1991).

the basis of an assessment of the market in the presence of the accused products.[153]

Speculative future lost sales may support a determination of an existing threat of substantial injury to a domestic industry.[154] Three additional factors are to be considered where "an assessment of the market in the presence of the accused imported products demonstrates relevant conditions or circumstances from which probable future injury can be inferred":

(1) foreign cost advantages and production capacity;
(2) the ability of the imported product to undersell the domestic product; or
(3) substantial foreign manufacturing capacity combined with the respondent's intention to penetrate the United States market.[155]

Furthermore, the threatened injury must be "substantive and clearly foreseen," and a causal nexus must exist between the unfair act and the alleged future injury.[156]

In *Digital Multimeters*, the ALJ found that the complainant had suffered and/or was threatened with substantial injury due to the importation of products infringing its trade dress.[157] Specifically, he determined that probable future injury existed based on a brief analysis of several of the factors listed above. The ALJ agreed with the complainant's assertions that (a) the respondents' products were directly competitive in the same distribution channels; (b) there was underselling by the respondents; and (c) the respondents had a large manufacturing capacity and

---

153. *See id.* at 248.

154. *See In re* Von Clemm, 229 F.2d 441, 445 (C.C.P.A. 1955) ("While the record does not show that [complainant] has as yet been substantially damaged by Von Clemm's action, in our opinion it sufficiently supports the holding that such actions have a tendency to injury substantially . . . within the meaning of section 337 . . . .").

155. *Digital Multimeters*, Order No. 22 (Initial Determination) (Pub. Version), at 8 (citations omitted); *see also Electric Power Tools,* Initial Determination (Pub. Version), at 248 (citation omitted) (citing *Certain Air Impact Wrenches (Air Impact Wrenches)*, Inv. No. 337-TA-311, Initial Determination, at 138 (May 6, 1991) (unreviewed) (stating that the 1988 Act did not affect the evaluative factors) (citation omitted)).

156. *Digital Multimeters,* Order No. 22 (Initial Determination), at 8 (quoting *Air Impact Wrenches*, Initial Determination, at 139).

157. *Id.* at 8–9.

maintained large inventories in the United States.[158] The ALJ also noted that the likelihood of post-purchase cognitive dissonance by consumers and the resulting harm to the complainant's goodwill and business reputation evinced probable future injury.[159]

3. Defining Substantial Injury

Direct economic competition is typically a sine qua non of a finding of substantial injury, existing or threatened. Defining the scope of the industry allegedly subject to the threat or effect of substantial injury—i.e., market segmentation, is sometimes a significant concern. For example, in *Characters with Gremlins Depictions*, no injury was found where the accused imports, although in competition with licensed imports, did not compete with domestically made licensed products.[160] Similarly, in *Rotary Wheel Printing Systems*, no injury was found where domestically produced articles competed in a different market segment from that of the accused imports.[161]

The CAFC has affirmed the Commission's general rule that an infringer must hold, or threaten to hold, either a significant share of the domestic market in the covered articles or have made a significant amount of sales of the articles at issue.[162] The CAFC held in *Corning Glass Works* that the respondent's several million dollars of infringing sales were not a "significant amount" of sales that could lead to a finding of substantial injury, because such a finding cannot be based in vacuo on the dollar amount of sales.[163] The court did find that a comparison between a respondent's sales and total U.S. sales—i.e., a market share comparison—is meaningful and may be indicative of a significant level of sales.[164]

---

158. *Id.* at 8.

159. *Id.*

160. *See Certain Prods. with Gremlins Character Depictions,* Inv. No. 337-TA-201, USITC Pub. 1815, Views of Comm'n, at 14–16 (Mar. 1986).

161. *See Certain Rotary Wheel Printing Sys.,* Inv. No. 337-TA-185, USITC Pub. 1857, Additional Views of Comm'n, at 56 (May 1986).

162. *See* Corning Glass Works v. U.S. Int'l Trade Comm'n, 799 F.2d 1559 (Fed. Cir. 1986).

163. *Id.* at 1569 ("[T]he amount of sales is highly relevant to the injury determination; however, whether the amount is 'significant' cannot be determined by the dollar amount in vacuo. 'Significant' requires some further inquiry once the amount of sales is found.").

164. *Id.*

However, lost sales could not be proven where the domestic industry had considerable production deficits and could not satisfy domestic demand.[165]

In sum, the determination of injury "necessarily must be based upon the particular facts of each [investigation]."[166] No arbitrary, fixed market-share benchmark has been imposed by either the Commission or the CAFC for a finding of substantial injury.

4. Causal Nexus

The Commission has declined to find injury where there was no direct evidence of a causal nexus between substantial injury to the domestic industry and unfair acts by respondents. For example, an intervening or superseding cause, such as a shift in consumer demand, may be the actual cause of injury, rather than the alleged or proven unfair act.[167] In *Vertical Milling Machines,* the Commission found false advertising in violation of subsection 43(a) of the Lanham Act, and consequent lost sales, a declining market share, and decreased employment.[168] However, it found no causal nexus between the unfair act and injury to the domestic industry, partially due to the presence of a substantial overall decline in demand in the industry contemporaneous with modifications in the complainant's supply chain.[169] The Commission further identified a decision by the complainant to increase production capacity, thereby increasing fixed costs and resulting in significant price increases during a period of contracting demand, as indicating that respondents' unfair act did not have the effect or tendency of substantially injuring the domestic industry.[170]

---

165. *See id.*

166. *Id.* at 1568.

167. *See Certain Large Video Matrix Display Sys.*, Inv. No. 337-TA-75, USITC Pub. 1158, Comm'n Op., at 25 (June 1981).

168. *Certain Vertical Milling Machs. & Parts, Attachments, & Accessories Thereto,* Inv. No. 337-TA-133, USITC Pub. 1512, Views of the Comm'n, at 42–45 (Mar. 1984).

169. *Id.* at 45–46.

170. *Id.* at 46–47.

CHAPTER 6

Commencement of the Investigation

A Section 337 investigation is instituted based upon a complaint filed by a private party with the Commission or by the Commission on its own motion.

A. PREPARING THE COMPLAINT

Commission rules require that the complaint be under oath and signed; include a statement of the facts constituting the alleged unfair methods of competition and alleged unfair acts; describe specific instances of alleged unlawful importations or sales; state the name, address and nature of the business of each person alleged to be violating Section 337; include a statement as to whether there is any litigation in another court or agency involving the alleged unfair methods of competition and unfair acts; a description of the complainant's business and its interest in the relevant domestic industry or the relevant trade and commerce; and a request for relief.[1] If an allegedly infringed patent is involved, the rules specifically require that the presentation of facts show the importation of the accused

---

1. 19 C.F.R. § 210.12 (2012). *See also* Rules of General Application, Adjudication, & Enforcement (Proposed Rules), 77 Fed. Reg. 41,122 (requiring the complainant to plead with particularity whether it alleges a domestic industry that exists or one that is in the process of being established, requires complainant to specify if it is requesting a general exclusion order, a limited exclusion order, and/or cease and desist orders, and requires complainant to identify the accused products in plain English so as to put the public on notice of the type of products involved) (proposed July 11, 2012) (to be codified at 19 C.F.R. pt. 210).

products, facts supporting infringement (including, "when practicable," a claim chart),[2] and facts that support the existence of a domestic industry. Moreover, the complaint should include copies of the patents at issue and their prosecution history, the status of foreign patent applications corresponding to the patents at issue, and license agreements relating to the patents at issue.

The rules also require that the complainant or its duly authorized officer, attorney, or agent verify that the factual contentions in the complaint have evidentiary support, that they are not presented for an improper purpose, and that the legal contentions are warranted.[3] The Commission has the authority to impose monetary sanctions for violating this duty of candor.

1. Public Interest Statement

On November 18, 2011, the Commission's Rules of Practice and Procedure were amended to require complainants to file a separate public interest statement concurrently with the complaint.[4] The statement must be no longer than five pages and should address how issuance of the requested relief (i.e., a general exclusion order, a limited exclusion order, and/or a cease and desist order), could affect the public health and welfare in the United States, competitive conditions in the United States economy, the production of like or directly competitive articles in the United States, or United States consumers.[5] Pre-institution comments about the public interest are also solicited from the public and potential respondents via a Federal Register notice.[6] The complainant may file reply submissions to these responses.[7]

Based on the submissions from the complaint, the public, and potential respondents, the Commission may delegate consideration of public interest issues to the administrative law judge by directing the ALJ to take evidence and to issue a recommended determination on the public

---

2. *See* 19 C.F.R. § 210.12(a)(9)(viii).

3. *See id.* at §§ 210.4(c)(1)–(3).

4. Rules and Regulations, 76 Fed. Reg. 64,803 (Oct. 19, 2011).

5. 19 C.F.R. § 210.8(b).

6. *See id.* at § 210.8(c)(1).

7. *See id.* at § 210.8(c)(2). *See also* Proposed Rules, 77 Fed. Reg. 41,122 (requiring public versions of any confidential submissions to be filed simultaneously) (proposed July 11, 2012) (to be codified at 19 C.F.R. pt. 210).

interest.[8] If this occurs, respondents are required to submit a statement of public interest with the response to the complaint, not exceeding five pages, if they have not already done so.[9] The ALJ is required to appropriately limit public interest discovery, with particular consideration for third parties.[10]

2. Amending the Complaint

The complaint may be amended at any time prior to the institution of the investigation.[11] After the investigation has been instituted, however, complainants must seek the ALJ's leave to amend the complaint, and must show good cause and that the public interest and rights of the parties will not be prejudiced.[12]

B. PREFILING REVIEW OF THE COMPLAINT

Prior to filing the complaint, the complaining party can present a draft complaint to the OUII for an informal evaluation to ensure the complaint complies with Commission rules. A staff attorney informally reviews the draft and provides feedback regarding the sufficiency of the complaint. Issues that arise during pre-filing review typically relate to the factual support for the allegations. The informal review process identifies issues that a party can quickly correct or supplement before formally filing the complaint.

---

8. *See* 19 C.F.R. § 210.10(b).

9. *See id.* at § 210.14(f).

10. *See id.* at § 210.10(c).

11. *See id.* at § 210.14(a). *But see* Proposed Rules, 77 Fed. Reg. 41,122 (adding a new sentence to the end of § 210.14(a) to provide that if a complainant significantly amends a complaint prior to institution, the amendment will restart the normal 30-day process for determining whether to institute the investigation) (proposed July 11, 2012) (to be codified at 19 C.F.R. pt. 210).

12. *See* 19 C.F.R. § 210.14(b). The proposed changes to § 210.14(b) will also add the requirement in § 210.15(a)(2), that motions to amend the complaint to add proposed respondents must be served on each proposed respondent. *See* Proposed Rules, 77 Fed. Reg. 41,122 (proposed July 11, 2012) (to be codified at 19 C.F.R. pt. 210).

C. PREPARING THE RESPONSE TO THE COMPLAINT

Respondents generally have 20 days from the date of service of the complaint and notice of investigation by either the Commission or a party in which to file a response to the complaint.[13] Computation of "days" is governed by Commission Rules 210.6, 201.14, and 201.16(d). Commission Rule 210.6 references Commission Rules 210.14 and 210.16(d), however, these references are typographical errors. The correct sections provide that "days" do not include Saturdays, Sundays, or federal holidays, and that three calendar days are added to the prescribed period for a response after service by mail if the respondent is in the United States, and 10 days if the respondent is outside the United States. When service is by overnight delivery, one day is added to the prescribed period.[14] Each respondent must respond to each allegation in the complaint and notice of investigation and must set forth a concise statement of the facts constituting each ground of defense. Respondents must specifically admit, deny, or explain each fact alleged in the complaint and notice, or state that they are without knowledge of any such fact. Allegations that are not answered in this way may be deemed admitted.[15] Further, each response must include, when available, statistical data on the quantity and value of imports of the involved article; importers must also provide the Harmonized Tariff Schedule item numbers for the accused imports. Each respondent must include a statement concerning its capacity to produce the subject article and the relative significance of the U.S. market to its operations. Respondents who are not manufacturing their accused products in the United States must state the name and address of the suppliers of those imports.[16]

Affirmative defenses must be pleaded with "as much specificity as possible" and must be timely raised.[17] When the alleged unfairness is

---

13. *See* 19 C.F.R. § 210.13(a).

14. *See id.* at § 201.16(e). *See also* Proposed Rules, 77 Fed. Reg. 41,121 (which would clarify that service by mail is equally applicable to service by the Commission as well as by the parties, expand subsection (c) to include and refer to applicable requirements for service other than certificates of service, and add five additional days to the response time where overnight delivery service is to a foreign country) (proposed on July 11, 2012) (to be codified at 19 C.F.R. pt. 201).

15. *See* 19 C.F.R. § 210.13(b). *See also* Proposed Rules, 77 Fed. Reg. 41,122 (proposed July 11, 2012) (to be codified at 19 C.F.R. pt. 210).

16. *See* 19 C.F.R. § 210.13(b).

17. *See id.*

based on the claims of a valid U.S. patent, respondents are encouraged to show how the accused products are not covered by the specified patent, including, when practicable, a claim chart and visual representations of the accused product.[18] When respondents assert that the U.S. patent involved is invalid or unenforceable, the basis for such assertion, including a showing of how any prior art renders the claim invalid or unenforceable, should be stated.[19]

Leave to amend a response is permissible under the regulations[20] and is routinely granted when the movant can show good cause and that there will be no prejudice to the opposing party or the public interest.[21] For example, in *Electronic Devices*, the ALJ granted Apple's motion to amend its response, stating that "Apple was diligent in proposing its amended response, as the proposed additions and clarifications to its defenses relate to matters that Apple has fleshed out during discovery."[22]

Respondents may file counterclaims in accordance with Section 337(c) of the Tariff Act of 1930 at any time after institution of the investigation, but no later than ten business days before the commencement of the evidentiary hearing.[23] However, counterclaims must be immediately removed to district court.[24]

D. INSTITUTION OF THE INVESTIGATION

When a complaint is filed, it is a public document, with the exception of confidential business information (CBI). Upon filing, respondents normally become quickly aware of the existence of the complaint, giving them up to 30 days to reach a state of adequate preparation when the complaint is formally instituted.[25] When filed, the Commission directs the complaint to staff attorneys in OUII who, during a 20-day period, investi-

---

18. *See id.* at §§ 210.13(b)(1)–(2).

19. *See id.* at § 210.13(b)(3).

20. *See id.* at § 210.14(b)(2).

21. *See Certain Elec. Devices, Including Mobile Phones, Portable Music Players, & Computers (Electronic Devices)*, Inv. No. 337-TA-701, Order No. 28 (Pub. Version), at 2 (July 30, 2010) ("Commission's Rules permit amendments to pleadings other than complaints upon a showing of good cause, provided that care is taken to avoid prejudice to the parties and the public") (citations omitted).

22. *Id.*

23. 19 C.F.R. § 210.14(e).

24. 19 U.S.C. § 1337(c) (2006).

25. 19 C.F.R. § 210.10.

gate the background of the complaint and determine whether it meets certain procedural rules. OUII then makes a recommendation to the Commission on whether the complaint meets the rules and presents a cause of action that should be considered by the Commission for investigation.

If the Commission determines, as it normally does, that an investigation should be instituted, a notice is published in the *Federal Register* and copies of the complaint are served upon those named as respondents in the investigation. In the case of foreign respondents, the respective embassies also receive service.[26] A staff attorney from OUII may be designated as a formal party to the investigation to participate in all phases of the proceeding. The investigation is assigned to an ALJ, who controls the conduct of the investigation until issuance of an initial determination on violation and a recommended determination on remedy and bonding.

E. PREHEARING PROCEDURES

The date of publication of the Notice of Investigation in the *Federal Register* begins the schedule for the Commission's investigation, including setting a target date for completion of the investigation.[27] Significantly, it is through the use of such target dates—normally in the range of 14 to 16 months—that the Commission has maintained its record of completing investigations in an expeditious manner.

Parties may begin discovery once notice of the investigation appears in the *Federal Register*. Due to the expedited schedule of these investigations, the time for answering interrogatories, producing documents, and conducting depositions is very short. The entire process of discovery normally takes place within approximately five to seven months. During this time, there may be one or more conferences with the ALJ. The ALJ controls the discovery process, rules upon motions, and handles requests of the parties, such as gaining additional information or being permitted to withhold information requested by an opposing party. With respect to CBI, protective orders are issued as a matter of course.[28] A protective order establishes the terms by which CBI is to be exchanged and handled by the parties during the course of the investigation. Accordingly, CBI is routinely exchanged among outside counsel and independent experts but protected from public disclosure or disclosure to the opposing party.

---

26. *See id.* at §§ 210.4(b), (c).

27. *See id.* at § 210.10(b).

28. *See id.* at § 210.34.

Immediate entry of a protective order allows discovery to commence immediately at the beginning of the investigation.

The ALJ will subsequently issue orders establishing the ground rules, procedural schedule, and target date for the investigation. The ground rules address the manner in which the ALJ will conduct the investigation.[29] Each ALJ issues separate ground rules, which, although similar, vary in their details. The ground rules govern all aspects of the investigation while it is before the ALJ, including motions practice, discovery (including discovery deadlines), expert witnesses and reports, settlement conferences, hearing procedures, and pre- and post-hearing briefing.

The schedule for the investigation is set forth in a procedural schedule issued by the ALJ, sometimes after receipt of proposals from the parties. The dates in the procedural schedule will generally be dictated by the target date for completion of the investigation set by the ALJ. On July 7, 2008, the Commission issued final regulations amending the Commission Rules of Practice and Procedure in several important areas.[30] Notably, the amended rules permit ALJs to set the target date for an investigation at up to 16 months by issuing an order.[31] Such an order does not have to be reviewed by the Commission.[32] Prior to the new regulations, a target date of 15 months was the maximum an ALJ could set without being subject to Commission review. Since these regulations went into effect, target dates of 16 months or longer are not uncommon.[33] In setting the target date, ALJs consider the complexity of the

---

29. *See id.* at § 210.5.

30. *See* Rules of General Application and Adjudication and Enforcement, 73 Fed. Reg. 38,316 (July 7, 2008).

31. 19 C.F.R. § 210.51(a). *But see* Proposed Rules, 77 Fed. Reg. 134,41125 (providing that ALJs set target dates of 12 months or less by order, but set target dates greater than 12 months by initial determination) (proposed July 11, 2012) (to be codified at 19 C.F.R. pt. 210).

32. 19 C.F.R. § 210.51(a). An ALJ can set the target date at greater than 16 months only by issuing an initial determination, which has to be reviewed by the Commission. *See id.* at § 210.42.

33. *See, e.g., Certain Integrated Circuits, Chipsets, & Prods. Containing Same, Including Televisions,* Inv. No. 337-TA-822, Order No. 8, at 1 (Feb. 17, 2012) (setting target date of sixteen months); *Certain Mobile Devices & Related Software,* Inv. No. 337-TA-750, Order No. 3, at 1 (Jan. 7, 2011) (same); *Certain Elec. Imaging Devices,* Inv. No. 337-TA-726, Order No. 4, at 3 (Aug. 13, 2010) (same); *Certain Game Devices, Components Thereof, & Prods. Containing the Same (Game Devices),* Inv. No. 337-TA-757, Order No. 4 (Initial Determination), at 1 (Mar. 1, 2011) (unreviewed) (setting target date of seventeen months); *Certain Gaming & Entm't Consoles, Related Software, & Com-*

issues at hand, the arguments set forth in the discovery statements and in the preliminary conference, courtroom availability, and the ALJ's commitments in other investigations.[34]

The procedural schedule sets forth a detailed timetable for the investigation. It includes dates for, inter alia, expert witness identification, prior art notices (in patent cases), witness lists, discovery deadlines, settlement conferences, motions to compel discovery, motions for summary determination, prehearing statements and briefs, and hearing and post-hearing briefs. Occasionally, parties will request that additional dates, such as dates for exchange of proposed claim construction or dates for responding to contention interrogatories, be included in the procedural schedule. Absent a stay (which is rarely granted) or some other event that requires an extension of the target date, the procedural schedule provides firm dates that will keep the investigation on track.

F. MODIFYING THE GROUND RULES OR THE PROCEDURAL SCHEDULE

The parties can seek to modify the terms of the ground rules or the procedural schedule by stipulation and/or motion. Some of the most common issues parties have addressed involve electronic service, electronic discovery, limits on discovery into draft expert reports, provisions addressing the inadvertent disclosure of privileged documents, protection of source code, preclusion of patent prosecution counsel from being admitted under the protective order, and, very rarely, access to CBI by in-house counsel. To minimize discovery disputes over sensitive information, in-house counsel, as well as foreign attorneys, are traditionally excluded from access to CBI. There is, however, an exception for foreign attorneys who are members of U.S. bars.[35]

---

ponents Thereof, Inv. No. 337-TA-752, Order No. 5 (Initial Determination), at 1 (Jan. 13, 2011) (unreviewed) (same); *Certain Digital Televisions & Components Thereof*, Inv. No. 337-TA-789, Order No. 5 (Initial Determination), at 1 (Aug. 2, 2011) (unreviewed) (setting target date of 18 months).

34. *See, e.g., Game Devices*, Order No. 4 (Initial Determination), at 2 (considering courtroom availability, arguments set forth in discovery statements and in the preliminary conference, the ALJ's schedule, and leaving sufficient time for discovery).

35. *See Certain L-Lysine Feed Prods., Their Methods of Prod. & Genetic Constructs for Prod.*, Inv. No. 337-TA-571, Order No. 4, at 4–5 (July 7, 2006) (allowing foreign attorney to receive CBI if attorney is a member in good standing of a U.S. state bar); *cf. Certain Sortation Sys., Parts Thereof & Prods.*

Parties frequently seek to modify the ground rules by agreeing by stipulation to electronic service and limitations on electronic discovery. For example, in *Flash Memory Controllers,* the ALJ adopted the parties' stipulation consenting to electronic service and a protocol for discovery requests and responses.[36] Issues commonly addressed in this manner include service of documents via e-mail, including a deadline for service on the day in question; exchange of discovery requests in Word format; the discoverability of metadata; and the electronic format (i.e., TIFF images versus PDF) in which document production will be provided.

Minor amendments to the procedural schedule can be made in a similar manner as long as the changes do not affect other dates in the schedule, particularly the hearing date. For example, in *Buffer Systems and Components Thereof,* the ALJ found good cause to amend the procedural schedule where the parties sought to extend dates to accommodate the expert deposition schedule.[37]

G. MODIFYING THE PROTECTIVE ORDER

Similarly, the parties might seek to modify the protective order to provide additional safeguards for the treatment of CBI. Such requests are often granted, particularly when the parties are in agreement. The most common issues that arise with respect to amending the protective order include the addition of a so-called "clawback" provision, a source code provision, a provision to preclude patent prosecution counsel from having access to CBI, and a provision permitting in-house counsel access to CBI.

A clawback provision protects against the inadvertent disclosure of privileged information, including information subject to attorney-client privilege, work-product doctrine, the common interest doctrine, and joint-defense agreements. Parties request a clawback provision with the under-

---

Containing Same, Inv. No. 337-TA-460, Order No. 9, at 3–4 (Nov. 20, 2001) (excluding foreign counsel who were not members of a U.S. state bar from receiving CBI because of the lack of options to enforce the protective order against those attorneys).

36. *See Certain Flash Memory Controllers, Drives, Memory Cards, & Media Players & Prods. Containing Same,* Inv. No. 337-TA-619, Order No. 17, at 1–2 (Feb. 19, 2008).

37. *See Certain Buffer Sys. & Components Thereof Used in Container Processing Lines (Buffer Systems),* Inv. No. 337-TA-609, Order No. 14, at 1–2 (Feb. 12, 2008); *see also Certain Semiconductor Chips with Minimized Chip Package Size & Prods. Containing Same (Semiconductor Chips),* Inv. No. 337-TA-605, Order No. 12, at 1–2 (Nov. 20, 2007).

standing that, when a privileged document is inadvertently produced to the opposing side, the producing party will contact the opposing party within a specified number of days and request that the opposing party return the privileged information.[38] If the requirements of the clawback provision are met, privilege is not waived. In a similar vein, parties can seek an amendment to the protective order to add a provision regarding the safeguarding and handling of source code.[39] In *GPS Devices*, the parties agreed on a source code provision that included restrictions on the production of source code, locations for review of the source code, and the parties who could access the code.[40]

Parties also have sought to add provisions to preclude patent prosecution counsel from being admitted under the protective order.[41] A "patent prosecution bar" seeks to screen out individuals prosecuting patents for one of the parties from obtaining confidential information under the protective order in the ITC investigation.[42] The patent prosecution bar attempts to alleviate parties' concerns that a patent attorney who obtains confidential information from the opposing side may use, even if only inadvertently, this information when drafting patent applications.[43] In

---

38. *See, e.g., Certain Digital Television Prods. & Certain Prods. Containing Same & Methods of Using Same (Digital Television Products)*, Inv. No. 337-TA-617, Order No. 7, at 7–8 (Dec. 17, 2007) (requiring that the producing party notify the receiving party in writing when inadvertent production of privileged or protected material is discovered, and requesting party return the privileged material within 10 business days); *Certain GPS Devices & Prods. Containing Same (GPS Devices)*, Inv. No. 337-TA-602, Order No. 3, at 1–2 (July 26, 2007) (amending Protective Order to include clawback provision).

39. *See, e.g., Digital Television Products*, Order No. 24, at 1; *GPS Devices*, Order No. 3, at 1–2.

40. *GPS Devices*, Order No. 3, at 1–2.

41. *See, e.g., Digital Television Products*, Order No. 7, at 8; *Certain Data Storage Sys. & Components Thereof (Data Storage Systems)*, Inv. No. 337-TA-471, Order No. 5, at 1–2 (July 12, 2002); *Certain Set-Top Boxes & Components Thereof*, Inv. No. 337-TA-454, Order No. 6, at 6 (May 17, 2001) ("The case law is well established that a patent attorney, who handles patent prosecution and who knows the confidential information under a protective order relating to certain products of a complainant or a respondent, may not be expected to unlearn that information eve when acting in the best of faith.").

42. *See id.*

43. *See Certain Microlithographic Machs. & Components Thereof (Microlithographic Machines)*, Inv. No. 337-TA-468, Order No. 5, at 1–3 (Mar. 21, 2002).

addition, a patent prosecution bar may preclude counsel involved in the investigation from prosecuting patents in the relevant field of technology for a specified amount of time.[44]

With respect to in-house counsel, the general rule is that, absent agreement between the parties, in-house counsel will not be permitted access to CBI under the protective order.[45] However, an ALJ will allow in-house counsel access to CBI if the parties reach a mutual agreement on the matter.[46] The parties may be very specific as to the types of CBI in-house counsel may access under the protective order. For example, in *Vehicle Security Systems*, respondent agreed to allow complainant's in-house counsel access to eight of respondents' proposed hearing exhibits.[47] The parties also obtained permission from a third-party supplier who was the owner of the documents.[48] The ALJ granted the complainant's motion to amend the protective order, finding that, because the motion was unopposed and accomplished the desires of the third-party supplier, complainant's in-house counsel could have access to the eight exhibits.[49] In *Coamoxiclav Products* the protective order was not amended, but the ALJ nonetheless recognized the parties' agreement that certain information could be seen by specified in-house counsel, subject to the protective order.[50]

---

44. *See id.*

45. *See Certain Auto. Parts*, Inv. No. 337-TA-557, Order No. 5, at 1 (Mar. 10, 2006) ("It is well established that in section 337 investigations, it is the exception rather than the rule to release confidential information to in-house counsel absent an agreement between the parties.") (internal quotations omitted).

46. *See Certain Vehicle Security Sys. & Components Thereof (Vehicle Security Systems)*, Inv. No. 337-TA-355, Order No. 15, 1994 WL 930093, at *1 (Feb. 2, 1994); *Certain Plastic Encapsulated Integrated Circuits*, Inv. No. 337-TA-315, Order No. 13, 1990 WL 710750, at *1–2 (Nov. 30, 1990); *see also Certain Coamoxiclav Prods., Potassium Clavulanate Prods., & Other Prods. Derived from Clavulanic Acid (Coamoxiclav Products)*, Inv. No. 337-TA-479, Order No. 5, at 1–3 (Nov. 12, 2002).

47. *Vehicle Security Systems*, Order No. 15, 1994 WL 930093, at *1.

48. *Id.*

49. *Id.*

50. *Coamoxiclav Products*, Order No. 5, at 2.

H. STAYS OF THE PROCEDURAL SCHEDULE

Parties in ITC proceedings often are interested in staying[51] proceedings before the Commission pending the outcome of concurrent, related proceedings in another forum. Non-ITC proceedings, such as patent reexaminations or district court cases, can affect claims before the ITC. Non-ITC proceedings can reduce the scope of claimed rights or solidify claims of injury. Parties may wish to avoid the pressures on time and cash flow that concurrent proceedings entail. The Commission has the power to stay proceedings before it, but that power and the Commission's willingness to use it have limits.

Prior to the 1994 Uruguay Round Agreement Acts (URAA), the Commission had the authority to suspend proceedings before it "because of proceedings in a court or agency of the United States involving similar questions concerning the subject matter of such investigation."[52] This gave the Commission broad power to suspend investigations before it. Perhaps such broad power was deemed necessary because the Commission had a strict deadline for completion of its investigations of "one year (18 months in more complicated cases) after the date of publication of notice of such investigation."[53] By suspending proceedings, which tolled its decision deadline,[54] the Commission could leverage the investigative powers of other tribunals if concurrent proceedings were under way. For example, the Commission could use this power "to suspend investigations in which the patent(s)-in-suit were undergoing a re-examination or re-issue proceeding before the U.S. Patent and Trademark Office (PTO) or were the subject of concurrent proceedings in a district court."[55]

The URAA eliminated the strict temporal deadline. It simply required that the Commission make its determination "at the earliest practicable time" and establish a target date for its final determination within

---

51. The terms "suspend" and "stay" are both used in ALJs' and Commission dispositions. The differences between these terms concern the Uruguay Round Agreements Act, discussed *infra*. Basically, "suspend" and "stay" carry out the same function and attain the same result.

52. 19 U.S.C. § 1337(b)(1) (prior to URAA) (1998).

53. *Id.*

54. *Id.*

55. *See Certain Personal Computer/Consumer Elec. Convergent Devices, Components Thereof, & Prods. Containing Same (Convergent Devices)*, Inv. No. 337-TA-558, Order No. 6 (Initial Determination), at 4 (Feb. 7, 2006) (unreviewed).

45 days after institution of the investigation.[56] Attached to this increased
flexibility came a reduction of power in another area: the Commission
lost much of the authority it had been granted under subsection 337(b)(1)
of the Tariff Act of 1930 to suspend investigations.[57]

The Commission, however, quickly asserted the authority to extend
the target date for completing investigations under "[c]ircumstances that
would have warranted suspension under the [pre-URAA] rules."[58] This
new authority to stay proceedings, rather than suspend them, has been
exercised by the Commission and judges at the ITC under "appropriate
circumstances."[59] Whether circumstances are appropriate to warrant a
stay ordinarily depends on consideration of multiple factors. These factors typically include "(1) the state of discovery and the hearing date; (2)
whether a stay will simplify the issues and hearing of the case; (3) the
undue prejudice or clear tactical disadvantage to any party; (4) the stage
of the parallel proceedings; and (5) the efficient use of Commission resources."[60] While ALJs present similar reasons to justify a stay, they weigh
the factors individually according to the particular facts of a case.

In the oft-cited *Semiconductor Chips (IV)*, the ALJ found that two of
the four patents-at-issue in the case were at issue in another ITC investigation in which the Commission had determined to review the ALJ's
initial determination.[61] The ALJ opined that a stay in the procedural schedule would simplify the issues at the hearing.[62] In contrast, the ALJ in
Integrated Circuits weighed the factors and denied the respondents' motion for a stay, specifically citing the fact that discovery was already well

---

56. Uruguay Round Agreements Act § 321, Pub. L. 103-465, 108 Stat.
4809 (1994).

57. *Id.*

58. *See Convergent Devices,* Order No. 6 (Initial Determination), at 7
(citing 59 Fed. Reg. 67,622, 67,626 (1994)).

59. *Id.*

60. *See, e.g., Certain Mobile Commc'ns & Computer Devices & Components Thereof (Mobile Communications & Computer Devices)*, Inv. No. 337-
TA-704, Order No. 58, at 1-2 (Oct. 25, 2010) (citing *Certain Semiconductor
Chips with Minimized Chip Package Size & Prods. Containing Same (Semiconductor Chips)*, Inv. No. 337-TA-605, Comm'n Op., at 3 (May 27, 2008)).

61. *Certain Semiconductor Chips with Minimized Chip Package Size
& Prods. Containing Same (IV)*, Inv. No. 337-TA-649, Order No. 18 (Initial
Determination), at 6 (Feb. 10, 2009) (unreviewed).

62. *Id.* ("[A]waiting the Commission's decision in [*Semiconductor Chips,*
Inv. No. 337-TA-605] will simplify the issues and hearing of this Investigation as well as be an efficient use of resources.").

underway, that the complainant could be prejudiced by a stay, and that a stay could add costs to the investigation.[63] The ALJ in *Blu-Ray Disc Players* came to the same conclusion, finding that four of the five factors weighed against a stay.[64]

Recently, a federal bankruptcy court granted a party's request to stay a hearing at the ITC pending the outcome of the bankruptcy decision. In *In re Qimonda AG*, the Bankruptcy Court of the Eastern District of Virginia granted a stay of the respondent's participation in an ITC case, holding that Chapter 15 filings automatically stayed other pending U.S. litigation under 11 U.S.C. § 362(a) and 11 U.S.C. § 1520. It further held that the "police and regulatory" exception to the automatic stay, found in 11 U.S.C. § 362(b) did not apply to ITC proceedings.[65] The U.S. District Court for the District of Virginia reversed, however, holding that the police and regulatory exception did apply.[66]

Parties may also file a motion to stay an ITC investigation due to concurrent PTO proceedings. Pursuant to 35 U.S.C. § 302, "[a]ny person at any time may file a request for re-examination." The PTO then will order a reexamination if it finds that a substantial new question of patentability exists.[67] In 1999, Congress passed amendments to the reexamination process that provided third parties with increased participation after filing the initial reexamination request.[68] In determining whether to

---

63. *Certain Integrated Circuits, Chipsets, & Prods. Containing Same Including Televisions, Media Players, & Cameras*, Inv. No. 337-TA-709, Order No. 13, at 3–4 (July 28, 2010).

64. *Certain Blu-Ray Disc Players, Components Thereof & Prods. Containing the Same*, Inv. No. 337-TA-824, Order No. 13, at 6-12 (Apr. 16, 2012).

65. *In re* Qimonda AG, 433 B.R. 547 (Bankr. E.D. Va. 2010) (staying Respondent Qimonda AG's participation in *Certain Semiconductor Integrated Circuits Using Tungsten Metallization & Prods. Containing Same*, Inv. No. 337-TA-648, Order No. 110 (July 15, 2009)).

66. U.S. Int'l Trade Comm'n v. Jaffe, 433 B.R. 538, 547 (E.D. Va. 2010) A similar thing happened in *In re* Spansion, Inc. where the U.S. Bankruptcy Court for the District of Delaware ordered the ITC to stay its investigation of the respondents. The District Court did not reach this argument on appeal, as it upheld a Letter Agreement in which the complainant agreed to dismiss and not refile its ITC action. *See In re* Spansion, Inc., 418 B.R. 84, 97 (Bankr. D. Del. 2009); *In re* Spansion, Inc., No. 09-1069 (KJC), 2011 WL 3268084, at *8 (D. Del. 2011).

67. *See* 35 U.S.C. § 304.

68. *See id.* at §§ 311–18 (1999). *See also* Lisa Norton & Steve Kelber, *Ex Parte Reexamination—What More Could a Patent Owner Ask For?* (2004),

grant a stay based on a patent reexamination, the Commission will weigh the same five factors it weighs when considering staying an investigation for other reasons. In *Semiconductor Chips*, the Commission overturned the ALJ's decision to stay the investigation pending a patent reexamination after weighing these five factors and concluding that a stay would effectively terminate the investigation because the patents at issue would almost certainly terminate before the reexamination was completed.[69]

Stays are also often requested and granted when two or more parties to the investigation have reached, or are in the process of reaching, a settlement agreement.[70] In such scenarios, the justification for the stay is avoidance of the "excessive and unnecessary costs" the parties might incur if they were forced to continue taking discovery or preparing for the hearing when an imminent settlement agreement, if concluded, would render those efforts moot and unwarranted.[71]

I. CONSOLIDATION OF INVESTIGATIONS

Pursuant to Commission Rule 201.7(a), "in order to expedite the performance of its functions," the Commission has the authority to "engage in investigative activities preliminary to and in aid of any authorized investigation, consolidate proceedings before it, and determine the scope and manner of its proceedings." The Commission rules do not clearly authorize an ALJ to consolidate investigations after being assigned to a particular investigation. However, ALJs have relied on Rule 201.7 to consolidate related investigations when there is substantial overlap in subject matter, products at issue, evidence to be presented, and issues to

---

available at http://www.dlapiper.com/files/Publication/eb70c44b-83f4-48c4-9be4-ee9ecd291d5a/Presentation/PublicationAttachment/b2456c80-2cbe-42b0-b8d5-f06e1fd758b9/ExParteReex.pdf.

69. *Certain Semiconductor Chips with Minimized Chip Package Size & Prods. Containing Same (Semiconductor Chips)*, Inv. No. 337-TA-605, Comm'n Op., at 4–5 (May 27, 2008)).

70. *See, e.g., Certain Buffer Sys. & Components Thereof Used in Container Processing Lines (Buffer Systems)*, Inv. No. 337-TA-609, Order No. 25, at 1 (May 7, 2008); *Certain Base Stations & Wireless Microphones*, Inv. No. 337-TA-653, Order No. 14, at 1–2 (Dec. 15, 2008); *Certain Lighting Prods., Components Thereof & Prods. Containing Same*, Inv. No. 337-TA-594, Order No. 4, at 1 (May 4, 2007); *Certain Tissue Converting Mach., Including Rewinders, Tail Sealers, Trim Removers, & Components Thereof*, Inv. No. 337-TA-548, Order No. 13, at 1 (Feb. 22, 2006); *Certain Digital Image Storage & Retrieval Devices*, Inv. No. 337-TA-527, Order No. 31, at 1 (Aug. 3, 2005).

71. *Buffer Systems*, Order No. 25, at 1.

be decided.[72] In one investigation, an ALJ denied the complainant's contention that, before an administrative law judge may consolidate investigations, there must be some direction from the Commission regarding the consolidation.[73] Instead, ALJs have held that whether or not the Commission stated in the notice of investigation that the ALJ is authorized to consolidate is merely a factor that weighs in favor of consolidation.[74] Other factors the ALJ may consider are whether the two investigations have the same complainant(s), the same respondent(s), the same patent(s), the same asserted claim(s), the same accused product(s), the same ALJ, and the same staff attorney.[75] For example, in *Liquid Crystal Display Devices*, the ALJ consolidated two investigations, noting that they both involved the same complainants, the same ALJ, and the same staff attorney, and that all of the patents asserted in the 749 investigation were also asserted in the 741 investigation.[76] "Thus, the two investigations will contain many overlapping legal issues, such as claim construction, domestic industry, invalidity, and unenforceability."[77] Similarly, the ALJ consolidated *Nitrile Gloves*, Inv. No. 337-TA-608, with *Nitrile Rubber Gloves*, Inv. No. 337-TA-612, because these two investigations were brought by the same complainant on the same patent and covered the same products.[78] The ALJ noted that "[t]he entirety of the 612 investigation overlaps the 608 investigation because the complainant in the 608

---

72. *See Certain Integrated Repeaters, Switches, Transceivers, & Prods. Containing Same (Integrated Repeaters)*, Inv. No. 337-TA-435, Order No. 3 (Aug. 24, 2000) (consolidating Inv. Nos. 337-TA-430 and 337-TA-435). In the notice of institution for *Integrated Repeaters*, the Commission stated: "The presiding administrative law judge is authorized to consolidate Inv. No. 337-TA-430 and this investigation if he deems it appropriate." Inv. No. 337-TA-435, Notice of Investigation, at 3 (Aug. 17, 2000).

73. *See Certain 3G Wideband Code Division Multiple Access (WCDMA) Handsets & Components Thereof*, Inv. No. 337-TA-613, Order No. 5, at 9 (Oct. 24, 2007).

74. *See Certain Motion-Sensitive Sound Effects Devices & Image Display Devices &Components & Prods. Containing Same*, Inv. No. 337-TA-787, Order No. 12, 2011 WL 2742559, at *1 (July 13, 2011).

75. *See Certain Elec. Devices Including Handheld Wireless Commc'n Devices*, Inv. No. 337-TA-673, Order No. 8, at 4 (Apr. 23, 2009).

76. *Certain Liquid Crystal Display Devices, Including Monitors, Televisions, & Modules, & Components Thereof (LCD Devices)*, 337-TA-749, Order No. 6, at 2 (Dec. 16, 2010).

77. *Id.*

78. The 612 investigation named additional companies as respondents.

investigation requested relief in the form of a general exclusion order that could have encompassed the respondents in the 612 investigation."[79] In the *Integrated Repeaters* investigations, the ALJ decided to consolidate two investigations, instituted approximately four months apart, that had been filed by the same complainant against the same respondent.[80] In granting the motion to consolidate, the ALJ noted the extensive overlap of issues between the two investigations, "especially in view of the efficiencies in time and resources that would result."[81]

Two fundamental concerns are cited by parties who oppose consolidation of investigations: potential confusion at the hearings and in the record presented to the Commission, and possible prejudice to complainant in the first-filed investigation due to delay. It was, in part, for these reasons that one ALJ denied a motion to consolidate when the party opposing consolidation was able to demonstrate sufficient differences in the patents at issue, the products at issue, and the domestic industry issues.[82] In particular, the number and scope of patents in a would-be consolidated investigation can weigh heavily against consolidation. In *Mobile Telephones*, the ALJ denied respondents' motion to consolidate an investigation involving two patents and 10 claims with another investigation involving three patents and 17 claims.[83] The ALJ stated that consolidating the two cases "would create an inordinately large and complex investigation" and that this weighed even more heavily against consolidation than the number of respondents in each investigation, which was also substantial.[84]

It is important to note that some of the benefits gained by consolidation can also be gained by partial consolidation or by other measures. For example, coordinating discovery, issuing a unified protective order, and

---

79. *Certain Nitrile Gloves*, Inv. No. 337-TA-608, Order 19 (Initial Determination), at 3 (Sept. 19, 2007) (unreviewed).

80. *Integrated Repeaters*, Order No. 3, at 5–6. The second-filed investigation involved an additional complainant, Intel Corp; however, the ALJ expressly noted that Intel was the other complainant's parent.

81. *Id.* at 5.

82. *See LCD Devices*, Order No. 7, at 4 (citing *Certain NAND Flash Memory Devices & Prods. Containing Same*, Inv. No. 337-TA-553, Order No. 3, at 7–8 (Dec. 21, 2005)); *see also Certain SDRAMs, DRAMs, ASICs, RAM & Logic Chips, Microprocessors, Microcontrollers, Processes for Mfg. Same & Prods. Containing Same*, Inv. 337-TA-404, Order No. 8 (Jan. 13, 1998).

83. *Certain Mobile Tels. & Wireless Commc'n Devices Featuring Digital Cameras, & Components Thereof*, 337-TA-663, Order No. 16 (June 11, 2009).

84. *Id.* at 4.

holding joint conferences can ease the burden on parties without unnecessarily confusing patent and other complex issues.[85] Similarly, a partial consolidation, in which some issues are consolidated and others left separate, can yield benefits of efficiency for both the parties and the ITC.[86] For example, in *Light-Emitting Diodes*, the Commission agreed to partially consolidate the 784 investigation with the 785 investigation before the two investigations were instituted.[87] After institution, respondents asked the ALJs in each investigation to fully consolidate the two. Both ALJs refused.[88]

J. TEMPORARY RELIEF PROCEEDINGS

Under some circumstances, complainants may request that the ITC conduct an expedited temporary relief investigation and issue a temporary exclusion order (TEO) or cease and desist order (CDO) prior to completion of an investigation.[89] TEOs are neither frequently pursued nor commonly granted. This is likely because of the already expedited nature of ITC proceedings and the analogous heightened standard used by federal courts in granting preliminary injunctions.[90] A TEO, however, is a valu-

---

85. *See, e.g., Certain Programmable Logic Devices & Prods. Containing Same*, 337-TA-453, Order No. 3, at 8 (Apr. 17, 2001) (denying the complainant's motion to consolidate but ordering parties to "meet and confer about coordinating discovery and discovery scheduling, discovery-related motions, judicial conferences, summary determination motions, pre-trial pleadings, exhibits, the proposed trial schedule, and post-trial briefings . . . as they may find necessary and appropriate in order to economize as much as possible in areas where the two investigations coincide.")

86. *See Mobile Commc'n & Computer Devices*, 337-TA-704, Order No. 5 (Apr. 26, 2010) (granting a partial consolidation and transferring the five overlapping patents to another ALJ).

87. *Certain Light-Emitting Diodes & Prods. Containing the Same*, Inv. No. 337-TA-784, Order No. 3, at 2–3 (Aug. 23, 2011); *Certain Light-Emitting Diodes & Prods. Containing the Same*, Inv. No. 337-TA-785, Order No. 4, at 2 (Aug. 23, 2011).

88. *Id.*

89. *See* 19 U.S.C §§ 1337(e)(1) & (f)(1).

90. There were 45 motions for temporary relief filed from 1976 to 2012, and only nine of them were granted, the last one in 1996. *See, e.g., Certain Apparatus for the Continuous Prod. of Copper Rod*, Inv. No. 337-TA-89, Comm'n Op. (Apr. 1981); *Certain Coin-Operated Audiovisual Games & Components Thereof*, Inv. No. 337-TA-105, Comm'n Op. (July 1982); *Certain Grooved Wooden Kitchen Utensils & Gadgets*, Inv. No. 337-TA-125, Comm'n

able remedy to consider for complainants who face substantial and immediate harm from widespread infringing imports.

Commission Rules 210.52 through 210.69 govern temporary relief proceedings. Pursuant to Rule 210.52(a), the ITC applies the same standards that the CAFC applies in determining whether to affirm lower court decisions granting preliminary injunctions. Requests for temporary relief must be made through a motion. The motion for temporary relief must contain a detailed statement of facts bearing on the factors the CAFC has stated a U.S. district court must consider in granting a preliminary injunction. These factors are:[91]

(1)   a reasonable likelihood of success on the merits;
(2)   irreparable harm to the domestic industry in the absence of temporary relief;[92]
(3)   the balance of harm tipping in complainant's favor; and
(4)   a tolerable effect on the public interest.

The CAFC has made it clear that, in a patent infringement case, a preliminary injunction (or other forms of temporary relief) should not

Op. (July 1983); *Certain Double-Sided Floppy Disk Drives & Components Thereof*, Inv. No. 337-TA-215, Comm'n Op. (Jan. 11, 1986); *Certain Reclosable Plastic Bags & Tubing*, Inv. No. 337-TA-266, Comm'n Op. (Jan. 1988) (motion was granted in part except bond and license part); *Certain Crystalline Cefadroxil Monohydrate*, Inv. No. 337-TA-293, Comm'n Op. (June 1991); *Certain Cellular Radiotelephones & Subassemblies & Component Parts Thereof*, Inv. No. 337-TA-297, Order No. 21 (Aug. 9, 1989); *Certain Dielectric Miniature Microwave Filters & Multiplexers Containing Same*, Inv. No. 337-TA-359, Comm'n Op. (June 1994); *Certain Hardware Logic Emulation Sys. & Components Thereof (Hardware Logic)*, Inv. No. 337-TA-383, Comm'n Op. (Sept. 1996). Most recently, a motion for temporary relief was denied in *Certain Muzzle-Loading Firearms and Components Thereof*, Inv. No. 337-TA-777, Initial Determination (Pub. Version), at 62-63 (Aug. 31, 2011) (*aff'd* on Comm'n review).

91. *See Hardware Logic*, Order No. 34 (Initial Determination), 1996 WL 965338, at *5 (July 8, 1996) (unreviewed) (citing Sofamor Danek Group, Inc. v. Depuy Motech, Inc., 74 F.3d 1216 (Fed. Cir. 1996)); *see also Certain Auto. Fuel Caps & Components Thereof*, Inv. No. 337-TA-532, Order No. 10 (Initial Determination), 2005 WL 1492510, at n.4 (June 10, 2005) (unreviewed).

92. In district court litigation the irreparable harm is to the patentee, not the domestic industry. *See* Tate Access Floors, Inc. v. Interface Architectural Res., Inc., 279 F.3d 1357, 1362 (Fed. Cir. 2002).

issue if the patentee fails to prove either of the first two factors. However, all four factors must be considered.[93]

Pursuant to Commission Rule 210.52(b), a movant for temporary relief must address the appropriateness of a bond. Therefore, the motion for temporary relief must also contain a detailed statement of facts as to whether the complainant should be required to post a bond as a prerequisite to the issuance of temporary relief. The motion must also state the appropriate amount of such a bond.

Because a motion for temporary relief can be decided without a hearing,[94] the complainant must lay out its complete case for relief in the motion papers. Therefore, pursuant to Commission Rule 210.52(d), the following documents and information also must be filed together with the motion for temporary relief:

(1) a memorandum of points and authorities in support of the motion;

(2) affidavits executed by persons with knowledge of the facts asserted in the motion; and

(3) all documents, information, and other evidence in complainant's possession that complainant intends to submit in support of the motion.[95]

Normally, a motion for temporary relief must be filed with the complaint.[96] The motion may be filed after the complaint, but must be filed prior to Commission determination under Section 210.10 on whether to institute an investigation. However, if the motion for temporary relief is filed after filing the complaint, the complainant must demonstrate extraordinary circumstances that justify such delayed filing.[97]

Commission Rule 210.54 governs service of the motion by the complainant. A signed certificate of service must accompany the complaint and motion for temporary relief; otherwise, the Office of the Secretary

---

93. *See* Amazon.com v. Barnesandnoble.com, Inc., 239 F.3d 1343, 1350 (Fed. Cir. 2001) (stating that "[o]ur case law and logic both require that a movant cannot be granted a preliminary injunction unless it establishes both of the first two factors, *i.e.*, likelihood of success on the merits and irreparable harm.").

94. 19 C.F.R. §§ 210.62, 210.50.

95. *See id.* at § 210.52.

96. *See id.*

97. *See id.* at § 210.53.

of the Commission will not accept the complaint or the motion.[98] Further, a notice must accompany each service copy of the complaint and motion for temporary relief containing the text set forth in Commission Rule 210.56 explaining the nature of the motion. In the event the complaint and motion for temporary relief are filed after the date specified in the notice, the complainant must serve a supplementary notice to all proposed respondents and embassies stating the correct filing date, together with a certificate of service.[99]

Pursuant to Commission Rule 210.57, a motion for temporary relief may be amended at any time prior to the institution of an investigation. However, such a motion may not be amended to expand the scope of the temporary relief inquiry after an investigation is instituted.[100]

The Commission determines whether to accept a motion for temporary relief at the same time it determines whether to institute an investigation on the basis of the complaint, pursuant to Commission Rule 210.58.[101] That determination is made within 35 days after the complaint and motion for temporary relief are filed, unless the 35-day period is restarted when a motion for temporary relief is filed after the complaint but before the Commission determines whether to institute an investigation.

Ordinarily, any party may file a response to a motion for temporary relief not later than 10 days after service of the motion by the Commission. The response must contain (1) a statement of objections with particularity; (2) a statement of specific facts concerning the four factors the CAFC has stated a U.S. district court must consider in granting a preliminary injunction; (3) a memorandum of points and authorities in opposition to the motion; and (4) affidavits by persons with knowledge of the facts specified in the response, if possible. In addition, each response to a motion for temporary relief must be accompanied by a response to the complaint and notice of investigation.[102]

A normal temporary relief request must be concluded within 90 days after publication of the notice of institution.[103] This statutory deadline is a

---

98. *See also* Proposed Rule, 77 Fed. Reg. 134,41125 (amending the rule to include mention of a motion for temporary relief in a sentence to provide antecedent basis for the phrase "both documents") (proposed July 11, 2012) (to be codified at 19 C.F.R. pt. 210).

99. *See* 19 C.F.R. § 210.54.

100. *See id.* at § 210.57.

101. *See id.* at § 210.58.

102. *See id.* at § 210.59.

103. *See id.* at. § 210.51(b).

vestige of certain similar statutory deadlines that existed before the 1994 amendments but had to be removed for investigations for permanent relief because of a ruling by the General Agreement on Tariffs and Trade.[104] Commission Rule 210.60 handles designation of an investigation deemed "more complicated" for purposes of adjudicating a motion for temporary relief. Generally, an investigation may be designated "more complicated" if the Commission makes such a designation for the purpose of obtaining up to 60 additional days to adjudicate the motion for temporary relief.[105] Alternatively, the ALJ may issue an order, sua sponte or on motion, designating the investigation "more complicated" for the purpose of obtaining additional time to adjudicate the motion for temporary relief. The order, whether entered by the Commission or the ALJ, constitutes the Commission's final determination on the matter. The Commission is required to publish notice of the order in the *Federal Register*.[106] For cases designated "more complicated," the timeframe is 150 days.[107]

Following the ruling on temporary relief, the case will move forward the same as other Section 337 cases. If a complainant's motion for temporary relief is granted, it may lose any bond money it had submitted if it ultimately fails to prevail in the underlying investigation. An order issued at the conclusion of a TEO proceeding is also subject to presidential review.[108]

---

104. *Compare* 19 U.S.C. § 1337(b) (1988) *with* 19 U.S.C. § 1337(b) (1994); *see also* Vastfame Camera, Ltd. v. U.S. Int'l Trade Comm'n, 386 F.3d 1108, 1113 (2004) (quoting legislative history: "The amendments are necessary to ensure that U.S. procedures for dealing with alleged infringements by imported products comport with GATT 1994 'national treatment' rules, while providing for the effective enforcement of intellectual property rights at the border." S. Rep. No. 103-412, at 120 (1994); H.R. Rep. No. 103-826, at 140–42 (1994)).

105. *See also* Proposed Rules, 77 Fed. Reg. 134,41125 (adding a definition of "more complicated" which had previously been deleted and clarifying that this only applies to the temporary relief phase, not the investigation) (proposed July 11, 2012) (to be codified at 19 C.F.R. pt. 210).

106. 19 C.F.R. § 210.60.

107. *See id.* at § 1337(e)(2).

108. *See id.* at §§ 1337(e) & (j).

CHAPTER 7

Discovery

Discovery in an ITC proceeding is similar to discovery in a federal district court, with one important exception—the accelerated pace. In ITC practice, responses to interrogatories and document requests are due within 10 calendar days of service. Discovery requests can be served almost from the outset of the investigation (beginning the day after publication of the notice of investigation in the *Federal Register*). The entire discovery process, including fact and expert discovery, and third-party discovery is typically completed within five to seven months. This accelerated process can work to the initial advantage of the complainant who is in a position to prepare its discovery in advance of filing the complaint. It behooves respondents to obtain counsel quickly so as to be able to respond in kind with early discovery requests directed to the complainant.

The ITC discovery rules, which are contained both in the Commission Rules and in the ground rules of the individual ALJs, are similar to the discovery rules contained in the Federal Rules of Civil Procedure. As such, ITC discovery practice will not be totally foreign to U.S. district court practitioners. However, while the ALJs may look to the Federal Rules for guidance, there are important differences between ITC and federal practice, and, ultimately, "the Commission Rules, not the Federal Rules, govern ITC proceedings and the Federal Rules serve only as guidelines for the interpretation and application of parallel Commission Rules."[1]

---

1. *Certain Network Interface Cards & Access Points for Use in Direct Sequence Spread Spectrum Wireless Local Area Networks & Prods. Containing Same*, Inv. No. 337-TA-455, Order No. 24, at 5 (July 26, 2001).

Practitioners are also well advised to pay close attention to individual ALJ's ground rules, which tend to contain subtle differences.

A. GROUND RULES

At the beginning of each investigation, the assigned ALJ will issue a set of procedural ground rules that supplement the Commission Rules found in 19 C.F.R. Part 20. The ground rules, which vary to some degree from ALJ to ALJ, typically address, among other things, filing and service requirements, contents and timing of motions, taking discovery, pre-hearing submissions, hearing procedures, and post-hearing submissions. The ground rules may include, for example, limitations on the number of interrogatories that can be served. Some ALJs require parties to establish a "discovery committee" to meet and confer regularly. All ALJs insist that parties make good faith efforts to facilitate discovery and to resolve discovery disputes without ALJ intervention. Compliance with the ALJ's ground rules is critical to successful practice at the ITC.[2]

B. PROTECTIVE ORDER

Unlike U.S. district court practice, the protective order in an ITC investigation is not a document negotiated by the parties and submitted to a judge. Rather, the ALJ issues a standard protective order without waiting for the parties' input. The protective order broadly defines the scope of the confidential information that shall be protected. The protective order also contains detailed rules for marking and handling confidential documents. Most notable about ITC protective orders is that access to confidential information is available only to government personnel, outside counsel for the parties, and experts who have submitted a written agreement to abide by the terms of the order.

The Commission Rules allow in-house counsel access to an opposing party's confidential business information only by agreement of the par-

---

2. *See, e.g., Certain Muzzle-Loading Firearms & Components Thereof,* Inv. No 337-TA-777, Order No. 17, at 3–8 (Nov. 7, 2011) (denying motion for leave to serve responses to requests for admission out of time for failure to comply with the ground rules while emphasizing that parties practicing at the ITC need to comply with the Commission Rules and ALJ's ground rules); *Certain Adjustable Keyboard Support Sys. & Components Thereof,* Inv. No. 337-TA-670, Order No. 13, at 1–4 (Sept. 18, 2009) (denying complainant's and respondents' motions to compel for failure to comply with the ground rules).

ties and after in-house counsel "signs on to the protective order." Alternatively, if both the complainant and respondent agree that their respective in-house counsel can view some or all of each other's confidential information exchanged during discovery, the ALJ may modify the protective order to reflect that agreement. The ALJ, however, will not generally entertain any amendment to the protective order to allow in-house counsel access to third-party information obtained by subpoena and marked confidential according to the protective order.

Parties can seek amendments to the protective order when deemed necessary and appropriate. Frequently, for example, source code is recognized as being highly sensitive and requiring special handling procedures to achieve adequate protection. ALJs are generally willing to amend protective orders to establish extra protection for source code materials, whereby a party needs to make those materials available only to a limited subset of attorneys and experts, under restrictive conditions.[3] Such amendments to the protective order should be negotiated among counsel for the parties.

C. STIPULATIONS

ALJs generally permit and encourage parties to stipulate to certain matters to streamline discovery and to help reduce the number of issues requiring litigation. Discovery stipulations may address, among other things, extensions of deadlines; electronic service; procedures for handling inadvertent disclosure of privileged material or failure to designate information as confidential business information subject to the protective order; exchange of privilege logs; production of electronically stored information; and limitations on expert discovery.

D. TIMING

The discovery process formally begins upon publication of the Notice of Investigation in the *Federal Register*. Parties may serve discovery the day

---

3. *See, e.g., Certain Flash Memory Controllers, Drives, Memory Cards, & Media Players & Prods. Containing Same*, Inv. No. 337-TA-619, Order No. 27, at 1–4 (Apr. 25, 2008); *Certain Digital Televisions & Certain Prods. Containing Same & Methods of Using Same*, Inv. No. 337-TA-617, Order No. 23, at 14–15 (Feb. 25, 2008); *Certain 3G Wideband Code Division Multiplier Access (WCDMA) Handsets & Components Thereof (3G WCDMA Handsets)*, Inv. No. 337-TA-601, Order No. 7, at 1–5 (July 10, 2007).

after the publication or at any such time after the publication as determined by the ALJ.[4] Thus, discovery requests may be served before the ground rules are in place, and even before the investigation is assigned to an ALJ. Fact discovery continues until the fact discovery deadline set by the ALJ in the procedural schedule. Expert discovery typically follows the fact-discovery period. The procedural schedule also typically sets a deadline for motions to compel discovery.

E. SERVICE METHODS

One of the distinctive aspects of ITC discovery practice is the relative ease of obtaining information from foreign parties to the investigation. There is no time spent waiting to perfect service of process or to obtain a determination on personal jurisdiction issues. Shortly after institution, discovery can be served directly on the opposing parties or their counsel of record. Foreign parties can be required to appear for deposition in the United States or at another location where depositions are permitted.[5] Foreign respondents have also been required to submit to plant inspections outside the United States.[6] Failure to provide discovery in response

---

4. 19 C.F.R. §§ 210.28(a), 210.29(b)(1), 210.30(b)(1), 210.31(a). Ground rules typically require the parties to wait at least 20 days after service of the complaint and notice of investigation before issuing requests for admission.

5. *Certain Hardware Logic Emulation Sys. & Components Thereof*, Inv. No. 337-TA-383, Order No. 69, at 13–14 (Jan. 28, 1997) ("Even in an investigation where a foreign government had barred a respondent from participating in discovery, the Commission found that an administrative law judge is 'not precluded from ordering discovery, including depositions and the production of documents, to take place in this country.'" (citing *Certain Mass Flow Devices*, 337-TA-91, Comm'n Op., at 7 (Apr. 21, 1981)); *see also Certain Rotary Printing Apparatus Using Heated Ink Composition Components Thereof, & Sys. Containing Said Apparatus & Components*, Inv. No. 337-TA-320, Order No. 2, 1991 WL 788584, at *1 (Jan. 17, 1991) ("If the Commission has personal jurisdiction over the foreign respondent, the judge can order the respondent to produce some types of foreign discovery.").

6. *See Certain R-134A Coolant (Otherwise Known As 1,1,1,2-Tetrafluoroethane)*, Inv. No. 337-TA-623, Order No. 8, at 1–2 (Apr. 29, 2008) (granting complainants' motion for issuance of a letter request to support complainants' request for Chinese governmental permission to conduct inspections of respondents' factories in China); *Certain Sucralose, Sweeteners Containing Sucralose, & Related Intermediate Compounds Thereof*, Inv. No.

to an ALJ's order may lead to discovery sanctions or even a default judgment.[7]

Another distinctive aspect of ITC discovery practice arises from the ITC's authority to effect service of process nationwide. Upon application by a party, the ALJ may issue a subpoena directed to third parties requesting documents or deposition testimony.[8] When issued, third-party subpoenas can be served anywhere in the United States because section 333(b) of the Tariff Act of 1930 authorizes nationwide service of process. If necessary, subpoenas can be enforced by the ITC via an action brought in the U. S. District Court for the District of Columbia.[9]

F. LIMITATIONS ON SCOPE OR NUMBER

Commission Rule 210.27 governs the scope of discovery.[10] A party "may obtain discovery regarding any matter, not privileged" relevant to the claims and defenses of the parties, including discovery of documents, things, and the identity of persons with relevant knowledge.[11] Additionally, an ITC practitioner should seek discovery related to the appropriate remedy[12] (for example, the existence of commercially significant amounts of domestic inventory of the accused products may be relevant to obtaining a cease and desist order), as well as the appropriate amount of the bond during the Presidential review period in the event a remedial order is issued.[13] Discovery is generally not permitted into "public interest"

337-TA-604, Order No. 31, at 1–2, 7–8 (Oct. 5, 2007) (granting in part complainants' motion to compel complete inspections of respondents' manufacturing facilities in China where complainants and respondents agreed that such inspections were appropriate but disagreed as to the scope of the inspections).

7. 19 C.F.R. § 210.33.

8. *Id.* § 210.32.

9. *See* U.S. Int'l Trade Comm'n v. ASAT, Inc., 411 F.3d 245, 246–56 (D.C. Cir. 2005) (acknowledging that the district court had subject matter and personal jurisdiction and was a proper venue to enforce the ITC subpoena, but reversing the district court's order for the subpoena's enforcement because of the lack of sufficient evidence to determine whether ASAT, Inc. had control over the subpoenaed documents); U.S. Int'l Trade Comm'n v. E. & J. Gallo Winery, 637 F. Supp. 1262, 1263, 1272–73 (D.C. Cir. 1985) (affirming the district court's enforcement order).

10. 19 C.F.R. § 210.27.

11. *Id.* § 210.27(b).

12. *Id.* § 210.42(a)(1)(ii)(A).

13. *Id.* § 210.42(a)(1)(ii)(B).

issues, except in investigations where the Commission has delegated such issues to the ALJ, which has happened more frequently under the Commission's recently revised rules.[14] In contrast to the Federal Rules, the Commission Rules do not limit the number of interrogatories. Some ALJs, however, do limit the number of interrogatories to 175, including discrete subparts.[15] Even if an ALJ does not set a numerical limit, a party may seek a protective order if faced with excessive or harassing discovery requests.[16]

G. ELECTRONIC DISCOVERY

Formal rules regarding e-discovery are not yet in place at the ITC as they are in federal district court.[17] The Commission is, however, in the process of adopting its own set of e-discovery rules, which may well reflect changes similar to those implemented in the Federal Rules of Civil Procedure. In 2010, Chief Judge Randall R. Rader of the U.S. Court of Appeals for the Federal Circuit tasked the Federal Circuit Advisory Council (FCAC) with studying e-discovery issues and developing a model order regarding the use of e-discovery in litigation, particularly patent cases. The result of this effort was an e-discovery model order that has been adopted in a number of district court litigations.[18]

---

14. *Id.* §§ 210.42(a)(1)(ii)(C), 210.50(b)(1); *see also, e.g., Certain Consumer Elecs., Including Mobile Phones & Tablets,* Inv. No. 337-TA-839, 77 Fed. Reg. 24,514, 24,515 (Apr. 24, 2012) (issuing notice of investigation and directing the presiding ALJ to take evidence and hear arguments with respect to the public interest in the investigation); *Certain Dynamic Random Access Memory & NAND Flash Memory Devices & Prods. Containing Same (Dynamic Random Access Memory Devices),* Inv. No. 337-TA-803, 76 Fed. Reg. 55,417, 55,418 (Sept. 7, 2011) (same).

15. *See, e.g,. Certain Elec. Devices For Capturing & Transmitting Images, & Components Thereof,* Inv. No. 337-TA-831, Order No. 4, at 15 (Mar. 23, 2012); *Certain Ink Application Devices & Components Thereof & Methods Of Using The Same,* Inv. No. 337-TA-832, Order No. 2, at 8 (Mar. 6, 2012); *Certain Dimmable Compact Fluorescent Lamps & Prods. Containing Same,* Order No. 2, at 12 (Feb. 28, 2012).

16. *See, e.g., Certain Anti-Theft Deactivatable Resonant Tags & Components Thereof,* Inv. No. 337-TA-347, Order No. 14 (May 28, 1993).

17. *See, e.g.,* FED. R. CIV. P. 16(b)(3)(iii), 26(b)(2)(B), 26(f)(3)(C), 33(d), 34, 37(e), 45.

18. *See, e.g.,* McGrath v. United States, 104 Fed. Cl. 658, 658–60 (2012) (issuing an e-discovery order); DCG Sys., Inc. v. Checkpoint Techs., LLC, No. C-11-03792 PSG, 2011 WL 5244356, at *1–2 (N.D. Cal. Nov. 2, 2011) (grant-

In January 2012, Chief Judge Rader and three members of the FCAC presented to the Commission a proposal to streamline 337 investigations through e-discovery limits.[19] If accepted, this initiative would require parties:

- to indicate whether or not electronic documents such as email are being sought;
- to preemptively limit the number of custodians (individuals who may have documents that are the subject of discovery requests) whose files will be searched, the locations of those documents, and the search terms that will be used (if litigants exceed the specified limits, they would assume the additional costs);
- to use focused search terms limited to specific contested issues; and
- to allow privileged documents to be exchanged without losing privilege.[20]

The FCAC is not the only group to offer suggestions on this issue to the Commission. In early 2012, the ITC Trial Lawyers Association presented a proposal to the Commission regarding potential e-discovery regulations.[21] The specific suggestions include amending the Commission's Rules to allow e-discovery within certain limits[22] and to allow for cost shifting when appropriate. The proposal also suggests that the ALJs include in their ground rules an early meet-and-confer by counsel regarding e-discovery issues, as well as a heightened standard for production of

---

ing a defendant's motion for an order adopting a version of the Model Order on E-Discovery in Patent Cases);

19. U.S. International Trade Commission, *E-Discovery Limits—USITC Considers Proposal to Streamline Section 337 Investigations,* http://www.usitc.gov/press_room/documents/featured_news/ediscovery_article.htm (last visited July 10, 2012).

20. *Id.*

21. *ITCTLA E-Discovery Proposal* (Jan. 20, 2012), http://pdfserver.amlaw.com/legaltechnology/ITCTLA_ediscovery_proposals.pdf.

22. These limits would include a provision that parties need not provide discovery of electronically stored information from sources identified as not reasonably accessible because of undue burden or cost, limitations on the discovery of unreasonably cumulative or duplicative information, limitations on discovery when the party seeking it has otherwise had ample opportunity to obtain the information in discovery, and limitations on discovery when the burden or expense would outweigh its likely benefit.

metadata. At the time of this writing, however, the ITC has not adopted any e-discovery rules.

H. INTERROGATORIES

After the Notice of Investigation is published in the *Federal Register*, a party may serve written interrogatories upon any other party.[23] The party served with the interrogatories must answer within 10 calendar days of service or within the time specified by the ALJ.[24] Agreements for extensions of time to respond are common; the ALJ's ground rules may, however, require a motion for leave.

Procedures for answering interrogatories are set forth in Commission Rules 210.29(b)(2), which states that:

(1) Parties answering interrogatories shall repeat the interrogatories being answered immediately preceding the answers.

(2) Each interrogatory shall be answered separately and fully in writing under oath, unless it is objected to, in which event the reasons for objection shall be stated in lieu of an answer.

(3) The answers are to be signed by the person making them, and the objections are to be signed by the attorney making them.

(4) The party upon whom the interrogatories have been served shall serve a copy of the answers and objections, if any, within ten days of service of the interrogatories or within the time specified by the administrative law judge.

(5) The party submitting the interrogatories may move for an order under section 210.33(a) with respect to any objection to or other failure to answer an interrogatory.[25]

A party may answer an interrogatory with detailed and specific references to documents or records from which an answer may be derived or ascertained.[26] In order to ensure completeness and correctness of the

---

23. 19 C.F.R. § 210.29(b)(1).

24. *Id.* § 210.29(b)(2).

25. *Id.*

26. *Id.* § 210.29(c); *see infra* Part 2 of this section for a more complete discussion of producing documents in lieu of answers. *See also* Rules of General Application, Adjudication, and Enforcement (Proposed Rules), 77 Fed. Reg. 41,124 (limiting the number of interrogatories to 175 including subparts, absent stipulation by the parties or grant of a written motion by a party to the presiding ALJ for good cause) (proposed July 11, 2012) (to be codified at 19 C.F.R. pt. 210).

record developed in the case, all parties are under an obligation to amend prior interrogatory responses when new, formerly unknown information comes to their attention.[27] The answers to interrogatories may be used to the extent permitted by the rules of evidence.[28]

Contention interrogatories often cause friction between the parties. There is a natural tension between the need for fact discovery before requiring a party to take a firm position, and the need for solidification of the parties' positions. Some ALJs set a deadline in the procedural schedule for initial and supplemental responses to contention interrogatories.

I. PRODUCTION OF DOCUMENTS

Similar to written interrogatories, any party may serve on any other party a request for production of documents and things after the Notice of Investigation is published in the *Federal Register*.[29] The recipient must serve a written response within 10 calendar days of service or other time specified by the ALJ.[30] Typically, of course, actual production of the requested documents does not occur within 10 days. The parties are expected to agree to a reasonable schedule for producing documents, but in cases of undue delay the intervention of the ALJ may be necessary.[31] ALJs do not typically limit the number of requests for production that a party may serve, and it is not uncommon for a party to serve hundreds of such requests.[32]

---

27. 19 C.F.R. § 210.27(c).
28. *Id.* § 210.29(a).
29. *Id.* § 210.30(b)(1).
30. *Id.* § 210.30(b)(2).
31. *See Certain Elec. Devices, Including Wireless Commc'n Devices, Portable Music & Data Processing Devices, & Tablet Computers*, Inv. 337-TA-794, Order No. 9, at 3–7 (Nov. 17, 2011) (ordering complainant to provide a specific timeline for completion of its document production and to produce certain categories of documents by dates set by the ALJ); *Certain Prods. Containing Interactive Program Guide & Parental Controls Tech.*, Inv. No. 337-TA-747, Order No. 11, at 2–5 (Apr. 8, 2011) (granting respondents' motion to compel discovery responses and documents from complainant where complainant tried to limit its production of documents to those that "can be reasonably retrieved" and failed to state when it would make the production); *Certain Absorbent Garments*, Inv. No. 337-TA-508, Order No. 22, at 3–6 (Aug. 26, 2004) (ordering respondents to supplement production of certain documents within five business days from the date of the order).
32. *See* 19 C.F.R. § 210.30.

1. Documents Kept in the Usual Course of Business

Pursuant to Commission Rule 210.30(b)(2), parties must organize documents either "as they are kept in the usual course of business" or so that they "correspond to the categories in the request."[33] Generally, the ALJs accept a party's representation that it turned over documents as they were kept in the usual course of business. The burden of proving otherwise lies with the requesting party. ALJs have compelled responding parties to reorganize documents or to provide information regarding the origin of documents when the documents were turned over in an obviously unreasonable form, or when the requesting party had legitimate suspicions that the responding party had performed an incomplete search for documents.

In *Video Graphics Display Controllers*, for example, the ALJ ordered the complainant to comply with Commission Rule 210.30(b)(2), requiring that "[a] party who produces documents for inspection shall produce them as they are kept in the usual course of business or shall organize and label them to correspond to the categories in the request."[34] The ALJ further stated that "[i]f [the complainant] produced documents as kept in the ordinary course, it has no further obligation in this regard; but if the documents were not produced as kept in the ordinary course, [the complainant] is ordered to designate . . . which documents correspond to which categories in the requests."[35]

In *Optical Disk Controller Chips and Chipsets*, the complainant turned over 29,000 pages of documents in electronic format with no page breaks.[36] The ALJ found the suggestion that the complainant kept the documents in this form in the usual course of business "ludicrous," and accordingly ordered the complainant to re-serve the documents with page breaks.[37]

In some cases, the ALJ has ordered responding parties to turn over information regarding the location, timing, and personnel involved in the searches underlying the responding parties' document production in order to determine whether they had performed complete and thorough searches. In *Integrated Repeaters*, the respondent moved to compel re-

---

33. *Id.* § 210.30(b)(2).

34. *Certain Video Graphics Display Controllers & Prods. Containing Same*, Inv. 337-TA-412, Order No. 11, at 13 (Oct. 5, 1998) (quoting 19 C.F.R. § 210.30(b)(2)).

35. *Id.* at 13–14.

36. *Certain Optical Disk Controller Chips & Chipsets & Prods. Containing the Same, Including DVD Players & PC Optical Storage Devices II*, Inv. No. 337-TA-523, Order No. 8, at 12–13 (Dec. 9, 2004).

37. *Id.* at 13.

sponses to a number of discovery requests, including twenty interrogatories regarding the complainants' document production.[38] The respondent argued that the small volume and superficial quality of the complainants' responses up to that point indicated that the complainants had not performed a complete search for documents.[39] Additionally, the respondent asked that the complainants list the "facilities and electronic storage devices [that] were searched, when these were searched, who conducted the searches, and what documents were discovered in each search."[40] Though the complainants objected on the grounds that the interrogatories were overly broad, vague, and ambiguous, the ALJ disagreed and granted the respondent's motion to compel, holding that the interrogatories were detailed, specific, and likely to lead to admissible evidence by highlighting any deficiencies in the complainants' search.[41]

By contrast, in a different investigation, the same ALJ did not compel the responding party to provide information regarding the origination of documents. The respondent contested the organization of the produced documents but did not make any arguments regarding the adequacy of the complainant's document search.[42] The respondent moved to compel the complainant to organize the produced documents according to Commission Rule 210.30(b)(2).[43] The respondent argued that the "often haphazard and random order of document groupings, as well as the failure to provide necessary information concerning the location and file from which the documents originated[]" was unacceptable, and that the complainant should be required to provide such information.[44] The OUII staff attorney, in opposing the respondent's motion, argued that Commission Rule 210.30(b)(2) "does not require labeling of origin that allows the recipient to avoid reviewing" documents.[45]

The ALJ denied the respondent's motion, holding that the respondent failed to meet its burden of showing that the complainants' documents were not turned over as they had been kept in the ordinary course

---

38. *Certain Integrated Repeaters, Switches, Transceivers, & Prods. Containing Same*, Inv. No. 337-TA-435, Order No. 7, at 37–38 (Dec. 21, 2000).

39. *Id.* at 37.

40. *Id.* at 37–38.

41. *Id.* at 38–39.

42. *Certain Ink Cartridges & Components Thereof*, Inv. No. 337-TA-565, Order No. 13, at 1 (July 19, 2006).

43. *Id.*

44. *Id.* at 3.

45. *Id.* at 4.

of business.[46] The ALJ further stated that "[t]he purpose of Commission [R]ule 210.30(b)(2), thus, is similar to Fed. R. Civ. P. 34(b), which is to 'prevent parties from deliberately [mixing] critical documents with others in the hope of obscuring significance' . . . [and] *not* to make it easier for recipient to review large volumes of material or to determine the integrity and completeness of the documents."[47]

2. Documents in Lieu of Answers

Analogous to Federal Rule of Civil Procedure 33(d), Commission Rule 210.29(c) states that:

> [w]hen the answer to an interrogatory may be derived or ascertained from the records of the party upon whom the interrogatory has been served . . . and the burden of deriving or ascertaining the answer is substantially the same for the party serving the interrogatory as for the party served, it is a sufficient answer to such interrogatory to specify the records from which the answer may be derived or ascertained and to [produce those records].[48]

The identification of records must "include sufficient detail to permit the interrogating party to locate and to identify . . . the documents."[49] For example, in *Neodymium-Iron-Boron Magnets*, a complainant replied to several interrogatories by producing 50 boxes of documents, with no explanation of where to locate the relevant answers.[50] Upon the respondent's motion to compel, the ALJ ordered that the complainant identify the specific documents containing the relevant answers, as well as provide several of the answers in narrative form.[51] The ALJ reasoned that, because the documents produced belonged to the complainant, it possessed superior knowledge of them.[52]

At least one ALJ has indicated that identifying documents in lieu of a narrative responses to interrogatories is appropriate only "where the

---

46. *Id.* at 5.

47. *Id.* at 4–5 (citations omitted).

48. 19 C.F.R. § 210.29(c).

49. *Id.*

50. *Certain Neodymium-Iron-Boron Magnets, Magnet Alloys, & Articles Containing the Same*, Inv. No. 337-TA-372, Order No. 16, 1995 WL 945744, at *1 (July 28, 1995).

51. *Id.*, at *2–14.

52. *Id.*, at *2.

most *complete* answer possible to the interrogatories can be found in such documents and where the burden is no greater on [the recipient] to derive the interrogatory answer from the documents than it would be on [the provider]."[53] In addition, the ALJ stated that if the specified documents do not contain all the responsive information known to the responding party, the responding party must supplement its answer to the interrogatory in narrative form.[54]

Numerous ALJ orders have addressed the sufficiency of interrogatory responses that refer the requesting party to documents under Commission Rule 210.29(c).[55] Such decisions are not always consistent. For

---

53. *Certain HSP Modems, Software, & Hardware Components Thereof, & Prods. Containing Same (HSP Modems)*, Inv. No. 337-TA-439, Order No. 51, at 4 (May 9, 2001)); *see also Certain Cigarettes & Packaging Thereof (Cigarettes)*, Inv. No. 337-TA-424, Order No. 46, at 3 (Feb. 11, 2000).

54. *HSP Modems*, Order No. 51, at 4; *see also Certain Prods. Containing Interactive Program Guide & Parental Controls Tech.*, Inv. No. 337-TA-747, Order No. 8, at 5 (Mar. 30, 2011).

55. *See, e.g., Certain Silicon Microphone Packages & Prods. Containing The Same (Silicon Microphone Packages)*, Inv. No. 337-TA-629, Order No. 9, at 3–4, 9 (May 22, 2008) (denying in part respondent's motion to compel interrogatory responses based on complainant's assertion that burden to derive the information from the documents identified in response to certain interrogatories was the same for complainant and respondent); *Certain Mech. Lumbar Supports & Prods. Containing Same (Mechanical Lumbar Supports)*, Inv. No. 337-TA-415, Order No. 27, at 2–4 (Jan. 26, 1999) (denying complainant's motion to compel in part relating to interrogatories answered pursuant to Commission Rule 210.29(c) by emphasizing that complainant failed—with two exceptions—to explain why the burden on complainant would be greater than on respondents to derive answers from the documents while noting that "[w]hile the creator of a document may at least initially have greater familiarity with it, this does not necessarily render a lighter burden on the creator than on others to derive the answers to specific questions"); *see also Cigarettes*, Order No. 14, at 1–3 (Nov. 17, 1999) (denying in part complainant's motion to compel respondent to fully respond to discovery requests by finding that the burden of ascertaining the requested information from the documents that respondent specified in response to two of complainant's interrogatories would be substantially the same for both parties); *Certain Hardware Logic Emulation Sys. (Hardware Logic)*, Inv. No. 337-TA-383, Order No. 56, at 9–10 (Oct. 24, 1996) (granting in part respondents motion to compel by noting that because the interrogatories at issue concerned claims of the patents asserted by complainant and related to the documents created by complainant, the burden of deriving the responses from the documents that complainant identified would not be substantively the same for complainant and for respondents).

example, ALJs have differed on whether the burden of deriving inter-rogatory answers from documents should be placed on the responding party when that party created the documents in question. In a number of investigations, this factor was a primary reason for issuing an order com-pelling a narrative response.[56] Some ALJs, however, have held that the burden of ascertaining an answer from documents is not necessarily re-duced just because the requesting party created the documents and have therefore refused to order narrative responses under similar facts.[57]

J. REQUESTS FOR ADMISSION

The Commission Rule governing requests for admission states in perti-nent part that:

> [a]ny party may serve on any other party a written request for admission of the truth of any matters relevant to the investiga-tion and set forth in the request that relate to statements or opin-ions of fact or of the application of law to fact, including the genuineness of any document described in the request. Copies of documents shall be served with the request unless they have been otherwise furnished or are known to be, and in the request are stated as being, in the possession of the other party.[58]

A party on whom requests for admissions have been served must provide answers within 10 days, or a period of time as determined by the ALJ.[59] If no response is served during this period, the matters addressed in requests for admission may be deemed admitted.[60]

The party to whom requests for admissions are directed may:

(1) admit the subject of a request for admission in its entirety; or

(2) deny the requested matter or object to it in its entirety; or

---

56. *See Hardware Logic,* Order No. 56, at 9–10.

57. *See Silicon Microphone Packages,* Order No. 9, at 3–4, 9; *Mechani-cal Lumbar Supports,* Order No. 27, at 2–4; *see also Cigarettes,* Order No. 14, at 1–3.

58. 19 C.F.R. § 210.31(a).

59. *Id.* § 210.31(b).

60. *Id.; see also Certain Muzzle-Loading Firearms & Components Thereof,* Inv. No. 337-TA-777, Order No. 17, at 2–8 (Nov. 7, 2011) (deeming requests for admission to be admitted because of complainants' failure to timely file a motion for leave to serve response to respondents' first set of requests for admission out of time).

(3)   admit only part of the matter and deny the rest.[61]

Any admissions made may only be used in the pending investigation and any related proceeding.[62] Related proceedings include preinstitution proceedings, sanction proceedings, bond forfeiture proceedings, proceedings to enforce, modify, or revoke a remedial or consent order, or advisory opinion proceedings.[63]

When objecting to or denying requests for admission, a responding party must set forth in detail the reasons why it cannot truthfully admit or deny the matter.[64] The responding party cannot cite lack of information or knowledge as a basis for the objection unless it states that it made a reasonable inquiry and that the information known or readily obtainable is insufficient to either admit or deny the request.[65] A party not satisfied with responses to requested admissions may move to determine the sufficiency of the answers or objections pursuant to Commission Rule 210.31(c).[66] A responding party must do more than provide mere blanket responses. In *Zero-Mercury-Added Alkaline Batteries*, the ALJ granted the complainant's motion to compel full and complete responses, indicating that the respondents' responses were "repetitive," "boilerplate," "unresponsive objections and denials,"[67] and"[i]t is an utter waste of litigation time and paper to produce responses to discovery requests like these."[68]

The ALJs may require parties to supplement their responses to requests for admissions, especially in the later stages of an investigation

---

61. *See* 19 C.F.R. § 210.31(b).

62. *Id.* § 210.31(d).

63. *Id.* § 210.3. *See also* Proposed Rules, 77 Fed. Reg. 134,41121 (supplying "ancillary proceeding" as a synonym for "related proceeding") (proposed July 11, 2012) (to be codified at 19 C.F.R. pt. 210).

64. *Id.* § 210.31(b).

65. *Id.*

66. *Id.* § 210.31(c); *see, e.g., Certain Set-Top Boxes, & Hardware & Software Components Thereof,* Inv. No. 337-TA-761, Order No. 16, at 7–9 (Aug. 16, 2011) (granting in part respondent's motion to compel complainant to provide complete responses to requests for admission and stating that "[respondent] is entitled to full and unqualified responses . . .").

67. *Certain Zero-Mercury-Added Alkaline Batteries, Parts Thereof, & Prods. Containing Same,* Inv. No. 337-TA-493, Order No. 58, at 1–3 (Dec. 24, 2003).

68. *Id.* at 3.

and where the requests are directed towards the parties' respective claim constructions.[69] An ALJ may also order a party to supplement its responses "if the party learns that the response is in some material respect incomplete or incorrect and if the additional or corrective information has not otherwise been made known to the other parties during discovery or in writing."[70] In addition, parties can informally agree to supplement their discovery responses pursuant to Commission Rule 210.27(b).

K. REQUESTS FOR ENTRY ON LAND OR INSPECTION

Any party may serve another party with a request to permit entry upon designated land for the purpose of inspecting a designated object or operation thereon.[71] Such a request is expected to be fairly specific, defining, among other things, the items to be inspected, either by individual item or category, and providing a description of each item and category with reasonable particularity. The request must also set forth a reasonable time, place, and manner of making the inspection.[72] The party served with the request must furnish a written response within 10 days or within any other time set out by the ALJ.[73] Such written response may convey the party's consent to the requested entry upon its property or plant for the purpose of inspection or may set forth objections with a detailed explanation as to why it cannot submit to the opposing party's inspection.[74] In some cases, the ALJs have ordered parties to attempt to obtain discovery through less intrusive means before compelling an inspection.[75]

---

69. *See, e.g., Certain Dynamic Random Access Memory Controllers & Certain Multi-Layer Integrated Circuits, as Well as Chipsets & Prods. Containing Same,* Inv. No. 337-TA-388, Order No. 10, at 1–2 (Jan. 13, 1997); *see also Certain Engines, Components Thereof, & Prods. Containing the Same,* Inv. No. 337-TA-585, Order No. 5, at 3 (Dec. 21, 2006); *Certain High-Brightness Light Emitting Diodes & Prods. Containing Same,* Inv. No. 337-TA-556, Order No. 20, at 1–2 (May 17, 2006).
70. 19 C.F.R. § 210.27(c).
71. *Id.* § 210.30(a)(2).
72. *Id.* § 210.30(b)(1).
73. *Id.* § 210.30(b)(2).
74. *Id.*
75. *See Certain Gemcitabine & Prods. Containing Same,* Inv. No. 337-TA-766, Order No. 10, at 8–9 (June 22, 2011).

Plant inspections, particularly in process patent and trade secret cases, have taken place, often without controversy, even in foreign countries.[76] This is one of the key advantages of Section 337 proceedings over district court litigation from the point of view of the complainant.

Anisotropically Etched One Megabit and Greater DRAMS sets forth some of the factors that an ALJ considers in deciding whether to grant a motion to compel relating to a plant inspection.[77] In that matter, the complainant filed a motion to compel the respondent to permit inspection and sampling from various stages of the etching process used in two fabrication facilities.[78] The respondent argued that the inspection and sampling were "not needed, unduly burdensome, disruptive, and in part irrelevant."[79] The ALJ emphasized that "[i]n a motion to compel, the party seeking discovery must establish relevance, and the party resisting discovery must demonstrate undue burden."[80] The ALJ found there was, at a minimum, a justifiable interest in the inspection and that the inspection appeared to be neither "unduly cumulative of previously supplied written discovery," nor unreasonable.[81] In granting the motion to compel, the ALJ, however, ordered certain conditions to the inspection, including: "[the complainant must] describe how it wants to inspect the

---

76. *See Certain R-134A Coolant (Otherwise Known As 1,1,1,2-Tetrafluoroethane)*, Inv. No. 337-TA-623, Order No. 8, at 1–2 (Apr. 29, 2008) (granting complainants' motion for issuance of a letter request to support complainant's request for Chinese governmental permission to conduct inspections of respondents' factories in China); *Certain Sucralose, Sweeteners Containing Sucralose, & Related Intermediate Compounds Thereof*, Inv. No. 337-TA-604, Order No. 31, at 1–2, 7–8 (Oct. 5, 2007) (granting in part complainants' motion to compel complete inspections of respondents' manufacturing facilities in China where complainants and respondents agreed that such inspections were appropriate but disagreed as to the scope of the inspections); *Certain Aramid Fiber Honeycomb, Unexpanded Block of Slice Precursors of Such Aramid Fiber Honeycomb, & Carved or Contoured Blocks or Bonded Assemblies of Such Aramid Fiber Honeycomb*, Inv. No. 337-TA-305, Order No. 20, 1990 WL 710659, at *1 (Mar. 23, 1990) (granting joint motion for an extension of the date for the inspection of respondent's plant in Luxembourg).
77. *Certain Anisotropically Etched One Megabit & Greater DRAMS, Components Thereof, and Prods. Containing Such DRAMS*, Inv. No. 337-TA-345, Order No. 5, 1993 WL 852621, at *1–2 (Mar. 24, 1993).
78. *Id.* at *1.
79. *Id.*
80. *Id.*
81. *Id.*

facilities (for example, will it want employees to be there to explain the process, will it have an interpreter, will it record what is said, etc.) and [the complainant must] specify where it wants each sample to be taken and when."[82]

L. DEPOSITIONS

Following publication in the *Federal Register* of a Commission notice instituting the investigation, any party may seek to take the testimony of any person, including a party, by deposition upon oral examination or written questions.[83] Practically speaking, however, in most cases few depositions take place until document production is substantially complete. The Commission Rules and most ALJ ground rules do not impose any limitations on the number of fact depositions that may be taken and do not impose a one-person/one-day presumptive limitation as the Federal Rules provide. Depositions are otherwise taken in a manner similar to depositions in U.S. district court litigation.

---

82. *Id.* at *2; *see also Certain Lens-Fitted Film Packages,* Inv. No. 337-TA-406, Order No. 108, at 1, 4 (Sept. 8, 2003) (granting in part respondent's motion for a protective order barring complainant from inspecting some of respondent's former suppliers' factories located in China and Hong Kong based, at least in part, on complainant's failure to establish that requested inspections appeared reasonably calculated to lead to the discovery of admissible evidence and complainant's failure to specify the burdens which would be imposed on respondent and its former suppliers by proposed inspections); *Certain Cigarettes & Packaging Thereof,* Inv. No. 337-TA-424, Order No. 34, at 1–4 (Jan. 28, 2000) (denying respondent's motion for a protective order to prevent complainant's inspection of its premises by finding that respondent offered no support for its assertion that "the only purpose for the requested inspection was to harass and burden [respondent] by disrupting its regular business operations").

83. 19 C.F.R. § 210.28(a). *See also* Proposed Rules, 77 Fed. Reg. 41,123 (creating a 10-day period in which parties may respond to and make objections to a notice of deposition, limiting the number of depositions a party may take to 10 unless stipulated otherwise, limiting the number of fact depositions taken to five per respondent or 20 as a group of respondents—whichever is greater. The proposed rule also limits any Commission investigative attorney to taking a maximum of 10 fact depositions. The number of depositions may be increased on written motion to the presiding ALJ for good cause shown.) (proposed July 11, 2012) (to be codified at 19 C.F.R. pt. 210).

1. Review and Alteration of Depositions

Unlike the Federal Rules of Civil Procedure, the Commission Rules do not specifically provide for a process of reviewing and amending a deposition transcript.[84] Parties typically follow federal practice in this regard. Disputes over amendments to deposition transcripts rarely arise at the ITC.

2. Corporate Witnesses

The Commission Rules do not contain a direct corollary to Federal Rule 30(b)(6) regarding the obligation of a corporate entity, in response to a deposition notice or subpoena, to designate a witness who is knowledgeable as to topics enumerated in the notice or subpoena. Nevertheless, parties in Section 337 investigations routinely serve and respond to corporate deposition notices that operate in the same manner as Rule 30(b)(6) notices in federal practice.[85] In an ITC investigation, a deposition of a party (i.e., testimony provided in response to a 30(b)(6) deposition notice) may be used by an adverse party for any purpose.[86]

3. Deposition Testimony as to Contentions

The question of whether a party witness must provide testimony as to the party's contentions is decided based on the particular facts of the case.[87] In *Integrated Repeaters*, the complainants moved to compel a respondent to prepare a knowledgeable Rule 30(b)(6) witness for deposition on top-

---

84. *Compare* 19 C.F.R. § 210.28, *with* FED. R. CIV. P. 30(e).

85. *Certain Steel Rod Treating Apparatus & Components Thereof*, 337-TA-97, Order No. 13, 1981 WL 178518, at *3 (May 8, 1981) ("The Commission's Rules of Procedure (19 C.F.R. § 210.1 et seq.) follow the general intent and often the letter of the Federal Rules of Civil Procedure and apply the Federal Rules of Civil Procedure when not inconsistent with the mandates of Section 337.").

86. 19 C.F.R. § 210.28(h)(2).

87. *See, e.g., Certain Integrated Repeaters, Switches, Transceivers, & Prods. Containing Same*, Inv. No. 337-TA-435, Order No. 16, at 20–21 (Feb. 13, 2001) (denying complainants' motion to compel in part relating to the production of a 30(b)(6) witness capable of responding to questions relating to the bases of [respondent's] defense of non-infringement based on the factual circumstances, including the higher cost, the more invasive nature of the deposition process, and difficulties in summarizing the information sought) (citing Exxon Research & Eng'g Co. v. United States, 44 Fed. Cl. 597 (1999)).

ics including the respondent's infringement contentions.[88] The respondent designated its marketing vice president as its witness and refused to permit answers on certain topics on the theory that the "complainants have the burden of proof on infringement."[89] The ALJ denied the complainants' motion to compel the production of a Rule 30(b)(6) witness capable of answering claim construction questions because he found that answering contention interrogatories was a less expensive and less invasive method to learn the requested information.[90] The ALJ further cited *Exxon Research and Engineering Co. v. United States* in which the court found that claim construction was a difficult issue to summarize by one deponent and "could lead to the deposition of one of the defendant's attorneys, which, although not prohibited, was clearly disfavored."[91] Though the ALJ denied the motion at issue, the complainants were permitted the opportunity to compel depositions if they were not satisfied with any of the responses to the contention interrogatories.[92]

In *Rechargeable Nickel Metal Hydride Anode Materials and Batteries*,[93] however, the ALJ held that "once a party's contentions have been stated, the party's witnesses may be deposed on the details of the facts on which the party intends to rely to prove its contentions."[94] In addition, the ALJ stated that "although the witness could not be asked a pure question of law, he could be asked to answer mixed questions of fact and law, and could be asked to give the factual basis for any contention."[95]

88. *Id.* at 3, 20–21.
89. *Id.* 3–6.
90. *Id.* at 20–21 (citing *Exxon Research*, 44 Fed. Cl. at 601).
91. *Id.* (citing *Exxon Research*, 44 Fed. Cl. at 601).
92. *Id.* at 21.
93. *Certain Rechargeable Nickel Metal Hydride Anode Materials & Batteries, & Prods. Containing Same*, Inv. No. 337-TA-368, Order No. 5, 1994 WL 930315, at *1 (Dec. 12, 1994).
94. *Id.*
95. *Id.; see also Certain GPS Chips, Associated Software & Sys., & Prods. Containing Same*, Inv. No. 337-TA-596, Order 13, at 2–4 (June 27, 2007) (granting respondent's motion to compel complainant to produce a witness to testify regarding prior art despite complainant's argument that prior art is a complex legal question by emphasizing that, while it is a question of law, it is based on underlying fact questions).

4. Depositions in Foreign Countries

ITC practitioners must be very aware of the rules that apply when attempting to take depositions in foreign countries. For example, deposition cannot be conducted in mainland China. Instead, depositions of Chinese witnesses are often taken in Hong Kong. Additionally, even where depositions are permitted, there may be restrictions on when and how to schedule and conduct a deposition. Depositions in Japan, for example, can only be conducted at a U.S. embassy or consulate. The noticing party must reserve space at the embassy or consulate and obtain a special visa, which requires a certified copy of a U.S. district court order, as Japan will not accept an order from an administrative law judge.[96] The U.S. Department of State website provides information regarding discovery abroad.[97]

M. EXPERT DISCOVERY

Expert discovery in an ITC investigation is almost the same as in federal district court, but it proceeds at a significantly faster pace. Expert reports are typically due within weeks from the close of fact discovery, with rebuttal reports typically due a week or two later. Expert depositions normally must be scheduled during a short window following the submission of rebuttal reports.

In addition to an expert's role as a hearing witness on the issues under dispute, experts can also play an important role in educating the ALJ about the technology at issue in the investigation. Frequently—in-

---

96. *See* U.S. Dep't of State, Bureau of Consular Affairs, Japan Judicial Assistance, http://travel.state.gov/law/info/judicial/judicial_678. html#courtorder (last visited 7/10/2012). For information regarding the actual steps to scheduling a deposition at either the U.S. Embassy in Tokyo or the American Consulate in Osaka, *see* http://tokyo.usembassy.gov/e/acs/tacs-7116.html (Taking Depositions in Tokyo) (last visited July 10, 2012) and http://tokyo.usembassy.gov/e/acs/tacs-osakadepositions.html (Taking Depositions in Osaka) (last visited July 10, 2012).

97. *See, e.g.,* U.S. Dep't of State, http://travel.state.gov /law/judicial/judicial_2514.html (general information regarding obtaining evidence abroad), http://travel.state.gov/law/judicial/judicial_678.html (information regarding judicial assistance, including taking deposition, in Japan), http://travel.state.gov/law/judicial/judicial_656.html (information regarding judicial assistance, including taking depositions, in Malaysia), http://travel.state.gov/judicial/judicial_650.html (information regarding judicial assistance, including taking depositions, in Hong Kong) (last visited July 10, 2012).

creasingly so in recent years—the ALJs will request, or grant the parties' request, to conduct a technology tutorial, which usually takes place around the time of the prehearing conference.[98] The ALJ often leaves it up to the parties how to conduct the tutorial, which is intended to educate the ALJ on the underlying technology. The technology tutorials should not, in theory, be used to argue the parties' positions. It has become increasingly popular for the parties' experts to present these tutorials. After the party's expert educates the ALJ about the relevant technology, the ALJ may find the expert's opinion testimony on the disputed issues easier to follow and more credible.

Expert reports are usually not admitted into evidence, although this can vary depending on the ALJ and on the investigation. For example, one ALJ generally does not allow expert reports into evidence,[99] but in at least one investigation he did require the parties to file their expert reports on claim construction in advance of a *Markman* hearing.[100]

Most Section 337 patent cases involve technical experts. An increasing number of investigations also involve economic experts, who may address domestic industry, remedy, or bonding issues, as well as public interest. Less commonly, legal experts are also employed. Legal experts' testimony is typically limited to PTO procedure.[101] ALJs enforce this rule by striking the portions of expert reports that go beyond PTO procedure,[102] or by excluding such testimony offered at a hearing.[103]

---

98. *See, e.g., Certain Blu-Ray Disc Players, Components Thereof & Prods. Containing the Same,* Inv. No. 337-TA-824, Order No. 2, 2012 WL 167443, at *2 (Jan. 19, 2012).

99. *Id.* at *22.

100. *Certain Dynamic Random Access Memory & NAND Flash Memory Devices & Prods. Containing Same,* Inv. No. 337-TA-803, Order No. 20, at 1 (Jan. 5, 2012).

101. *See, e.g., Certain Ink Application Devices & Components Thereof & Methods Of Using The Same,* Inv. No. 337-TA-832, Order No. 2, at 13 (Mar. 6, 2012) ("Legal experts may only testify as to procedures of the U.S. Patent and Trademark Office."); *Certain Blu-Ray Disc Players,* Order No. 2, 2012 WL 167443, at *21 (Jan. 19, 2012) (same); *Certain Composite Wear Components & Prods. Containing the Same,* Inv. No. 337-TA-644, Order No. 2, at 20 (May 5, 2008) (same).

102. *See, e.g., Certain Equip. for Telecomms. or Data Commc'n Networks, Including Routers, Switches, & Hubs, & Components Thereof,* Inv. No. 337-TA-574, Order No. 21, at 4–9 (May 8, 2007).

103. *See, e.g., Certain NOR & NAND Flash Memory Devices & Prods. Containing Same,* Inv. No. 337-TA-560, Order No. 32, at 2–3 (Oct. 11, 2006).

N. THIRD-PARTY DISCOVERY

The ITC allows broad discovery from third parties. The Commission has stated, however, that a requesting party must first seek discovery from other parties to the investigation before seeking the same information from third parties.[104]

1. Obtaining Discovery from Third Parties by Means of Subpoena

The ITC is authorized to issue subpoenas "[f]or the purposes of carrying out its functions and duties in connection with any investigation authorized by law."[105] This broad power extends throughout the United States and its territories.[106] Each ALJ's ground rules detail the procedure for obtaining and serving an ITC subpoena. Generally, the requesting party submits, ex parte, a subpoena application explaining the relevance and scope of the information sought. If the ALJ approves the application and signs the subpoena, the subpoena is returned to the requesting party for service.[107] After the subpoena is served, the responding party has 10 days to move to quash or limit the subpoena.[108]

When considering a motion to quash:

> Commission rules 210.34(a) and 210.34(a)(7) provide that the administrative law judge may make "any order that may appear necessary and appropriate for the protection of the public interest" and has the authority, "when justice requires," to protect a party or person from "annoyance, embarrassment, oppression,

---

104. *See, e.g.,* Haworth, Inc. v. Herman Miller, Inc., 998 F.2d 975, 978 (Fed. Cir. 1993) (requiring party to seek discovery from opposing party before burdening third party); *Certain Foam Footwear,* Inv. No. 337-TA-567, Order No. 16, at 1, 3 (Aug. 2, 2006) (granting four third parties' motions to quash or otherwise limit respondents' subpoena duces tecum and ad testificandum based, in part, on the availability of the information that the respondents sought to obtain from the third parties directly from the complainant).

105. 19 U.S.C. § 1333(a).

106. *See id.*

107. Ground rules differ as to whether the application must subsequently be served on opposing counsel, along with the subpoena.

108. Responding parties frequently request, and are usually given, extensions of time to file their motions to quash/limit.

or undue burden or expense." . . . *The fact of non-party status may be considered with any motion to limit.*[109]

In addition, ALJs have held that a subpoena should be quashed if it imposes an undue burden on a third party.[110]

When a third party refuses to comply with an ITC subpoena, the requesting party may seek judicial enforcement by the ITC.[111] Pursuant to Commission Rule 210.32(g), a party requesting judicial enforcement of a third-party subpoena must first file a motion to the ALJ for certification to the Commission.[112] The third party generally has at least 10 days to respond to such a request. If the ALJ finds that the subpoenaed party has failed to reasonably comply, he may certify a request for enforcement to the Commission.[113] The Commission may seek additional briefing before issuing a notice as to whether it will seek judicial enforcement.

If the Commission determines to seek judicial enforcement, it "may invoke the aid of any district court or territorial court of the United States . . . within the jurisdiction of which such inquiry is carried on" to enforce the subpoena.[114] This statutory language authorizes nationwide

---

109. *Certain Optical Disk Controller Chips & Chipsets & Prods. Containing Same*, Inv. No. 337-TA-506, Order No. 39, at 2 (Feb. 7, 2005) (citing *Certain Set-Top Boxes & Components Thereof*, Inv. No. 337-TA-454, Order No. 16, at 1–2 (July 2, 2001) (emphasis added).

110. *See Certain Authentication Sys., Including Software & Handheld Elect. Devices*, Inv. No. 337-TA-697, Order No. 8, at 3–4 (Apr. 15, 2010) (rejecting a third party's motion to quash respondents' subpoena ad testificandum and decus tecum, at least in part, because the discovery that the respondents sought was not unduly burdensome).

111. *See Certain Portable Elec. Devices & Related Software*, Inv. No. 337-TA-797, Order No. 54 (corrected), at 1–6 (May 23, 2012) (certifying to the Commission complainant's request for enforcement of its subpoena ad testificandum issued to a non-party regarding certain characteristics of accused products relevant to complainant's infringement allegations); *Certain Elec. Devices, Including Handheld Wireless Commc'n Devices*, Inv. No. 337-TA-667/673, Order No. 26C, at 13–14 (Aug. 17, 2009) (certifying to the Commission respondents' request for judicial enforcement of a subpoena duces tecum by finding that the information that respondents sought from a third-party law firm regarding the prosecution of two patents, one of which was not asserted in the investigation, concerned the production of relevant information because respondents expected that information to support their inequitable conduct defense and was reasonable in scope and non-burdensome).

112. *See* 19 C.F.R. § 210.32(g).

113. *See id.*

114. 19 U.S.C. § 1333(b).

service of process and, thus, personal jurisdiction by the U.S. district courts for subpoena enforcement actions under 19 U.S.C. § 1333(a).[115] The Commission, through its general counsel, typically initiates the enforcement proceeding by filing a petition with the U.S. District Court for the District of Columbia.[116]

In determining whether to enforce an ITC subpoena, the district court's role is "strictly limited."[117] Specifically, this role consists of deciding (1) whether the subpoena was issued for a lawful purpose within the statutory authority of the issuing agency; (2) whether the demand is sufficiently definite and not unduly burdensome; and (3) whether the subpoena seeks information reasonably relevant to the agency's investigation.[118] If the district court finds that each of these elements is satisfied, it will issue an order compelling the third party to produce documents and information in response to the subpoena. Judicial enforcement of third party subpoenas can be a lengthy process and in some cases has led to delays in the resolution of Section 337 investigations.[119]

2. Obtaining Discovery from Third Parties under the Control of Named Parties

Commission Rule 210.30(a)(1), which is similar to Federal Rule of Civil Procedure 34(a), provides in pertinent part that "[a]ny party may serve on any other party a request to produce . . . any designated documents . . . or tangible things that are in the possession, custody or control of the party

---

115. *See* U.S. Int'l Trade Comm'n v. ASAT, Inc., 411 F.3d 245, 246, 250–52 (D.C. Cir. 2005).

116. *See, e.g., id.* at 245.

117. *Id.* at 253 (citing FTC v. Texaco, Inc., 555 F.2d 862, 872 (D.C. Cir. 1977)).

118. *See id.* (citing United States v. Morton Salt Co., 338 U.S. 632, 652–53 (1950)).

119. *See Certain Encapsulated Integrated Circuit Devices & Prods. Containing Same*, Inv. No. 337-TA-501, Notice of Comm'n Final Determination of No Violation of Section 337, at 2 (July 20, 2010) (noting that "[c]ompletion of this investigation has been delayed because of difficulty in obtaining from third party . . . certain documents that [respondent] asserted were crucial for its affirmative defenses[]" where it took over four years between the issuance of a subpoena *duces tecum* and *ad testificandum* and the order of the U.S. District Court for the District of Columbia granting the ITC's second enforcement petition).

upon whom the request is served."[120] When the issue of control arises in parent-subsidiary situations, the Commission has determined that "a litigating parent corporation has control over documents in the physical possession of its subsidi[ary] corporation."[121]

The Commission's rulings in the parent-subsidiary context are consistent with federal district court precedent. The Commission frequently relies upon the *Camden Iron and Metal v. Marubeni America* decision, which sets forth standards for finding control of documents.[122] The court defined control as "the legal right, authority, or ability to obtain documents upon demand."[123] Moreover, the "federal courts construe 'control' very broadly."[124] With respect to a parent corporation's control over a subsidiary, the court noted that "a litigating parent corporation has control over documents in the physical possession of its subsidiary corporation where the subsidiary is wholly owned or controlled by the parent."[125]

Additionally, a parent has control over its subsidiary when there is a "sufficient structural interlocking of the two companies."[126] A seminal case that analyzed control within the context of the corporate structure of two corporations is *In re Uranium Antitrust Litigation*.[127] When determining the level of control between parent and subsidiaries, courts examine factors such as (1) the parent's ownership share in the subsidiary

---

120. *Compare* 19 C.F.R. § 210.30(a)(1), *with* FED. R. CIV. P. 34(a) ("[a] party may serve on any other party a request [for the following] within the . . . responding party's possession, custody, or control:. . . any designated documents or . . . any designated tangible things[]"), *and* FED. R. CIV. P. 34(c) ("a nonparty may be compelled to produce documents and tangible things or to permit an inspection[]").

121. *Certain NAND Flash Memory Circuits & Prods. Containing Same*, Inv. No. 337-TA-526, Order No. 6, at 3 (Mar. 8, 2005); *see also Certain Wiper Blades*, Inv. No. 337-TA-816, Order No. 24, 2012 WL 1892236, at *1–2 (May 10, 2012).

122. *See* Camden Iron & Metal, Inc. v. Marubeni America Corp., 138 F.R.D. 438, 441 (D.N.J. 1991).

123. *Id.*

124. *Id.*

125. *Id.* (citing Gerling Int'l Ins. Co. v. Comm'r of Internal Revenue, 839 F.2d 131, 140 (3d Cir. 1988)); *see also* 8A CHARLES ALAN WRIGHT & ARTHUR R. MILLER, FEDERAL PRACTICE AND PROCEDURE: CIVIL, § 2210 n.8 (2008) (and decisions cited therein).

126. Gen. Envtl. Sci. Corp. v. Horsfall, 136 F.R.D. 130, 133 (N.D. Ohio 1991) (citing *Gerling Int'l Ins. Co.*, 839 F.2d at 140–41)).

127. *In re* Uranium Antitrust Litig., 480 F. Supp. 1138, 1138–56 (N.D. Ill. 1979).

corporation,[128] (2) whether the corporations have interlocking management structures,[129] and (3) the degree of control exercised by the parent over the subsidiary's directors, officers, and employees.[130] Furthermore, courts normally take into consideration whether the subsidiary of the litigating parent is involved in the business operations that are subject of the present investigation. If it is determined that the third party is indeed the wholly owned subsidiary of the litigating parent, and the litigating parent refuses to search for and produce responsive documents and information in the possession, custody, and control of such third party, it can be compelled to do so.[131]

Obtaining upstream discovery from the parent company of a subsidiary acting as a complainant is also possible. In *Transport Vehicle Tires*, the

---

128. *See id.* at 1151 (concluding that a corporation's total ownership of its subsidiaries gave it effective control over the subsidiaries' documents); Hubbard v. Rubbermaid, Inc., 78 F.R.D. 631, 637 (D.C. Md. 1978) (determining that documents in the possession of wholly owned subsidiaries were subject to discovery in view of the fact that they were in the custody or under control of corporate parent, which was a defendant to the case); *see also Certain Lens-Fitted Film Packages (LFFPs)*, Inv. No. 337-TA-406, Order No. 12, at 7–8 (Aug. 20, 1998) (granting a subpoena directed at the production of relevant documents in the possession of complainant's foreign subsidiaries where the complainant had not denied that it was in control of its foreign subsidiaries).

129. *See Gen. Envtl. Sci. Corp.*, 136 F.R.D. at 133–34 (holding that a corporation controlled a non-party corporation where the corporation owned a majority of the non-party's equity and both companies shared the same owners and directors).

130. *Id.*

131. *See In re Richardson-Merrell, Inc.*, 97 F.R.D. 481, 483 (S.D. Ohio 1983) (holding that the parent corporation was obliged to conduct a foreign search for documents in the hands of its foreign subsidiaries and to "produce all documents, responsive to plaintiff's requests, in the care, custody or control of its foreign subsidiaries[]"); *LFFPs*, Order No. 12, at 7–8 (ordering the parent corporation to determine if its foreign subsidiaries had any responsive documents, what it would take to produce the requested documents, and to provide a report detailing complainant's search efforts by a designated date); *see also Certain NAND Flash Memory Circuits & Prods. Containing Same*, Inv. No. 337-TA-526, Order No. 6, at 2–4 (Mar. 8, 2005) (noting that two subsidiaries who had resisted a third-party subpoena had not conducted any search for responsive documents in their possession and ordering that the subsidiaries had to produce any responsive documents within their possession and control).

respondents sought an order to compel complainant, a subsidiary of a parent company, to provide discovery of information in the possession of the parent company and its affiliates.[132] While the subsidiary argued it was a separate entity and that discovery from its parent company should not be granted, the ALJ found that the "documents and things in the possession, custody or control of other [parent company] entities should be considered within the control of [the subsidiary] for discovery purposes" because the subsidiary "was able to secure documents from [the parent company's] entities for use in [the] investigation."[133]

In *Cast Steel Railway Wheels,* the ALJ concluded that respondents were entitled to discovery from two third parties—Datong ABC Castings Company Limited (DACC) and ABC Rail Products China Investment Corporation (ABC Rail)—that were related to the named complainant.[134] The complainant had pleaded trade secret misappropriation, which was alleged to have occurred from or at DACC, which in turn was a joint venture of ABC Rail (a wholly owned subsidiary of the complainant) and another Chinese company.[135] The ALJ noted that while "DACC and ABC Rail are not presently named complainants in this investigation, in considering the overall relationship between [the complainant], ABC Rail, and DACC and the connection of each to the . . . subject of this trade secrets investigation[], it would be manifestly unfair to respondents to shield DACC and ABC Rail from the obligation of providing information directly relevant to the heart of this investigation."[136]

3. *Obtaining Discovery from Foreign Third Parties*

The ITC's subpoena power does not extend beyond the United States.[137] Accordingly, the ALJs will not issue subpoenas seeking documents and

---

132. *Certain Transp. Vehicle Tires,* Inv. No. 337-TA-390, Order No. 8, 1996 WL 965776, at *1 (Nov. 12 1996).

133. *Id.* at *12–13 (citing *Camden Iron & Metal, Inc.,* 138 F.R.D. at 441–42 (reasoning that a subsidiary to possess control over a parent's records when "the relationship [was] such that the agent-subsidiary [could] secure documents of the principal-parent to meet its own business needs and documents helpful for use in litigation," or alternatively when "there [was] access to documents when the need [arose] in the ordinary course of business").

134. *Certain Cast Steel Ry. Wheels, Certain Processes for Mfg. or Relating to Same & Certain Prods. Containing Same,* Inv. No. 337-TA-655, Order No. 16, at 1–4 (Mar. 4, 2009).

135. *Id.* at 1–2.

136. *Id.* at 2–3.

137. *See* 19 U.S.C. § 1333.

information from foreign third parties unless those parties maintain an agent in the United States who is authorized to accept service.[138] There are, however, other options available to parties seeking discovery from foreign third parties.[139]

A requesting party may be able to obtain documents and information from the domestic affiliate or subsidiary of a foreign third party if it can show that the affiliate/subsidiary maintains possession, custody, or control over the documents or information in question.[140] The U.S. Court of Appeals for the District of Columbia has explained that a subsidiary corporation has the requisite control of documents that are in a foreign parent company's possession where:

(1) the alter ego doctrine . . . warranted "piercing the corporate veil";

(2) the subsidiary was an agent of the parent in the transaction giving rise to the lawsuit;

(3) [t]he relationship is such that the agent-subsidiary can secure documents of the principal-parent to meet its own business needs and documents helpful for use in litigation;

(4) [t]here is access to documents when the need arises in the ordinary course of business;

(5) [the] subsidiary was [a] marketer and servicer of the parent's product . . . in the United States.[141]

The same analysis also applies to documents in the possession of sister or affiliated companies.[142]

---

138. *See, e.g., Certain Encapsulated Integrated Circuit Devices,* Inv. 337-TA-501, Order No. 29, at 3, 6 (Apr. 13, 2004).

139. *See Certain Optical Disk Controller Chips & Chipsets & Prods. Containing Same, including DVD Players & PC Optical Storage Devices,* Inv. No. 337-TA-506, Order No. 11, at 2 (Aug. 26, 2004) (finding that a subpoena was not effectively served under the Hague Convention, but permitting the subpoena to remain in effect for documents that the foreign third party was willing to produce).

140. *See* 19 C.F.R. § 210.32(b).

141. U.S. Int'l Trade Comm'n v. ASAT, Inc., 411 F.3d 245, 254 (D.C. Cir. 2005) (quoting *Camden Iron & Metal, Inc.,* 138 F.R.D. at 441–42).

142. *See, e.g., Gerling Int'l Ins. Co.,* 839 F.2d at 141 ("The few cases involving sister corporations . . . follow the same pattern."); Alimenta (U.S.A.) Inc. v. Anheuser-Busch Cos., 99 F.R.D. 309, 313 (N.D. Ga. 1983).

An ALJ's finding of possession, custody, or control is subject to review by the Commission, the district court adjudicating the enforcement proceeding, and the court of appeals overseeing any appeal from the district court.[143] As such, seeking documents from a domestic subsidiary of a foreign third party is a difficult and potentially lengthy process.

When obtaining the relevant discovery from a domestic entity is not possible, a party may be able to use the Hague Convention on Taking Evidence Abroad in Civil or Commercial Matters, which was adopted to create a uniform protocol for the collection of evidence from parties of the various signatory states. The Hague Convention purports to reconcile different and, often conflicting, discovery procedures in common-law and civil-law countries. For example, the Hague Convention provides for a letter of request to be issued from the judicial authority of one signatory state to another for the purpose of obtaining evidence to be used in judicial proceedings.[144] Pursuing discovery under the Hague Convention can be time-consuming and expensive.[145] Moreover, a genuine issue exists as to whether the Hague Convention applies to service issued by a U.S. government agency, including the ITC.[146] As with taking depositions in foreign countries, the U.S. Department of State website generally provides a good starting point for practitioners seeking information regarding international judicial assistance for overseas discovery issues.[147]

Where the Commission has personal jurisdiction over a foreign non-party, the Hague Convention need not apply. Under a "comity analysis," serving a subpoena on a foreign third party would be permitted in the United States if there is personal jurisdiction, whether or not that

---

143. *See generally ASAT, Inc.*, 411 F.3d at 245–56.

144. The Hague Evidence Convention only binds signatory states. South Korea, for example, is not a signatory to the Convention.

145. *See* Societe Nationale Industrielle Aerospatiale v. U.S. District Court, 482 U.S. 522, 560–63 (1987); *see also Certain Hardware Logic Emulation Sys.*, Inv. No. 337-TA-383, Order No. 65, at 13–19 (Jan. 16, 1997).

146. *See* F.T.C. v. Compagnie De Saint-Gobain-Pont-a-Mousson, 636 F.2d 1300, 1323–27 (D.C. Cir. 1980).

147. *See, e.g.*, http://travel.state.gov/law/judicial/judicial_678.html (information regarding judicial assistance, in Japan), http://travel.state.gov/law/judicial/judicial_656.html (information regarding judicial assistance in Malaysia), http://travel.state.gov/judicial/judicial_650.html (information regarding judicial assistance in Hong Kong) (last visited July 10, 2012).

party is willing to comply.[148] Where there is no personal jurisdiction, a party can make concurrent requests for the ALJ's recommendation to the district court to order that a deposition take place and to issue a letter rogatory pursuant to the Hague Convention or some other bilateral or multilateral agreement between the countries involved. Finally, if the foreign non-party is willing to assist in the investigation, but the foreign country has a "blocking statute" or has taken an exception to relevant parts of the Hague Convention, the deposition may take place in another country to eliminate the risk that the deponent is subject to criminal liability.

4. Obtaining Information Subject to Nondisclosure Agreement

The Commission protective order is generally considered sufficient protection for sensitive third-party information.[149] Thus, the ALJ may order

---

148. *See Societe Nationale Industrielle Aerospatiale,* 482 U.S. at 540–44 (finding that, where a tribunal has personal jurisdiction over a foreign entity, the Hague Convention is not the mandatory or exclusive means for obtaining discovery, and that "the concept of international comity requires in this context a more particularized analysis of the respective interests of the foreign nation and the requesting nation"); *see also Certain HSP Modems, Software, & Hardware Components Thereof, & Prods. Containing Same,* Inv. No. 337-TA-439, Order No. 23, at 4 (Mar. 16, 2001) (finding that the Commission Rules applied and the Hague Convention did not apply, because the foreign non-party had sufficient minimum contacts and had "not offered any particularized countervailing interest to offset the interest of the United States in facilitating proper and expedient discovery in th[e] . . . investigation") (citing *Societe Nationale Industrielle Aerospatiale,* 482 U.S. at 541–43).

149. *See Certain Microsphere Adhesives, Process for Making Same, & Prods. Containing Same, Including Self-Stick Repositionable Notes,* Inv. No. 337-TA-366, Order No. 13, 1994 WL 930346, at *1 (Oct. 26, 1994) (ordering complainant to produce all documents and things in its possession or under its control that disclosed or related to any settlement agreements or negotiations thereof that arose from any proceeding in which the validity or infringement of the involved patent was at issue, and "[i]f this information includes the confidential business information of a third party, it can be produced under the protective order"); *see also Certain Memory Devices with Increased Capacitance & Prods. Containing Same,* Inv. No. 337-TA-371, Order No. 48, at 1–2 (June 28, 1995) (issuing an order compelling discovery based on a finding the third-party discovery sought appeared to have some relevance and could lead to admissible evidence and the respondent made no assertion

the production of third-party confidential information despite the existence of a nondisclosure agreement.

As a general rule, the compelled party should make every effort to
procure the consent of a third party with which it has a nondisclosure
agreement allowing the production of documents containing confidential
business information. Inability to secure such consent does not, however,
constitute an adequate basis for outright refusal to provide the requested
documents, particularly if they contain relevant information or information reasonably calculated to lead to the discovery of admissible evidence.[150] The ALJs may allow production of such information to be delayed
so that the parties may be given a chance to obtain consent for disclosure
from the third party. If consent, however, is withheld for so long a period
of time that it threatens to impede the discovery process, the party may
be compelled to produce such information despite the absence of approval by the third party.[151]

O. PRIVILEGE

1. *Application of Privilege and the Work Product Doctrine*

The work product doctrine, as codified under Rule 26(b)(3) of the Federal Rules of Civil Procedure and as applied in Section 337 investigations, protects from discovery documents and other tangible things

---

of undue burden with respect to production of the discovery requested, and
that there was no indication that sensitive third-party information was not
adequately protected by the protective order entered); *Hardware Logic*, Inv.
No. 337-TA-383, Order No. 9, at 1–3 (Apr. 1, 1996).

150. *See Certain Baseband Processor Chips & Chipsets, Transmitter &
Receiver (RADIO) Chips, Power Control Chips & Prods. Containing Same*,
Inv. No. 337-TA-543, Order No. 8, at 2 (Nov. 28, 2005) (ordering the respondent to make every attempt to obtain the permission of third parties to release the relevant information that was sought by the complainant and that
was in the respondent's possession and further ordering that absent such
consent, the respondent was compelled to produce such information).

151. *See Certain Point of Sale Terminals & Components Thereof*, Inv. No.
337-TA-524, Order No. 17, at 2 (Nov. 29, 2004) (granting respondent's motion to compel complainant to produce unredacted documents relating to
agreements assigning or licensing the asserted patent despite the
complainant's previously stated argument that it was unable to secure third
parties' consent for production of those documents).

prepared by a party or its counsel in anticipation of litigation.[152] Information protected by the work product doctrine is generally only discoverable upon a showing that the opposing party has a substantial need for the materials in the preparation of its case and is unable without undue hardship to obtain the substantial equivalent of the materials by other means.[153]

Included within the purview of work-product protection are "[t]ests conducted specifically for the purpose of [the] investigation at the instance of counsel, and not performed for other purposes within the regular course of business."[154] Such tests, if "generated specifically for litigation," are not viewed as "preexisting facts," and thus are protected as work product even where performed by in-house technical personnel and not by counsel.[155] Similarly, data collected from the testing of samples that was conducted before filing a complaint are protected by the work product doctrine.[156] For example, in *Polyethylene Terephthalate Yarn,* the ALJ refused to grant the respondent's request for production of the complainant's testing data because the testing of samples was "for the sole purpose of filing [the] complaint that ultimately led to the institution of the present investigation."[157] Because the testing data was regarded as trial preparation material, prepared in anticipation of litigation and conducted at the insistence of counsel, the testing data was protected as work product pursuant to Rule 26(b)(3).[158]

The attorney-client privilege "protects confidential communications made between clients and their attorneys when the communications are for the purpose of securing legal advice or services."[159] In order to assert

---

152. *Certain Coenzyme Q10 Prods. & Methods of Making Same,* Inv. No. 337-TA-790, Order No. 17, at 3–4 (Mar. 21, 2012) (citing FED. R. CIV. P. 26(b)(3)).

153. FED. R. CIV. P. 26(b)(3).

154. *Certain Polyethylene Terephthalate Yarn & Prods. Containing Same (Polyethylene Terephthalate Yarn),* Inv. No. 337-TA-457, Order No. 29, at 2 (Sept. 13, 2001) (citing *Certain Phenylene Sulfide Polymers & Polymer Compounds & Prods. Containing Same (Phenylene Sulfide Polymers),* Inv. No. 337-TA-296, Order No. 13, 1989 WL 609026, at *5 (July 12, 1989)).

155. *Phenylene Sulfide Polymers,* Order No. 13, 1989 WL 609026, at *5.

156. *Polyethylene Terephthalate Yarn,* Order No. 29, at 1–3.

157. *Id.* at 2–3.

158. *Id.* (citing FED. R. CIV. P. 26(b)(3)).

159. *Certain Elec. Devices With Multi-Touch Enabled Touchpads & Touchscreens,* Inv. No. 337-TA-714, Order No. 30, at 2 (Feb. 9, 2011) (quoting *In re Lindsey,* 148 F.3d 1100, 1103 (D.C. Cir. 1998)).

this privilege, a lawyer must be "acting in the capacity of a lawyer . . . for the primary purpose of securing legal advice or legal services provided that the privilege has been properly asserted and has not been waived."[160] The Commission has stated that the "seminal expression of the conditions necessary for invoking the attorney-client privilege" is the following:

> The privilege applies only if (1) the asserted holder of the privilege is or sought to become a client; (2) the person to whom the communication was made (a) is a member of the bar or of a court, or his subordinate and (b) in connection with this communication is acting as a lawyer; (3) the communication relates to a fact of which the attorney was informed (a) by his client (b) without the presence of strangers (c) for the purpose of securing primarily either (i) an opinion on law or (ii) legal services or (iii) assistance in some legal proceedings, and not (d) for the purpose of committing a crime or tort; and (4) the privilege has been (a) claimed and (b) not waived by the client.[161]

By asserting the attorney-client privilege, a complainant will not be compelled to divulge the particular reasons why it chose not to make a claim of infringement against certain entities. For example, respondents in *Acid-Washed Denim Garments* asked complainant to divulge the reasons an infringement action was not filed against any particular entity.[162] Because the ALJ found it "difficult to imagine a response that would not reveal the content of [legal] communication between [c]omplainants and their counsel," he deemed those reasons to be protected by the attorney-client privilege.[163] Thus, if an investigation was conducted on the advice

---

160. *Certain Optical Disk Controller Chips II,* Inv. No. 337-TA-523, Order No. 56, at 2–3 (May 18, 2005) (citing Hartford Fire Ins. Co. v. Garvey, 109 F.R.D. 323, 327 (N.D. Ca. 1985)).

161. *Certain Coenzyme Q10 Prods.,* Inv. No. 337-TA-790, Order No. 17, at 3 (March 12, 2012) (citing *Certain Anisotropically Etched One Megabit & Greater DRAMS,* Inv. No. 337-TA-345, Comm'n Op. (Aug. 30, 1993) (quoting United States v. United Shoe Mach. Corp., 89 F. Supp. 357, 358–59 (D. Mass. 1950)); *see also Certain Semiconductor Chips With Minimized Chip Package Size & Prods. Containing Same (III),* Inv. No. 337-TA-630, Order No. 32, at 1–2 (Sept. 16, 2008).

162. *Certain Acid-Washed Denim Garments & Accessories,* Inv. No. 337-TA-324, Order No. 11, 1991 WL 788738, at *1 (June 1, 1991).

163. *Id.* at *2.

of counsel and specifically for determining whether to charge entities with infringement, the facts surrounding the investigation should be protected by the attorney-client privilege.[164]

2. Foreign Privilege Laws

"The attorney-client privilege generally extends to communications with a foreign attorney or patent agent about a patent prosecution in a foreign country provided the foreign country extends the attorney-client privilege to such communications."[165] The party asserting the privilege must prove the existence of the foreign privilege law. Further, the law must not be contrary to the public policy of the United States.[166] "[P]rivilege may attach to documents involving patent agents in one country and not to documents involving patent agents in another country."[167] Applying these principles, a former Chief ALJ stated that a communication is privileged if:

> [t]he person from whom advice was asked or given [is] either a member of the bar, or a member of a class recognized in foreign law as capable of giving or receiving privileged communications to or from persons in that country, provided that persons claiming the privilege are subject to the laws of that country and the advice given involves legal actions or patent prosecutions in that country.[168]

---

164. *Id.*

165. *Certain Short Wavelength Semiconductor Lasers & Prods. Containing Same (Short Wavelength Semiconductor Lasers)*, Inv. No. 337-TA-627, Order No. 21, at 2–3 (Nov. 19, 2008) (citing *Certain Diltiazem Hydrochloride & Diltiazem Preparations,* Inv. No. 337-TA-349, Order No. 24 (Oct. 29, 1993).

166. *Id.* ("the burden is on the party claiming privilege 'to establish that, as to each country, the attorney-client privilege extends to patent attorneys and/or patent agents and that the communications were intended to be confidential . . .'") (quoting *Certain Microlithographic Machs. & Components Thereof,* Inv. No. 337-TA-468, Order No. 37 (July 25, 2002)).

167. *Certain Scanning Multiple-Beam Equalization Sys. for Chest Radiography & Components Thereof,* Inv. No. 337-TA-326, Order No. 17, 1991 WL 788663, at *1 (July 9, 1991); *see also Short Wavelength Semiconductor Lasers,* Order No. 31, at 3 (Dec. 19, 2008).

168. *Certain Tape Dispensers,* Inv. No. 337-TA-354, Notice to All Parties, 1993 WL 852372, at *1 (July 19, 1993); *see also Short Wavelength Semiconductor Lasers*, Order No. 31, at 3; *Certain Sortation Sys., Parts Thereof, &*

Some ALJs have established procedures for dealing with foreign privilege laws, particularly as they relate to privilege logs, normally following *Duplan Corp. v. Deering Milliken Inc.*[169] For example, one ALJ's ground rules required that each party create a privileged document list in which they would identify specific information regarding each privileged document.[170] Similarly, another ALJ's ground rules listed the information that the parties must identify for each privileged document.[171]

3. Communications between Clients and Foreign Patent Agents

"[M]ost countries have a clear body of law indicating whether a non-attorney patent agent can give advice in confidence in connection with a patent application in that country, and U.S. courts treat these confidential communications in the same way that the country in which these patent agents practice treat them."[172] The ALJs have generally held that the attorney-client privilege extends to confidential communications between a patent agent and the client if the communication has been made in connection with a patent prosecution and meets the requirements of the privilege laws

---

Prods. Containing Same, Inv. No. 337-TA-460, Order No. 9, at 2–3 (Nov. 20, 2001) (denying Dutch counsel access to CBI because the protective order provided no real threat of sanctions).

169. 397 F. Supp. 1146, 1146–202 (D.S.C. 1974). Multiple ALJs cite directly to *Duplan Corp.* in their ground rules when laying out the rule that each document a party withholds, claiming privilege as justification, must be separately identified in a privilege list. *See, e.g., Certain Power Supplies,* Inv. No. 337-TA-646, Order No. 2, at 9 n.2 (May 8, 2008); *Certain Composite Wear Components & Prods. Containing the Same,* Inv. No. 337-TA-644, Order No. 2, at 13 n.5 (May 5, 2008).

170. *See Certain Lighting Control Devices Including Dimmer Switches and/or Switches & Parts Thereof,* Inv. No. 337-TA-599, Order No. 2, at 13 (Apr. 6, 2007) ("If the author/sender, addressee or recipient [of the privileged document] is an attorney or foreign patent agent, he or she shall be so identified.").

171. *See Certain 3G Wideband Code Division Multiple Access (WCDMA) Handsets & Components Thereof,* Inv. No. 337-TA-601, Order No. 1, at 7 (Apr. 26, 2007) ("If the sender or recipient is an attorney or foreign patent agent, he or she should be so identified. In the case of a foreign patent agent, there should be a statement of whether the laws of the agent's country grant privileged status to a patent agent's communication.").

172. *Certain Fluidized Bed Combustion Sys.,* Inv. No. 337-TA-213, Order No. 14, 1985 WL 303731, at *1 (June 21, 1985).

of that foreign jurisdiction.[173] This extension of privilege is based on the doctrine of comity.[174] The principle of privilege for qualified foreign patent agent communications has been invoked before the Commission to protect communications between American attorneys and foreign patent agents, provided that the "communication[s] and the law under which the patent would be issue [sic] grants a privilege to communications between clients and non-lawyer patent agents."[175] Currently, some ALJs' ground rules contain a provision to address just this situation.

4. Motions to Compel

When parties have reached an impasse on a discovery dispute, they may file a motion to compel. Most ALJs have specific meet-and-confer requirements that the parties must meet before they file motions to compel. Some ALJs also make themselves available for conference calls to address discovery issues.

P. SANCTIONS

The Commission Rules authorize the ALJ to impose a variety of sanctions for failure to comply with discovery orders.[176]

---

173. *Certain Commercial Food Portioners, Components Thereof, Including Software, & Process Thereof*, Inv. No. 337-TA-339, Order No. 32, 1992 WL 811804, at *2 (Dec. 22, 1992).

174. *See Certain Short Wavelength Semiconductor Lasers & Prods. Containing Same*, Inv. No. 337-TA-627, Order No. 21, at 3 (Nov. 19, 2008).

175. *Certain Integrated Circuit Telecomm. Chips & Prods. Containing Same, Including Dialing Apparatus (Integrated Circuit Telecommunication Chips)*, Inv. No. 337-TA-337, Order No. 109, 1992 WL 811794, at *4 (Nov. 23, 1992) (referencing *Integrated Circuit Telecommunication Chips*, Order No. 88, 1992 WL 811715, at *1 (Oct. 16, 1992)).

176. *See* 19 C.F.R. §§ 210.4(d) (sanctions for abuse of process), 210.25 (general sanctions provision), 210.27 (sanctions for abuse of discovery), 210.33 (sanctions for failure to make or cooperate in discovery), 210.34 (sanctions for violation of a protective order); *see also* 19 U.S.C. § 1337(h) (stating that the Commission may prescribe sanctions for abuse of discovery and abuse of process to the extent authorized by the Federal Rules of Civil Procedure 11 and 37). "Because the Commission's Rules implementing the sanction authority must be consistent with . . . the Federal Rules of Civil Procedure, the interpretation and application of Rules 210.25, 210.27, and 210.33 are guided by the Advisory Committee Notes to the Federal Rules and Federal case law." *Certain Hardware Logic Emulation Sys. & Components Thereof (Hardware*

Commission Rule 210.4(d) is analogous to Federal Rule of Civil Procedure 11 and addresses violations of the duty to make a reasonable inquiry under the circumstances prior to making a representation before the ALJ or the Commission.[177] It includes a "safe harbor" provision, which requires that the moving party first provide a copy of the motion to the allegedly sanctionable party before the motion is filed with the ALJ or the Commission.[178] The rule notes that "a representation need not be frivolous in its entirety," and that "[i]f any portion of a representation is found to be false, frivolous, misleading, or otherwise in violation of paragraph (c), a sanction may be imposed."[179] The sanctions may be monetary and non-monetary, although monetary sanctions are more common, and they must be "limited to what is sufficient to deter repetition of such conduct or comparable conduct by others similarly situated."[180] Major considerations include whether the representation was objectively reasonable under the circumstances and the harm to the opposing party or parties, the staff, and the Commission.[181] There is particular focus on the

Logic)*, Inv. No. 337-TA-383, Order No. 96, at 33 n.29 (July 31, 1997). Parties often move for sanctions under more than one Commission Rule. *See, e.g., Hardware Logic*, Inv. No. 337-TA-383, Order No. 96, at 32 (noting that complainant moved for sanctions under Commission rules 210.25, 210.27, and 210.33 for a number of allegedly sanctionable actions by respondent); *Certain Point of Sale Terminals & Components Thereof (Point of Sale Terminals)*, Inv. No. 337-TA-524, Order No. 40, at 24-29 (Apr. 11, 2005) (addressing respondents' motions for sanctions under 210.4(d), 210.27(d)(2), and 210.33(b) and (c)).

177. *See Certain CD-ROM Controllers & Prods. Containing Same – II*, Inv. No. 337-TA-409, Recommended Determination Concerning Respondents' Motion for Sanctions, at 22 (Aug. 10, 1999) (noting that Commission Rule 210.4 is based upon Federal Rule of Civil Procedure 11); *Certain Salinomycin, Biomass & Preparations Containing Same*, Inv. No. 337-TA-370, Recommended Determination Concerning Respondents' Motion for Sanctions, at 49 (May 14, 1997) ("[T]he instant motion for sanctions was brought under Commission Rule 210.4, which is similar to Federal Rule of Civil Procedure 11."); *see also Point of Sale Terminals*, Order No. 63, at 30 (Feb. 6, 2007) ("As required by Rule 11 and 19 C.F.R. § 210.4, a party must refrain from all misrepresentations in its pleadings, whether it is satisfying minimal requirements or not.").

178. 19 C.F.R. § 210.4(d)(1)(i).

179. 19 C.F.R. § 210.4(d).

180. 19 C.F.R. § 210.4(d)(2).

181. *See, e.g., Wireless Commc'n Devices, Portable Music & Data Processing Devices, Computers & Components Thereof*, Inv. No. 337-TA-745, Order No. 34, at 4 (Apr. 24, 2012) (imposing monetary sanctions where "(1) the facts

harm to these participants and the integrity of the Commission's proceedings in light of the fast-paced nature of Section 337 cases. For example, in *Point of Sale Terminals,* the ALJ noted:

> A [party] in a Section 337 proceeding is expected to be truthful, honest and forthcoming. Half-truths, misleading statements and deceptive filings have no place in these proceedings. Section 337 investigations are massive, expedited proceedings usually involving highly technical issues, and the Administrative Law Judges expect that all parties, particularly a complainant seeking relief from the Commission, will be completely forthright and open. Even literally truthful but misleading statements cannot be tolerated.[182]

Commission Rule 210.33 corresponds to Federal Rule 37, and provides for monetary and non-monetary sanctions related to a party's failure to make or cooperate in discovery.[183] Unlike motions for sanctions under Commission Rule 210.4(d), these motions have no "safe harbor" prerequisite.[184] In practice, these sanctions are relatively rare, because

---

were misrepresented; (2) Respondent's counsel should have known better; (3) no satisfactory explanation for the misrepresentation exist[ed]; and (4) Complainant was harmed by Respondent's misrepresentation," but not imposing evidentiary sanctions because the issue was clarified and the harm to complainant was limited); *Certain Laser Bar Code Scanners & Scan Engines, Components Thereof & Prods. Containing Same (Laser Bar Code Scanners),* Inv. No. 337-TA-551, Initial Determination & Recommended Determination, at 11 (Jan. 29, 2007) (imposing monetary sanctions in light of respondents' being "less than forthcoming" regarding its ability to obtain relevant source code, "which ha[s] served to delay and frustrate the Commission's processes and [complainant's] discovery").

182. *Point of Sale Terminals,* Order No. 63, at 33 (Feb. 6, 2007); *see also Laser Bar Code Scanners,* Initial Determination & Recommended Determination (finding sanctions were warranted in light of the respondents' actions, "which . . . served to delay and frustrate the Commission's processes and [complainant's] discovery," and noting that "numerous judicial resources have been wasted. Such discovery tactics cannot be tolerated, especially for investigations with tight discovery deadlines where cooperation between parties is essential").

183. 19 C.F.R. §§ 210.33(b) (non-monetary sanctions), 210.33(c) (monetary sanctions).

184. *Compare* 19 C.F.R. 210.33(c), (d) *with* 19 C.F.R. 210.4(d)(2); *see also Point of Sale Terminals,* Inv. No. 337-TA-524, Order No. 40 (Apr. 11, 2005)

they cannot issue unless a discovery order is both issued and violated.[185] In *Encapsulated Integrated Circuit Devices*, for example, the ALJ denied respondent's motion for sanctions because the respondent "did not file a motion to compel . . . was not granted an order to compel . . . [and so] the motion for sanctions fail[ed] to satisfy the prerequisites for its own filing."[186] By contast, in *Agricultural Tractors Under 50 Power Take-Off Horsepower*, the ALJ granted complainant's motion for evidentiary sanctions against the respondent, recognizing that "it is undisputed that [respondent] has failed to comply with Order No. 15."[187] The ALJ sanctioned

---

(noting that "[u]nlike motions for sanctions under Commission Rule 210.4(d), motions for sanctions for discovery abuse have no 'safe harbor' prerequisite," and as a result, "the 'bad faith' standard of culpability for sanctions proceedings initiated *sua sponte* by a judge is not applicable to proceedings for discovery abuse").

185. *See* 19 C.F.R. §§ 210.33 (b) ("If a party or an officer or agent of a party fails to comply with an order . . ."), 210.33(c) ("If a party or an officer, director, or managing agent of the party or person designated to testify on behalf of a party fails to obey an order to provide or permit discovery. . ."); *but see Certain Zero-Mercury-Added Alkaline Batteries, Parts Thereof, & Prods. Containing Same*, Inv. No. 337-TA-493, Order No. 20, at 4 (Aug. 27, 2003) (denying complainants' motion for sanctions despite respondents' "failure to fully comply with the intended purpose of [an] [o]rder," instead choosing to issue a more comprehensive order compelling discovery, and cautioning that "[f]ailure to adhere to this order [would] result in evidentiary sanctions").

186. *Certain Encapsulated Integrated Circuit Devices & Prods. Containing Same*, Inv. No. 337-TA-501, Order No. 74, at 7 (June 18, 2004) (citing *Certain Agric. Tractors, Lawn Tractors, Riding Lawnmowers, & Components Thereof*, USITC Pub. No. 3625, Inv. No. 337-TA-486, Comm'n Op., at 19 n.14 (Aug. 2003) ("[a]n order compelling discovery is a prerequisite to all sanctions under Commission Rule 210.33")); *see also Certain Protective Cases & Components Thereof*, Inv. No. 337-TA-780, Order No. 27 (Mar. 19, 2012) (denying complainant's motion for sanctions finding, in part, the instruction given by the ALJ in a ground rule 3.5 telephone conference was "not an order, it [was] a warning").

187. *Certain Agricultural Tractors Under 50 Power Take-Off Horsepower (Tractors Under 50 Power)*, Inv. No. 337-TA-380, Order No. 51, at 11 (Sept. 6, 1996); *see also Certain Cigarettes & Packaging Thereof*, Inv. No. 337-TA-424, Order No. 38, at 2–6 (Feb. 2, 2000) (granting the a motion for evidentiary sanctions after an intervenor failed to comply with an order compelling it to "fully respond to certain interrogatories and document requests" before the set deadline, precluding intervenor from introducing evidence related to the interrogatories or claiming privilege as to certain documents); *see also Tractors Under 50 Power*, Order No. 51, at 11 (granting adverse inferences to the extent that the complainants' "specific discovery requests relat[ed] to the specific adverse inferences requested").

the respondent by entering several adverse inferences and precluding the respondent from presenting testimony, introducing certain evidence, and objecting to the complainant's use of secondary evidence.[188]

Commission Rule 210.27(d)(3) coincides with Rule 26(g) of the Federal Rules of Civil Procedure and provides for "appropriate" sanctions if a certification regarding a discovery request, response, or objection is made to the ALJ or Commission "without substantial justification."[189] The sanction may be imposed "upon the person who made the certification, the party on whose behalf the request, response, or objection was made, or both,"[190] and may be monetary and non-monetary. In *Light-Emitting Diodes*, the ALJ imposed a number of evidentiary sanctions on a complainant under 210.27(d)(3) after finding that the complainant had failed to answer interrogatories fully after a reasonable inquiry, in violation of Commission Rules and his ground rules and prejudicing the opposing parties.[191] In *Starter Motors*, the ALJ chose not to impose monetary or evidentiary sanctions against a complainant after it supplemented an interrogatory response with information not "thereafter acquired" in violation of Commission Rule 210.27(c), but ordered the new interrogatory responses to be stricken.[192] The ALJ did not impose sanctions because the moving party had not offered evidence regarding the extent of the complainant's factual inquiry when responding to the related interrogatories and had offered no evidence that the initial interrogatory responses were made in bad faith or for the purpose of causing unnecessary delay or needless increase in the cost of litigation.[193]

---

188. *Id.* at 12; *see also Certain Cloisonne Jewelry*, Inv. No. 337-TA-195, Initial Determination, 1984 WL 273698, at *15 (1984) (ruling "that the failure of the respondents . . . to provide discovery ordered in Order No. 8 warrants the imposition of [] sanctions" by preclusion from introducing evidence or objecting to movant's use of secondary evidence).

189. 19 C.F.R. § 210.27(d)(3) ("If without substantial justification a request, response, or objection is certified in violation of paragraph (d)(2) of this section, the administrative law judge or the Commission, upon motion or sua sponte . . . may impose an appropriate sanction . . .").

190. *Id.*

191. *Certain Light-Emitting Diodes & Prods. Containing Same*, Inv. No. 337-TA-785, Order No. 31, at 24–25, 28–29 (May 16, 2012).

192. *Certain Starter Motors & Alternators*, Inv. No. 337-TA-755, Order No. 25, at 5 (Aug. 23, 2011) .

193. *Id.* (stating that "[w]ithout more, I find that [respondents are] not entitled to monetary or evidentiary sanctions pursuant to Commission Rule 210.27(d)(3)").

Commission Rule 210.34 provides sanctions related to violations of the protective order.[194] The issue of sanctions can be "raised on a motion by a party, the administrative law judge's own motion, or the Commission's own initiative in accordance with § 210.25(a)(2)."[195] If sanctions are imposed, they are "of the sort enumerated in § 210.33(b), or such other action as may be appropriate."[196] While these sanctions are rare because adherence to protective orders is taken extremely seriously by ITC practitioners, when they are imposed, they can be severe. In *Plasma Display Panels*, the ALJ imposed sanctions under 210.34(c) "[i]n order to address the potential significant harm done by the unauthorized disclosure . . . of CBI [by both counsel and client]" and "to preserve the integrity of Commission proceedings under protective orders and to deter future violations of the protective order."[197] The ALJ barred the subject attorney from further access to CBI in the investigation, recommended that the Commission issue a public reprimand of the law firm involved, and ordered that a related subpoena be stricken from the record and that the sanctioned party be precluded from introducing into evidence any documents obtained from the subpoenaed party in that case.[198]

---

194. 19 C.F.R. § 210.34. *See also* Proposed Rule, 77 Fed. Reg. 41,124 (proposed July 11, 2012) (to be codified at 19 C.F.R. pt. 210).

195. Note to 19 C.F.R. § 210.34(c).

196. 19 C.F.R. § 210.34(c)(5).

197. *Certain Plasma Display Panels & Prods. Containing Same (Plasma Display Panels)*, Inv. No. 337-TA-445, Order No. 15, at 8 (May 8, 2001) (adopted by the Commission); *see also Plasma Display Panels*, Notice of Comm'n Determination to Adopt Two Recommended Determinations Concerning Sanctions (Feb. 15, 2002) (adopting Order No. 15 and a subsequent recommended determination denying a motion by complainants for costs, including attorney fees in connection with their motion for sanctions).

198. *Plasma Display Panels*, Order No. 15, at 8–11.

CHAPTER 8

Termination Prior to Hearing

Prior to the hearing, Section 337 investigations may be terminated, in whole or in part, for a variety of reasons, including settlement, agreement to a consent order, default, arbitration, or withdrawal of the complaint. Any party may move, at any time, to terminate the investigation as to any or all of the respondents, in whole or in part.[1] Termination of the investigation on the basis of settlement, consent order, arbitration, or withdrawal does not constitute a determination of violation of Section 337.[2] Since close to half of all Section 337 investigations are terminated by settlement or consent order,[3] participants in a Section 337 investigation should be familiar with this process.

A. SETTLEMENT

Under 19 C.F.R. § 210.21(b), an investigation may be terminated on the basis of a licensing or other settlement agreement.[4] If the complainant

---

1. 19 C.F.R. § 210.21(a) (2012).

2. The concept of terminating a party from an investigation "without prejudice" does not exist under the Commission's Rules, but as a practical matter, once a party is terminated based on a settlement or consent order agreement, that party cannot be added back into the investigation and another investigation will likely not be instituted based on the same accused products.

3. *See* Chapter 1, "Introduction to Section 337 Investigations."

4. *See also* Rules of General Application, Adjudication, and Enforcement (Proposed Rule), 77 Fed. Reg. 41,123 (adding that the parties must provide a copy of any documents referenced in the settlement agreements because these documents are considered part of the settlement agreement) (proposed July 11, 2012) (to be codified at 19 C.F.R. pt. 210).

and a respondent reach a settlement, by license agreement or otherwise, and wish to remove that respondent from the investigation, those parties must move for termination. Typically, the settling parties are required to include both confidential and non-confidential versions of any settlement agreement with their motions to terminate, to be served on the Commission and any parties subject to the protective order.[5] If the licensing or other form of settlement agreement contains confidential business information within the meaning of Commission Rule § 201.6(a), a public copy of the agreement with such information deleted must accompany the motion. The motion must also include "a statement that there are no other agreements, written or oral, express or implied between the parties concerning the subject matter of the investigation."[6]

Where complainants have been able to establish that they would suffer prejudice if the non-settling respondents were to receive full, unredacted versions of the settlement agreement, ALJs have granted protective orders or otherwise protected against the disclosure of the financial terms of settlement agreements to the non-settling respondents.[7] For example, ALJs have protected specific royalty rates from disclosure in settlement agreements to non-settling counsel.[8] In these situations, the parties must still provide the ALJ and OUII with a complete, unredacted copy of the settlement agreement.

When deciding a motion to terminate based upon settlement, the ALJ must consider whether terminating the investigation on the basis of

---

5. 19 C.F.R. § 210.21(b).

6. *Id.*

7. *See Certain Variable Speed Wind Turbines & Components Thereof,* Inv. No. 337-TA-641, Order No. 14, at 4 (Pub. Version) (Oct. 23, 2008) (holding that disclosure of the financial terms of a settlement could be harmful to complainant and give unfair advantage to the respondents); *Certain Silicon Microphone Packages & Prods. Containing Same (Silicon Microphone Packages),* Inv. No. 337-TA-629, Order No. 9, at 6 (Pub. Version) (Sept. 11, 2008) (denying disclosure of the financial terms of license agreements and reasoning that "the public interest favors settlement to avoid needless litigation and to conserve public and private resources") (citing *Certain Buffer Systems & Components Thereof Used in Container Processing Lines,* Inv. No. 337-TA-609, Order No. 8 (Sept. 7, 2007)); *Certain Semiconductor Integrated Circuits Using Tungsten Metallization & Prods. Containing Same,* Inv. No. 337-TA-648, Order No. 30 (Dec. 23, 2008) (granting a protective order against disclosure to the non-settling respondents of the financial terms of a settlement agreement with a respondent).

8. *See Silicon Microphone Packages,* Order No. 9, at 6.

the settlement agreement reached between the parties is contrary to the public interest.[9] In rare instances, ALJs have rejected motions to terminate based on settlement agreements. In a pending case, the ALJ refused to approve a settlement where he concluded that it "appears that the agreements may have been structured to bypass U.S. income tax laws."[10]

If the ALJ issues an order granting the motion, the order constitutes an initial determination pursuant to Commission Rule § 210.21(b)(2). As with any other ID, the Commission has discretion in determining whether to review the ID. Generally, both Commission policy and the public interest favor settlement agreements, since they preserve resources of the Commission and the private parties. Motions to terminate based upon a settlement agreement are thus, with the exception noted above, normally routinely granted.[11]

That there is a general policy favoring settlements is demonstrated by the authority to mandate settlement conferences. Pursuant to Section 556(c)(6) of the Administrative Procedure Act, ALJs may "hold conferences for the settlement or simplification of issues by consent of the parties . . . ."[12] It is typical for ALJs to exercise this authority, and most ALJs set forth dates in the procedural schedule by which the parties must conduct and report upon settlement conferences. Such conferences are generally set at regular intervals during the pretrial process. Some ALJs are very hands-on in establishing their settlement procedures, while others leave it largely to the parties.

---

9. 19 C.F.R. § 210.50(b)(2).

10. *Certain Dynamic Random Access Memory & NAND Flash Memory Devices & Prods. Containing Same,* Inv. No. 337-TA-803, Order No. 25, Denying Motion to Terminate Nanya Respondents from the Investigation (Feb. 23, 2012); *see also* Order No. 18 (Initial Determination Granting Mot. to Terminate Pantech Respondents from the Investigation) (Dec. 7, 2011) (unreviewed)(approving settlement only after similar concerns were alleviated).

11. *See, e.g., Certain Digital Televisions & Components Thereof,* Inv. No. 337-TA-742, Order No. 7 (Initial Determination) (Jan. 28, 2011) (unreviewed); *Certain GPS Devices & Prods. Containing Same,* Inv. No. 337-TA-602, Order No. 6 (Initial Determination) (Jan. 28, 2011) (unreviewed) (terminating enforcement proceeding based on a settlement agreement); *Certain Flat Panel Digital Televisions & Components Thereof,* Inv. No. 337-TA-733, Order No. 10 (Initial Determination) (Jan. 26, 2011) (unreviewed).

12. 5 U.S.C. § 556(c)(6) (2006).

B. MEDIATION PROGRAM

The Commission established a pilot mediation program for Section 337 investigations in 2008,[13] which became a permanent agency program on August 30, 2010, upon the issuance of a revised User Manual.[14] The program is modeled on the U.S. Court of Appeals for the Federal Circuit Mediation Program. All Section 337 investigations are eligible for the program,[15] though the Secretary of the Commission has stated that investigations with a limited number of large, sophisticated companies are those most likely to be recommended for the program.[16] The parties to a Section 337 investigation may individually or jointly participate in the program, or an administrative law judge may nominate the investigation for participation. There is a roster of mediators in the Commission's mediation brochure,[17] though parties may select non-roster mediators if they so choose.[18]

The program is designed to facilitate the settlement of disputes that underlie Section 337 investigations by resolving a matter entirely or by reducing the number of issues, patent claims, and/or respondents in a particular investigation. Based on feedback received by the Commission, mediations occurring after the completion of a *Markman* hearing, after the filing of hearing briefs (particularly after the filing of the Commission investigative staff's brief), or at the conclusion of the hearing (but

---

13. Initiation of Pilot Mediation Program for Investigations Under Section 337 of the Tariff Act of 1930, 73 Fed. Reg. 65,615 (Nov. 4, 2009).

14. Issuance of Revised Users' Manual for Commission Mediation Program for Investigations Under Section 337 of the Tariff Act of 1930, 75 Fed. Reg. 52,976 (Aug. 30, 2010); *see also* U.S. INT'L TRADE COMM'N, USER MANUAL FOR COMMISSION MEDIATION PROGRAM FOR SECTION 337 INVESTIGATIONS, *available at* http://www.usitc.gov/intellectual_property/documents/Manual_for_Commission_Mediation_Program_337.pdf.

15. Complainants receive materials explaining the Commission's mediation program upon filing a complaint; named respondents are served these materials together with the complaint. USER MANUAL FOR COMMISSION MEDIATION PROGRAM FOR SECTION 337 INVESTIGATIONS, contained in "Section 337 Mediation Program, Second Update" (Nov. 2011) at p. 7, *available at* http://www.usitc.gov/intellectual_property/documents/Mediation_Brochure_FINAL_Pub4275.pdf.

16. Michael B. Powell & Isaac E. Chao, *337 Mediation: Emerging Trends in a Promising Program*, ITCTLA 337 REPORTER SUMMER ASSOCIATE EDITION, 2011, at 118–19.

17. *See* "Section 337 Mediation Program, Second Update," *supra* note 15.

18. Powell & Chao, *supra* note 16, at 119.

before the ALJ issues a final determination) offer the best chance of reaching settlement.[19] The Commission program provides for mediation of one-half day, which, in most cases, is conducted at no cost to the parties; if the mediation continues beyond the initial session, however, the parties are expected to compensate the mediator.[20] Participation by a person from each party with actual settlement authority is required.[21]

The mediator, as well as the parties and their representatives,[22] are required to sign a non-disclosure agreement,[23] which places the participants under the Standing Commission Protective Order for Mediation and the protective order issued by the ALJ.[24] The mediator is required to maintain in confidence all information disclosed to him/her by each party. The mediator communicates exclusively with the Secretary to the Commission, who does not communicate with the Commission, the ALJ or the Commission investigative attorney assigned to the investigation to which the mediation is related.[25]

Recently, the Chief Administrative Law Judge has required the parties to participate in mediation in lieu of a required settlement conference.[26] As a result, the parties to 21 percent of Section 337 investigations

---

19. Holbein, James R., Secretary to the Commission, "Status Report on USITC Section 337 Mediation Program," March 16, 2012, at 3.

20. Powell & Chao, *supra* note 16, at 119.

21. As explained in the Commission brochure at p.5, a person with "actual settlement authority" means "the party representative should be a person who can make independent decisions and has the knowledge necessary to generate and consider creative solutions, e.g., a business principal."

22. Party representatives include any in-house counsel as well as outside counsel. "Section 337 Mediation Program," User Manual, *supra* note 15, at 7.

23. *See* "Non-Disclosure Confidentiality Agreement for Mediators," *available at* http://www.usitc.gov/intellectual_property/documents/Non-Disclosure_Confidentiality_Agreement_for_Mediators.pdf; "Non-Disclosure Confidentiality Agreement for Parties, or Employees or Inside Counsel Thereof," *available at* http://www.usitc.gov/intellectual_property/documents/Non-Disclosure_Confidentiality_Agreement_for_Parties_or_Employees_or_Inside_ Counsel_Thereof.pdf; and "Non-Disclosure Confidentiality Agreement for Authorized Representatives of Parties (Outside Counsel)," *available at* http://www.usitc.gov/intellectual_property/documents/Non-Disclosure_Confidentiality_Agreement_for_Authorized_ Representatives_of_Parties_ (Outside%20Counsel).pdf.

24. "Section 337 Mediation Program," User Manual, *supra* note 15, at 9.

25. *Id.*

26. "Status Report on USITC Section 337 Mediation Program," *supra* note 19, at 2.

now participate in mediation.[27] This program could well become mandatory once the Commission has gained more experience in its use.

C. CONSENT ORDER

Under 19 C.F.R. § 210.21(c), an investigation may be terminated on the basis of a consent order stipulation. A consent order is enforced in the same manner as Commission remedial orders.[28]

Any party may move for termination based on a consent order stipulation, either unilaterally or jointly.[29] A joint motion is typically based on a settlement agreement between complainant and respondent. A respondent can also seek to end its participation in the investigation, regardless of the wishes of the complainant, via a unilateral consent order stipulation agreeing to the relief sought by the complainant. The statute sets forth specific requirements that must be included in a consent order, including an admission of all jurisdictional facts and an express waiver of all rights to seek judicial review or otherwise to challenge the order's validity, among others.[30] If the investigation is based on intellectual property claims, additional content must be included, such as a statement that the order will not apply regarding any expired or invalid patent claims and a statement that the stipulating respondent will not challenge the validity of the IP.[31] These requirements are strictly enforced.[32] If a consent order is based on a settlement or license agreement, such agreement should be attached as an exhibit to the motion for a consent order and incorporated by reference into the proposed consent order and stipulation.[33]

---

27. *Id.*

28. 19 C.F.R. § 210.21(c)(3)(ii).

29. 19 C.F.R. § 210.21(c)(1).

30. *See* 19 C.F.R. § 210.21(c)(3) for a complete list of the required contents of a consent order. *See also* Proposed Rules, 77 Fed. Reg. 41,123 (proposed July 11, 2012) (to be codified at 19 C.F.R. pt. 210).

31. *See* 19 C.F.R. § 210.21(c)(3)(i)(B) for a complete list of the additional requirements of a consent order for an intellectual property–based investigation.

32. *See Certain Integrated Circuits, Chipsets, & Prods. Containing Same Including Televisions*, Inv. No. 337-TA-786, Order No. 25, Denying Complainant Freescale & Respondent Funai's Joint Mot. to Terminate the Inv. on the Basis of a Consent Order (Apr. 6, 2012) (denying motion to terminate on the basis that statement does not comply with 19 C.F.R. § 210.21(c)(3)).

33. *See Certain Purple Protective Gloves*, Inv. No. 337-TA-500, Order No. 16 (Initial Determination) (June 1, 2004) (unreviewed).

The ALJ will decide a motion to terminate via entry of an order that constitutes an ID. As with terminations based on settlement, the Commission, in making its determination on review, must decide whether termination on the basis of a consent order is in the public interest.

The parties may submit motions for termination based on a consent order at any time prior to the commencement of the hearing in an investigation.[34] The ALJ may also consider a motion to terminate based on a consent order during or after the hearing if the parties so move and are able to show good cause.[35] Once the parties have submitted a consent order stipulation, they may not withdraw from it without a showing of good cause.[36]

After an investigation has been terminated, a complainant that believes a consent order has been violated may file a complaint asking the Commission to institute an enforcement proceeding.[37] In an enforcement proceeding, the Commission may (1) modify the consent order, (2) impose civil penalties (up to $100,000 per day of violation) for violating the consent order,[38] and/or (3) revoke the consent order and impose a cease and desist and/or a limited exclusion order.[39]

D. DEFAULT

19 U.S.C. § 1337(g) provides the Commission the authority to find respondents in default.[40] Commission Rule § 210.16(a)(1) provides that a respondent shall be found in default if it fails to respond to the complaint

---

34. 19 C.F.R. § 210.21(c)(1)(ii).
35. *Id.*
36. *Id.*
37. 19 C.F.R. § 210.75(b). *See also* Proposed Rules, 77 Fed. Reg. 134,41125 (requiring ALJs to issue an enforcement initial determination no later than three months before the target date for formal enforcement proceedings and changing the length of time for the Commission to determine whether to review an enforcement initial determination from 90 days to 45 days) (proposed July 11, 2012) (to be codified at 19 C.F.R. pt. 210).
38. According to 19 U.S.C. § 1337(f)(2) and 19 C.F.R. § 210.75(b), although the Commission may impose a civil penalty, it may only recover such penalties in a U.S. district court. In other words, the Commission does not have the authority to collect the amount owed to it without first going to a district court for enforcement.
39. *See* 19 C.F.R. §§ 210.75(b)(4)(i)–(iii); *see also* San Huan New Materials High Tech, Inc. v. U.S. Int'l Trade Comm'n, 161 F.3d 1347 (Fed. Cir. 1999).
40. 19 U.S.C. § 1337(g)(1).

and notice of investigation in the manner prescribed in Commission Rule § 210.13 or § 210.59(c), or otherwise fails to answer the complaint and notice and fails to show cause that it should not be found in default. If a respondent is found in default, the Commission presumes the facts in the complaint to be true and, after considering the statutory public interest factors, may enter a limited exclusion order or, if the factors listed in Section 337(g)(2) are met, a general exclusion order.

To initiate a finding of default, a complainant would file a motion for an order to show cause why one or more respondents should not be found in default. Generally, grounds to grant a "show cause order" will exist where a respondent has failed to respond to a properly served complaint and notice of investigation, or has otherwise failed to participate in the proceedings. If a respondent fails to respond to an order to show cause, the ALJ will issue an ID finding the respondent in default.[41] A respondent may also be found in default as a sanction for abuse of process or for failure to make or cooperate in discovery.[42] Notably, the threat of default in Section 337 proceedings exists even where a respondent would not be subject to personal jurisdiction in a U.S. district court, thereby making Section 337 actions an attractive vehicle for intellectual property owners whose rights have been infringed by foreign entities not subject to personal jurisdiction in district court.

Commission Rule § 210.16(c)(1) permits a complainant to seek immediate entry of an exclusion order and/or a cease and desist order against a respondent found in default.[43] The Commission, however, typically does not grant immediate relief against a respondent in default when active respondents remain in the investigation.[44] The Commission's practice of delaying immediate entry of relief stems from a concern that it could be forced to vacate a prematurely issued limited exclusion order in

---

41. 19 C.F.R. § 210.16(a)(1). This rule states that "[a] party *shall* be found in default if it fails to respond to the complaint and notice of investigation in the manner prescribed in § 210.13 or § 210.59(c), or otherwise fails to answer the complaint and notice, and fails to show cause why it should not be found in default" (emphasis added). *See also* Proposed Rules, 77 Fed. Reg. 41,123 (proposed July 11, 2012) (to be codified at 19 C.F.R. pt. 210).

42. 19 C.F.R. § 210.16(a)(2).

43. 19 C.F.R. § 210.16(c)(1); *Certain Hydraulic Excavators & Components Thereof*, Inv. No. 337-TA-582, Order No. 8 (Initial Determination), at 4 (Dec. 1, 2006) (unreviewed).

44. *See Certain Lens-Fitted Film Packages (LFFPs)*, Inv. No. 337-TA-406, Order No. 24 (Initial Determination), at 3 (Sept. 25, 1998) (unreviewed).

the event that, for example, the patent at issue is found invalid or unenforceable.[45] Additionally, the Commission has denied requests for immediate entry of relief based on concerns about the administrative burdens that might accrue from the premature issuance of an exclusion order.[46] The Commission has, at a minimum, generally waited until the "adjudication of any defenses by participating respondents that may have a bearing on the public interest factors."[47]

Once an investigation reaches the stage of issuance of a final ID on violation and recommended determination on remedy, the ALJ will presume the pleaded facts to be true against any defaulting respondents and will find those respondents in violation of Section 337 (assuming the asserted patent(s) have not been found invalid or unenforceable). Typically, the Commission will then issue a limited exclusion order against the defaulting respondents. If a complainant seeks a general exclusion order in an investigation in which all respondents default (or settle), it must present "substantial, reliable, and probative evidence" of a violation of Section 337 (in addition to satisfying the other more strenuous requirements for issuance of a general exclusion order).[48]

E. ARBITRATION

Commission Rule § 210.21(d) provides for the termination of an investigation on the basis of an arbitration agreement.[49] Motions to terminate investigations on the basis of an arbitration agreement are often contested where the parties disagree about whether the arbitration agreement pre-

---

45. *See Certain Oscillating Sprinklers, Sprinkler Components, & Nozzles (Oscillating Sprinklers)*, Inv. No. 337-TA-448, Order No. 7 (Initial Determination), at 3 (May 22, 2001) (unreviewed).

46. *See, e.g., Certain Plastic Grocery & Retail Bags*, Inv. No. 337-TA-492, Order No. 27 (Initial Determination), at 2 (Jan. 21, 2004) (unreviewed).

47. Proposed Final Rules Governing Investigation and Enforcement Procedures Pertaining to Unfair Practices in Import Trade, 57 Fed. Reg. 52,830, 52,837 (Nov. 5, 1992); *Certain Laminated Floor Panels*, Inv. No. 337-TA-545, Order No. 18 (Initial Determination), at 2 n.1 (Mar. 3, 2006) (unreviewed); *Oscillating Sprinklers*, Inv. No. 337-TA-448, Order No. 7, at 3; *LFFPs*, Order No. 24, at 2–3.

48. 19 U.S.C. § 1337(g)(2); 19 C.F.R. § 210.16(c)(2).

49. The statutory power to terminate an investigation based on an arbitration agreement, found in Section 337(c), was added via amendment in 1994. *See* Uruguay Round Agreements Act of 1994, H.R. Doc. No. 316, 103rd Cong. 2d Sess., Vol. 1.

cludes a Commission investigation.[50] Once the complainant and/or one or more respondents present the matter for arbitration and reach an agreement pursuant to such arbitration, the parties must file a motion to terminate if they wish to end the ITC investigation. As with settlements and consent orders, a copy of the agreement must be included with this motion. The ALJ will consider the motion and issue an ID either granting or denying termination. The Commission will then have an opportunity to review the ID before it becomes the final determination.

If parties agree to outside arbitration, the Commission may terminate the investigation without determining whether a Section 337 violation exists. Any party at any time may move to terminate based on an existing arbitration agreement between parties.[51]

Termination of Section 337 proceedings based on arbitration agreements differs from the effect of arbitration in U.S. district courts. In district court, the court will typically stay the proceedings pending arbitration. By contrast, in Section 337 proceedings, the presence of an arbitration agreement will typically lead the Commission to terminate the investigation upon motion by the parties, assuming such an agreement does not conflict with the public interest.

F. WITHDRAWAL

Once an investigation has been instituted, a complainant may seek to terminate the investigation based upon withdrawal of the complaint pursuant to 19 C.F.R. § 210.21(a).[52] Complainants may withdraw the complaint at any time prior to the issuance of an ID on violation.[53] Absent extraordinary circumstances, the Commission generally grants motions

---

50. *See, e.g., Certain Composite Wear Components & Prods. Containing Same,* Inv. No. 337-TA-644, Order No. 20, Denying Respondent's Mot. to Terminate the Inv. on the Basis of a Previously Unasserted Arbitration Agreement (Mar. 5, 2009).

51. Mitsubishi Motors Corp. v. Soler Chrysler-Plymouth, Inc., 473 U.S. 614, 631 (1985).

52. 19 C.F.R. § 210.21(a). Similar to termination by settlement, a motion for termination by withdrawal must "contain a statement that there are no agreements . . . between the parties concerning the subject matter of the investigation, or if there are any agreements concerning the subject matter of the investigation, all such agreements shall be identified."

53. *Id.* Prior to institution, the complainant may withdraw the complaint as a matter of right at any time prior to the Commission vote on whether to institute the investigation. 19 C.F.R. § 210.10(a)(5)(i).

to terminate on this basis.[54] Indeed, to deny such a motion would force an unwilling patent holder to exercise its patent monopoly rights in a Section 337 investigation.[55] Additionally, such motions are typically granted because public policy favors the conservation of public and private resources that result from the avoidance of litigation.[56]

Such motions are typically denied only when they raise "substantial public interest concerns."[57] The Commission has found that "extraordinary circumstances" sufficient to justify denial of a complainant's motion to terminate based on withdrawal of the complaint are not present where, for example, a respondent opposes the motion and termination of the investigation because it wants a ruling on patent validity or because significant discovery has already taken place.[58] As with other orders pertaining to motions to terminate on other bases, the ALJ's order to terminate based on withdrawal of the complaint constitutes an ID.

Termination of an investigation on the basis of withdrawal of the complaint is without prejudice, unlike proceedings before U.S. district courts.[59] The Commission has held that "whether termination of an investigation is styled with or without prejudice will have no effect on whether another investigation will be instituted upon a subsequently filed

---

54. *See Certain Digital Televisions & Components Thereof*, Inv. No. 337-TA-789, Order No. 17 (Initial Determination) (Oct. 17, 2011) (granting joint motion to terminate investigation with respect to one respondent) (unreviewed) (citing *Certain Ultrafiltration Membrane Sys. & Components Thereof, Including Ultrafiltration Membranes*, Inv. No. 337-TA-107, Comm'n Action & Order, at 2 (Mar. 11, 1982) ("[I]n the absence of extraordinary circumstances, termination of the investigation will be readily granted to a complainant during the pre-hearing stage of an investigation")).

55. *Certain Starter Kill Vehicle Sec. Sys. (Starter Kill Vehicle)*, Inv. No. 337-TA-379, Order No. 13 (Mar. 5, 1996).

56. *Certain Integrated Circuits, Chipsets, & Prods. Containing Same Including Televisions, Media Players, & Cameras*, Inv. No. 337-TA-709, Order No. 48 (Initial Determination) (Feb. 7, 2011) (terminating the investigation as to certain parties) (unreviewed).

57. *Id.* (citing *Starter Kill Vehicle*, Order No. 13).

58. *See, e.g., Certain Single In-Line Memory Modules & Prods. Containing Same*, Inv. No. 337-TA-336 (June 18, 1992); *Starter Kill Vehicle*, Order No. 13.

59. *See Certain Bar Clamps, Bar Clamp Pads, & Related Packaging, Display, & Other Materials*, Inv. No. 337-TA-429, Comm'n Op. (Pub. Version), at 7 (Feb. 13, 2001); *Certain Hand-Held Meat Tenderizers (Meat Tenderizers)*, Inv. No. 337-TA-647, Order No. 6 (Initial Determination) (Sept. 5, 2008).

complaint," as the Commission is bound under the statute to evaluate each complaint filed.[60] Nevertheless, the Commission would likely not react favorably to an attempt to re-submit a complaint substantially similar to one previously withdrawn, unless the withdrawal occurred very early in the investigation.

G. MOTIONS FOR SUMMARY DETERMINATION

As in U.S. district court, the parties to a Section 337 proceeding may move to resolve issues where they can prove that undisputed facts of the case support such a resolution. Pursuant to Commission Rule 210.18, any party may move for summary determination on all or part of the issues present in a Section 337 investigation. Complainants may file a motion for summary determination at any time after 20 days following service of the complaint and notice of investigation.[61] Respondents or any other party may move for summary determination at any time after the date the notice of investigation is published in the *Federal Register*.[62] All summary determination motions must be filed at least 60 days before the hearing date, although the ALJ has the authority to permit a summary determination motion to be filed after this time under exceptional circumstances if good cause exists and a party so moves.[63] After a motion for summary determination is served, the nonmoving parties have 10 days to respond.[64] The ALJ has the power to hold oral argument and call for the submission of additional briefs or memoranda.[65] This power is rarely exercised in practice, however.

Also, as in district court, motions for summary determination at the ITC must be supported by the facts and are often accompanied by declarations. The requirements of what must be included with a motion for summary determination are normally specified in the ground rules issued by the ALJ presiding over the investigation. Certain ALJs require a moving party to accompany such a motion with a separate statement of material facts to which the moving party contends there is no genuine issue,

---

60. *Meat Tenderizers*, Order No. 6 (Initial Determination), at 3 (citing *Certain Multibrand Infrared Remote Control Transmitters*, Inv. No. 337-TA-363, Comm'n Op., at 5–7 (June 1994)).

61. 19 C.F.R. § 210.18(a).

62. *Id.*

63. *Id.*

64. *Id.* at § 210.18(b).

65. *Id.* at § 210.18(a).

thus making summary determination justifiable as a matter of law.[66] Some ALJs do not impose this requirement.[67] Thus, unlike U.S. district court practice, motions for summary determination are not always filed with an accompanying statement of undisputed facts.

The summary determination standard of the Commission is analogous to that for motions for summary judgment in U.S. district court. Pursuant to Commission Rule 210.18, an ALJ must grant a motion for summary determination if the "pleadings and any depositions, answers to interrogatories, and admission on file, together with the affidavits, if any, show that there is no genuine issue as to any material fact and that the moving party is entitled to summary determination as a matter of law."[68] As in district court, the evidence should be viewed in the light most favorable to the party opposing the motion, with any doubt resolved in favor of the nonmovant.[69] Additionally, the ALJ should "assure itself that there is no reasonable version of the facts, on the summary judgment record, whereby the nonmovant could prevail, recognizing that the purpose of summary judgment is not to deprive a litigant of a fair hearing, but to avoid an unnecessary trial."[70] Any ALJ order granting summary determination constitutes an initial determination, which must be certified to the Commission.[71] By contrast, a denial is appealable only if certified by the ALJ.[72]

The fact of importation, along with the existence of a domestic industry with respect to the economic prong of that statutory requirement, are issues often resolved through summary determination.[73] Motions for

---

66. *See, e.g., Certain Elec. Devices Including Handheld Wireless Commc'ns Devices*, Inv. No. 337-TA-673, Order No. 2, at 4–5 (Mar. 26, 2009).

67. *See, e.g., Certain Variable Speed Wind Turbines & Components Thereof*, Inv. No. 337-TA-641, Order No. 2 (Apr. 2, 2008).

68. 19 C.F.R. § 210.18(b).

69. *Certain Auto. Parts*, Inv. No. 337-TA-651, Order No. 21 (Initial Determination) (Pub. Version), at 2 (Mar. 6, 2009) (unreviewed).

70. *Certain Laser Imageable Lithographic Printing Plates (Lithographic Printing Plates)*, Inv. No. 337-TA-636, Order No. 22 (Pub. Version), at 3 (Feb. 23, 2009) (citing EMI Group N. Am., Inc. v. Intel Corp., 157 F.3d 887, 891 (Fed. Cir. 1998)).

71. 19 C.F.R. §§ 210.18(f), 210.42(c).

72. 19 C.F.R. § 210.24(b).

73. *See, e.g., Certain Flash Memory & Prods. Containing Same*, Inv. No. 337-685, Order No. 44 (Initial Determination Granting Complainant's Motion for Summary Determination that the Alpine Respondents have met the Impor-

summary determination are also common where all remaining respondents have been found in default.[74]

Motions for summary determination based on patent issues such as infringement or validity are also frequently made, but less commonly granted.[75] This is likely due to timing, if the motion is filed before the ALJ issues a claim construction for the patent-at-issue, or to the high burden to show invalidity by clear and convincing evidence.[76] If a respondent is successful in a motion for summary determination of invalidity, however, this dispositive finding can lead to termination of the investigation if there are no valid patents left in the investigation.

Summary determination is a particularly useful tool at the ITC, given the condensed schedule under which investigations proceed. The disposition of issues through summary determination allows more time to deal with other issues at the hearing and can also help streamline discovery. Even if a party is not successful in obtaining summary determination to the full extent sought, the ALJ may partially grant such motions to the extent the facts are not in dispute. And even if the motion is denied, it might help educate the ALJ about the issues in dispute. Thus, summary determination can be a valuable part of any party's strategy to streamline an investigation and advance its case.

---

tation Requirement of 19 U.S.C. § 1337) (Dec. 22, 2010) (unreviewed); *Certain Handheld Elec. Computing Devices, Related Software, & Components Thereof*, Inv. No. 337-TA-769, Order No. 34 (Initial Determination Granting Microsoft's Mot. for Summary Determination that it Has Satisfied the Economic Prong of the Domestic Industry Req't) (Feb. 6, 2012) (unreviewed).

74. *See, e.g., Certain Hydraulic Excavators & Components Thereof*, Inv. No. 337-TA-582, Order No. 67 (Initial Determination Granting Mot. for Summary Determination Concerning Violation of Section 337, Remedy, Bonding, and the Pub. Interest) (Pub. Version) (Feb. 6, 2009) (unreviewed) (granting complainant's motion for summary determination of a violation of Section 337 where the only two respondents remaining in the investigation had been found in default).

75. *See, e.g., Lithographic Printing Plates*, Order No. 22, at 4.

76. *Id.* at 2–4.

CHAPTER 9

Prehearing Preparation

Once the period for discovery is closed, preparation begins in earnest for the hearing before the ALJ. Typically, the procedural schedule provides for one to two months between the close of discovery and the beginning of the hearing, during which pretrial briefs and exhibits are prepared, motions in limine are filed, and, in some investigations, a technical tutorial is conducted.

A. PREHEARING STATEMENTS

Prior to the hearing, the ALJ generally requires each party to submit a prehearing statement, including or in addition to a prehearing brief. Some ALJs require these to be submitted a month or more in advance of the hearing, while others schedule the submission deadline much closer to the start of the hearing. In investigations involving multiple respondents, the ALJ may encourage or require respondents to file a single, consolidated submission.

The prehearing statement is generally intended to provide the ALJ with a roadmap for the hearing, while the prehearing brief sets forth, in detail, the parties' positions on the contested issues. Absent unusual circumstances, parties are bound by the positions set forth in their prehearing briefs.[1] Page limits for the prehearing brief are at the discretion of the ALJ;

---

1. *See, e.g., Certain Protective Cases & Components Thereof*, Inv. No. 337-TA-780, Order No. 24, at 18 (Dec. 30, 2011) ("Any contentions not set forth in detail as required herein shall be deemed abandoned, or withdrawn, except for contentions of which a party is not aware and could not be aware in the exercise of reasonable diligence at the time of filing the prehearing statements.").

at least two ALJs have set page limits in their ground rules,[2] while others have done so in individual cases in response to a motion from a party.[3]

The deadline for the OUII's prehearing statement/brief is typically set for at least few days after the deadline for the private parties to allow OUII to take the parties' briefs into account. This marks the first time that OUII takes positions on the substantive issues in the investigation (other than issues previously raised in summary determination motions). Absent unusual circumstances that would cause it to change its views (such as newly discovered evidence at the hearing), OUII will advocate the positions set forth in its prehearing statement before both the ALJ and the Commission for the remainder of the investigation. For this reason, parties are well advised to meet with OUII in advance of the deadline for submission of prehearing statements to ensure that the OUII attorney is fully informed of the merits of the party's positions on the issues in dispute.

The required contents of the prehearing statement and prehearing brief are generally set out in the ALJ's ground rules and typically include some or all of the following items.

1. List of Testifying Witnesses

To assist with scheduling issues and to provide notice to the opposing parties, ALJs typically require each party to list the witnesses they intend to call at trial, sometimes including a description of their expected testimony and an estimate of the time needed for each witness. If the parties' witnesses are too numerous in light of the scheduled hearing time, the ALJ may ask the parties to reduce the number of live hearing witnesses through the use of stipulations or by designating portions of deposition testimony in lieu of live testimony for certain witnesses. The majority of ALJs require the parties to introduce their witnesses' direct testimony through written witness statements, which limit those witnesses' live testimony to cross-examination and possible redirect.

---

2. *See Certain Set-Top Boxes, & Hardware & Software Components Thereof*, Inv. No. 337-TA-761, Order No. 26, at 16 (Nov. 21, 2011); *Certain Dimmable Compact Fluorescent Lamps & Prods. Containing Same*, Inv. No. 337-TA-830, Order No. 2, at 17 (Feb. 28, 2012) (both setting page limits of 175 pages for the body of the prehearing brief and 50 pages for the attachments).

3. *See Certain Semiconductor Chips & Prods. Containing Same*, Inv. No. 337-TA-753, Order No. 51 (Sept. 15, 2011); *Certain Portable Elec. Devices & Related Software*, Inv. No. 337-TA-721, Order No. 44 (Apr. 4, 2011).

2. List of Exhibits

Under the typical procedural schedule, the parties exchange exhibit lists prior to submitting their prehearing statements. The list submitted with the prehearing statement is primarily for administrative convenience and the benefit of the ALJ.

3. Stipulations

ALJs generally encourage the parties to stipulate to non-controversial issues, such as importation, to streamline the hearing and allow the judge to focus on the contested issues. The parties are typically required to list in their prehearing statement any agreed-upon stipulations, and in some cases are also asked to list any proposed stipulations that the other side has not agreed to.

4. Positions on the Issues

The substantive heart of the prehearing statement (sometimes submitted as a separate, stand-alone "prehearing brief") is a description of the issues to be decided by the ALJ and an explanation of the party's contentions on those issues, including citations to supporting legal authority. In a patent case, for example, the parties are expected to set forth in detail all of their claim constructions, infringement/non-infringement and validity/invalidity contentions, as well as their contentions on any other case-specific issues or defenses. Although the ALJ does not decide any issues on the merits based on the prehearing statement alone—such decisions are made only after the receipt of evidence at the hearing and consideration of extensive post-hearing briefing—the prehearing statement's exposition of a party's positions on the issues is still extremely important in framing the contested issues for the ALJ. Perhaps even more important, as previously explained, any contentions not expressed in the prehearing statement may be deemed abandoned or waived.

5. Proposed Agenda for the Prehearing Conference

The parties are expected to disclose in their prehearing statement the issues they intend to raise at the prehearing conference. Items typically addressed at prehearing conferences include rulings on outstanding motions, including motions in limine, rulings on high priority objections, resolution of questions regarding hearing protocol, and the scheduling of witnesses.

6. Statement Regarding Use of Depositions

The parties are typically asked to state their position regarding the use of deposition testimony in lieu of live testimony. Some ALJs establish a separate deadline for submissions of statements regarding use of depositions rather than including this item in the prehearing statement.

7. Statement Regarding Opening and Closing Arguments

Some ALJs ask the parties to state whether they wish to make opening statements or closing arguments. ALJs vary in their preferences regarding such statements or arguments. Brief opening statements are typically allowed, while closing arguments are rarely held.

B. EXHIBITS

Procedures for handling exhibits vary somewhat among the ALJs as set forth in their ground rules. Typically, the procedural schedule will include deadlines for exchange of initial and rebuttal exhibits, and for the submission of objections to them, at least one week before the hearing. Most ALJs require identification of a sponsoring witness and a purpose for each exhibit. Confidential exhibits must be clearly designated as such.

Parties are expected to remove duplicate exhibits and fix curable problems (such as legibility, lack of a translation for foreign language documents, etc.) without the intervention of the ALJ. Physical exhibits are generally listed and dealt with separately; for obvious reasons, these are typically not served on the opposing parties but must be made available for inspection. Parties frequently obtain leave to identify and serve demonstrative exhibits shortly before their use at the hearing. In investigations before ALJs who require written witness statements, these must typically be exchanged at or near the deadlines for submission of exhibits. Preparing witness statements as exhibits is a major undertaking that requires a considerable amount of time and effort.

Some ALJs prefer to rule on objections to exhibits at the outset of the hearing, in some cases requiring the parties to submit a list of "high-priority" objections to streamline the process. Others use a more traditional trial-style approach of ruling on the admission of exhibits into evidence only after they are discussed by a witness on the stand or in a witness statement. After the close of the evidentiary record, the parties must submit a final list of exhibits showing which were admitted and which were rejected or not offered. An official set of admitted exhibits must be compiled for the record. The Commission has gradually moved towards the submission of exhibits in electronic rather than paper form, but the ALJs' ground rules must still be consulted as to their individual preferences. Even exhibits that the ALJ rejects travel with the record for Commission and possible Federal Circuit review. The Commissioners may decide that the ALJ incorrectly precluded a party from admitting an exhibit into the record and may base their decision on such an exhibit.

C. MOTIONS IN LIMINE

Motions in limine can be filed in advance of the hearing, typically according to a deadline established in the procedural schedule. Some ALJs set limits on the number of motions in limine the parties may file.[4] Motions in limine are used to preclude admission of evidence in the form of testimony or exhibits that a party contends is irrelevant or unfairly prejudicial. For example, a complainant might seek to preclude the testimony of a "patent law expert" with respect to a claim of inequitable conduct. Parties are well advised to address motions in limine to specific, discrete evidentiary issues. Broadly worded motions (e.g., a motion to preclude expert testimony to the extent not disclosed in the expert's reports) are sometimes granted but are of limited practical value, because objections must still be raised and ruled upon when offending testimony is offered at the hearing. Motions in limine based on underlying substantive issues (e.g., a motion to preclude expert testimony of infringement based on incorrect claim construction) are rarely granted.[5]

Motions in limine frequently cite to and rely upon the Federal Rules of Evidence (FRE), but it should be remembered that the FRE are not strictly applicable to administrative hearings before an ALJ. Instead, the admission of evidence in a Section 337 proceeding is governed by Commission Rule 210.37, which provides that "[r]elevant, material, and reliable evidence shall be admitted. Irrelevant, immaterial, unreliable, or

---

4. *See Certain Protective Cases & Components Thereof,* Inv. No. 337-TA-780, Order No. 24, at 20 (Dec. 30, 2011) (setting a limit of 10 motions in limine for each side, including when an investigation involves multiple respondents).

5. Such issues should generally be raised in a motion for summary determination rather than a motion in limine.

unduly repetitious evidence shall be excluded." Nevertheless, the Commission does look to the FRE for guidance on evidentiary issues.[6]

D. *MARKMAN* HEARINGS

The decision by the U.S. Supreme Court in *Markman v. Westview Instruments*[7] established that claim construction is a matter of law. Since that decision, it has become the practice of many U.S. district courts to hold separate "*Markman* hearings" to construe the patent claims at issue prior to a jury trial. At the Commission, however, the ALJ decides both legal and factual issues, so one of the primary rationales for conducting a separate claim-construction hearing is absent in a Section 337 investigation. For this reason and others, including the rapid pace of Section 337 investigations, *Markman* hearings have traditionally been the exception rather than the rule at the Commission.[8] However, the instance of *Markman* hearings has recently been increasing. Of the 40 investigations instituted in the second half of 2011, 15 were scheduled to conduct *Markman* hearings.[9] If a party believes a *Markman* hearing is appropriate in a particular investigation, the issue should be raised with the ALJ at an early stage of the proceeding so that the procedural schedule can be crafted accordingly. The decision whether or not to conduct a *Markman* hearing is ultimately at the discretion of the ALJ and can be scheduled over the objection of a party.[10] Some ALJs specifically address the procedures for

---

6. See *Certain Coenzyme Q10 Prods. & Methods of Making Same*, Inv. No. 337-TA-790, Order No. 14, 2012 WL 595607, at *2 (Feb. 22, 2012) ("Although the Federal Rules of Evidence are not strictly applicable to administrative hearings before an Administrative Law Judge, the Commission does look to the Federal Rules of Evidence for guidance on evidentiary issues." (citing *Certain Semiconductor Chips with Minimized Chip Package Size & Prods. Containing Same (III)*, Inv. No. 337-TA-630, Order No. 46 (Initial Determination) (Aug. 28, 2009) (unreviewed))).

7. Markman v. Westview Instruments, 517 U.S. 370 (1996).

8. *See, e.g., Certain Home Vacuum Packaging Machs.*, Inv. No. 337-TA-496 (2003), for an example of an investigation that included a *Markman* hearing.

9. *See* Inv. Nos. 337-TA-781, 337-TA-782, 337-TA-785, 337-TA-789, 337-TA-792, 337-TA-794, 337-TA-796, 337-TA-797, 337-TA-803, 337-TA-806, 337-TA-808, 337-TA-810, 337-TA-816, 337-TA-819, 337-TA-820.

10. *See, e.g., Certain Elec. Devices, Including Wireless Commc'n Devices, Portable Music & Data Processing Devices, & Tablet Computers*, Inv. No. 337-TA-794, Order No. 5, at 1 (Oct. 17, 2011) (*Markman* hearing scheduled despite Complainant's objections).

potential *Markman* hearings in their ground rules.[11] In deciding whether to hold a *Markman* hearing, the ALJ may consider such factors as the number of patents and asserted claims, the complexity of the technology, and the ALJ's overall docket.[12] When a *Markman* hearing is held, the ALJ's claim construction ruling is an order, not an initial determination, and may not be immediately appealed to the Commission.[13] This practice is consistent with federal court practice where a court's interim claim construction order is not immediately appealable to the Federal Circuit.

E. TUTORIALS

At the discretion of the ALJ, tutorials are sometimes conducted in cases involving complex technology. The purpose of a tutorial is to instruct the ALJ on the technology of the case. The parties are not expected to use the tutorial to argue the merits of their positions. The tutorial may take place on the eve of the hearing or a week or more in advance. The ALJs frequently leave it up to the parties to determine the length of time they need and the manner in which the tutorial will be conducted. Most commonly, the tutorial is conducted by the parties' respective experts in equal allotments of time, either in a lecture style or in a question-and-answer format, but without cross-examination. The parties should discuss with the ALJ and reach an understanding on whether visual aids (such as a PowerPoint presentation) used during the tutorial become part of the record. In addition to or in lieu of a technology tutorial, the ALJ may instruct the parties to prepare and agree to a technology stipulation set-

---

11. *See Certain Auto. GPS Navigation Sys., Components Thereof, & Prods. Containing Same,* Inv. No. 337-TA-814, Order No. 4, at 7–8 (Feb. 9, 2012).

12. *See, e.g., Certain LED Photographic Lighting Devices & Components Thereof,* Inv. No. 337-TA-804, Order No. 10, at 1–2 (Nov. 28, 2011) ("While the number of patents and asserted claims could certainly benefit from a *Markman* hearing, that alone does not warrant holding the hearing especially since it is not clear that the technology is so complex that holding an early tutorial and *Markman* hearing would provide some benefit. In addition, under the ALJ's current schedule . . . it is highly unlikely the ALJ will be able to construe claims in a timely manner given his docket and responsibilities in other investigations.").

13. *See Certain Mobile Tels. & Wireless Commc'n Devices Featuring Digital Cameras, & Components Thereof,* Inv. No. 337-TA-703, Notice of Comm'n Determination That June 22, 2010 Initial Determination is an Order Rather Than an Initial Determination (Oct. 20, 2010).

ting forth undisputed background information about the technology at issue in the asserted patents.[14]

F. PREHEARING CONFERENCE

ALJs typically[15] schedule a prehearing conference for the morning of the first scheduled hearing day, but in some cases the prehearing conference may occur earlier. In the prehearing conference, the ALJ will provide final instructions regarding the conduct of the hearing, address any scheduling concerns regarding the order of witnesses, and answer any procedural questions. The ALJ will also frequently rule upon pending motions, with or without oral argument. The ALJ may also inquire about settlement discussions and press the parties to streamline the hearing through the use of stipulations.

---

14. *See, e.g., Certain Dynamic Random Access Memory & NAND Flash Memory Devices & Prods. Containing Same*, Inv. No. 337-TA-803, Order No. 21 (Jan. 5, 2012).

15. 19 C.F.R. § 210.35 authorizes the ALJ to conduct prehearing conferences at any time prior to the hearing. Some ALJs hold "preliminary conferences" at an early stage of an investigation. Others hold conferences at various points during an investigation to hear argument on substantive, discovery, or procedural motions. The prehearing conference is generally conducted immediately prior to the hearing.

CHAPTER 10

Hearing and Post-Hearing

Commission Rule § 210.36(a) provides that "an opportunity for a hearing shall be provided in each investigation . . . ." The purpose of the hearing is to allow the presiding "administrative law judge [to] take evidence and hear argument for the purpose of determining whether there is a violation of section 337 of the Tariff Act of 1930, and for the purpose of making findings and recommendations, as described in §210.42(a)(1)(ii), concerning the appropriate remedy and the amount of the bond to be posted by respondents during Presidential review of the Commission's action, under section 337(j) of the Tariff Act."[1]

Pursuant to this rule—except in the case of investigations resolved by settlement, consent, default, or by way of summary determination—an evidentiary hearing, which may last from a few days to several weeks, is conducted before the ALJ in a courtroom at the ITC.[2] Though similar in some ways to a U.S. district court bench trial, a Section 337 hearing is governed neither by the Federal Rules of Civil Procedure nor by the Federal Rules of Evidence. (However, when there is a gap in the Commission's rules of practice or precedent, the ALJs will look to those

---

1. 19 C.F.R. § 210.36 (a)(1) (2012).
2. *See* 19 C.F.R. § 210.36(c): *Expedition.* Hearings shall proceed with all reasonable expedition, and, insofar as practicable, shall be held at one place, continuing until completed unless otherwise ordered by the administrative law judge; 19 C.F.R. § 210.36(e): *Presiding official.* An administrative law judge shall preside over each hearing unless the Commission shall otherwise order.

federal rules.[3]) Instead, the hearing is governed by the requirements of the Administrative Procedure Act.[4]

Commission Rule § 210.36(b) provides that all hearings "shall be public unless otherwise ordered by the administrative law judge." Nevertheless, because much of the testimony in a typical Section 337 hearing involves confidential business information, in most cases significant portions of the hearing are conducted on the confidential record, with only those persons covered by the protective order, or the party whose confidential information is being discussed, allowed in the courtroom.

A. OPENING STATEMENTS

At the ALJ's discretion, the parties may present brief opening statements. Because the parties' positions are already set forth in detail in the prehearing statements and hearing time is precious, lengthy opening statements are generally disfavored.

B. ORDER OF PRESENTATION

Typically, the hearing begins with the complainant's case-in-chief, followed by the respondent's case, the OUII's case,[5] and concluding with

---

3. *See, e.g., Certain Coenzyme Q10 Prods. & Methods of Making Same,* Inv. No. 337-TA-790, Order No. 14, at 4 (Feb. 22, 2012) ("Although the Federal Rules of Evidence are not strictly applicable to administrative hearings before an Administrative Law Judge, the Commission does look to the Federal Rules of Evidence for guidance on evidentiary issues.") (citing *Certain Semiconductor Chips with Minimized Chip Package Size & Prods. Containing Same (III),* Inv. No. 337-TA-630, Order No. 46 (Initial Determination) (Aug. 28, 2009) (unreviewed)); *Certain Cold Cathode Fluorescent Lamp (CCFL) Inverter Circuits & Prods. Containing the Same,* Inv. No. 337-TA-666, Order No 28, at 6 (Sept. 16, 2009) (quoting *Certain Composite Wear Components & Prods. Containing Same,* Inv. No. 337-TA-644, Order No. 16, at 2-3 (Jan. 22, 2009)); *Certain Indomethacin,* Inv. No. 337-TA-183 (Ancillary proceeding), Comm'n Op., at 4 n.8 (June 30, 1988) ("Although Commission Practice is not governed by the Federal Rules of Civil Procedure, it often looks to those rules for guidance.").

4. *See* 19 C.F.R. § 210.36(d): *Rights of the parties.* Every hearing under this section shall be conducted in accordance with the Administrative Procedure Act (i.e., 5 U.S.C. §§ 554 through 556). Hence, every party shall have the right of adequate notice, cross-examination, presentation of evidence, objection, motion, argument, and all other rights essential to a fair hearing.

5. OUII typically presents its case through cross-examination of the private parties' witnesses, but it reserves the right to call witnesses on its own behalf.

the complainant's rebuttal case. The order of presentation may be altered to accommodate the schedules of the witnesses. This can include taking witnesses out of order, interrupting one witness to allow another to take the stand, and allowing a witness to appear on the stand only once even if he would otherwise appear in both the complainant's and the respondent's case.

C. WITNESS EXAMINATION

A significant divide exists between the practices of the ALJs with respect to the examination of witnesses. Five of the six current ALJs follow the practice used in certain other administrative agencies and require the parties to present direct testimony, with the exception of that of adverse witnesses, by way of written witness statements. These witness statements are typically submitted to the other parties before the hearing when documentary exhibits are exchanged. The other parties then raise their objections to the testimony when providing objections to the documentary exhibits. In these hearings, there is no live direct testimony with the exception noted above; instead, the witness is sworn in, attests to the witness statement, and then is subjected to cross-examination, examination by OUII, and redirect examination.

The ALJ will not decide the case on the merits immediately upon conclusion of the hearing. Instead, the ALJ will issue an initial determination (ID) approximately two months later, after receiving initial and reply post-hearing briefs. Subsequent to the ALJ's decision, the Commission may review that decision, relying only on the written record. For these reasons, while it is certainly desirable to make a favorable impression on the ALJ at the hearing, it is perhaps even more important to create a clear written record of the evidence so that it can be cited and understood after the hearing. These considerations should be kept in mind when preparing witness statements and conducting live examinations.

D. ADMISSION OF EVIDENCE

Section 337 hearings are governed by Commission Rule § 210.37(b), which simply states that all "relevant, material, and reliable evidence shall be admitted," and that "irrelevant, immaterial, unreliable, or unduly repetitious evidence shall be excluded." Notably, this definition allows for the admission of hearsay.[6] For this reason, and because the ALJ is both the finder of fact and decides the legal issues, in comparison to a U.S. district court jury trial, hearings are typically more lenient with respect to admitting evidence into the record. In lieu of making border-line evidentiary rulings, ALJs often err on the side of admitting objected-to testimony with the understanding that the ALJ will be able to sort out and disregard unreliable evidence and that the objectionable evidence will, therefore, also be available to the Commission should it review the initial determination. For example, objections that challenge the reliability of the proffered testimony are sometimes denied on the ground that the objection "goes to weight." Because hearing time is limited, however, ALJs will cut off irrelevant or redundant questioning fairly quickly.

In those instances where evidence is excluded by the ALJ, the affected party is well advised to make an offer of proof to preserve the issue for appeal.[7] The Commission Rules also provide that exhibits rejected by the ALJ should be retained with the record for consideration by any reviewing authority.[8] Formal exceptions to adverse evidentiary rulings are not required, however.[9] Finally, the fact that evidence is admitted does not prevent a party from arguing that it should be given no weight; to the contrary, ALJs often encourage the parties to address the credibility and reliability of the evidence in their post-hearing briefing.

Depending on the ALJ's practice, exhibits are submitted into evidence either en masse or individually. Most commonly, at the conclusion of a witness's testimony, all of the exhibits discussed by the witness, either live or in the witness statement, are offered into evidence. Demonstrative exhibits used by a witness are not substantive evidence, but they

---

6. *See Certain Light-Emitting Diodes & Prods. Containing Same*, Inv. No. 337-TA-512, Initial Determination (Pub. Version), at 137 n.576 (May 10, 2005) (unreviewed in pertinent part) ("With respect to Dominant's hearsay objection, hearsay evidence is not *per se* excludable in administrative proceedings but is an argument affecting the weight to be given certain evidence.") (citing Richardson v. Perales, 402 U.S. 389, 402 (1972)).

7. 19 C.F.R. § 210.37(g): *Excluded evidence.* When an objection to a question propounded to a witness is sustained, the examining party may make a specific offer of what he expects to prove by the answer of the witness, or the administrative law judge may in his discretion receive and report the evidence in full. Rejected exhibits, adequately marked for identification, shall be retained with the record so as to be available for consideration by any reviewing authority.

8. *Id.*

9. 19 C.F.R. § 210.37(f).

should still be made part of the record to facilitate understanding the witness's testimony.

E. COMMISSION RECORD

The hearing is transcribed by the official reporter of the Commission and becomes part of the Commission record.[10] The record, for purposes of appeal to the CAFC, also includes:

> all pleadings, the notice of investigation, motions and responses, all briefs and written statements, and other documents and things properly filed with the Secretary, in addition to all orders, notices, and initial determinations of the administrative law judge, orders and notices of the Commission, hearing and conference transcripts, evidence admitted into the record (including physical exhibits), and any other items certified into the record by the administrative law judge or the Commission.[11]

At the conclusion of the hearing, the ALJ typically closes the evidentiary record, which is the record upon which the ID is based. The ALJ nevertheless retains the power to reopen the record and receive additional evidence at any time prior to the issuance of the ID,[12] and will generally do so based on a showing of good cause.[13] For example, it is not uncommon for the record to be reopened to allow for the inclusion of exhibits that were inadvertently not moved into evidence at the hearing.[14]

---

10. 19 C.F.R. § 210.38(b).

11. *Id.* at § 210.38(a).

12. *Id.* at § 210.37(g).

13. *See, e.g., Certain Semiconductor Chips & Prods. Containing Same,* Inv. No. 337-TA-753, Order No. 61 (Feb. 10, 2012) (reopening the evidentiary record to receive an exhibit for good cause shown).

14. *See, e.g., Certain Protective Cases & Components Thereof (Protective Cases),* Inv. No. 337-TA-780, Order No. 33 (May 9, 2012) (granting complainant's motion to reopen the evidentiary record for admission of an exhibit inadvertently not recorded as admitted into evidence); *Certain Laminated Floor Panels,* Inv. No. 337-TA-545, Order No. 32 (May 1, 2006) (reopening the evidentiary record and admitting additional evidence identified during witness testimony).

After the ALJ issues the ID, he no longer has the authority to reopen the evidentiary record.[15]

F. POST-HEARING BRIEFS

Following completion of the hearing, the ALJ will establish a schedule for the submission of post-hearing briefs, typically over a three- to five-week period. The schedule normally includes initial post-hearing briefs followed by reply post-hearing briefs. OUII submits its post-hearing briefs on the same deadlines as the private parties. Page limits are usually established for the briefs, with reply briefs typically half the length of the initial briefs.

The parties may submit proposed findings of fact and conclusions of law at the close of the evidentiary hearing in accordance with Commission Rule 210.40. None of the current ALJs requires the parties to submit proposed findings of fact and conclusions of law. Some ALJs do not address findings of fact and conclusions of law in their ground rules. The ALJs that address these submissions make them an optional filing at the time of initial post-hearing briefs. The parties should cite to the specific exhibits or portions of the hearing transcript that support their proposed findings. The parties may submit objections and rebuttal findings to the other parties' proposed findings with their reply post-hearing briefs. Although some ALJs impose specific rules about findings of fact and conclusions of law, no ALJ deems a proposed finding admitted because the other parties do not include a separate statement of objections or rebuttal to a proposed finding.[16] The ALJs typically do not impose page limits on the initial or rebuttal findings.

Post-hearing briefing offers the parties their final and best opportunity to convince the ALJ of the merits of their case by linking their legal arguments to the evidence in the record. The parties are expected to provide citations to testimony or exhibits that support their specific contentions. ALJs who require findings of fact often require the parties to cite to particular findings of fact rather than the exhibits or hearing transcript. The ALJ will not comb through the record in search of relevant evidence.

---

15. *See Certain Display Controllers with Upscaling Functionality & Prods. Containing Same*, Inv. No. 337-TA-481 (Remand), Order No. 40 (Feb. 19, 2004).

16. *See, e.g., Certain Auto. GPS Navigation Sys., Components Thereof, & Prods. Containing Same*, Inv. No. 337-TA-814, Order No. 4, at 28–29 (Feb. 9, 2012); *Protective Cases*, Order No. 24, at 35–36 (Dec. 30, 2011).

G. CLOSING ARGUMENTS

At the discretion of the ALJ, closing arguments may occur following the conclusion of post-hearing briefing. In the majority of investigations, closing arguments are not held.

H. INITIAL DETERMINATION AND RECOMMENDED DETERMINATION

After the receipt and consideration of the post-hearing briefing, the ALJ issues an ID as to whether there is a violation of Section 337.[17] The ID addresses all of the substantive issues in the investigation, including the unfair act, importation, the existence of a domestic industry, and, where at issue, injury to the domestic industry.[18] The ID is issued in the form of an opinion stating findings of fact, conclusions of law, and an explanation of the ALJ's reasoning.[19] Until recently, the ALJ did not frequently address the issue of the public interest. Public interest discussions in IDs will likely increase, however, after the November 2011 amendments to the Commission Rules requiring complainants to file a public interest statement concurrently with the complaint, which may prompt the Commission more regularly to direct the ALJ to consider public interest issues.[20] The ID becomes the determination of the Commission unless the Commission determines to review the ID within 60 days of issuance.[21]

The ALJ also issues a recommended determination (RD) concerning the appropriate remedy should the Commission find a violation of Section

---

17. The ID is filed no later than four months before the target date set by the Commission for completion of the investigation. 19 C.F.R. § 210.42(a)(1)(i). *See also* Rules of General Application, Adjudication, and Enforcement (Proposed Rules), 77 Fed. Reg. 134,41124 (proposed July 11, 2012) (to be codified at 19 C.F.R. pt. 210).

18. The 1988 amendments to Section 337 removed the requirement of proof of injury to the domestic industry in patent, trademark, and copyright cases. *See supra* Chapter 1, "Introduction to Section 337 Investigations."

19. *See* 19 C.F.R. § 210.42(d).

20. The November 2011 public interest amendments to the Commission Rules are discussed in Chapter 6, Section A. Since the *Kyocera* case, which essentially required all potential downstream infringers to be named as respondents, public interest considerations have played a more specific role in hearings. The impact of the *Kyocera* case is discussed in Chapter 12, Section F.

21. *See* 19 C.F.R. § 210.42(h)(2).

337, and the amount of the bond to be posted during the presidential review period.[22] The RD is taken into consideration by the Commission in making its remedy and bonding determination, but, unlike the ID, the RD will not become the determination of the Commission; instead, the Commission always receives submissions from the parties, interested persons, and other government agencies before issuing any form of remedy.[23]

---

22. 19 C.F.R. § 210.42(a)(1)(ii)(A)–(B). The RD is filed by the ALJ within 14 days of the issuance of the ID. 19 C.F.R. § 210.42(a)(1)(ii).

23. *See* 19 C.F.R. § 210.50(a). *See also* Proposed Rules, 77 Fed. Reg. 41,124 (proposed July 11, 2012) (to be codified at 19 C.F.R. pt. 210).

CHAPTER 11

Types of Relief and Bonding

The Commission has broad discretion in selecting the form, scope, and extent of the remedy in a Section 337 proceeding.[1] One of the main attractions to the ITC is the potent exclusion remedy that is available. An exclusion order directs U.S. Customs and Border Protection (Customs) to stop infringing imports from entering the United States. When a complainant prevails on the merits, the Commission will seek to fashion a remedy that balances the complainant's interest in receiving protection from all infringing imports against the risk of disrupting legitimate trade. Once the Commission has selected a remedy, judicial review is limited.[2]

A complainant can obtain four types of remedy in a Section 337 investigation.[3] A limited exclusion order (LEO) instructs Customs to exclude from entry into the United States infringing goods manufactured or distributed by a named respondent.[4] A general exclusion order (GEO) instructs Customs to exclude from entry all goods covered by the as-

---

1. Viscofan, S.A. v. U.S. Int'l Trade Comm'n, 787 F.2d 544, 548 (Fed. Cir. 1986).

2. Hyundai Elecs. v. U.S. Int'l Trade Comm'n, 899 F.2d 1204, 1207–09 (Fed. Cir. 1990) (holding that the standard of review of an ITC decision on remedy is whether that "choice of remedy was arbitrary, capricious, abuse of discretion, or otherwise not in accordance with law").

3. 19 U.S.C. § 1337(c) (2006).

4. *See Certain Semiconductor Chips Having Synchronous Dynamic Random Access Memory Controllers & Prods. Containing Same*, Inv. No. 337-TA-661, Initial Determination & Recommended Determination on Remedy and Bond (Pub. Version), at 123 (Apr. 26, 2010).

serted intellectual property, regardless of their source or manufacturer.[5] The Commission may, in lieu of or in addition to an exclusion order, issue a cease and desist order (CDO) prohibiting named respondents from engaging in the unfair methods or acts involved in the investigation, i.e., marketing, distributing, or selling infringing goods that enter the country before imposition of an exclusion order.[6] In addition to these permanent orders, temporary exclusion orders (TEO) and cease and desist orders are also available during the pendency of the investigation (comparable to a preliminary injunction in federal district court), though relatively rare. Remedial orders typically include a reporting requirement, directing the respondent to file statements with the ITC at regular intervals describing any activity that has occurred with respect to the subject goods.[7]

A. LIMITED EXCLUSION ORDER

If the Commission determines that there is a violation of Section 337, "it shall direct that the articles concerned, imported by any person violating the provision of this section, be excluded from entry into the United States," unless such relief would be contrary to the statutory public interest factors.[8] Exclusion "shall be limited to persons determined by the Commission to be violating [Section 337]," unless certain conditions are met such that the Commission is satisfied that a general exclusion order should issue.[9] Nonetheless, the Commission "has broad discretion in selecting the form, scope and extent of a particular remedy."[10] The chosen remedy must have "a reasonable relation to the unlawful practices found to exist" and balance the complainant's interest in obtaining effective relief against the risk of disrupting trade in legitimate products.[11]

---

5. *See id.*

6. *Certain Digital Multimeters, & Prods. with Multimeter Functionality*, Inv. No. 337-TA-588, Order to Cease & Desist (May 14, 2008).

7. *See, e.g., Certain Ground Fault Interrupters & Prods. Containing Same*, Inv. No. 337-TA-615, Order to Cease & Desist, at 4 (Mar. 9, 2009).

8. *See* 19 U.S.C. § 1337(d)(1).

9. *See* 19 U.S.C. § 1337(d)(2).

10. *Certain Integrated Repeaters, Switches, Transceivers & Prods. Containing Same*, Inv. No. 337-TA-435, Comm'n Op., at 3–4 (Aug. 16, 2002) (citing *Viscofan*, 787 F.2d 548).

11. *Certain Self-Cleaning Litter Boxes & Components Thereof*, Inv. No. 337-TA-625, USITC Pub. 4259, Comm'n Determination, at 94 (Oct. 2011) (citing *Hyundai Elecs. v. U.S. Int'l Trade Comm'n*, 899 F.2d 1204, 1209 (Fed. Cir. 1990).

Determining the scope of an exclusion order can be contentious, particularly, for example, if the infringing product consists of several components. In that case, the Commission must decide how narrowly to tailor the exclusion—whether only certain components or the complete product should be excluded. Regardless, the decision whether to exclude components of an accused product, assuming a violation, is dependent on the scope of the investigation.[12] In *Systems for Detecting and Removing Viruses or Worms,* the parties disagreed as to whether the exclusion order should include all respondent products, including hardware, components and software, or be limited to respondent's hardware when combined with the infringing software module.[13] The Commission held that, because the notice of investigation identified the infringing products as "systems for detecting and removing viruses or worms, components thereof, and products containing same," an order covering respondent's hardware components was appropriate, but only in instances where an infringing anti-virus software module was installed.[14]

However the LEO is fashioned, it will almost certainly not include product names or model numbers. The Commission has reasoned that the order should cover all of a respondent's infringing products within the scope of the investigation and that LEOs should not necessarily be limited to the models specifically considered in the investigation.[15] To hold otherwise would provide a loophole for respondents to simply change their product names or model numbers.

However, exclusion orders may include a certification provision, particularly where the infringing nature of the article is not easily determined

12. *See, e.g., Certain Sys. for Detecting & Removing Viruses or Worms, Components Thereof, & Prods. Containing Same*, Inv. No. 337-TA-510, Comm'n Op., at 4 (Aug. 23, 2005) (citing *Certain Insect Traps*, Inv. No. 337-TA-498, Order No. 7 (Apr. 2004)).

13. *Id.*

14. *Id.* ("We determine to issue both a limited exclusion order which prohibits the importation of any infringing FortiGate products, including software that would result in infringement of the '600 patent whether alone or when combined with other Fortinet components.")

15. *See Certain Integrated Repeaters, Switches, Transceivers & Prods. Containing Same*, Inv. No. 337-TA-435, Comm'n Op., at 22–23 (Aug. 16, 2002); *Certain Hardware Logic Emulation Sys. & Components Thereof*, Inv. No. 337-TA-383, Comm'n Op., at 13 (Mar. 1, 1998) ("[T]he Commission's long-standing practice is to direct its remedial orders to all products covered by the patent claims as to which a violation has been found, rather than limiting its orders to only those specific models selected for the infringement analysis.").

by visual inspection.[16] "[A] certification provision is appropriate . . . [if it] will aid Customs in determining whether imports infringe the asserted patents."[17] Under such a provision, respondents can certify, under penalty of perjury, that the goods it seeks to import do not fall within the scope of the Commission's exclusion order.

B. GENERAL EXCLUSION ORDER

The Commission may issue a GEO that applies to all infringing products, regardless of manufacturer, instead of an LEO directed only to persons determined to be in violation of Section 337, when:

(A)   a general exclusion from entry of articles is necessary to prevent circumvention of an exclusion order limited to products of named persons; or

(B)   there is a pattern of violation of this section and it is difficult to identify the source of infringing products.[18]

The Commission may issue a general exclusion order when either one of the statutory provisions is met.[19] Since a general exclusion order is directed to the infringing products, it can reach articles from suppliers and manufacturers not named in the original investigation.[20] The sweeping scope of a GEO makes it more difficult for a complainant to obtain than an LEO.

When the general exclusion order provision (Section 337(d)(2)) of the statute was amended in 1994, it codified prior Commission practice

---

16. *See, e.g., Certain Semiconductor Chips with Minimized Chip Package Size & Prods. Containing Same,* Inv. No. 337-TA-605, Comm'n Op., at 72 (June 3, 2009).

17. *Id.* at 72–73.

18. 19 U.S.C. § 1337(d)(2); *see also Certain Toner Cartridges & Components Thereof,* Inv. No. 337-TA-740, Order No. 26, at 22 (June 1, 2011); *Certain Hair Irons & Packaging Thereof,* Inv. No. 337-TA-637, Issuance of a General Exclusion Order; Termination of the Investigation (June 29, 2009).

19. *See, e.g., Certain Cigarettes & Packaging Thereof,* Inv. No. 337-TA-643, Comm'n Op. (Pub. Version), at 24–27 (Oct. 1, 2009).

20. *See* Vastfame Camera, Ltd. v. U.S. Int'l Trade Comm'n, 386 F.3d 1108 (Fed. Cir. 2004) (holding that entities that were not party to an investigation, yet are affected by a general exclusion order, may raise all legal and equitable defenses in a subsequent enforcement proceeding).

under *Airless Paint Spray Pumps*.[21] While the factors set forth in *Spray Pumps* guided the GEO analysis for some time, "[t]he focus now is primarily on the statutory language [of subsection (d)(2)] itself and not an analysis of the *Spray Pump* factors."[22] That is, "[w]hile *Spray Pumps* factors may be considered, they cannot be viewed as 'imposing additional requirements beyond those identified in Section 337(d)(2).'"[23]

A determination to grant relief under Section 337(d)(2) must be anchored in substantial, reliable, and probative evidence.[24] The statute further empowers the Commission to issue a GEO even when "no person appears to contest an investigation concerning violation of this section," provided that such a violation is established by substantial, reliable, and probative evidence.[25] The Commission has issued GEOs under these circumstances in investigations with at least one defaulting respondent and other settling respondents.[26] The Commission has also issued GEOs on

---

21. *Certain Airless Paint Spray Pumps & Components Thereof (Spray Pumps)*, Inv. No. 337-TA-90, USITC Pub. 119, Comm'n Op., at 18–19, (Nov. 1981); s*ee also Certain Neodymium-Iron-Boron Magnets, Magnet Alloys, & Articles Containing the Same*, USITC Pub. 2964, Inv. No. 337-TA-372, Comm'n Op., at 5 (May 1996)) (statutory standards "do not differ significantly" from the standards set forth in *Spray Pumps*).

22. *Certain Inkjet Ink Supplies & Components Thereof*, Inv. No. 337-TA-691, USITC Pub. 4290, Initial Determination on Violation, at 29 (Nov. 2011) (citing *Certain Ground Fault Interrupters & Prods. Containing Same*, Inv, No. 337-TA-615, Comm'n Op., at 25 (Mar. 26, 2009)); *Certain Coaxial Cable Connectors & Components Thereof & Prods. Containing Same*, Inv. No. 337-TA-650, Initial Determination (unreviewed in relevant part) (Pub. Version), at 119 n.42 (Nov. 4, 2009) (declining to implement *Spray Pumps* factors).

23. *See Certain Hair Irons & Packaging Thereof (Hair Irons)*, Inv. No. 337-TA-637, Comm'n Op. (Pub. Version), at 3–5 (July 20, 2009) (citing to Initial Determination).

24. 19 U.S.C. § 1337(g)(2).

25. *See Certain Digital Multimeters, & Prods. with Multimeter Functionality*, Inv. No. 337-TA-588, Comm'n Op. (Pub. Version), at 4 (June 3, 2008) (stating the standards for finding a violation under 337(d)(2) are the same as those for finding a violation under 337(g)(2)).

26. *Id.* (finding the Commission's authority to issue a GEO arises under Section 337(d)(2) given that several respondents made appearances and have settled or entered into consent orders); *see also Certain Toner Cartridges & Components Thereof*, Inv. No. 337-TA-740, Comm'n Op. (Pub. Version), at 5 n.2 (Oct. 5, 2011) (finding Lexmark properly moved for a GEO under Section 337(d)(2) rather than Section 337(g)(2) because some of the respondents ap-

summary determination where there were no active respondents due to a combination of default and other resolutions.[27]

Continued infringement despite the efforts of the IP holder to police the market is indicative of the need for a GEO.[28] The Commission recently issued a GEO finding the statutory requirements for a general exclusion order satisfied under both Sections 337(d)(2)(A) and (B).[29] Under Section 337(d)(2)(A), the ALJ in *Towel Dispensers* determined the "conditions are ripe for circumvention of a limited exclusion order" due to evidence of low barriers to enter the U.S. market, a large number of potential entrants to the U.S market, well-established distri-

---

peared before electing to default); *Certain Plastic Molding Machs. with Control Sys. Having Programmable Operator Interfaces Incorporating Gen. Purpose Computers, & Components Thereof,* Inv. No. 337-TA-462, Comm'n Op., at 14 (Apr. 2, 2003).

27. *See Hair Irons,* Comm'n Op. (Pub. Version), at 3–5 (issuing GEO in investigation where three respondents defaulted and two others entered into consent orders); *Certain Inkjet Ink Supplies & Components Thereof,* Inv. No. 337-TA-691, Initial Determination (Pub. Version), at 3–4, 32 (Aug. 30, 2010) (unreviewed) (recommending GEO in investigation where seven respondents defaulted, three respondents settled, and one respondent was terminated on the basis of a consent order); *Certain Energy Drink Prods.,* Inv. No. 337-TA-678, Initial Determination (Pub. Version), at 39 (Mar. 30, 2010) (unreviewed) ("The Commission has recognized that it has the authority to issue a general exclusion order under 19 U.S.C. § 1337(d)(2)(A) and (B) upon summary determination where . . . the last respondents have failed to appear.").

28. *Certain Handbags, Luggage, Accessories & Packaging Thereof,* Inv. No. 337-TA-754, Order No. 16, Initial Determination Granting Complainants' Motion for Summary Determination of Violation & Recommended Determination on Remedy & Bonding, at 21 (Mar. 5, 2012) (unreviewed), (citing *Certain Toner Cartridges & Components Thereof (Toner Cartridges),* Inv. No. 337-TA-740, Order No. 26, at 35 (June 1, 2011) (relying on evidence of efforts to police violations as support for a general exclusion order)); *see also Hair Irons,* Initial Determination (Pub. Version), at 27 (Nov. 19, 2010) (unreviewed) (finding complainant's numerous district court cases to enforce its patent rights was indicative of a pattern of violation); *Certain Cigarettes & Packaging Thereof,* Inv. No. 337-TA-643, Comm'n Op., at 25 (Oct. 1, 2009) (finding pattern of violation where infringing activity continued despite complainant's enforcement efforts).

29. *Certain Elec. Paper Towel Dispensing Devices (Towel Dispensers),* Inv. No. 337-TA-718, Comm'n Op. (Pub. Version), at 16 (Jan. 20, 2012).

bution channels, and heavy U.S. consumption of, and demand for, the patented product.[30]

A GEO may also issue in cases where there is a widespread pattern of violation of Section 337 and it is difficult to identify the source of infringing products.[31] A "pattern of violation may be explained, in whole or in part, by the business conditions found to exist . . . relating to circumvention of a limited exclusion order, including the ease of market entry, low manufacturing costs, an attractive and growing U.S. market, . . . well-established distribution channels, heavy U.S. consumption, [and] demand for [the patented product] . . . ." A lucrative market for the protected product, low barriers to entry, established demand for the patented product, and availability of online market places are also evidence of a pattern of violation. In addition to demonstrating a pattern of violation of Section 337 regarding infringing products, a complainant must further show it is difficult to identify the source of the infringing products.[32]

The Commission may not exclude products of unnamed respondents unless the heightened requirements of a general exclusion order in Sections 337(d)(2)(A) or (B) are satisfied.[33] The Commission addressed the use of GEOs to obtain downstream relief against unnamed third parties in

---

30. *Towel Dispensers*, Recommended Determination, Order No. 36, at 3–4 (July 12, 2011); *see also Towel Dispensers*, Comm'n Op., at 6.

31. 19 U.S.C. § 1337(d)(2)(B).

32. *Toner Cartridges*, Comm'n Op., at 6 (finding the "sale of accused [products] over the Internet allows for anonymity of source and ease of domestic penetration"). *See also Hair Irons*, Comm'n Op. (Pub. Version), at 5 (stating that distributing products over the Internet "lends itself to anonymity and makes it difficult to determine the source of the infringing products"); *Certain Hydraulic Excavators & Components Thereof*, Inv. No. 337-TA-582, Comm'n Op. (Pub. Version), at 19 (Feb. 3, 2009) (finding complainant established it is difficult to identify the source of infringing products based on deposition testimony from settled respondents); *Certain Inkjet Ink Supplies & Components Thereof*, Inv. No. 337-TA-691, Comm'n Op. (Pub. Version), at 12 (Jan. 28, 2011) (finding complainant "met its burden" by showing "products are packaged in unmarked, generic packaging, including the use of private label services"); *Certain Inkjet Ink Supplies & Components Thereof*, Inv. No. 337-TA-730, Final Initial Determination (Pub. Version), at 31 (Aug. 3, 2011) (unreviewed).

33. *See* Section F, *infra,* on downstream relief; Kyocera Wireless Corp. v. U.S. Int'l Trade Comm'n, 545 F.3d 1340, 1358 (Fed. Cir. 2008).

Semiconductor Chips with Minimized Chip Package Size.[34] The Commission declined to issue a GEO to address downstream imports.[35] The complainant failed to show that it was difficult to identify the source of the infringing products or that there was a pattern of violation.[36] In fact, although the complainant argued that extensive and time-consuming discovery was required to identify the sources of downstream products, the Commission noted that the complainant could have moved to amend its complaint once the additional infringing entities were identified.[37]

The Commission also reemphasized that a GEO is not an appropriate remedy to exclude infringing downstream products of entities that were incorporating the accused product into their products prior to the investigation.[38] Selling the accused product for incorporation into a downstream product was a preexisting practice and, thus, not evidence of "circumvention." Further, the Commission was "not persuaded by [the complainant]'s hypothetical argument that Respondents could circumvent an LEO by 'transferring the remainder of their infringing assemblies to their customer's facilities overseas, instead of in the United States, for incorporation into finished products that are then imported into the United States.'"[39] The Commission noted that proof of a substantial magnitude of transfer would need to be clear and a complainant's mere assertion of and concern for the possibility of such a transfer was insufficient.[40] The Commission has maintained its position that a GEO is not an appropriate remedy to exclude infringing downstream products of entities that were incorporating the accused product into their products prior to the investigation.[41]

---

34. *Certain Semiconductor Chips with Minimized Chip Package Size & Prods. Containing Same,* Inv. No. 337-TA-605, Comm'n Op. (Pub. Version) (June 3, 2009).

35. *See id.* at 66–70.

36. *Id.* at 68.

37. *Id.* at 69.

38. *Id.*

39. *Id.* at 67.

40. *Id.*

41. *Semiconductor Chips with Minimized Chip Package Size & Prods. Containing Same (III),* Inv. No. 337-TA-630, Initial Determination (Pub. Version), at 162–64 (Aug. 28, 2009) (adopted in relevant part by Comm'n); *Semiconductor Chips Having Synchronous Dynamic Random Access Memory Controllers & Prods. Containing Same,* Inv. No. 337-TA-661, Comm'n Op. (Pub. Version), at 12 (Aug. 10, 2010).

C. CEASE AND DESIST ORDER (CDO)

The ITC may issue CDOs in addition to, or instead of, exclusion orders. The Commission's authority to issue CDOs derives from subsection 1337(f)(1).[42] Unlike exclusion orders that only require in rem jurisdiction, CDOs are in personam orders directed to individual respondents. These orders may issue where the respondent maintains a commercially significant inventory of infringing goods, imported prior to the Commission's determination of a Section 337 violation.

A CDO is not necessarily limited to barring the sale of inventory. For example, the Commission has also ordered companies to cease specific marketing practices and certain types of anticompetitive conduct.[43] Where a respondent maintains an e-commerce website, the Commission has issued CDOs that specifically addressed those sites.[44]

Generally, CDOs are issued only with respect to domestic respondents that maintain commercially significant domestic inventories of the infringing product.[45] Complainants bear the burden of showing the existence of commercially significant inventories of infringing products in the United States.[46] Domestic respondents that default are presumed to

---

42. 19 U.S.C. § 1337(f)(2); *Certain Abrasive Prods. Made Using a Process for Powder Preforms, & Prods. Containing Same,* Inv. No. 337-TA-449, Comm'n Op. (Pub. Version), at 6 (July 26, 2002).

43. *See, e.g., Certain Laminated Floor Panels,* Inv. No. 337-TA-545, Order to Cease & Desist (Jan. 22, 2007).

44. *See Certain Ink Cartridges & Components Thereof (Ink Cartridges),* Inv. No. 337-TA-565, Final Initial & Recommended Determinations, at 363 (Mar. 30, 2007) (*aff'd* on Comm'n review); *see also id.* (Enforcement Proceeding), Comm'n Op., at 45–47 (Sept. 24, 2009) (assessing civil penalties to respondents who sold the accused products online after the CDO was issued).

45. *See, e.g., Certain Composite Wear Components & Prods. Containing Same (Composite Wear Components),* Inv. No. 337-TA-644, Comm'n Op., at 4 (Nov. 24, 2009).

46. *Certain Flash Memory Chips & Prods. Containing Same,* Inv. No. 337-TA-664, Initial Determination, at 124–25 (Nov. 5, 2010) (citing *Certain Integrated Repeaters, Switches, Transceivers & Prods. Containing Same,* Inv. No. 337-TA-435, Comm'n Op. (Aug. 16, 2002)); *Certain Condensers, Parts Thereof & Prods. Containing Same, Including Air Conditioners for Automobiles,* USITC Pub. 3063, 337-TA-334 (Remand), Comm'n Op., at 27 (Sept. 1997) ("The well-established purpose of cease and desist orders is to ensure complete relief to complainants when infringing goods are held in inventory in the United States, and, therefore, beyond the reach of an exclusion order.").

maintain commercially significant inventories of accused products in the United States and, therefore, are subject to CDOs.[47]

It is has been the established practice of the Commission not to issue CDOs against foreign entities, because a "cease and desist order is typically an *in personam* order directed to a party in the United States and enforced by the Commission in U.S. district courts. Thus, unless a party in the United States can be compelled to do some act or refrain from doing some act by U.S. courts, a cease and desist order is inappropriate."[48]

Despite the Commission's practice, there is no express prohibition in 19 U.S.C. § 1337 against the issuance of a CDO against a foreign entity. If anything, the language of 19 U.S.C. § 1337—stating that a CDO can be issued against *"any person"*—suggests the contrary.[49] Thus, in the last few years, the Commission has issued CDOs against foreign entities in limited circumstances. For example, in *Abrasive Products*, the Commission issued a CDO against a Taiwanese respondent because it kept a do-

---

47. 19 C.F.R. § 210.16(c); *Ink Cartridges*, Comm'n Determination, at 61 (Dec. 2010) (citing *Certain Video Game Sys.*, Inv. No. 337-TA-473, Comm'n Op., at 2 (Dec. 2, 2002)); *Composite Wear Components*, Comm'n Op., at 4 (Nov. 24, 2009) (describing the Commission practice of presuming that defaulting domestic respondents "maintain significant inventories of infringing products in the United States") (citations omitted); *Certain Agric. Tractors*, USITC Pub. 3026, Inv. No. 337-TA-380, Comm'n Op., at 44 n.124 (Mar. 12, 1997).

48. *Certain Microsphere Adhesives, Process for Making Same, & Prods. Containing Same, Including Self-Stick Repositionable Notes*, USITC Pub. 2949, Inv. No. 337-TA-366, Comm'n Op. (Pub. Version), at 22 (Jan. 16, 1996); *accord, Certain Curable Fluroelastomer Compositions & Precursors Thereof*, USITC Pub. 2890, Inv. No. 337-TA-364, Comm'n Op., at 5 (May 1, 1995) ("[U]nless a party in the United States can be compelled to do some act or to refrain from doing some act, a cease and desist order is inappropriate since the jurisdiction of the Commission (and United States courts) does not extend abroad."); *see also Certain Flash Memory Circuits & Prods. Containing Same*, USITC Pub. 3046, Inv. No. 337-TA-382, Comm'n Op., at 39 (June 26, 1997) (stating that, "in light of the difficulty of enforcing such orders" the Commission does not typically issue CDOs against foreign respondents); *Certain Reclosable Plastic Bags & Tubing*, USITC Pub. 2058, Inv. No. 337-TA-266, Comm'n Op., at 5 (Jan. 1987) (refusing to issue a cease and desist order against several foreign respondents in light of "the potential difficulty of enforcing a cease and desist order issued to a foreign entity").

49. 19 U.S.C. § 1337; *see also* 19 U.S.C. § 1337(f)(1) ("[T]he Commission may issue and cause to be served on *any person* violating this section . . . an order directing such person to cease and desist from engaging in the unfair methods or acts involved . . . .") (emphasis added).

mestic agent, which sold the accused products on consignment for the respondent.[50] In *Reclosable Plastic Bags and Tubing*,[51] the presiding ALJ found that in personam jurisdiction over two foreign entities had been established where the foreign respondents responded to the investigation in some fashion, without asserting the defense of lack of personal jurisdiction.[52] In *Toner Cartridges*, the Commission accepted the ALJ's recommendation to issue CDOs against defaulting a foreign respondent where "that respondent's domestic distributor has maintained a commercially significant inventory in the United States."[53]

Thus, while it has not been tested that one may obtain a CDO against a foreign respondent, it is certainly not without precedent.

D. TEMPORARY EXCLUSION ORDER

Upon proper motion filed with the complaint, a TEO may be imposed after an early determination by the Commission that there is reason to believe a violation of Section 337 is occurring, under a standard identical to that for a preliminary injunction in district court.[54] The decision on entry of a TEO must be issued within 90 days after initiation of the investigation or, in more complicated cases, within 150 days.[55] The ITC may also issue temporary cease and desist orders if it issues a TEO.[56]

---

50. *Certain Abrasive Prods. Made Using a Process for Powder Preforms, & Prods. Containing Same*, Inv. No. 337-TA-449, Comm'n Op., at 7 (July 26, 2002); *see also Certain Semiconductor Memory Devices & Prods. Containing Same*, Inv. No. 337-TA-414, 1999 WL 1267282, at *5 (Dec. 13, 1999) (recommending CDO against foreign respondent to "prevent it from transferring infringing products to the United States").

51. Inv. No. 337-TA-266, Initial Determination (Jan. 29, 1988).

52. *Id.*

53. *Certain Toner Cartridges & Components Thereof,* Inv. No. 337-TA-740, Comm'n Op., at 7 (Oct. 5, 2011).

54. 19 U.S.C. § 1337(e)(2); 19 C.F.R. § 210.52(a).

55. These statutory time limits are a hold-over from the 1974 amendments to Section 337 not modified by the Uruguay Amendments Act of 1994. S. Rep. 1298, 93d Cong., 2d Sess. 198 (1974).

56. *Certain Hardware Logic Emulation Systems & Components Thereof*, Inv. No. 337-TA-383, Notice of Comm'n Decision Not to Modify or Vacate an Initial Determination Granting Temporary Relief, and Issuance of a Temporary Limited Exclusion Order & a Temporary Cease & Desist Order, Subject to Posting of Bond by Complainant, 61 Fed. Reg. 41,652 (Aug. 9, 1996).

A complainant seeking a TEO bears a heavy burden of proving that it is likely to prevail in the permanent relief phase of this investigation.[57] The motion must contain a detailed statement of specific facts bearing on: (1) the likelihood of the patentee's success on the merits; (2) irreparable harm to the petitioner if the injunction is not granted; (3) the balance of hardships between the parties; and (4) the public interest."[58]

As is the case with preliminary injunctions in district court, TEOs are infrequently granted because of this high burden.[59] Irreparable harm is usually the most disputed issue in a hearing on a motion for a TEO. Temporary relief at the ITC may be granted *only* where irreparable harm is likely to occur during the temporary relief period itself.[60] Harm is considered irreparable when "monetary damages cannot be calculated with a reasonable degree or certainty or will not adequately compensate the injured party."[61] Where monetary damages are available in district court, however, there is no likelihood of irreparable harm.[62] A complainant must also show that the accused products, and not some other factor—such as another competitor or market conditions—will cause the irreparable harm.[63]

---

57. Nat'l Steel Car, Ltd. v. Canadian Pac. Railway, Ltd., 357 F.3d 1319, 1324 (Fed. Cir. 2004) ("A preliminary injunction is a 'drastic and extraordinary remedy that is not to be routinely granted.'") (citation omitted).

58. 19 C.F.R. § 210.52(a); Procter & Gamble Co. v. Kraft Foods Global, Inc., 549 F.3d 842, 847 (Fed. Cir. 2008).

59. The last successful attempt at obtaining a TEO was in 1996 in *Certain Hardware Logic Emulation & Systems & Components Thereof,* Inv. No. 337-TA-483.

60. *Certain Vacuum Packaging Machs.,* Inv. No. 337-TA-496 Order No. 36: Initial Determination [Denying] Temporary Relief (adopted in relevant part by the Commission), 2003 WL 23210691, at *6 (Dec. 16, 2003); *see also* Mikohn Gaming Corp. v. Acres Gaming, Inc., 165 F.3d 891, 895 (Fed. Cir. 1998) ("Thus, the proper inquiry during the temporary relief phase of a section 337 investigation is what irreparable harm, if any, a complainant will suffer during the pendency of an investigation if temporary relief is not granted.").

61. *Certain Silicon Microphone Packages & Prods. Containing Same,* 337-TA-695, Initial Determination, at 92-103 (Mar. 24, 2010) (aff'd on Comm'n review) (citations omitted) (denying temporary relief and finding complainant failed to prove irreparable harm likely).

62. Automated Merch. Sys., Inc. v. Crane Co., 357 Fed. Appx. 297, 301 (Fed. Cir. 2009) (holding that the burden is on the patentee to prove that its potential losses cannot be compensated by monetary damages).

63. *See Certain Muzzle-Loading Firearms & Components Thereof (Muzzle-Loading Firearms),* Inv. No. 337-TA-777, Initial Determination [Denying]

Moreover, to discourage frivolous requests, the ITC may require complainants to post a bond as a prerequisite to receiving temporary relief.[64] Section 337(e)(2) provides that "[t]he Commission may require the complainant to post a bond as a prerequisite to the issuance of an order under this subsection." In determining whether to require complainants to post a bond, the Commission will "be guided by practice under Rule 65 of the Federal Rules of Civil Procedure," which requires bond set at an amount appropriate to offset the costs and damages sustained if a party is later found wrongfully enjoined.[65]

E. BOND

As set forth in both Section 337 and the Commission's regulations, respondents can continue to import during the 60-day period for Presidential review of Commission remedial orders, if a bond is posted sufficient to "protect complainant from any injury."[66] Long-standing Commission precedent makes clear that "[t]he bond should not be set so high as to effectively prevent importation during the Presidential review period."[67] Additionally, it is "[t]he complainant [that] has the burden of supporting any proposition it advances, including the amount of bond."[68] An ALJ is

---

Compl. Mot. for Temp. Relief, at 46–54 (Aug. 31, 2011) (unreviewed); *see also Certain Dynamic Sequential Gradient Compression Devices & Components & Parts Thereof,* Inv. No. 337-TA-335, Comm. Op., at 69, 72 (June 22, 1992) (finding Respondents' sales cannot automatically be considered lost sales of Complainant, where there were other market factors); *Certain Pressure Transmitters,* Inv. No. 337-TA-304, Comm'n Op., at 35 (1990) (finding it unlikely that any market share gained by Respondents would be entirely at complainant's expense, where there were other market factors).

64. 19 C.F.R. § 210.68; *see also Muzzle-Loading Firearms,* Initial Determination [Denying] Compl. Mot. for Temp. Relief, at 60; *Certain Crystalline Cefadroxil Monohydrate,* USITC Pub. No. 2240, Inv. No. 337-TA-293, Comm'n Op., at 50 (Nov. 1989).

65. 19 C.F.R. § 210.52(c); FED. R. CIV. P. 65(c).

66. 19 U.S.C. § 1337(j)(3); *see also* 19 C.F.R. § 210.50(a)(3).

67. *Certain Digital Televisions & Certain Prods. Containing Same & Methods of Using Same,* Inv. No. 337-TA-617, Comm'n Op., at 19 (Apr. 23, 2009).

68. *Certain Rubber Antidegradants, Components Thereof & Prods. Containing Same,* USITC Pub. 3975, Inv. No. 337-TA-533, Comm'n Op., at 40 (July 21, 2006); *see also Certain Silicone Microphone Packages & Prods. Containing Same,* Inv. No. 337-TA-629, Initial Determination, at 222 (Feb. 10, 2009) (aff'd on Comm'n review) (finding complainant had "failed to meet its burden in supporting its argument that a 100% bond is appropriate").

not required to recommend any bond amount if the complainant does not, as a threshold matter, establish the need for a bond.[69]

1. Determination of the Appropriate Bond

The purpose of the bond is to protect the complainant from any injury.[70] "When reliable price information is available, the Commission has often set the bond by eliminating the differential in sales price between the domestic product and the lower price of the infringing imported product."[71] For example, in *Electrical Connectors*, the Commission found that respondent's connectors typically sold for 15-20 percent below complainant's product, and thus ordered respondents to pay a 20 percent bond on the entered value of any imported infringing products.[72] In contrast, "where . . . variations in pricing make price comparisons complicated and difficult, the Commission typically has set a 100 percent bond."[73] For example, in circumstances where "there are a vast number of websites selling" the infringing article, the Commission has set a 100 percent bond.[74]

69. *Certain Liquid Crystal Display Devices and Prods. Containing Same*, Inv. No. 337-TA-631, Final Initial & Recommended Determination, at 223–25 (Jan. 26, 2009) (aff'd in relevant part on Comm'n review).

70. 19 C.F.R. §§ 210.42(a)(1)(h), 210.50(a)(3).

71. *Certain Cigarettes & Packaging Thereof (Cigarettes)*, Inv. No. 337-TA-643, Order No. 23, Recommended Determination as to Remedy & Bonding, 2009 WL 809540, at *8 (Mar. 18, 2009) (citing *Certain Microsphere Adhesives, Process for Making Same, & Prods. Containing Same, Including Self-Stick Repositionable Notes (Microsphere Adhesives)*, USITC Pub. 2949, Inv. No. 337-TA-366, Comm'n Op., at 24 (Dec. 15, 1995)).

72. *Certain Elec. Connectors & Prods. Containing Same*, USITC Pub. 2981, Inv. No. 337-TA-374, Comm'n Op., at 20–22 (July 1996).

73. *Cigarettes*, Order No. 23, 2009 WL 809540, at *8 (citing *Microsphere Adhesives*, Comm'n Op., at 24); *Digital Multimeters, & Prods. with Multimeter Functionality (Digital Multimeters)*, Inv. No. 337-TA-588, Comm'n Op., at 12–13 (June 3, 2008) (finding 100 percent bond where each respondent set its price differently, preventing clear differentials between the complainant's products and the infringing imports).

74. *Cigarettes*, Comm'n Op., at 8–9 (Oct. 1, 2009); *see also Digital Multimeters*, Comm'n Op., at 12–13 (June 3, 2008) (finding 100 percent bond where each respondent set its price differently, preventing clear differentials between the complainant's products and the infringing imports); *Certain Variable Speed Wind Turbines & Components Thereof*, Inv. No. 337-TA-376, Comm'n Op., at 46 (Sept. 23, 1996) (setting the bond at 100% "because of the difficulty in quantifying the cost advantages of respondents' imported Enercon wind turbines and because of price fluctuations due to exchange rates and market fluctuations due to exchange rates and market conditions").

Alternatively, the Commission may rely on royalty rates in order to set the appropriate bond.[75] For example, where the respondent's prices are equal to or greater than those of the complainant, the Commission has set the bond at a reasonable royalty rate.[76]

2. Bond Forfeiture Proceedings

Assuming, as is typically the case, that the President does not set aside the Commission's remedial order(s), "proceedings to determine whether a respondent's bond should be forfeited to a complainant in whole or part may be initiated upon the filing of a motion by a complainant within 30 days after expiration of the Presidential review period [(PRP)] under 19 U.S.C. § 1337(j)."[77] Conversely, a "respondent may file a motion for the return of its bond."[78] The issues adjudicated during a bond forfeiture proceeding are limited to bond coverage and the amount owed under the Commission's bond order.[79]

---

75. *See, e.g., Certain Mobile Tel. Handsets, Wireless Commc'n Devices, & Components Thereof,* Inv. No. 337-TA-578, Final & Initial Determinations, 2007 WL 4872686, at *138 (Dec. 12, 2007) ("The Commission may also rely on royalty rates established on the basis of license agreements or other reliable evidence of an appropriate royalty rate for the patents at issue."); *Certain Semiconductor Chips with Minimized Chip Package Size & Prods. Containing Same,* Inv. No. 337-TA-432, Recommended Determination on Remedy & Bonding (Oct. 1, 2001); *Certain Integrated Circuit Telecomm. Chips & Prods. Containing Same, Including Dialing Apparatus,* Inv. No. 337-TA-337 (1993) (setting bond at 8% per infringing chip based on a reasonable royalty rate); *Certain Acid-Washed Denim Garments & Accessories,* Inv. No. 337-TA-324, Comm'n Op., at 28 (Aug. 6, 1992) (basing 3.75% bond on previous royalty rate).

76. *Certain Abrasive Prods. Made Using a Process for Power Preforms & Prods. Containing Same,* USITC Pub. 3530, Inv. No. 337-TA-449, Comm'n Op. on Remedy, the Public Interest, and Bonding, at 9–10 (July 26, 2002).

77. 19 C.F.R. § 210.50(d)(1)(i). *See also Certain Semiconductor Chips with Minimized Chip Package Size & Prods. Containing Same,* Inv. No. 337-TA-605, Comm'n Notice (May 18, 2012) (determining not to review an ID denying respondent's motion for return of its bond).

78. 19 C.F.R. § 210.50(d)(1)(ii). *See also* Proposed Rules, 77 Fed. Reg. 41,124 (adding that a motion for return or forfeiture of a bond may be made, if an appeal is taken from the Commission determination, within 30 days of the resolution of the appeal) (proposed July 11, 2012) (to be codified at 19 C.F.R. pt. 210).

79. *Certain Lens-Fitted Film Packages (LFFPs),* Inv. No. 337-TA-406 (Bond Forfeiture Proceeding), Order No. 52, at 5 (Oct. 14, 1999).

The amount of the bond forfeited to the complainant can be the full amount posted for covered articles imported during the Presidential review period.[80] In deciding on the amount of forfeiture, the ALJ and the Commission are guided by the principles of Rule 65 of the Federal Rules of Civil Procedure, which concerns recovery of preliminary injunction bonds.[81] It is important to note that under Rule 65, a "party's proof of damages 'd[oes] not need to be to a mathematical certainty.'"[82] Moreover, "[w]hen the amount of the damages cannot be ascertained with precision, any doubts regarding the amount must be resolved against the infringer."[83]

In *Lens-Fitted Film Packages*, the ALJ analyzed the number of covered products sold and covered products imported and sold during the PRP, as well as the nature of the market for those products, in order to determine the appropriate level of bond forfeiture.[84] The respondent argued that the complainant had not proven damages, an argument the ALJ rejected because the respondent admittedly imported and sold covered products for consumption during the PRP.[85] To determine the complainant's damages for the covered products, the ALJ turned for guidance to the Federal Circuit's opinion in *Panduit v. Stahlin Brothers Fibre Works,* which set forth the following analysis:

---

80. *See Certain Semiconductor Chips with Minimized Chip Package Size & Prods. Containing Same (Semiconductor Chips)*, Inv. No. 337-TA-605, Order No. 68 (Initial Determination), at 9 (Apr. 2, 2012) (unreviewed) (noting that certain respondents had agreed to forfeit the entirety of its posted bond amount); *see also generally Semiconductor Chips*, Inv. No. 337-TA-605, Order No. 71 (Initial Determination) (Apr. 24, 2012) (unreviewed) (granting joint motion of complainant and certain respondents requesting an initial determination after the respondents agreed to pay complainant the bond amount posted during the presidential review period).

81. 19 C.F.R. § 210.50(d)(3); *LFFPs* (Bond Forfeiture Proceeding), Initial Determination, at 14, 39 (May 29, 2003) (damages accrued are "assessed under Rule 65 and limited to actual damages directly attributable to the Commission's remedial orders").

82. Nokia Corp. v. Interdigital, Inc., 645 F.3d 553, 559 (Fed. Cir. 2011) (citing Global NAPs, Inc. v. Verizon New Eng., Inc., 489 F.3d 13, 24 (1st Cir. 2007)).

83. Gyromat Corp. v. Champion Spark Plug Co., 735 F.2d 549, 554–55 (Fed. Cir. 1984).

84. *LFFPs* (Bond Forfeiture Proceeding), Order No. 52, at 5 (Oct. 14, 1999).

85. *LFFPs* (Bond Forfeiture Proceeding), Initial Determination, at 10.

To obtain as damages the profits on sales he would have made absent the infringement, i.e., the sales made by the infringer, a patent owner must prove: (1) demand for the patented product, (2) absence of acceptable noninfringing substitutes, (3) his manufacturing and marketing capability to exploit the demand, and (4) the amount of the profit he would have made.[86]

The ALJ found that all four of the requirements were met, given: (1) that demand existed, as the respondent sold the covered products during the PRP; (2) an absence of acceptable non-infringing substitutes because the respondent, complainant, and complainant's licensee all competed for sales of the covered products; (3) that the complainant and its licensee would have been able to exploit the increased demand in the absence of the respondent's infringing sales; and (4) the complainant had previously profited from sales of the covered products and could therefore fairly estimate its lost profits and royalties.[87] Additionally, a recovering complainant is entitled to pre-judgment interest, which is calculated based on Moody's AAA monthly average corporate bond rate.[88]

F. DOWNSTREAM RELIEF

In *Kyocera Wireless Corp. v. U.S. International Trade Commission*, the Federal Circuit determined that, contrary to its long-standing practice, the Commission does not have the statutory authority in an LEO to exclude "downstream" products, i.e., products of unnamed respondents that incorporate infringing products of named respondents.[89] The Federal Circuit held that the Commission's authority to exclude products in an LEO is restricted to products of the named respondents in an investigation.[90] The Commission may not exclude products of unnamed respondents unless the heightened requirements of a GEO in Sections 337(d)(2)(A) or (B) are satisfied.[91] However, the Commission may still exclude down-

---

86. *LFFPs* (Bond Forfeiture Proceeding), Initial Determination, at 40 (citing Panduit Corp. v. Stahlin Bros. Fibre Works, Inc., 575 F.2d 1152, 1156 (6th Cir. 1978)).

87. *Id.* at 41.

88. *Id.* at 51–53.

89. Kyocera Wireless Corp. v. U.S. Int'l Trade Comm'n, 545 F.3d 1340, 1355–58 (Fed. Cir. 2008).

90. *Id.* at 1356.

91. *Id.* at 1358.

stream products of the named respondents in a limited exclusion order after weighing the "*EPROM* factors."[92] The Commission has historically used the nine *EPROM* factors in determining whether to extend exclusion orders to downstream products of named respondents[93]:

(1) the value of the infringing products compared to value of the downstream products in which they are incorporated;

(2) whether the downstream products are manufactured by the party found to have committed the unfair act, or by third parties;

(3) the incremental value to complainant of the exclusion of downstream products;

(4) the incremental detriment to respondents of such exclusion;

(5) the burdens imposed on third parties by excluding downstream products;

(6) the availability of alternative downstream products that do not contain the infringing articles;

(7) the likelihood that imported downstream products actually contain the infringing articles and are thereby subject to exclusion;

(8) the opportunity for evasion of an exclusion order that does not include downstream products; and

(9) the enforceability of an order by Customs.[94]

---

92. *See, e.g., Certain Semiconductor Chips & Prods. Containing Same,* Inv. No. 337-TA-753, Initial Determination, at 372 (Mar. 2, 2012) (unreviewed in relevant part); *Certain Liquid Crystal Display Modules, Prods. Containing Same, & Methods Using Same,* Inv. No. 337-TA-634, Comm'n Op., at 4 (Nov. 24, 2009) (adopting the ALJ's *EPROM* analysis stating "[i]n determining whether an exclusion order should extend to downstream products, the Commission applies a test first articulated in [*EPROM*]"; *Certain Semiconductor Chips with Minimized Chip Package Size & Prods. Containing Same (III) (Semiconductor Chips III),* Inv. No. 337-TA-630, USITC Pub. 4209, Initial Determination on Violation, at 166–67 (Sept. 25, 2009) (unreviewed).

93. *Certain Baseband Processor Chips & Chipsets, Transmitter, & Receiver (Radio) Chips, Power Control Chips, & Prods. Containing Same, Including Cellular Tel. Handsets,* Inv. No. 337-TA-543, Comm'n Determination, at 31–115 (Oct. 2011).

94. *See Certain Erasable Programmable Read-only Memories, Components Thereof, Prods. Containing Such Memories, & Processes for Making Such Memories (EPROM),* USITC Pub. 2196, Inv. No. 337-TA-276, Comm'n Op. (Pub. Version), at 125 (May 1989); *see also Semiconductor Chips III,* Initial Determination on Violation, at 165–66.

In the wake of *Kyocera*, the need to consider the *EPROM* factors has been diminished. In *Flash Memory*, the ALJ stated that the *EPROM* factors were not relevant to the investigation because the downstream entity at issue was a named respondent.[95] Subsequently in *Flash Memory Chips*, the ALJ denied complainant's motion to supplement its expert report regarding *EPROM* factors because the respondents accused of incorporating the products at issue were named in the investigation.[96] The ALJ further stated "[t]he Commission's concern articulated in EPROMs has been obviated by the [*Kyocera* decision] . . . . Because a limited exclusion order only applies to named respondents in an investigation, there is no worry that a limited exclusion order will "disrupt legitimate trade in products which were not themselves the subject of a finding of violation of section 337."[97]

Since *Kyocera*, the Commission has also addressed the use of a GEO to obtain downstream relief against unnamed third parties. In *GPS Devices*, the Commission found insufficient evidence to issue a GEO and denied complainant's request for downstream relief against any unnamed respondent.[98] Specifically, the Commission held "the overwhelming majority of infringing SiRF GPS chips enter the United States as components of 'downstream' products rather than as individual chips" and the "non-respondent manufacturers that continue to import products incorporating infringing articles cannot be deemed to have 'circumvented' an exclusion order by merely continuing their pre-existing practice."[99] The Commission did note, however, that:

---

95. *Certain Flash Memory & Prods. Containing Same*, Inv. No. 337-TA-685, Initial Determination, at 109 n.36 (Feb. 28, 2011) (unreviewed due to parties' settlement).

96. *Certain Flash Memory Chips & Prods. Containing Same*, Inv. No. 337-TA-735, Order No. 32, at 8–9 (May 9, 2011) (unreviewed due to parties' settlement).

97. *Id.* at 8 (citing *EPROM*, Inv. No. 337-TA-276, Comm'n Op. at 125 (stating the purpose of the *EPROM* factors)); *see also Certain Elec. Devices with Image Processing Sys., Components Thereof, & Associated Software*, Inv. No. 337-TA-724, Order No. 25 (Mar. 4, 2011), (stating that expert testimony concerning the *EPROM* factors is irrelevant to the determination of the scope of a limited exclusion order).

98. *Certain GPS Devices & Prods. Containing Same*, Inv. No. 337-TA-602, Comm'n Op. (Pub. Version), at 17–18 (Jan. 27, 2009).

99. *Id.* (further holding that complainant had not shown a pattern of violation or that it would be difficult to identify the source of the infringing products).

We do not view the Court's opinion in *Kyocera* as affecting the issuance of LEOs that exclude infringing products made by respondents found to be violating Section 337, but imported by another entity. The exclusionary language in this regard that is traditionally included in LEOs is consistent with 19 U.S.C. § 1337(a)(1)(B)–(D) and 19 U.S.C. § 1337(d)(1).[100]

As noted above, the Commission has maintained its position that a GEO is not an appropriate remedy to exclude infringing downstream products of entities that were incorporating the accused product into their products prior to the investigation.[101] In light of the Commission's post-*Kyocera* decisions on downstream relief and heightened requirements of a GEO under Sections 337(d)(2)(A) or (B), complainants should name as respondents any known importer of infringing products, including downstream products, in order to obtain full and complete relief.[102]

G. TEMPORARY RESCISSION OF REMEDY

The Commission has the authority to rescind or temporarily rescind a remedial order. Section 337(k)(l) provides that any exclusion order or cease and desist order continues in effect until the conditions that led to the order no longer exist.[103] Section 337(k)(2) specifically allows the Commission to modify or rescind a remedial order when the Federal Rules of Civil Procedure "would permit relief from a judgment or order."[104] Relief is available under the Federal Rules of Civil Procedure when, subsequent to a judgment, conditions that led to the judgment

---

100. *Id.* at 17 n.6.
101. *Certain Semiconductor Chips with Minimized Chip Package Size & Prods. Containing Same,* Inv. No. 337-TA-605, Comm'n Op. (Pub. Version) (June 3, 2009); *Certain Semiconductor Chips with Minimized Chip Package Size & Prods. Containing Same (III),* Inv. No. 337-TA-630, Initial Determination, at 162–64 (Aug. 28, 2009); *Semiconductor Chips Having Synchronous Dynamic Random Access Memory Controllers & Prods. Containing Same,* Inv. No. 337-TA-661, Comm'n Op. (Pub. Version), at 12 (Aug. 10, 2010).
102. For an in-depth discussion of these issues in the post-*Kyocera* context, *see* V. James Adduci II & Michael L. Doane, *Availability of General Exclusion Orders Providing Downstream Relief After Semiconductor Chips, in* THE COMPUTER AND INTERNET LAW (Nov. 2009).
103. 19 U.S.C. § 1337(k)(1).
104. *Id.* at § 1337(k)(2)(B); *see also* 19 C.F.R. § 210.76(a)(2).

have changed.[105] Petitions under Section 337(k) and 19 C.F.R § 210.76 to rescind the Commission's remedial orders are filed before the Commission, not the ALJ who presided over the investigation.[106]

In *Composite Wear Components*, the Commission determined to temporarily rescind its limited exclusion order and cease and desist order pending resolution of an appeal at the Federal Circuit.[107] The respondent chose to not to participate in the ITC investigation filed against it and, instead, informed the ALJ that it intended to seek redress against complainant's allegations in the U.S. district court by initiating an action seeking a declaratory judgment that its products do not infringe and that the asserted patent is invalid and unenforceable. Consequently, the ALJ found the respondent in default, and the Commission issued an LEO and CDO against respondent. Subsequently, the district court found the asserted patent invalid, and the complainant filed a notice of appeal with the Federal Circuit.[108]

In granting respondent's petition, the Commission determined to temporarily rescind the remedial orders, rather than to do so permanently, taking into account the possibility the Federal Circuit could reverse the district court's invalidity finding. The Commission did state, however, that the remedial orders would be permanently rescinded if the Federal Circuit affirmed the district court and would, conversely, be reinstated if the Federal Circuit reversed the district court.[109]

The Commission distinguished its determination from that in *Steel Rod* where the Commission revoked its prior exclusion order, issued a

---

105. A judgment may be set aside or modified if: (1) The judgment was subject to modification by its own terms or by applicable law, and events have occurred subsequent to the judgment that warrant modification of the contemplated kind; or (2) There has been such a substantial change in the circumstances that giving continued effect to the judgment is unjust. RESTATEMENT (SECOND) OF JUDGMENTS § 73 CHANGED CONDITION.

106. *See* Proposed Rules, 77 Fed. Reg. 41,125 (proposing that parties may submit comments within 10 days of service of the recommended determination, and may submit responses thereto within 5 business days from service of any comments) (proposed July 11, 2012) (to be codified at 19 C.F.R. pt. 210).

107. *Certain Composite Wear Components & Prods. Containing Same (Composite Wear Components)*, Inv. No. 337-TA-644, Comm'n Op. (Pub. Version), at 1 (Feb. 10, 2011).

108. *Id.* at 5.

109. *Id.* at 9.

new order under Section 337(e),[110] and allowed importation under bond pending final determination of the district court's ruling.[111] In *Steel Rod*, the district court in a parallel proceeding declared the asserted patent invalid during the Presidential review period. In issuing a new exclusion order under 100% bond pursuant to then-existing Section 337(e), the Commission emphasized that there was a direct conflict between the Commission's determination and the district court's decision regarding invalidity of the patent that turned on differing interpretations of law, which was to be resolved by the Federal Circuit.[112] Unlike the facts of *Steel Rod*, the respondent in the *Composite Wear Components* investigation was found in default and the ALJ did not reach the merits of the case. Thus, unlike *Steel Rod*, there was no contradiction between the Commission and district court's interpretation of the law, and temporary rescission of the remedial orders until final ruling by the Federal Circuit was appropriate.[113]

---

110. Section 337(e) applies the preliminary injunction standard for the federal courts for temporary relief granted by the Commission. Section 337(e) states, "The Commission may grant preliminary relief under this subsection or subsection (f) of this section to the same extent as preliminary injunctions and temporary restraining orders may be granted under the Federal Rules of Civil Procedure." 19 U.S.C. §1337(e)(3).

111. *Composite Wear Components*, Comm'n Op., at 7 (citing *Certain Steel Rod Treating Apparatus & Components Thereof* ("*Steel Rod*"), Inv. No. 337-TA-97, Comm'n Op., at 6 (Jan. 15, 1982)).

112. *Id.* at 11 (citing *Steel Rod*, Comm'n Op., at 9–13).

113. *Id.* at 12 (providing further that the 1988 Amendments to Section 337 changed the standard for granting temporary relief since *Steel Rod*, adding the federal court preliminary standard to 337(e)(3)).

CHAPTER 12

Interlocutory Appeals of ALJ Decisions, Commission Review, Public Interest, and Presidential Review

A. INTERLOCUTORY APPEALS OF ALJ DECISIONS

While the Commission has the final decision-making power in Section 337 proceedings, the ALJ is charged with conducting the day-to-day progress of an investigation. Typically, an ALJ's rulings may not be appealed to the Commission prior to the ALJ's issuance of a final ID on the merits of the investigation, unless the ruling is in the form of a non-final ID.[1] The issuance of any ID, whether a final ID on violation or

---

1. The Commission Rules provide that certain ALJ determinations should be issued in the form of an ID. 19 C.F.R. §§ 210.42(a)–(c) (2012). Unless an ALJ determination is among the types enumerated, an ALJ's determination is not an ID, even if an ALJ attempts to issue it in the form of an ID. Notably, an ALJ's effort to obtain interlocutory review on the issue of claim construction was rejected by the Commission. In that investigation, *Mobile Telephones and Wireless Communication Devices Featuring Digital Cameras*, the ALJ issued a *Markman* ruling as an ID. *Certain Mobile Tels. & Wireless Commc'n Devices Featuring Digital Cameras, & Components Thereof,* Inv. No. 337-TA-703, Notice of Comm'n Determination, at 2 (Oct. 20, 2010). The Commission declined to address the substance of the *Markman* ruling, finding that claim construction is not included in the list of issues that must be decided by ID and is not properly the subject of a motion for summary determination because claim construction "is not an 'issue' or 'any part of an issue'" within

another type of ID defined by the Commission Rules,[2] invokes the standard mechanism by which parties may petition for review of an ID.[3]

Under a specific set of limited circumstances, however, a party may also appeal ALJ decisions that are issued as orders, not as IDs. Commission Rule 210.24 states that a party may seek an interlocutory appeal provided it does not pertain to a motion for temporary relief decided by the ALJ prior to the issuance of an ID on that form of relief.[4] There are two types of interlocutory appeals—appeals without leave of the ALJ, which are also referred to as appeals by right, and appeals with leave of the ALJ. The Commission exercises its discretion to allow interlocutory appeals, whether by right or with leave of the ALJ, very rarely. The parties have an appeal by right in a very limited set of circumstances. The Commission has discretion to hear appeals without leave of the ALJ when an ALJ ruling either (1) requires the disclosure of Commission records or the appearance of government officials under Commission Rule 210.32(c)(2), or (2) denies an application for intervention under Commission Rule 210.19.[5] However, even where a party has an appeal by right, the Commission may not necessarily grant the appealing party's application.[6]

A party may also seek leave from the ALJ to file an interlocutory appeal of the ALJ's orders with the Commission. A party seeking such an appeal must file a request with the ALJ, and the ALJ must find (1) that the ruling "involves a controlling question of law or policy as to which there is substantial ground for difference of opinion," and (2) "that either an immediate appeal from the ruling may materially advance the ultimate completion of the investigation or subsequent review will be an

---

the meaning of Commission Rule 210.18. Accordingly, claim construction and other issues not explicitly included on the list of issues that must be decided as an ID and not covered by Commission Rule 210.18 regarding summary determination are unavailable for interlocutory review, except through the limited interlocutory appeal procedures available to litigants under Commission Rule 210.24.

2. 19 C.F.R. §§ 210.42(a)–(c). *See also* Rules of General Application, Adjudication, and Enforcement (Proposed Rules), 77 Fed. Reg. 41,124 (proposed July 11, 2012) (to be codified at 19 C.F.R. pt. 210).

3. 19 C.F.R. § 210.42(h).

4. *See* 19 C.F.R. §§ 210.24, 210.64.

5. *Id.* at § 210.24(a).

6. *See id.* (noting that the Commission "may" entertain interlocutory appeals in these two situations).

inadequate remedy."[7] The moving party bears the heavy burden of showing that these two criteria are satisfied.[8] If the ALJ so finds, he or she will certify the matter to the Commission. Any application for review under Commission Rule 210.24(b) must be less than 16 pages in length and must be filed within five business days after service of the ALJ's ruling.[9]

A question of law is considered controlling "if its resolution is quite likely to affect the further course of the litigation, even if not certain to do so."[10] If there is substantial ground for a difference of opinion, an issue of first impression to the Commission,[11] or unprecedented action by the Commission, the question of law might be deemed controlling.[12] Merely arguing that an ALJ applied the law to the facts incorrectly is insufficient to meet this first prong of Commission Rule 210.24(b).

The second prong necessary to obtain interlocutory review requires a finding that the appeal will materially advance the investigation toward ultimate completion or that future review will be inadequate. In *Bearings*,

---

7. *Id.* at § 210.24(b); *see also Certain Integrated Circuits, Chipsets, and Prods. Containing Same Including Televisions, Media Players, & Cameras*, Inv. No. 337-TA-709, Order No. 12 (July 28, 2010); *Certain Personal Computer/Consumer Elec. Convergent Devices, Components Thereof, & Prods. Containing Same*, Inv. No. 337-TA-558, Order No. 17 (Sept. 8, 2006); *Certain Bearings & Packaging Thereof (Bearings)*, Inv. No. 337-TA-469, Order No. 16 (July 10, 2002).

8. 19 C.F.R. § 210.24(b); *see also Bearings*, Order No. 16; *Certain Network Interface Cards & Access Points for Use in Direct Sequence Spread Spectrum Wireless Local Area Networks & Prods. Containing Same*, Inv. No. 337-TA-455, Order No. 28, at 4 (Aug. 17, 2001).

9. 19 C.F.R. § 210.24(b)(3).

10. *Certain Personal Computer/Consumer Elec. Convergent Devices, Components Thereof, & Prods. Containing Same*, Inv. No. 337-TA-558, Order No. 17, at 5 (Sept. 8, 2006) (quoting Sokaogon Gaming Enter. Corp. v. Tushie-Montgomery Assoc., Inc., 86 F.3d 656, 659 (7th Cir. 1996) (internal quotations omitted)).

11. *Certain Catalyst Components & Catalysts for the Polymerization of Olefins*, Inv. No. 337-TA-307, Order No. 15, at 6–7 (Apr. 11, 1990).

12. *Certain Network Interface Cards & Access Points for Use in Direct Sequence Spread Spectrum Wireless Local Area Networks & Prods. Containing Same (Network Interface Cards)*, Inv. No. 337-TA-455, Order No. 28, at 7– 8 (Aug. 17, 2001); *Bearings,* Order No. 16, at 11–12; *Certain Home Vacuum Packaging Machs.*, Inv. No. 337-TA-496, Order No. 52, at 5 (Mar. 17, 2004); *see also* Michael Lindinger, *Interlocutory Appeals of Administrative Law Judge Orders*, 22 ITCTLA 337 REPORTER 81, 81–86 (2006) (4th Summer Assoc. Ed.).

the ALJ found that interlocutory review is appropriate where resolution of the question at hand would "greatly affect the scope and course of [the] investigation," such as eliminating an entire claim under Section 337 from the investigation.[13] In that instance, the ALJ held that significantly narrowing the issues for discovery and at the scheduled hearing constituted a material advance toward the completion of the investigation.[14]

If the ALJ determines in writing that the issue presented meets these two criteria, the party seeking appeal may file an application within five days after service of the ALJ's determination.[15] The nonmoving parties then have five business days after service of the application to file a reply, after which time the Commission may permit an appeal.[16] This decision is completely within the Commission's discretion. Unless the Commission orders otherwise, any appeal will be confined to the application for review, along with any response filed by the nonmoving parties, with no further briefing or oral arguments.[17] The filing of an application for review under Commission Rule 210.24 does not stay an investigation unless the ALJ or Commission so orders.[18]

An alternative to filing an application for interlocutory review during an investigation is to file a motion for reconsideration. Instead of petitioning the Commission to review the order, this motion requests that the ALJ reconsider his own ruling. Even if the ALJ grants a motion to reconsider, however, he or she may still arrive at the same conclusion on the matter.[19]

B. COMMISSION REVIEW

Commission review gives the Commission the opportunity to place its imprimatur on every decided case. While the ALJ is the fact finder and

---

13. *Bearings*, Order No. 16, at 3, 13 (granting interlocutory review of an order denying a motion for a partial summary determination that a complainant's "unfair pecuniary benefits" claim does not allege an unfair act under Section 337 and that the investigation should therefore be terminated as to this claim).

14. *Id.* at 13.

15. 19 C.F.R. § 210.24(b)(3).

16. *Id.*

17. *Id.*

18. *Id.* at § 210.24(c).

19. *Network Interface Cards*, Order No. 67 at 3 (Dec. 10, 2001) (citing *Network Interface Cards*, Order No. 26, at 8 (Aug. 17, 2001)).

decides all issues in the first instance, the final decision is that of the Commission, which may adopt, revise, reverse, or take no position on each of the ALJ's determinations.

Pursuant to Commission Rule 210.43(b), parties may appeal the ID of the ALJ by filing a petition for review with the Commission. A petition for review shall specify the issues upon which review of the ID is sought. Also, a petition shall, with respect to each such issue, specify one or more of the following grounds upon which review is sought: (i) that a finding or conclusion of material fact is clearly erroneous; (ii) that a legal conclusion is erroneous, without governing precedent, rule or law, or constitutes an abuse of discretion; or (iii) that the determination is one affecting Commission policy.[20] The petition for review must set forth a concise statement of the facts material to consideration of the stated issues and must present a concise argument that review by the Commission is necessary or appropriate to resolve an important issue of fact, law, or policy.[21] If review is granted, the Commission may request further briefing, but the petition (along with any response(s)), could be the only pleadings filed.

Failure to file a petition waives any future right of appeal.[22] Thus, even a successful party should file a contingent petition for review pursuant to Commission Rule 210.43(b)(3) to preserve an appeal on any issues on which it was unsuccessful before the ALJ. The deadline to petition for review depends on the type of motion upon which the ID rules.[23]

---

20. 19 C.F.R. § 210.43(b).

21. *Id.*

22. *Id.* at § 210.43(b)(4).

23. The circumstances under which the ID issues dictate the amount of time allowed to petition for review, which ranges widely. For example, petitions for review of an ID on violation of Section 337 must be filed within 12 days of service of the ID. 19 C.F.R. § 210.43. However, petitions regarding an ID granting a motion for summary determination that terminates the investigation in its entirety must be filed within 10 *business* days, and petitions to review an ID on a motion for forfeiture or return of respondent's or complainant's bond must be filed within 10 *calendar* days. *Id. But see* Proposed Rules, 77 Fed. Reg. 41,123 (changing 10 *business* days to 10 *calendar* days) (proposed July 11, 2012) (to be codified at 19 C.F.R. pt. 210). Other deadlines are as short as five business days (e.g., for IDs issued under Commission Rule 210.42(c) on matters other than summary determination).

The Commission may grant or deny petitions for review and also may review the ID on its own initiative. [24] The Office of General Counsel plays a direct role in advising the Commission regarding review and represents the Commission before the Court of Appeals for the Federal Circuit (CAFC) in the event an appeal is taken. Only one Commissioner's vote is required to initiate review, although a vote is typically taken on a consensus basis. [25]

Pursuant to 19 C.F.R. § 210.43(d), within 60 days of service of the ID or by such other time as the Commission may order, the Commission will issue a notice announcing its decision whether to review the ID. If the Commission determines not to review, the ID becomes the final determination of the Commission. If the ID found no violation, the investigation is terminated immediately. If the ID found a violation, the Commission will take briefing on the appropriate remedy, the public interest, and bonding, as explained below, before issuing any remedial orders.

If the Commission decides to review the ID, it will specify the scope of review and the issues to be considered and may make provisions for the filing of briefs and for oral argument if deemed appropriate. [26] Regardless of whether briefing on the issues under review is requested, the Commission will solicit written submissions from parties, interested government agencies, and interested persons on the issues of remedy, the public interest, and bonding. The Commission will also consult with the Department of Health and Human Services, the Department of Justice, the Federal Trade Commission, Customs and Border Protection, and other departments and agencies as the Commission deems appropriate. [27]

Pursuant to Commission Rule 210.45, in the event the Commission orders review of an ID, the parties may be requested to file briefs on the issues under review. Within the time provided for filing the review briefs, the parties may submit a written request for a hearing to present oral argument before the Commission. [28]

---

24. The Commission has rarely initiated review of an ID on its own initiative. *See* Michael Diehl, *Does ITC Review of Administrative Law Judge Determinations Add Value in Section 337 Investigations?*, 21 FED. CIR. B.J. 119, 136 (2011-12).

25. 19 C.F.R. § 210.43(d)(3).

26. *Id.* at § 210.43(d)(2).

27. *Id.*

28. *Id.* at § 210.45(a). In fact, it has been many years since the Commission last heard oral argument in a Section 337 investigation. *See, e.g., Certain Sputtered Carbon Coated Computer Disks & Prods. Containing Same, Including Disk Drives*, Inv. No. 337-TA-350, USITC Pub. 2701 (Nov. 1993).

"On review, the Commission may affirm, reverse, modify, set aside or remand for further proceedings, in whole or in part, the initial determination . . . ."[29] The CAFC provided an interpretation of these sections in *Beloit Corp. v. Valmet Oy*.[30] The court determined that when the Commission specifically states that it has taken "no position" on a particular finding or portion of the ALJ's determination, that finding or portion of the ID does not automatically become part of the final Commission determination.[31] The court reasoned that, because the Commission is at "perfect liberty to reach a no violation determination on a single dispositive issue," the Commission need not take a position on any other issue.[32] When the Commission makes a "no position" decision on any issue, the CAFC may not review that issue on appeal.[33] However, if the CAFC reverses a Commission finding, the Commission may need "to revisit one or more portions of the initial determination on which it had taken no position."[34] Furthermore, the Commission "may also make any findings or conclusions that in its judgment are proper based on the record in the proceeding. If the Commission's determination on review terminates the investigation in its entirety, a notice will be published in the *Federal Register*."[35]

When the Commission takes no position on an issue within an ID, that issue is not appealable. In *Beloit*, the Commission's Notice of Review stated that it adopted the ALJ's non-infringement portion of the ruling but took no position on any other issue because the non-infringement ruling was dispositive.[36] The Commission's practice of taking no position on certain issues was recently criticized in an opinion by the CAFC in *General Electric Co. v. U.S. International Trade Commission*,

---

29. 19 C.F.R. § 210.45(c).

30. Beloit Corp. v. Valmet Oy, 742 F.2d 1421 (Fed. Cir. 1984); *see also* Finnigan Corp. v. U.S. Int'l Trade Comm'n, 180 F.3d 1354, 1360 n.3 (Fed. Cir. 1999).

31. *Beloit*, 742 F.2d at 1423.

32. *Id.*

33. *See id.* (stating that "this court does not sit to review what the Commission has not decided. Nor will it review determinations of presiding officers on which the Commission has not elected to provide the court with its views.").

34. *Id.*

35. *Id.*

36. *Id.* ("The [CAFC] has not been constituted a 'Surrogate Commission' to review portions of a presiding officer's determination on which the Commission has 'taken no position.'").

although that portion of the opinion was later withdrawn.[37] In this case, the Commission's Notice of Review stated that it would review all issues with regard to one asserted patent, with the exception of importation and the "intent" element of the ALJ's inequitable conduct ruling.[38] However, the Commission ultimately decided only the domestic industry question with respect to that asserted patent and took no position on any other issue. On appeal, the Commission argued that the other issues were not subject to judicial review because they did not constitute the Commission's final determination.[39] The CAFC's original opinion reversed the Commission's domestic industry ruling and noted that the Commission's failure to take a position on the other issues required an otherwise unnecessary remand.[40]

After the CAFC's opinion was issued, the ITC filed a combined petition for panel rehearing and rehearing en banc, and a response was filed by the General Electric Company. The petition for panel rehearing was granted for the limited purpose of withdrawing the portion of the original opinion that criticized the Commission's taking of no position in that case.[41] Judge Newman dissented regarding the withdrawal, arguing that the Commission had stated it would review certain issues, but instead it did not decide those issues, which "prevented completion of the Section 337 action," and deprived the losing party of its right to "full judicial review and final resolution," thereby "fail[ing] the requirement that Section 337 actions be expeditiously completed."[42] This issue may well arise again if it comes before a different panel of the CAFC.

The Commission typically renders its final decision on the issues under review 120 days after the issuance of the ID. Pursuant to Commission Rule 210.47, within 14 days after service of a Commission determination, any party may file a petition for reconsideration of such determination setting forth the relief desired and the grounds in support

---

37. General Elec. Co. v. U.S. Int'l Trade Comm'n, 670 F.3d 1206 (Fed. Cir. 2012), *opinion withdrawn and superseded by* General Elec. Co. v. U.S. Int'l Trade Comm'n, No. 2010-1223, 2012 WL 2626902 (Fed. Cir. July 6, 2012).

38. *Certain Variable Speed Wind Turbines & Components Thereof*, Inv. No. 337-TA-641, Notice of Comm'n Determination to Review a Final Initial Determination of the Administrative Law Judge, at 2 (Oct. 8, 2009).

39. *General Elec. Co.*, 670 F.3d 1219.

40. *Id.*

41. *General Elec. Co.*, 2012 WL 2626908, at *1 (Order Granting a Rehearing En Banc).

42. *Id.* at *1–6.

thereof. Any petition filed under this section must be confined to new questions raised by the determination and upon which the petitioner had no previous opportunity to submit arguments. Oppositions to such a petition are due within five days after service of the petition. The filing of a petition for reconsideration does not stay the effective date of the determination or toll the running of any statutory time period affecting the determination, unless specifically ordered by the Commission. In response to a petition, the Commission may affirm, set aside, or modify its determination, including any action ordered by it to be taken thereafter. When appropriate, the Commission may order the ALJ to take additional evidence. It should be noted that petitions for reconsideration are routinely denied.[43] The Commission, however, has granted petitions for reconsideration when the petitioner persuaded the Commission that there were new questions for which the petitioner had no previous opportunity to submit arguments.[44] Some issues, however, may be waived unless they were properly raised in the petition for review.[45]

---

43. *See, e.g., Certain Liquid Crystal Display Modules, Prods. Containing Same, & Methods for Using the Same*, Inv. No. 337-TA-634, Comm'n Order (Oct. 20, 2009).

44. *See, e.g., Certain Silicon Microphone Packages & Prods. Containing the Same*, Inv. No. 337-TA-629, Comm'n Order (Aug. 18, 2009) (complainant and respondents both argued that certain of the Commission's wording in its opinion was incorrect). *See also Certain Digital Set-Top Boxes & Components Thereof*, Inv. No. 337-TA-712, Comm'n Op. (Sept. 23, 2011) (granting respondent's petition for reconsideration of the Commission's determination not to review the ALJ's finding of a violation of Section 337 for infringing a patent claim which had been found by a U.S. district court to be invalid).

45. For example, although claim construction is an issue of law, the petitioning party must still raise the claim construction arguments in the petition for review. *See* Finnigan Corp. v. U.S. Int'l Trade Comm'n, 180 F.3d 1354, 1362 (Fed. Cir. 1999) ("A party seeking review in this court of a determination by the Commission must 'specifically assert' the error made by the ALJ in its petition for review to the Commission."). *But see* Warner Bros. v. U.S. Int'l Trade Comm'n, 787 F.2d 562, 564 (Fed. Cir. 1986) (a party may not necessarily need to preserve an argument in the petition for review if it does not file a petition for review). Note that addressing an issue in the reply brief has been found insufficient to preserve the issue. *See* Enercon GmbH v. U.S. Int'l Trade Comm'n, 151 F.3d 1376, 1385 (Fed. Cir. 2010) (finding an argument waived when it was considered by the ITC, but not raised on appeal until the reply brief (citing FED. R. APP. P. 28(c); Amhil Enters. Ltd. v. Wawa, Inc., 81 F.3d 1554, 1563 (Fed. Cir. 1996))).

C. PUBLIC INTEREST

Before the Commission grants an exclusion order, subsections (d), (e), and (f) of Section 337 require the Commission to consider certain public interest factors. Specifically, the Commission must consider the effect that relief under the statute would have on the public health and welfare, competitive conditions in the U.S. economy, the production of like or directly competitive articles in the United States, and U.S. consumers.[46]

According to the legislative history of the Trade Act of 1974, the Commission must give overriding consideration to the effect of an exclusion order on the public interest.[47] In particular, the legislative history provides:

> Should the Commission find that issuing an exclusion order would have a greater adverse impact on the public health and welfare; on competitive conditions in the United States economy; on production of like or directly competitive conditions in the United States economy; or on the United States consumer, than would be gained by protecting the patent holder (within the context of the U.S. patent laws), then . . . such exclusion order should not be issued.[48]

Since the enactment of subsections (d), (e), and (f) of Section 337, the Commission has invoked the public interest as a basis for denying relief to a prevailing complainant on only three occasions: *Automatic Crankpin Grinders*,[49] *Inclined-Field Acceleration Tubes*,[50] and *Fluidized Supporting Apparatus*.[51] While the last instance was almost three decades ago, there is a recently renewed interest in public interest considerations.

Automatic Crankpin Grinders[52] afforded the Commission the first opportunity to consider whether to preclude the imposition of a remedy based on public interest factors, despite its determination that the accused

---

46. 19 U.S.C. §§ 1337(d), (e), (f) (2006).

47. *See* Trade Act of 1974, S. Rep. No. 93-1298, at 197 (1974).

48. *Id.*

49. *Certain Automatic Crankpin Grinders (Crankpin Grinders)*, Inv. No. 337-TA-60, USITC Pub. 1022, Comm'n Op., at 18 (Dec. 1979).

50. *Certain Inclined-Field Acceleration Tubes & Components Thereof (Acceleration Tubes)*, Inv. No. 337-TA-67, USITC Pub. 1119, Comm'n Op., at 29 (Dec. 1980).

51. *Certain Fluidized Supporting Apparatus & Components Thereof*, Inv. Nos. 337-TA-182/188, USITC Pub. 1667 (Oct. 1984).

52. *Crankpin Grinders*, Comm'n Op., at 18.

product infringed a valid and enforceable patent. The primary reason for the Commission's decision not to impose a remedy was the inability of the domestic industry to supply the demand for new orders of the patented product. With a view to the then-existing energy crisis, the Commission was persuaded that domestic vehicle manufacturers would not be able to meet the fuel economy standards mandated by Congress if the accused products were excluded from the United States.[53] More specifically, the Commission found that the "public as a whole has an interest in conserving fuel through the provision of energy efficient alternatives represented in this case by automobiles with more efficient engines which are produced with the assistance of crankpin grinders which are the subject of this investigation."[54] Accordingly, the Commission determined that such public interest concerns were greater than the interest in protecting the asserted patent, and denied relief to the complainant.[55]

Likewise, in *Inclined-Field Acceleration Tubes*,[56] the Commission declined to impose a remedy despite its finding of patent infringement. In that case, the Commission established a two-pronged test to determine whether public interest factors preclude the imposition of a remedy for a Section 337 violation. First, the Commission must determine whether a remedy under Section 337 would have an adverse impact on the public health and welfare.[57] Should that be determined in the affirmative, the Commission must then balance the damage to the patent holder's rights against the adverse impact of the remedy on the "public health and welfare and the competitive conditions in the United States economy."[58]

In addressing the first inquiry, the Commission was persuaded by submissions from the National Science Foundation, three research universities, and one prominent laboratory detailing the devastating impact that an exclusion and/or cease and desist order would have on scientific research. In particular, the Commission was affected by the beneficial use of acceleration tubes for nuclear weapons development, paleontological purposes, and archaeological applications.[59] According

---

53. *Id.* at 18–19.

54. *Id.* at 20.

55. *Id.* at 21.

56. *Certain Inclined-Field Acceleration Tubes & Components Thereof,* Inv. No. 337-TA-67, USITC Pub. 1119, Comm'n Op., at 29 (Dec. 1980).

57. *Id.* at 22.

58. *Id.* (quoting S. REP. No. 93-1298, at 197 (1974)).

59. *Id.* at 23.

to the Commission, the importance of such research was reinforced by congressional enactment of the National Science Foundation Act, which provided financial support for much of the research carried out with domestic and imported tubes.[60] With respect to the second inquiry, the devastating impact on scientific research was sufficient to deny the patentee the rewards of developing the patented product.[61] In coming to this conclusion, the Commission found it dispositive that the patented product was expensive and incompatible with existing research programs in contrast to the accused product.[62] In addition, a *non-infringing* feature of the accused product offered "significant operational advantages, at lower cost" and made "significant progress toward a solution of the technical problem that the invention of the patent was designed to solve."[63] Therefore, the public interest in scientific research outweighed the patent holder's entitlement to an effective remedy.[64]

In *Fluidized Supporting Apparatus*,[65] the Commission found reason to believe there was a violation of Section 337, but that the public interest factors relevant to the discretionary grant of temporary relief dictated the non-issuance of a remedy. At issue in that investigation were specialized beds, which were adapted for use by patients with severe burns.[66] In finding that an overriding public interest existed, the Commission focused on the unique benefits of the burn beds and the inability of the complainant to meet existing domestic demand.[67] Additionally, the Commission was persuaded by the ALJ's determination that decreasing competition would "result in a price increase which would effectively deny these beds to patients with limited means."[68]

---

60. *Id.*

61. *Id.* at 29.

62. *Id.* at 26–27.

63. *Id.* at 29.

64. It is worthy of note that the *Acceleration Tubes* balancing test only focused on the first public interest consideration, i.e., the effect a remedy would have on the public health and welfare, and neglected to mention whether such a two-pronged analysis would apply to the other Section 337 public interest factors. Despite this oversight, it is logical to infer that such a balancing test applies equally to the effect a remedy would have on the competitive conditions in the U.S. economy, the production of like or directly competing articles in the United States, and U.S. consumers.

65. *Certain Fluidized Supporting Apparatus & Components Thereof*, Inv. Nos. 337-TA-182/188, USITC Pub. 1667 (Oct. 1984).

66. *Id.* at 1.

67. *Id.* at 23.

68. *Id.*

Thus, the Commission concluded that public interest concerns necessitated the preclusion of a remedy.[69]

Several common characteristics are present in this limited list of cases in which the Commission precluded a remedy despite finding a violation of Section 337 or need for temporary relief. Each case reflects the Commission's firm adherence to the public interest factors delineated in Section 337.[70] First, the accused product in each investigation provided a *clear* and *valuable* benefit to the public health and welfare, i.e., clean air, scientific research, and medical equipment, respectively. Second, the complainant in each investigation was unable to meet the domestic demand for the patented product. As a result, public health and welfare were jeopardized, which sufficed to preclude a remedy. Finally, in two of the three investigations, an act of Congress reinforced the importance of the public interest considerations.[71]

Recently, the Commission conducted a thorough analysis of the four statutory public interest factors when considering the appropriate remedy in *Personal Data and Mobile Communications Devices*, concluding that they did not weigh against the issuance of a limited exclusion order.[72] Nonetheless, the Commission did not immediately exclude the accused products; rather, the exclusion of articles subject to the order commenced four months after the opinion was issued, after considering the competitive conditions in the U.S. economy.[73] In addition, the Commission allowed the respondent to import refurbished products as replacements under warranty or pursuant to an insurance contract—regardless of who offered the warranty or contract—because it was believed existing consumers expected to receive the same model for replacement.[74]

Importantly, the CAFC has affirmed that the factors governing issuance of injunctive relief in federal court, per *eBay Inc. v. MercExchange, L.L.C.*, do not apply to Commission remedy determinations.[75] One of the

---

69. *Id.* at 24.

70. *See* 19 U.S.C. §§ 1337(d), (f).

71. *Certain Automatic Crankpin Grinders*, Inv. No. 337-TA-60, USITC Pub. 1022, Comm'n Op., at 18 (Dec. 1979); *Certain Inclined-Field Acceleration Tubes & Components Thereof*, Inv. No. 337-TA-67, USITC Pub. 1119, Comm'n Op., at 23 (Dec. 1980).

72. *Certain Personal Data & Mobile Commc'ns Devices & Related Software*, Inv. No. 337-TA-710, Comm'n Op., at 83 (Dec. 29, 2011).

73. *Id.* at 79–83.

74. *Id.* at 69–73.

75. These four factors are: (1) that the plaintiff has suffered an irreparable injury; (2) that remedies available at law, such as monetary damages, are inad-

many respondents in *Semiconductor Chips with Minimized Chip Package Size*[76] argued to the CAFC that the Commission failed to give meaningful consideration to the public interest factors before issuing limited exclusion and cease and desist orders. The respondent further argued that the public interest inquiry is similar to the *eBay* test for injunctive relief. The CAFC rejected these arguments, holding that the statutory standards governing Commission remedial orders are distinct from the equitable framework set up by *eBay*, and that the Commission had appropriately addressed the statutory public interest factors.[77]

In 2011, the Commission amended certain procedural rules regarding public interest.[78] The new rules do not affect the Commission's substantive practice with respect to its consideration of the statutory public interest factors, but are intended to "increase efficiency" and "improve procedures" for ensuring a complete record on the public interest.[79] According to these new rules, complainants must file a separate statement of public interest, limited to five pages, concurrently with the complaint.[80] The statement should: (1) include an explanation of how articles potentially subject to the requested remedy are used in the U.S.; (2) identify any public health, safety or welfare concerns; (3) identify like or directly competitive articles that could replace excluded articles; (4) indicate whether the complainant, its licensees, and/or third parties have the capacity to replace the volume of articles subject to the requested remedial orders in a commercially reasonable time in the United States; and (4) describe the effect of the requested remedy on consumers.[81]

---

equate to compensate for that injury; (3) considering the balance of hardships between the plaintiff and defendant, a remedy in equity is warranted; (4) that the public interest would not be disserved by a permanent injunction. eBay Inc. v. MercExchange, L.L.C., 547 U.S. 388, 391 (2006).

76. *Certain Semiconductor Chips with Minimized Chip Package Size & Prods. Containing Same*, Inv. No. 337-TA-605, USITC Pub. 4282 (Nov. 2011).

77. Spansion, Inc. v. U.S. Int'l Trade Comm'n, 629 F.3d 1331, 1358–60 (Fed. Cir. 2010).

78. *See* Notice of Final Rulemaking, 76 Fed. Reg. 64,803 (Oct. 19, 2011). The new rules took effect on Nov. 18, 2011.

79. *Id.*

80. 19 C.F.R. § 210.8(b). *See also* Proposed Rules, 77 Fed. Reg. 41,122 (requiring the filing of a public version of any confidential submission) (proposed July 11, 2012) (to be codified at 19 C.F.R. pt. 210).

81. 19 C.F.R. § 210.8(b).

After a complaint is filed, the Commission will publish a notice inviting comments from the public and proposed respondents on the public interest.[82] At the time of institution of an investigation, the Commission may order the ALJ to take evidence and to issue an RD on the public interest.[83] If the Commission orders the ALJ to take evidence with respect to the public interest, respondents must submit a statement concerning the public interest, specifically responding to any issues raised by the complainant in its public interest submission at the same time as their response to the complaint is due.[84] Since the new rules took effect in November 2011, the Commission has directed the ALJ to take evidence on public interest in several investigations.[85]

Despite the Commission addressing the public interest factors in *Personal Data and Mobile Communications Devices*, discussed above, it is still too early to tell whether the increased attention to the public interest factors will have a significant impact on the Commission's remedy decisions. Also, public interest is being discussed as an element of the current debate over the role of non-practicing entities as complainants and patents subject to FRAND (fair, reasonable, and non-discriminatory) terms by virtue of being incorporated in standards established by voluntary standard-setting organizations.[86] The Commission will, undoubtedly, have the opportunity to address public interest in these contexts in the near future.[87]

---

82. *Id.* at § 210.8(c)(1).

83. *Id.* at § 210.10(b).

84. *Id.* at § 210.14(f).

85. *See, e.g.*, Commission Notice of Institution of 337-TA-779, 76 Fed. Reg. 36576 (June 22, 2011); Commission Notice of Institution of 337-TA-803, 76 Fed. Reg. 55,418 (Sept. 7, 2011); Commission Notice of Institution of 337-TA-811, 76 Fed. Reg. 69,284 (Nov. 8, 2011); Commission Notice of Institution of 337-TA-814, 76 Fed. Reg. 72,442 (Nov. 23, 2011); and Commission Notice of Institution of 337-TA-817, 76 Fed. Reg. 76,436 (Dec. 7, 2011).

86. See Chapter 16, Section D for a discussion of FRAND agreements (also referred to as "RAND"). *See also Certain Wireless Commc'n Devices, Portable Music & Data Processing Devices, Computers & Components Thereof*, Inv. No. 337-TA-745, Notice of Comm'n Determination to Review in Part a Final ID Finding a Violation of Section 337; Request for Written Submissions (June 25, 2012) (requesting briefing on a number of RAND-related issues, and specifically requesting a discussion of the public interest in relation to the RAND issues).

87. *See Certain Gaming & Entm't Consoles, Related Software, & Components Thereof*, Inv. No. 337-TA-752, Notice of Comm'n Determination to Review a Final Initial Determination Finding a Violation of Section 337; Remand of the Investigation to the ALJ (June 29, 2012) (determining to review and

D. PRESIDENTIAL REVIEW

Because Section 337 is a trade statute affecting international relations of the United States, after the Commission finds a violation of Section 337 and issues a remedy, its determination is published in the *Federal Register* and transmitted to the President, together with the record upon which it is based.[88] While the Commission determination becomes effective upon publication in the *Federal Register*, it does not become final until after the Presidential review period.[89] It should be noted, however, that the President has only exercised his authority to disapprove a Commission remedy for violation of Section 337 "for policy reasons" in five instances, the last time being more than two decades ago.[90]

---

remand a final initial determination finding a violation of Section 337 regarding alleged FRAND patents, and noting a number of public interest statements filed in response to the recommended determination).

88. 19 U.S.C. § 1337(j)(1); 19 C.F.R. § 210.49.

89. During the Presidential review period, articles directed to be excluded from entry are entitled to entry under bond. 19 U.S.C. § 1337(j)(3); 19 C.F.R. § 210.49. *See also* Chapter 11, Section E, "Bond," *supra*.

90. *See* Notice of Presidential Disapproval, 43 Fed. Reg. 17,789–90 (Apr. 26, 1978) (rejecting the Commission's issuance of a cease and desist order in *Certain Welded Stainless Steel Pipe & Tube*, Inv. No. 337-TA-29 (1978), issued on the basis of four policy considerations, including (1) the detrimental effect the remedy would have on the national economic interest; (2) the detrimental effect of the imposition of the remedy on the international economic relations of the United States; (3) the need to avoid duplication and conflicts in the administration of unfair trade practice laws in the United States; and (4) the probable lack of any significant benefit to U.S. producers or consumers to counterbalance the above considerations); Notice of Presidential Disapproval, 46 Fed. Reg. 22,083 (1981) (recommending a narrower exclusion order directed only at the infringing foreign manufacturer's products in *Certain Headboxes & Papermaking Machine Forming Sections for the Continuous Production of Paper & Components Thereof*, Inv. No. 337-TA-82 (1981)); Notice of Presidential Disapproval, 47 Fed. Reg. 19,485 (1982) (disapproving of cease and desist orders issued in *Certain Molded-In Sandwich Panel Inserts & Methods for Their Installation*, Inv. No. 337-TA-99 (1982), and indicating that the orders were likely not in compliance with U.S. international obligations); Notice of Presidential Disapproval, 50 Fed. Reg. 1655 (1985) (rejecting a general exclusion order issued in *Certain Alkaline Batteries*, Inv. No. 337-TA-165 (1984) because the President was in the process of reviewing policy on gray market importations); Notice of Presidential Disapproval, 52 Fed. Reg. 46,011 (1987) (disapproving of a limited exclusion order issued in *Certain Dynamic Random Access Memories*, Inv. No. 337-TA-242 (1986) because of the order's disruptive effect on legitimate trade).

Pursuant to Commission Rule 210.49, the Commission transmits its determination to the President for review. The determination is initially submitted to the White House clerk's office, which then forwards copies to the Office of the United States Trade Representative (USTR).[91] The USTR, on behalf of the President, has 60 days to review the determination of violation and approve or disapprove the remedy for policy reasons.

Congress provided for Presidential review of Commission remedial orders because:

> It is recognized by the Committee that the granting of relief against imports could have a very direct and substantial impact on United States foreign relations, economic and political. Further, the President would often be able to best see the impact which the relief ordered by the Commission may have upon the public health and welfare, competitive conditions in the United States economy, the production of like or directly competitive articles in the United States, and United States consumers.[92]

Therefore, it was deemed necessary by Congress to permit the President to intervene before such determination and relief become final, if he determines that policy reasons require it. The President's power to intervene would not be for the purpose of reversing a Commission finding of a violation of Section 337; such finding is determined solely by the Commission, subject to judicial review.[93]

As this legislative history and the subsequent Section 337 investigations in which the President intervened make clear, the "policy reasons" considered during Presidential review are not limited to the public interest factors set forth in the statute but may include national economic interests and foreign relations. Moreover, there is no right of review of the President's decision.[94] If the President does not disapprove the rem-

---

91. In 2005 the President delegated the authority to disapprove Commission exclusion orders to the U.S. Trade Representative. *See* 70 Fed. Reg. 43,251 (July 26, 2005).

92. S. REP. No. 93-1298, at 199 (1974).

93. *Id.*

94. Duracell, Inc. v. U.S. Int'l Trade Comm'n, 778 F.2d 1578, 1580 (Fed. Cir. 1985) ("Nothing in section 337(g) [the predecessor to section 337(j)] or elsewhere in the statute provides a litigant with a right of review of the *President's* decision per se.").

edy within the 60 days, the determination becomes final on the day after the close of the 60-day period.[95]

While lobbying of Commission officials is forbidden, there is no such prohibition against lobbying USTR during the Presidential review period. Counsel for the parties, as well as interested non-parties, may arrange presentations, as appropriate, before designated officials of USTR and of those executive departments whose views might be sought by USTR with respect to a particular order.

---

95. 19 U.S.C. § 1337(j)(4).

CHAPTER 13
_____

Federal Circuit Review of Section 337 Decisions

The Court of Appeals for the Federal Circuit (CAFC) has sole statutory jurisdiction over appeals from Commission decisions regarding matters under Section 337. Parties adversely affected by the Commission's determination, including a non-party to the investigation, can appeal to the CAFC. The CAFC gives deference to the Commission in the areas of its expertise, as it must give deference "to an interpretation of a statute by the agency charged with its administration,"[1] though it does reverse Commission decisions when the Commission has overreached its authority.[2]

_____

1. Corning Glass Works v. U.S. Int'l Trade Comm'n, 799 F.2d 1559, 1565 (Fed. Cir. 1986). *See also* Chevron v. Natural Res. Defense Council, 467 U.S. 837, 844 (1984) ("We have long recognized that considerable weight should be accorded to an executive department's construction of a statutory scheme it is entrusted to administer.").

2. As discussed in Chapter 11, Section F, one of the most recent examples of the CAFC taking such action occurred in Kyocera Wireless Corp. v. U.S. Int'l Trade Comm'n, 545 F.3d 1340 (Fed. Cir. 2008). In *Kyocera*, the CAFC reversed a Commission determination on remedy that resulted in a limited exclusion order that reached the products of parties that had not been named in the complaint, but that nonetheless manufactured products containing the accused products of named respondents. The CAFC held that limited exclusion orders could only reach the products of named respondents, and to the extent the exclusion order reached the products of unnamed parties, the complainants would have to satisfy the higher standard used for general exclusion orders. *Id.* at 1345, 1358. *See also* VastFame Camera v. U.S. Int'l Trade Comm'n, 386 F.3d 1108, 1110 (Fed. Cir. 2004).

A. JURISDICTION

28 U.S.C. § 1295(a)(6) grants the CAFC exclusive jurisdiction to review the Commission's final determinations in investigations under Section 337.[3] The "final determinations" appealable to the CAFC are specified in Section 1337(c). That provision states, in relevant part: "[a]ny person adversely affected by a final determination of the Commission under subsection (d), (e), (f), or (g) of this section [which govern, respectively, permanent exclusion orders, temporary relief, cease and desist orders, and relief in investigations involving defaulting respondents] may appeal such determination, within 60 days after the determination becomes final, to the U.S. Court of Appeals for the Federal Circuit for review in accordance with chapter 7 of Title 5."[4] Further, CAFC precedent has established that a final determination as stated in 28 U.S.C. § 1295 is "a final administrative decision *on the merits*, excluding or refusing to exclude articles from entry" under 19 U.S.C. §§ 1337 (d), (e) or (f).[5]

1. Adversely Affected Parties

To file an appeal before the CAFC from a Commission determination under Section 337, the filing party must meet the statutory requirements. 19 U.S.C. § 1337 allows any person who is adversely affected by the Commission's final determination to file an appeal.

Whether a complainant or a respondent is considered "adversely affected" typically depends only on the Commission's final determination excluding or refusing to exclude articles from entry into the United States. On the one hand, a complainant is typically "adversely affected" only by a finding of no violation. By the same token, a respondent is typically "adversely affected" only upon a finding of violation.[6] In situations where a party wins on one issue and not another, e.g., a complainant wins on one patent but not another or a respondent wins on non-infringement but

---

3. "[T]o review the final determinations of the United States International Trade Commission relating to unfair practices in import trade, made under section 337 of the Tariff Act of 1930 (19 U.S.C. § 1337)." 28 U.S.C. § 1295(a)(6) (2006).

4. 19 U.S.C. § 1337(c) (2006).

5. *See* Crucible Mat'ls Corp. v. U.S. Int'l Trade Comm'n, 127 F.3d 1057, 1060 (Fed. Cir. 1997) (emphasis in original).

6. *See* Krupp Int'l, Inc. v. U.S. Int'l Trade Comm'n, 626 F.2d 844, 846 (Fed. Cir. 1980) ("ITC Respondents . . . are not 'adversely affected' by a determination that they did not violate section 337.").

not on invalidity, that party may not appeal the patent or issue on which it has lost if the overall result has not left it adversely affected.[7]

There are two factors, however, that can result in the prevailing complainant nevertheless being "adversely affected" by the Commission's determination to exclude articles: (1) the length of the entered remedy and (2) the scope of the entered remedy. As for the length of the remedy, a complainant that prevails on the basis of one patent, but loses as to another patent, may be considered "adversely affected" if the patent for which there is no violation expires at a later date than the patent for which there is a violation.[8] As for the scope of the remedy, a prevailing complainant may be "adversely affected" if the Commission enters only a limited exclusion order when the complaint sought the broader remedy of a general exclusion order.[9]

Notably, the appellant does not have to have been a party to the original investigation. In *LSI Computer Systems, Inc. v. U.S. International Trade Commission*, the CAFC interpreted the "adversely affected" language of Section 337 and held that a non-party to the original investigation was adversely affected by a Commission finding of infringement.[10] The non-party's products were not the same as those in the investigation, but they were in the same class as those found to be infringing. The CAFC reasoned this was sufficient to meet the requirements of the statutory language, explaining its belief that Congress had intended to permit outsiders to the investigation to appeal as long as they proved that they were adversely affected by the Commission's determination.

---

7. *See* Surface Tech., Inc. v. U.S. Int'l Trade Comm'n, 780 F.2d 29, 30 (Fed. Cir. 1985) (alleged infringer lacked standing to challenge a Commission finding that certain requirements of Section 337 were satisfied when the non-infringement finding made the alleged infringer the prevailing party); Krupp Int'l, Inc. v. U.S. Int'l Trade Comm'n, 626 F.2d 844, 846 (C.C.P.A. 1980).

8. *See* Yingbin-Nature (Guangdong) Wood Indus. Co., Ltd v. U.S. Int'l Trade Comm'n, 535 F.3d 1322, 1331 (Fed. Cir. 2008) (deeming an appeal as to the validity of certain patents not moot where it could affect the expiration date of the entered remedy). While Yingbin addressed how the timing of the remedy can render an appeal moot as to certain issues from the perspective of a respondent, the same logic applies to a successful complainant that would be "adversely affected" as to a finding of violation on one patent but not as to another with a later expiration date.

9. *See* John Mezzalingua Assocs., Inc. v. U.S. Int'l Trade Comm'n, 660 F.3d 1322, 1326–27 (Fed. Cir. 2011) (finding standing to appeal on the basis of seeking a broader remedy than entered by the Commission).

10. LSI Computer Sys., Inc. v. U.S. Int'l Trade Comm'n, 832 F.2d 588, 591 (Fed. Cir. 1987).

2. Determination on the Merits

The CAFC has no jurisdiction to hear appeals from Commission determinations that are not final decisions on the merits of a Section 337 investigation. For example, in *Seagate Technologies, Inc. v. U.S. International Trade Commission*, the Commission terminated the Section 337 investigation based on settlement agreements between the parties.[11] The CAFC refused to hear an appeal, filed by one of the respondents, of an interlocutory Commission decision on a jurisdictional issue,[12] holding that there was no appealable "final determination" because the Commission had not issued a decision excluding or refusing to exclude articles from entry into the United States.[13] However, in *Amgen, Inc. v. U.S. International Trade Commission*, the CAFC found the Commission's dismissal of Amgen's complaint for lack of subject matter jurisdiction appealable, holding that the determination at issue "clearly reaches the merits of Amgen's complaint and determinatively decides Amgen's right to proceed in a section 1337 action."[14] The CAFC concluded that, because the issue of importation is both jurisdictional and substantive, the ITC should not have dismissed it for lack of subject matter jurisdiction due to no importation, but rather should have assumed jurisdiction and decided the investigation, including the issue of importation, on the merits.[15]

Significantly, because the CAFC may only review determinations reaching the merits of a Section 337 investigation, the CAFC may not review a "no position" determination issued by the Commission.[16] A "no

11. Seagate Tech., Inc. v. U.S. Int'l Trade Comm'n, No. 94-1348, 36 F.3d 1113, at *1 (Fed. Cir. 1994) (unreported).

12. *Id.* The appealing respondents argued that it was adversely affected by the jurisdictional ruling because of its "possible preclusive effect."

13. *Id.* at *3. *See also* Joanna B. Gunderson, *Appellate Review of Section 337 Actions in the Court of Appeals for the Federal Circuit: It's Not as Broad as You Might Think!*, 20 ITCTLA 337 REPORTER 127, 130 (2d Summer Assoc. ed.) (2004).

14. Amgen, Inc. v. U.S. Int'l Trade Comm'n, 902 F.2d 1532, 1535 (Fed. Cir. 1990).

15. *Id.* at 1536, 1540.

16. As discussed in Chapter 12, Section B, the parties to appeals before the CAFC must limit the issues to those decided by the Commission. *See* Beloit Corp. v. Valmet Oy, 742 F.2d 1421, 1423 (Fed. Cir. 1984) ("This court does not sit to review what the Commission has not decided. Nor will it review determinations of presiding officers on which the Commission has not elected to provide the court with its views.").

position" decision is not actually a decision and thus cannot be a decision on the merits.[17]

3. Final Determination

The CAFC will not review a Commission decision before it becomes a final determination.[18] According to Commission Rule 210.42, the ID of an ALJ becomes the final determination of the Commission within 45 days, unless the Commission orders review of the ID or certain issues therein.[19]

The finality of a Commission determination for purposes of appeal depends on the nature of the determination. Upon a finding of no violation, a Commission determination is immediately final and appealable. However, upon an affirmative finding of a violation, Section 1337(j) establishes a 60-day window in which the President considers whether to approve the remedy issued in connection with the Commission's final affirmative determination.[20] Thus, an affirmative determination of violation does not become final for purposes of appeal to the CAFC until the 60-day period expires without the President disapproving the remedy. If the President overturns the Commission's remedy during the 60-day period, the Commission's determination has no force or effect and is not appealable to the CAFC.

17. *But see* Chapter 12, Section B, "Commission Review," for a discussion of Judge Newman's criticism of the Commission's practice of taking no position in General Elec. v. U.S. Int'l Trade Comm'n, 670 F.3d 1206 (Fed. Cir. 2012).

18. *See* Tessera, Inc. v. U.S. Int'l Trade Comm'n, 646 F.3d 1357, 1367–69 (Fed. Cir. 2011). The Commission and intervenor Elpida argued that Tessera did not timely appeal the Commission's decision on a patent exhaustion issue. The CAFC, however, rejected the Commission's argument, based on Commission Rule 210.42(h)(2), which provides that an initial determination becomes the final determination of the Commission "unless the Commission . . . shall have ordered review of the initial determination or certain issues therein . . . ." Because the Commission decided to review certain issues with respect to another asserted patent in its Notice to Review, the Initial Determination did not become final until the Commission issued its Final Determination. The 60 days starts from the date of issuance of *Final Determination*, not *Notice to Review*. Tessera's notice of appeal, though more than 60 days from the Notice to Review, was timely because it was within 60 days from the Final Determination.

19. 19 C.F.R. § 210.42(h)(1).

20. The President has delegated this authority to the U.S. Trade Representative. See Memorandum for the U.S. Trade Representative, 70 Fed. Reg. 43,251 (July 26, 2005).

Because the CAFC only hears appeals of the Commission's final decisions, interlocutory and collateral issues are not appealable to the CAFC because there is no final order excluding or refusing to exclude articles from entry into the United States, which, as previously mentioned, is a requirement for the CAFC to assume jurisdiction.[21]

4. *Writs of Mandamus*

The CAFC has exclusive jurisdiction to hear appeals from the Commission.[22] As discussed above, the ability to appeal Commission decisions is available only upon a final determination of the Commission. However, it is possible to petition the CAFC for a writ of mandamus regarding a Commission decision during the course of an investigation.

The CAFC has held that mandamus is available only "in extraordinary situations to correct a clear abuse of discretion or usurpation of judicial power."[23] The petitioning party bears the burden of proving (a) that a writ of mandamus is the only means of attaining the desired relief, and (b) that the right to issuance of the writ is "clear and indisputable."[24] The CAFC has denied a party's petition for a writ of mandamus where other remedies are available.[25] Similarly, the CAFC has denied petitions for a writ of mandamus where the underlying determination involved a discovery dispute.[26]

---

21. *See* 28 U.S.C. § 1295 (2006); Crucible Mat'ls Corp. v. U.S. Int'l Trade Comm'n, 127 F.3d 1057, 1060 (Fed. Cir. 1997).

22. 28 U.S.C. § 1295(a)(6).

23. *In re* Freescale Semiconductor, Inc., 290 Fed. Appx. 326, 327 (Fed. Cir. 2008) (citing *In re* Calmar, Inc., 854 F.2d 461, 464 (Fed. Cir. 1988)). The CAFC grants mandamus only rarely because of this high standard; however, such grants are not entirely unheard of. *See In re* TS Tech USA Corp., 551 F.3d 1315, 1319–23 (Fed. Cir. 2008) (granting mandamus with regard to district court ruling refusing to transfer the case to another venue).

24. *Freescale Semiconductor,* 290 Fed. Appx. at 327 (quoting Allied Chem. Corp. v. Daiflon, Inc., 449 U.S. 33, 35 (1980)).

25. *See, e.g., Freescale Semiconductor,* 290 Fed. Appx. 326 (Fed. Cir. 2008); *In re* RAD Data Commc'ns, Ltd., Misc. No. 461, 91 F.3d 169, at *2 (Fed. Cir. 1996) (unreported) (also denying the writ on the grounds that petitioner's right to a writ was not clear and indisputable).

26. *In re* Meta Sys., Misc. No. 501, 111 F.3d 142, *2–3 (Fed. Cir. 1997) (unreported) (holding that it takes exceptional circumstances for a petitioner's right to a writ to be "clear and indisputable" when it involves matters within the court's discretion, such as discovery).

In *In re RAD Data Communications, Ltd.*, the petitioner sought a writ of mandamus to direct the ITC to cease its investigation of RAD's importation of self-powered fiber-optic interconnect systems.[27] RAD argued that the patent extension terms and remedy limitations of the Uruguay Round Agreements Act (URAA) applied to Section 337 investigations and, because permanent relief would not likely be awarded in the case until after the expiration of the original patent term, the ITC had no power to grant relief against an "invested infringer" such as itself.[28] The ITC opposed the writ, arguing that the URAA limited other statutory infringement remedies only, and that the URAA limitations were not applicable to Section 337.[29] The CAFC denied the writ, reiterating its decision in *In re Cordis Corp.* that, when "a rational and substantial legal argument can be made in support of the rule in question, the case is not appropriate for mandamus, even though on normal appeal, a court might find reversible error."[30]

B. STANDARDS OF REVIEW

The CAFC varies in the level of deference it gives to the findings and decisions of the Commission. For instance, the CAFC grants no deference to Commission claim construction,[31] but grants broad deference in factual matters and, normally, to the Commission's interpretation of Section 337 itself.

1. *Claim Construction*

The CAFC does not grant deference to the claim construction of the Commission because claim construction is a matter of law.[32] Still, while the CAFC may not defer to the Commission's claim construction, the

---

27. *In re* RAD Data Commc'ns, Ltd., 91 F.3d 169.
28. *Id.* at *1.
29. *Id.* at *2.
30. *Id.* (quoting *In re* Cordis Corp., 769 F.2d 733, 737 (Fed. Cir. 1985)).
31. *See* General Protecht Grp., Inc. v. U.S. Int'l Trade Comm'n, 619 F.3d 1303, 1307 (Fed. Cir 2010) ("Claim construction is an issue of law and is subject to de novo review.") (citing Cybor Corp. v. FAS Tech., Inc., 138 F.3d 1448, 1451 (Fed. Cir. 1998) (en banc)).
32. *Id.*

court will not disturb such construction if no party challenged it during the Section 337 investigation.[33]

2. Factual Findings

Commission factual findings are reviewed under the "substantial evidence" standard.[34] This "standard is satisfied by 'such relevant evidence as a reasonable mind might accept as adequate to support a conclusion.'"[35] While the "substantial evidence" standard of review is highly deferential, the CAFC adjusts the threshold for "substantial evidence" based on the burden of proof that was required in the proceedings below.

When the CAFC reversed a Commission finding of patent invalidity in *Finnigan Corp. v. U.S. International Trade Commission*, it demonstrated the significant flexibility of the "substantial evidence" standard.[36] The CAFC relied on the presumption of validity set forth in 35 U.S.C. § 282 (1994) and the fact that the "burden is on the party asserting invalidity to prove it with facts supported by clear and convincing evidence."[37] Based on this heightened burden of proof and a review of the record, the CAFC "determined that the invalidity determination was not based upon substantial evidence which [was] clear and convincing."[38]

While the "substantial evidence" standard may be flexible in some circumstances, that is not always so. Specifically, the CAFC may not:

> conduct a *de novo* investigation of the evidence on the record before it and reach an independent conclusion; rather, the court's review is limited to deciding whether there is sufficient evidence in the record considered as a whole to support the [Commission's] findings. The mere fact that a reasonable person

---

33. *See* Finnigan Corp. v. U.S. Int'l Trade Comm'n, 180 F.3d 1354, 1363 (Fed. Cir. 1999) (while the CAFC has the "ability to *review* claim construction de novo, it [is not required] to effectively *retry* claim construction de novo by consideration of novel arguments not first presented to the tribunal whose decision is on review").

34. *See* Enercon GmbH v. U.S. Int'l Trade Comm'n, 151 F.3d 1376, 1381 (Fed. Cir. 1998).

35. *Id.* (citing Consol. Edison Co. v. Nat'l Labor Relations Bd., 305 U.S. 197 (1938)).

36. *Finnigan Corp.*, 180 F.3d at 1354.

37. *Id.* at 1365 (citing SSIH Equip. S.A. v. U.S. Int'l Trade Comm'n, 718 F.2d 365, 375 (Fed. Cir. 1983)).

38. *Id.*

might reach some other conclusion is insufficient for [the CAFC] to overturn the [Commission's] conclusions.[39]

Appeals that hinge on finding error in the Commission's findings of fact must show that, in light of the relevant evidentiary requirements, the Commission's "determination, on the record, is arbitrary, capricious, or an abuse of discretion."[40]

3. Interpreting Section 337

While in practice the CAFC generally reviews Commission interpretations of law de novo, its official position is that as "the agency charged with the administration of section 337, [the Commission is entitled] to appropriate deference to its interpretation of the statute."[41] This deference affects the CAFC's review of Commission remedies and proceedings.

The limits of such deference were explored in *VastFame Camera v. International Trade Commission*. VastFame had been brought before the Commission in a post-determination enforcement proceedings with regard to a general exclusion order.[42] The ALJ refused to hear VastFame's patent invalidity argument, as a "defense [that] could not be raised in the enforcement proceeding."[43] VastFame had not been a party to the initial proceedings and argued that the enforcement proceedings were legally a new investigation, entitling VastFame to raise its defense under the statutory language of 19 U.S.C. § 1337(c).[44] The Commission, which agreed with its ALJ, argued that the words "all cases" in Section 337(c) meant only original investigations before the Commission and not "advisory and enforcement proceedings."[45] The Commission further argued to the

---

39. Akzo N.V. v. U.S. Int'l Trade Comm'n, 808 F.2d 1471, 1479 (Fed. Cir. 1986).

40. *Id.* at 1486 (citing Corning Glass Works v. U.S. Int'l Trade Comm'n, 799 F.2d 1559, 1568 (Fed. Cir. 1986).

41. Enercon GmbH v. U.S. Int'l Trade Comm'n, 151 F.3d 1376, 1381 (Fed. Cir. 1998) (citing Chevron U.S.A., Inc. v. Natural Res. Def. Council, Inc., 467 U.S. 837, 844 (1984)).

42. VastFame Camera v. U.S. Int'l Trade Comm'n, 386 F.3d 1108, 1110 (Fed. Cir. 2004); *see also* Kyocera Wireless Corp. v. U.S. Int'l Trade Comm'n, 545 F.3d 1340 (Fed. Cir. 2008).

43. *Id.*

44. *Id.* at 1113 ("All legal and equitable defenses may be presented in all cases" before the Commission.).

45. *Id.* at 1114.

CAFC that its enforcement proceedings were being exercised as a matter of inherent authority, thus falling outside Section 337.[46]

Ultimately, both Commission positions were reversed by the CAFC, which held that the Commission did have the power to conduct enforcement proceedings under 19 U.S.C. § 1337(b),[47] and that those enforcement proceedings fell under the rubric "all cases."[48] In turning aside the Commission's interpretation of Section 337, the CAFC voiced concern about the impact of a general exclusion order, which "broadly prohibits entry of articles that infringe the relevant claims of a listed patent without regard to whether the persons importing such articles were parties to, or were related to parties to, the investigation that led to the issuance of the general exclusion order."[49]

In interpreting Section 337 in *Kinik Company* v. *U.S. International Trade Commission*, the CAFC affirmed the Commission's ruling that the defenses established in 35 U.S.C. § 271(g) are not available in Section 337 investigations.[50] Kinik Company (Kinik) was the importer of products manufactured overseas in a manner accused of infringing a U.S. process patent in a Section 337 investigation. Kinik argued that because 19 U.S.C. § 1337(c) stated that all legal and equitable defenses may be presented in Commission investigations, it should be able to use the defenses under recently enacted 35 U.S.C. § 271(g). The Commission, siding with the ALJ, disagreed. Relying on Congress's interpretation of the Process Patent Amendments Act of 1988 that "[t]he amendments made by this subtitle shall not deprive a patent owner of any remedies available. . . under section 337 of the Tariff Act of 1930, or under any other provision of law" and the statement in the clause introducing the new defense to infringement by overseas practice of Section 271(g) that the new defenses were "for purposes of this title," the Commission concluded that the new defenses under Section 271(g) were to authorize district courts to adjudicate and impose liability for infringement based on the overseas practice of U.S. process patents.[51] The new defenses,

---

46. *Id.* at 1112.
47. *Id.*
48. *Id.* at 1115.
49. *Id.* at 1114.
50. Kinik Co. v. U.S. Int'l Trade Comm'n, 362 F.3d 1359, 1361–63 (Fed. Cir. 2004).
51. Prior to the enactment of § 271(g), patent owners facing overseas infringement of U.S. patents could only seek remedy by exclusion action under the Tariff Act. *Kinik*, 362 F.3d at 1362.

however, were not intended to be available in the Commission's Section 337 investigations. Kinik appealed to the CAFC, but the court upheld the Commission's ruling.

In *Amgen, Inc. v. U.S. International Trade Commission*, the CAFC affirmed the Commission's ruling that the safe harbor provision of 35 U.S.C. § 271(e)(1) applies in Section 337 investigations relating to process patents as well as to product patents, for imported products that are used for exempt purposes.[52] The CAFC also upheld the Commission's jurisdiction to investigate and remedy infringement with respect to products imported for purposes of obtaining federal approval, regardless of whether or not there was an actual sale in the United States or contract for sale of the imported product.[53] Amgen filed a complaint before the Commission, claiming certain importation of recombinant human erythropoietin and derivatives thereof (collectively, EPO) were in violation of Section 337. The producer and importer of the accused EPO, Roche, moved for summary determination of non-infringement as to all claims, on the ground that the imported EPO was exempt from infringement by operation of 35 U.S.C. § 271(e)(1),[54] the "safe harbor" statute, because the accused EPO was used for purposes that fell within this safe harbor. Amgen argued that the court in *Kinik* confirmed that no change was made in the Commission's authority under the Tariff Act to exclude products made abroad by a process infringing a U.S. process patent by the enactment of § 271(g)(1) and (2). The Commission disagreed with Amgen and granted Roche's motion. Amgen appealed to the CAFC. The court concluded that the Commission's decision that the safe harbor provided by § 271(e)(1) applied in "proceedings under the Tariff Act relating to process patents as well as product patents, for imported product that is used for exempt purposes" was consistent with congressional policy as set forth in enactment of § 271(g) and as shown by the Supreme Court precedent implementing the congressional policy.[55]

---

52. Amgen, Inc. v. U.S. Int'l Trade Comm'n, 565 F.3d 846, 856 (Fed. Cir. 2009).

53. *Id.* at 854.

54. 35 U.S.C. § 271(e)(1) states, "It shall not be an act of infringement to make, use, offer to sell, or sell within the United States or import into the United States a patented invention . . . solely for uses reasonably related to the development and submission of information under a Federal law which regulates the manufacture, use, or sale of drugs or veterinary biological products . . . ."

55. *Amgen*, 565 F.3d 848–51.

With respect to limits on the Commission's remedial powers, in *Spansion, Inc. v. U.S. International Trade Commission,*[56] the CAFC distinguished the discretionary injunctive relief in district court pursuant to 35 U.S.C. § 283 from the mandatory issuance of an exclusion order by the Commission in Section 337 investigations and agreed with the Commission that the statutory factors governing ITC remedial orders are not limited by the equitable framework established by *eBay.*[57] This decision has undoubtedly contributed to the Commission's increased caseload in recent years.[58]

In a test of the Commission's enforcement authority, a Chinese producer of ink printer cartridges and its U.S. subsidiary, Ninestar, challenged the Commission's imposition of a civil penalty as a result of Ninestar's deliberate violation of Commission remedial orders, arguing that the Commission's statute is "an unconstitutional monstrosity" by depriving it of a jury trial.[59] The CAFC disagreed. The court explained that the Commission is one of the administrative agencies to which Congress assigned adjudicatory authority with which trial by jury would be incompatible. The court stated, "Section 337 proceedings are integral to the control of unfair competition in trade, and the provision of a civil penalty is within regulatory authority and is appropriately assigned to the administrative agency."[60]

A significant 2011 CAFC decision addressed the Commission's authority with respect to foreign misappropriation of trade secrets. The CAFC was asked to decide whether the Commission exceeded its statutory power by finding a violation of Section 337 based on misappropriation of trade secrets occurring outside the United States.[61] The CAFC affirmed the Commission's ruling in favor of its authority over such misappropriation by a 2-1 vote. As an initial matter, the court held that a uniform federal standard, not a particular state's laws, controls what con-

---

56. Spansion, Inc. v. U.S. Int'l Trade Comm'n, 629 F.3d 1331, 1358–59 (Fed. Cir. 2011).

57. eBay Inc. v. MercExchange, L.L.C., 547 U.S. 388, 391 (2006).

58. The number of Commission's investigations more than doubled from calendar 2006 to 2011. Data from http://www.usitc.gov/ intellectual_property/documents/cy_337_institutions.pdf (last visited June 12, 2012).

59. Ninestar Tech. Co., Ltd. v. U.S. Int'l Trade Comm'n, 667 F.3d 1373, 1383 (Fed. Cir. 2012).

60. *Id.* at 1384.

61. TianRui Grp. Co. v. U.S. Int'l Trade Comm'n, 661 F.3d 1322 (Fed. Cir. 2011).

stitutes a misappropriation of trade secrets sufficient to establish an "unfair method of competition" under the statute.[62] On the question of extraterritoriality, the court held that the "Commission has authority to investigate and grant relief based in part on extraterritorial conduct insofar as it is necessary to protect domestic industries from injuries arising out of unfair competition in the domestic marketplace."[63] The court further ruled that the presumption against extraterritorial application of U.S. law did not govern this case for three reasons: (1) Section 337 is directed at "importation of articles," which is an "inherently international transaction"; (2) the regulated conduct is not purely "extraterritorial" because, if the goods manufactured using misappropriated trade secrets were not imported to the United States, Section 337 would not apply to conduct that occurred outside the United States; and (3) legislative history and flexible statutory language supports interpreting Section 337 as applicable to acts of trade secret misappropriation occurring overseas.[64] Finally, the court held that a domestic company injured by trade secret misappropriation that occurred abroad may seek relief from the Commission even if the company is not using those trade secrets in the U.S.[65]

C. ISSUE PRECLUSION

Congress did not intend decisions of the Commission on patent issues to have preclusive effect.[66] However, a Commission finding will have attributed to it "whatever persuasive value [the district court] consider[s] justified."[67] When the CAFC upholds the ITC on appeal, it strengthens the persuasive effect of the Commission's holding. On the other hand, when trademarks, as opposed to patents, are at issue, "courts have consistently recognized the commission's trademark determinations as having preclusive effect in subsequent cases."[68] Regardless, a district court, hear-

---

62. *Id.* at 1327–28.
63. *Id.* at 1324.
64. *Id.* at 1328–31.
65. *Id.* at 1335–37.
66. Minnesota Mining & Mfg. Co., Inc. v. Beautone Specialties Co., Ltd., 117 F. Supp. 2d 72, 82 (citing Texas Instruments v. Cypress Semiconductor Corp., 90 F.3d 1558, 1569 (Fed. Cir. 1996)).
67. *Id.*
68. V. James Adduci II & Michael L. Doane, *Curbing Counterfeit Goods*, LEGAL TIMES (week of Sept. 8, 1997) (citing Union Mfg. Co. v. Han Baek Trading Co., 763 F.2d 42 (2d Cir. 1985)).

ing a case that has also come before the Commission, cannot ignore a Commission decision that has been affirmed by the CAFC.

D. TIMING ISSUES

As is the case with appeals to any federal court, the briefing schedule is dependent upon receipt of the certified record—in this case, from the Commission. Because a United States agency is a party, under Federal Rule of Appellate Procedure 4(a)(1)(B), the notice of appeal must be filed within 60 days after the judgment or order is entered from which an appeal is sought. Pursuant to Federal Circuit Rule of Practice 17, no later than 40 days after the court serves a petition or notice of appeal on the Commission, the Commission must send to the clerk the certified list or index and a copy of the order or decision being appealed. Pursuant to Federal Circuit Rule 31, the appellant must serve and file a brief within 60 days after the certified list or index is filed. The appellee must serve and file a response brief within 40 days after service of the appellant's brief. The appellant may then file and serve a reply brief within 14 days after service of the appellee's brief. Intervenors' briefs are due within the same time as the appellee's brief—40 days after the appellant's brief is served.

E. WAIVER

One last, key timing issue to consider is that winning an appeal at the CAFC starts long before the first brief, or even the notice of appeal, becomes due. The CAFC is an appellate court that reviews decisions. As such, it does not consider a party's new theories, argued first on appeal, with only a few notable exceptions.[69] "In short, the CAFC does not 're-

---

69. In *Forshey v. Principi*, the CAFC articulated an exemplary set of exceptions where new arguments presented on appeal could be allowable: (1) "[w]hen new legislation is passed while an appeal is pending, courts have an obligation to apply the new law if Congress intended retroactive application even though the issue was not decided or raised below"; (2) "when there is a change in the jurisprudence of the reviewing court or the Supreme Court after consideration of the case by the lower court"; (3) "appellate courts may apply the correct law even if the parties did not argue it below and the court below did not decide it, but only if an issue is properly before the court"; (4) "where a party appeared pro se before the lower court, a court of appeals may appropriately be less stringent in requiring that the issue have been raised explicitly below." 284 F.3d 1335, 1355–57 (Fed. Cir. 2002) (en banc) (superseded by statute on other grounds).

view' that which was not presented to the district court."[70] Similarly, the Commission clearly states that "[i]n order to preserve an issue for review by the Commission or the U.S. Court of Appeals for the Federal Circuit that was decided adversely to a party, the issue must be raised in a petition for review, whether or not the Commission's determination on the ultimate issue, such as a violation of [S]ection 337, was decided adversely to the party."[71] The CAFC, on the basis of the Commission rules, has declined to hear issues first raised by the parties in petitions to the court.[72] Normally, the prevailing party before the ITC becomes and intervenor before the CAFC on the side of the ITC appellee.

When a party to an administrative proceeding, like a Section 337 investigation before the ITC, fails to assert an issue during that proceeding, other parties are not given an opportunity to present arguments on that issue before the agency. Moreover, the agency is not afforded the opportunity to consider the issue in the first instance.[73] "A party seeking review in [the CAFC] of a determination by the Commission must 'specifically assert' the error made by the ALJ in its petition for review to the Commission."[74] By comparison, adversely affected persons who were not parties to the ITC proceedings may have more leeway before the CAFC.

---

70. Sage Prods., Inc. v. Devon Indus., Inc., 126 F.3d 1420, 1426 (Fed. Cir. 1997).

71. 19 C.F.R. § 210.43(b)(3).

72. *See* Mag Instrument, Inc. v. U.S. Int'l Trade Comm'n, No. 88-1313, 868 F.2d 1278, n.2 (1989), (Fed. Cir. 1989) (declining to consider the patent invalidity issue due to the party's failure to raise that issue in its petition for review of the ALJ's ID before the Commission under a prior version of the Commission rule (citing Allied Corp. v. U.S. Int'l Trade Comm'n, 850 F.2d 1573, 1580 (Fed. Cir. 1988)).

73. The Commission insisted that complainant Tessera waived the right to petition respondents' patent exhaustion defense because it did not present the argument to the ALJ during the course of the investigation to afford him an opportunity to consider the argument and make appropriate findings. Further, Tessera did not raise the issue in its petition for review to the Commission. *Certain Semiconductor Chips with Minimized Chip Package Size, & Prods. Containing Same* (III), Inv. No. 337-TA-630, Comm'n Op. at 27 n.6 (Feb. 24, 2010).

74. Finnigan Corp. v. U.S. Int'l Trade Comm'n, 180 F.3d 1354, 1363 (Fed. Cir. 1999) (citing Checkpoint Sys., Inc. v. U.S. Int'l Trade Comm'n, 54 F.3d 756, 760 (Fed. Cir. 1995)).

CHAPTER 14

Parallel and Subsequent District Court Litigation

Parallel proceedings before the ITC and U.S. district court often arise when IP owners seek to use multiple avenues to protect their IP.[1] Under 28 U.S.C. § 1659(a), a respondent that finds itself in such parallel proceedings can move the district court, as a matter of right, to stay its proceedings until the Commission's determination on the claims that are common to both the Section 337 investigation and the district court action become final.[2] Further, after dissolution of the stay, 28 U.S.C. § 1659(b) allows the parties to use the record from the ITC proceeding in the district court proceeding. However, the use of this record does not necessarily guarantee an identical outcome in the district court proceeding. The Court of Appeals for the Federal Circuit (CAFC) has declined to give Commission determinations preclusive effect in district court patent cases.[3] Nonetheless, U.S. district courts frequently assign persua-

---

1. *See, generally,* Jeremiah B. Frueauf, *A Comparison of Section 337 Decisions at the Commission and Parallel District Court Proceedings: The Commission's Decisions Affect Dispositions at the District Courts,* 337 RE-PORTER, vol. XXII, Summer 2006, at 31.

2. In *In re Princo,* the Federal Circuit determined that the statutory language "until the determination of the Commission becomes final," means that the Commission's determination is no longer subject to judicial review. 478 F.3d 1345, 1355 (Fed. Cir. 2007) (determining that because the Commission proceedings were still ongoing before the appellate court, that the statute requires the a stay of pending district court infringement proceedings so long as the requirements of the statute are otherwise met).

3. Texas Instruments, Inc. v. Cypress Semiconductor Corp., 90 F.3d 1558 (Fed. Cir. 1996).

sive value to Commission determinations and findings when deciding parallel proceedings.[4]

A. STAY

28 U.S.C. § 1659(a) states:

> In a civil action involving parties that are also parties to a proceeding before the United States International Trade Commission . . . , at the request of a party to the civil action that is also a respondent in the proceeding before the Commission, the district court shall stay, until the determination of the Commission becomes final, proceedings in the civil action with respect to any claim that involves the same issues involved in the proceeding before the Commission, but only if such request is made within . . . 30 days after the party is named as a respondent in the proceeding before the Commission.

Under this statute, a stay of the district court action is mandatory with respect to claims involving the same issues as those in the ITC proceeding. Frequently, however, the district court action may include claims not present in the ITC. In these circumstances, district courts have discretion over whether to stay the non-parallel portion of the case. In *FormFactor, Inc. v. Micronics Japan Co., Ltd.*,[5] for example, the court set forth the following elements of inquiry in deciding to stay the entire case or only that portion of the case subject to 28 U.S.C. § 1659(a): (1) possible damage that may result from the granting of a stay; (2) the hardship or inequity that a party may suffer in being required to go forward; and (3) the orderly course of justice measured in terms of simplifying or complicating issues, proof, and questions of law that could be expected to result from a stay.[6] In that case, the plaintiff asserted four

---

4. *See* Fuji Photo Film Co. v. Jazz Photo Corp., 173 F. Supp. 2d 268, 274 (D.N.J. 2001) (granting summary judgment to the plaintiff and stating that "this Court is mindful of the findings and opinions rendered by the ALJ and Commission, as well as the opinion rendered by the Federal Circuit on appeal from the Commission").

5. No. CV-06-07159 JSW, 2008 WL 361128, at *1, *4 (N.D. Cal. Feb. 11, 2008).

6. *Id.* at *1.

patents in the district court, two of which were not at issue in the ITC proceeding. After considering the three factors, the court stayed the entire district court action. The court noted that the ITC proceeding could narrow the issues in the district court case, that continuing the district court action on the two patents not at issue at the ITC could result in duplicative discovery, and that staying the case would promote judicial efficiency, particularly because some of the issues at the ITC could bear on the issues in the district court case.[7]

In *Advanced Analogic Technologies, Inc. v. Linear Tech Corporation*, the court granted a complainant's motion to stay pending resolution of the investigation before the Commission, finding that it would conserve the resources of the parties and the court.[8] Also, in *ILJIN U.S.A. v. NTN Corporation*, the court granted complainant's motion to stay a declaratory judgment proceeding after considering numerous factors, including the following:

(1) the claim at the Commission was filed earlier than the district court complaint;

(2) the Commission proceedings were more advanced than those in the district court;

(3) there had not been substantial discovery in the case;

(4) there would be a conservation of judicial resources by allowing the Commission investigation to proceed—which could also lead to the benefit of avoiding conflicting decisions;

(5) the Commission had more experience adjudicating patent disputes; and

(6) the complainant did not present a persuasive reason why the stay should not have been granted.[9]

In *Micron Technology, Inc. v. Mosel Vitelic Corp.*, the defendants moved to stay the district court proceedings as to the claims that were not at issue before the Commission.[10] The defendants argued that, due to the significant overlap of legal and factual issues among the four claims before the Commission and the seven remaining infringement claims, staying the remaining claims "would enhance judicial economy and potentially stream-

---

7. *Id.* at *2–3.

8. No. C-06-00735 MMC, 2006 WL 2850017, at *3 (N.D. Cal. Oct. 4, 2006).

9. No. 06-10145, 2006 WL 568351, at *2 (E.D. Mich. Mar. 7, 2006).

10. No. CIV 98-0293-S-LMB, 1999 WL 458168 (D. Idaho Mar. 31, 1999).

line future proceedings in the instant action once the ITC action [was] resolved."[11] Defendants further argued that staying the district court action until resolution of the Commission proceedings "would provide the Court with the benefit of the findings, conclusions and views of the ITC," that they would be prejudiced by defending actions in multiple fora, and that the plaintiffs would not be prejudiced by a stay because the claims before the Commission would be resolved in a timely manner.[12]

The court denied the defendants' motion, stating that "[d]efendants [had] not established that a stay of the instant proceedings is necessary to prevent undue hardship or injustice."[13] The court noted that:

> [t]he Supreme Court of the United States has clearly indicated that "the power to stay proceedings is incidental to the power inherent in every court to control the disposition of the causes on its docket with economy of time and effort for itself, for counsel, and for litigants. How this can best be done calls for the exercise of judgment, which must weigh competing interests and maintain an even balance."[14]

The court went on to note that "the moving party 'must make out a clear case of hardship or inequity in being required to go forward, if there is even a fair possibility that the stay for which he prays will work damage to some one [sic] else.'"[15] The *Micron Technology* court ultimately ordered that discovery related to patent infringement claims not at issue in the ITC proceeding could continue, even while the rest of the action before it was stayed.[16]

---

11. *Id.* at *4.

12. *Id.*

13. *Id.* at *5.

14. *Id.* at *4 (quoting Landis v. N. Am. Co., 299 U.S. 248, 254–55 (1936)).

15. *Id.* (quoting *Landis*, 299 U.S. at 255). In the Fifth Circuit, a district court "certainly possesses the authority to regulate its flow of cases" through the imposition of a stay authorized by any statute. Coastal (Berm.) Ltd. v. E.W. Saybolt & Co., 761 F.2d 198, 204 n.6 (5th Cir. 1985). The court in *Coastal* stated, "Generally, the moving party bears a heavy burden to show why a stay should be granted absent statutory authorization, and a court should tailor its stay so as not to prejudice other litigants unduly." *Id.* (internal citation omitted). It stated further, "Where a discretionary stay is proposed, something close to genuine necessity should be the mother of its invocation." *Id.*

16. Micron Tech., Inc. v. Mosel Vitelic Corp., No. CIV 98-0293-S-LMB, 1999 WL 458168, at *5 (D. Idaho Mar. 31, 1999).

In *Alloc, Inc. v. Unilin Décor, N.V.*, the court adopted the alternative position and entered a stay, reasoning that:

> [e]ven though the '579 patent does not contain precisely the same claims of the other patents that are under review or reexamination, there is a sufficient correlation among all of the patents for the court to conclude that a stay is appropriate.

Additionally, with regard to the issue of efficiency, it is beyond dispute that the court would benefit from a narrowing of the numerous complex issues relating to claims which, if clearly defined, would streamline discovery and subsequent litigation.[17]

Finally, the court noted that discovery in the case had not yet begun, nor had a discovery schedule been entered at that time. Likewise, the court had not yet set a trial date. Therefore, the stay was entered before any party incurred substantial litigation-related expenses.[18]

B. PRECLUSION

The doctrines of claim and issue preclusion support similar policy considerations—namely, the need for finality and fairness in judicial proceedings and "to secure the peace and repose of society by the settlement of matters capable of judicial determination."[19] Claim preclusion prevents a party from suing on a claim that has been previously litigated to a final judgment by the party or such party's privies and precludes the assertion by such parties of any legal theory, cause of action, or defense that could have been asserted in that action.[20] Issue preclusion, also known as collateral estoppel, prevents relitigation of issues actually litigated and necessary to the outcome of the prior suit, even if the current action involves different claims or different parties.[21]

---

17. No. Civ. A. 03-253-GSM, 2003 WL 21640372, at *2 (D. Del. July 11, 2003).

18. *Id.* at *2–3.

19. Southern Pacific Ry. Co. v. United States, 168 U.S. 1, 49 (1897).

20. 18 Moore's Federal Practice § 131.10[1][a] (3d ed. 2007). Claim preclusion is also known as "res judicata." Although "res judicata" has often been used more broadly to encompass both claim and issue preclusion, it is used in the narrow sense. *Id.* at § 131.10[1][b].

21. *Id.*

1. Claim Preclusion

a. Preclusive Effect of Commission Determinations in District Court

The CAFC has established that the Commission's determinations on patent issues, i.e., validity and infringement, are not entitled to preclusive effect in subsequent patent infringement actions in U.S. district court. This holding includes patent-based defenses, e.g., patent validity[22] or patent misuse. For example, a district court giving preclusive effect to an ITC ruling on a patent misuse defense would directly conflict with the language of 28 U.S.C. § 1338, which specifically states that federal courts have original and exclusive jurisdiction of a civil action "arising under any *Act of Congress* relating to patents."[23] The legislative history of Section 337 provides:

> The Commission's findings neither purport to be, nor can they be, regarded as binding interpretations of the U.S. patent laws in particular factual contexts. Therefore, it seems clear that any disposition of a Commission action by a Federal Court should

---

22. *See, e.g., Certain Semiconductor Chips with Minimized Chip Package Size & Prods. Containing Same*, Inv. No. 337-TA-650, Comm'n Op., at 9–10 (July 29, 2009) ("[T]he Commission does not make final binding rulings on any action relating to patents, including determining their validity. That task is exclusively relegated to federal district courts (28 U.S.C. § 1338) and the USPTO. Rather, the Commission makes validity findings when considering defenses to a complainant's allegations that there has been a violation of Section 337. These validity rulings have no collateral estoppel effect outside of the Commission's own investigations." (citing Texas Instruments, Inc. v. Cypress Semiconductor Corp., 90 F.3d 1558, 1569 (Fed. Cir. 1996); Corning Glass Works v. U.S. Int'l Trade Comm'n, 799 F.2d 1559, 1570 n.12 (Fed. Cir. 1986))); *Certain Self-Inflating Mattresses*, Inv. No. 337-TA-302, Initial Determination, 1990 WL 710637, at *3 (Mar. 9, 1990) ("Congress has stated expressly that the Commission's patent validity determinations are not binding on district courts.").

23. 28 U.S.C. § 1338 (2006) (emphasis added). Additionally, the Federal Circuit has held that, because the Commission "considers, for its own purposes under section 337, the status of imports with respect to the claims of U.S. patents," an appeal of a Commission determination to the Federal Circuit "does not estop fresh consideration by other tribunals." Tandon Corp. v. U.S. Int'l Trade Comm'n, 831 F.2d 1017, 1019 (Fed. Cir. 1987) (citing Lannom Mfg. Co., Inc. v. U.S. Int'l Trade Comm'n, 799 F.2d 1572, 1577–78 (Fed. Cir. 1986)).

not have a res judicata or collateral estoppel effect in cases before such courts.[24]

It bears noting, however, that one circuit court of appeals concluded that the Commission's determinations on *non-patent* issues, such as trademark infringement, must be given res judicata effect in subsequent U.S. district court actions.[25] In another example, preclusive effect was given to a Commission determination that respondents failed to establish antitrust and unclean hands defenses, barring a subsequent claim of unfair competition that would have amounted to relitigation of those defenses.[26]

b. Preclusive Effect of District Court Determinations Before the Commission

The logical converse of the question of whether an ITC decision has preclusive effect in district court is the effect of district court decisions on the issues of validity and infringement at the Commission in Section 337 investigations. Addressing this issue, the CAFC concluded that when a claim "which is the basis for the Section 337 investigation is a claim which would be barred by a prior judgment if asserted in a second infringement suit, that . . . claim may also be barred in a § 1337 proceeding."[27] Prior U.S. district court decisions, therefore, have preclusive effect in Section 337 investigations.[28]

The Commission is required to give preclusive effect even with respect to subsequent district court decisions.[29] There is no preclusive ef-

---

24. S. REP. No. 93-1298, at 19 (1974).

25. Union Mfg. Co., Inc. v. Han Baek Trading Co., Ltd., 763 F.2d 42, 46 (2d Cir. 1985).

26. Baltimore Luggage Co. v. Samsonite Corp., 727 F. Supp. 202, 205 (D. Md. 1989), *aff'd*, 977 F.2d 571 (4th Cir. 1992).

27. Young Eng'rs, Inc. v. U.S. Int'l Trade Comm'n, 721 F.2d 1305, 1316 (Fed. Cir. 1983).

28. A "final judgment on the merits of an action precludes the parties or their privies from relitigating issues that were or could have been raised in that action." *Certain Hybrid Elec. Vehicles & Components Thereof*, Inv. No. 337-TA-688, Initial Determination, at 3 (May 21, 2010) (citing Federated Dep't Stores Inc. v. Moitie, 452 U.S. 394, 398 (1981)), *aff'd*, Comm'n Op. at 3–5 (June 22, 2010).

29. *See* SSIH Equip. S.A. v. U.S. Int'l Trade Comm'n, 718 F.2d 365, 370 (Fed. Cir. 1983) (affirming Commission's modification of an exclusion order to suspend the portion referring to two patents subsequently found by a district court to be invalid). Note, however, the Federal Circuit generally does not

fect, however, if the "specific device" at issue in the investigation is materially different from the device at issue in the prior district court action.[30] In *Universal Transmitters for Garage Door Openers*, for example, it was argued that a U.S. district court decision had no preclusive effect when the facts upon which that decision was rendered had materially changed in some way before they reached the Commission.[31] However, the ALJ in that case determined that a claim based on facts that had been before the district court was precluded, even though the district court did not address those facts in its decision.

2. Issue Preclusion

The CAFC has held that applying issue preclusion (or collateral estoppel) against a plaintiff is appropriate only if "(1) the issue is identical to one decided in the first action; (2) the issue was actually litigated in the first action; (3) resolution of the issue was essential to a final judgment in the first action; and (4) plaintiff had a full and fair opportunity to litigate the issue in the first action."[32] Such preclusion applies even if the issue was raised as an affirmative defense in one action and as a claim in a subsequent action.[33] The ITC, like any court, has discretion to decide whether issue preclusion applies,[34] but it may be found inapplicable to Commission proceedings subsequent to U.S. district court determinations if these four elements are not met.

---

apply preclusive effect to vacated judgments. *Certain Semiconductor Integrated Circuits Using Tungsten Metallization & Prods. Containing Same*, Inv. No. 337-TA-648, Comm'n Op. (Feb. 18, 2009) (affirming ALJ's finding that complainants were not precluded from asserting patent at the Commission after the district court's invalidity ruling on the same patent was vacated pursuant to a settlement agreement).

30. Foster v. Hallco Mfg. Co., 947 F.2d 469 (Fed. Cir. 1991).

31. *Certain Universal Transmitters for Garage Door Openers (Universal Transmitters)*, Inv. No. 337-TA-497, Order No. 14, at 6 (Jan. 14, 2004).

32. A.B. Dick Co. v. Burroughs, 713 F.2d 700, 702 (Fed. Cir. 1983).

33. Baltimore Luggage Co. v. Samsonite Corp., 727 F. Supp. 202, 205 (D. Md. 1989), *aff'd*, 977 F.2d 571 (4th Cir. 1992).

34. *Certain Semiconductor Integrated Circuits Using Tungsten Metallization & Prods. Containing Same*, Inv. No. 337-TA-648, Comm'n Op., at 3 (Feb. 18, 2009) ("The application of issue preclusion is discretionary and the court must determine if its application is appropriate in view of any equitable considerations.") (citing *In re* Freeman, 30 F.3d 1459, 1467 (Fed. Cir. 1994).

In the context of claim construction, the Commission has held that district court findings are due preclusive effect in subsequent infringement suits only to the extent that the determination is essential to a final judgment on the question of validity or infringement.[35] For example, the ALJ in *Electronic Devices with Multi-Touch Enabled Touch Pads and Touchscreens* ruled that the complainant was collaterally estopped from challenging certain claim constructions from a prior district court litigation, noting that the claim construction ruling was essential to the final judgment on infringement because "an infringement analysis *requires* determining the meaning and scope of the patent claims."[36] However, the CAFC has stated that determinations regarding the scope of patent claims made in former adjudication should be narrowly construed.[37] Further, to apply issue preclusion to a claim interpretation issue decided in a prior infringement adjudication, the interpretation of the claim must be the reason for the loss on the issue of infringement.[38] In the case of *EPROM*, the Commission denied the respondent's motion for preclusive effect because it was unclear whether the U.S. district court's claim construction order was subject to appeal.[39]

D. TRANSFER OF RECORD

When a Section 337 investigation is completed, the record of the Commission's proceedings may be presented to the district court for entry into evidence either (1) pursuant to a formal request by the district

---

35. *Universal Transmitters*, Order No. 14, at 10.
36. *Certain Elec. Devices with Multi-Touch Enabled Touch Pads and Touchscreens*, Inv. No. 337-TA-714, Order No. 16, at 5–6 (Sept. 29, 2010) (emphasis in original) (citing Markman v. Westview Instruments, 52 F.3d 967, 976 (Fed. Cir. 1995)).
37. A.B. Dick Co. v. Burroughs, 713 F.2d at 704.
38. Jackson Jordan, Inc. v. Plasser American Corp., 747 F.2d 1567, 1577 (Fed. Cir. 1984).
39. *Certain EPROM, EEPROM, Flash Memory, & Flash Microcontroller Semiconductor Devices & Prods. Containing Same*, Inv. No. 337-TA-395, Comm'n Op., at 79 (Dec. 11, 2000). The Commission acknowledged the district court's claim construction was necessary to the district court's proceeding at the time and noted that the construction could later be relegated to mere dictum. *Id.* at n.87. In other words, the preclusive effect of the claim construction depended on whether it could be appealed later. "In view of these uncertainties," the Commission concluded, "we deny [Respondent]'s motion for preclusive effect." *Id.*

court or (2) by agreement among the parties, including third-party suppliers of CBI. Confidential discovery obtained in the investigation, however, may not be used in the district court litigation absent an agreement of the parties, again, including third-party suppliers of CBI.

Transfer of the Commission record to a U.S. district court is governed by 28 U.S.C. § 1659(b). This statute provides that, after dissolution of a stay in the district court, the record of the proceeding before the Commission *"shall be transmitted* to the district court and shall be admissible in the civil action."[40] The Commission, however, has implemented regulations such that the transfer of the Commission record to the district court does not occur automatically.

Pursuant to Commission Rule 210.39(b), the Commission "shall certify to the district court such portions of the record of its proceeding *as the district court may request.*"[41] Accordingly, the district court must request that the Commission transfer the investigatory record to it.

1. *Proper Request by the District Court*

The plain language of Commission Rule 210.39(b)—"as the district court may request"—suggests that a request directed to the Commission by a U.S. district court is the proper method to effect transfer of the investigation record to that court.[42] The district court may request the Commission's record, or any portion thereof, on its own or as a result of a motion or other request by a party to the district court proceeding.[43] However, the Commission does not simply accede to the request, but will first determine whether the request is proper, which may lead to additional delay and expense.[44] If the Commission determines that the request is appropriate under 28 U.S.C. § 1659(b), it will permit the Commission secretary to provide the district court with a certified copy of the investigation's docket list.[45] The secretary's office will thereafter provide any item from that docket list that the district court specifically requests.[46]

---

40. 28 U.S.C. § 1659(b) (2011) (emphasis added).

41. 19 C.F.R. § 210.39(b) (2012) (emphasis added).

42. *Id.*

43. Steven Anzalone & Paul C. Goulet, *Use of International Trade Commission's Evidentiary Record in a District Court Proceeding: The Mechanism's Implication of Transfer of the Commission Record*, 337 Reporter vol. XIX, Winter 2003, at *3.

44. *Id.*

45. *Id.*

46. *Id.*

2. Record Proffered by the Parties

Parties often avoid the requirement of the formal request and proffer their own copies of certain items from the Commission's proceedings to the district court.[47] Suppliers of CBI subject to a protective order, particularly parties to the investigation, often stipulate that discovery obtained or evidence entered in the Commission proceedings may be used in discovery or offered into evidence before the district court.[48] In addition, parties will cite Commission rulings as matters of public record.[49] A party that seeks to use this method to transfer the investigation record to the district court must obtain (1) the consent of the parties and third-party suppliers of confidential business information prior to proffering documents containing such information, and (2) permission from the supplier to retain CBI, despite the standard destruction clause of the Commission's protective order.

3. Use of Confidential Business Information

Section 337 provides:

> Information submitted to the Commission or exchanged among parties in connection with proceedings under this section which is properly designated as confidential pursuant to Commission rules may not be disclosed (except under a protective order issued under regulations of the Commission which authorizes disclosure of such information) to any person (other than a person described in paragraph (2)) without the consent of the person submitting it.[50]

This statutory language is implemented by Commission Rules 210.5(b), restricting disclosure of CBI, and 210.39(a), governing in camera treatment of CBI—as well as by protective orders issued by the ALJs to whom Section 337 investigations are assigned.[51] Protective orders include standard language requiring written agreement that the signatory will use CBI obtained in the investigation "solely for purposes of [that] investigation." Accordingly, counsel to a Section 337 investigation are

---

47. *Id.* at *4.
48. *Id.*
49. *Id.*
50. 19 U.S.C. § 1337(n)(1) (2006).
51. 19 C.F.R. §§ 210.5(b), 210.39(a).

not entitled to use confidential discovery obtained in that investigation in any other action absent consent of the supplier.

4. *Protective Order Destruction Clause*

Commission protective orders typically require destruction of CBI documents obtained during a Section 337 investigation, upon final termination of the investigation. For purposes of retaining CBI, the Commission has defined "final termination of the investigation" as exhaustion of the appellate process.[52]

Thus, in addition to the issues discussed above, parties that proffer copies of documents from Commission proceedings to a district court, or otherwise retain CBI obtained in a Section 337 investigation, may inadvertently find themselves in violation of this destruction clause. Accordingly, parties seeking to use CBI in a U.S. district court should seek to obtain permission from the supplier prior to the final termination of the investigation.

---

52. Notice of Proposed Rulemaking Concerning Post-Investigation Retention and Use of Confidential Business Information from Investigations on Unfair Practices in Import Trade, 60 Fed. Reg. 27,723–24 (Feb. 9, 1995) (codified at 19 C.F.R. 210).

Enforcement, Advisory Opinions, and Design-Arounds

A. COMMISSION ENFORCEMENT OF SECTION 337 REMEDIES

The Commission has the authority to impose a monetary penalty if a respondent fails to comply with a cease and desist order, or a consent order, issued in a Section 337 investigation.[1] The maximum amount of the penalty is the greater of either $100,000 for each day the proscribed activities or imports occur or twice the domestic value of the imported items.[2] The ability to impose monetary sanctions serves as a powerful tool for the ITC to ensure compliance with its orders.

The Commission's authority to impose civil penalties on parties in violation of cease and desist orders and consent orders was challenged,

---

1. *See, e.g., Certain Lens-Fitted Film Packages,* Inv. No. 337-TA-406, Comm'n Op. (Sept. 12, 2007). The CAFC affirmed the Commission's authority to enjoin respondents' officers, employees and agents from engaging in violations of Section 337 and to impose civil penalties for their violation of cease and desist orders, but remanded the case to the Commission for the actual amount of penalty that should be imposed. Fuji Photo Film Co. v. U.S. Int'l Trade Comm'n, 474 F.3d 1281 (Fed. Cir. 2007). Following the court's ruling, the Commission adjusted the civil penalty of $13,675,000 to $13,128,000 for violation of cease and desist orders; *see also* San Huan New Materials High Tech, Inc. v. U.S. Int'l Trade Comm'n, 474 F.3d 1281 (Fed. Cir. 2007). Following the court's ruling, the Commission, 161 F.3d 1347 (1998) (upholding civil penalty of $1.55 Million for violation of a consent order issued in Investigation No. 337-TA-372, *Certain Neodymium-Iron-Boron Magnets, Magnet Alloys, and Articles Containing Same*).

2. 19 U.S.C. § 1337 (f)(2) (2006).

and upheld, in *Ink Cartridges*.[3] In that investigation, the complainant filed an enforcement complaint after the Commission's final determination of a violation was affirmed by the Federal Circuit. In the enforcement proceeding, the Commission found that certain respondents had either violated the Commission's cease and desist orders or a consent order. Accordingly, the Commission ordered the respondents to pay civil fines ranging from $55,000 per violation day to the maximum penalty of $100,000 per violation day, with total penalties up to $11 million for one particular group of respondents.[4] On appeal, those respondents argued that the penalties were "of such magnitude as to be criminal in nature and that a procedure whereby an administrative agency levies a criminal penalty is an unconstitutional violation of separation of powers."[5] The Federal Circuit rejected the argument and affirmed the Commission's imposition of civil penalties for violation of its remedial orders, stating that "Section 337 proceedings are integral to the control of unfair competition in trade, and the provision of a civil penalty is within regulatory authority and is appropriately assigned to the administrative agency."[6]

Civil penalties are not available for violations of exclusion orders, the enforcement of which is primarily the responsibility of U.S. Customs and Border Protection (Customs). Given that the exclusion orders provided to Customs by the Commission typically lack particularity and Customs' limited resources available for enforcement, the infringing products may continue to be imported into the United States and compete with the complainant's products in the U.S. market despite the existence of the exclusion orders. If a complainant believes that infringing products covered by such an order are entering the United States, the complainant may ask the Commission to institute an enforcement proceeding.[7]

---

3. *Certain Ink Cartridges & Components Thereof (Ink Cartridges)*, Inv. No. 337-TA-565, Comm'n Op. (Sept. 24, 2009).

4. *Id.*, at 44–45.

5. Ninestar Tech. Co. v. U.S. Int'l Trade Comm'n, 667 F.3d 1373, 1384 (Fed. Cir. 2012).

6. *Id.*

7. 19 C.F.R. § 210.75 (2012). *See* Tom Schaumberg, *Advantages of ITC Practice*, Keynote Address at AIPLA Annual Meeting (Oct. 18, 2007); *see also Certain Personal Data & Mobile Commc'ns Devices & Related Software*, Inv. No. 337-TA-710, Enforcement Complaint (June 4, 2012); *Certain Liquid Crystal Display Devices & Prods. Containing Same*, Inv. No. 337-TA-631, Enforcement Complaint (Dec. 1, 2009); *Ink Cartridges*, Enforcement Complaint (Mar. 18, 2008); *Certain Automated Mechanical Transmission Sys. for Medium-Duty & Heavy-Duty Trucks & Components Thereof*, Inv. No. 337-TA-503, Enforcement Complaint (May 11, 2005).

If the Commission finds a violation of an exclusion order, it may modify the existing order to cover the infringing products to stop the continuance of importation of infringing items.[8] In addition, the Commission may issue an order directing the seizure and forfeiture of any imported items subject to an exclusion order where the Commission finds that the party has (1) previously attempted to import the product; (2) has been denied entry because of a final exclusion order; and (3) has received written notice of the exclusion order and the risk of seizure and forfeiture.[9]

B. CUSTOMS ENFORCEMENT OF EXCLUSION ORDERS

Customs is primarily responsible for enforcing exclusion orders issued by the Commission in Section 337 investigations. Customs has stated that it "is without legal authority to determine patent infringement."[10] Nevertheless, exclusion orders are typically directed to articles "that infringe" the patents at issue, so to enforce an exclusion order, Customs must in essence determine whether imported merchandise infringes.

When the ITC issues an exclusion order, it sends a copy of the order to the IP Rights Branch of Customs Headquarters in Washington, D.C. The attorneys in the IP Rights Branch consult with the ITC regarding any questions about the language of the order and any technical questions. Then, the branch forwards the order to Customs' Office of Field Operations. The Office of Field Operations enters the information contained in the order into Customs' selectivity criteria database so that it is available electronically to Customs officers at all of the ports of entry into the United States. Customs' IP Rights Branch also provides training to import specialists and other Customs officials

---

8. 19 C.F.R. § 210.75(b)(4).

9. 19 C.F.R. § 210.75(b)(6).

10. U.S. CUSTOMS AND BORDER PROTECTION, WORKING WITH U.S. CUSTOMS AND BORDER PROTECTION (CBP) AND CUSTOMS IN THE EUROPEAN UNION (EU) TO PROTECT YOUR INTELLECTUAL PROPERTY RIGHTS (IPR), *available at* http://www.cbp.gov/linkhandler/cgov/trade/trade_outreach/trade_symposium_archive/symposium08/event_materials/ipr/joint_guide.ctt/joint_guide.pdf (last visited July 5, 2012).

at the ports of entry.[11] These enforcement procedures are set forth in a Customs directive:

> ENFORCEMENT. In general, Exclusion Orders issued by the ITC are administered by the Office of Regulations & Rulings, IPR Branch, but are processed by the Office of Field Operations. Upon receipt of orders from the ITC, an "Exclusion Order Notice" is released to the field through the Office of Field Operations . . . via the U.S. Customs Bulletin Board . . . and will provide details relative to the enforcement of a particular order . . .
>
> 4.1 Procedures. The strategic operational analysis staff (SOAS) will update cargo and/or summary selectivity criteria to include exclusion order information.
>
> * * *
>
> 4.1.2. Where goods determined to be subject to an Exclusion Order are presented to Customs, field officers must exclude the goods from entry into the United States and permit export.[12]

C. CUSTOMS ADMINISTRATIVE RULINGS REGARDING EXCLUSION ORDERS

Customs has administrative procedures under which importers may file a request for a ruling with respect to the applicability of customs and related laws to a specific set of facts. These procedures can be used by importers to obtain rulings on the scope of Commission exclusion orders. Significantly, these ruling procedures are confidential and ex parte, meaning that the complainant in the underlying ITC matter may not participate in them. Several examples of such rulings are discussed below.

---

11. Munford Page Hall II, *US: ITC: Obtain Maximum Results from Exclusion Orders, in* MANAGING INTELLECTUAL PROPERTY, Oct. 2009, *available at* http://www.managingip.com/Article/2328151/US-ITC-Obtain-maximum-results-from-exclusion-orders.html.

12. OFFICE OF REGULATIONS AND RULINGS, U.S. CUSTOMS AND BORDER PROTECTION, CUSTOMS DIRECTIVE NO. 2310-006A, at 2 (Dec. 16, 1999), *available at* http://www.cbp.gov/linkhandler/cgov/trade/legal/directives/2310-006a.ctt/2310-006a.pdf.

In Headquarters Rulings (HQ) 470783, 470784, and 470875, Customs held that a "redesign" of certain semiconductor devices did not take them outside the scope of the exclusion order issued in *EPROM,* Investigation Number 337-TA-395.[13] Customs reviewed product samples and documentation submitted by the ruling requesters and determined that, because the claim of the patent at issue was "especially broad[,]" the redesign did not eliminate probable patent infringement.

In HQ 475295 (Feb. 20, 2004), Customs held that the exclusion order in *Audible Alarm Devices for Divers,* Investigation Number 337-TA-365, was applicable to a company determined to be an affiliate of the respondent on the basis of allegations by the complainant and a review of the Web site of one of the companies.[14]

Lens-Fitted Film Packages, Investigation Number 337-TA-406, has been the subject of numerous Customs rulings.[15] In HQ 474939 (Jan. 6, 2004), for example, Customs held that a sample single-use camera was a lens-fitted film package but was not within the scope of any of the claims and, therefore, was not within the scope of the exclusion order.[16]

In HQ H067500 (Aug. 5, 2009), Customs held that three "redesigned" semiconductor chip samples submitted by or on behalf of certain respondents whose products were found to be infringing in *Digital Televisions*, Investigation Number 337-TA-617, were not subject to the ITC's exclusion order. Funai, the complainant in the Commission investigation, then brought suit against Customs before the Court of International Trade, seeking a temporary restraining order and preliminary injunction to enforce the exclusion order, and to enjoin Customs from permitting importers from bringing any "redesigned" products into the U.S. The court, however, held that it did not have subject matter jurisdiction to review challenges to Customs rulings related to the administration of

---

13. HQ 470783 (April 10, 2001), *available at* 2001 WL 456817; HQ 470784 (Apr. 10, 2001), *available at* 2001 WL 456840; HQ 470785 (April 10, 2001), *available at* 2001 WL 456841.

14. HQ 475295 (Feb. 20, 2004), *available at* 2004 WL 527438.

15. Customs has issued over 40 rulings regarding the applicability of this exclusion order to newly constructed cameras, not including refurbished single-use cameras, of which 32 rulings held the exclusion order inapplicable, eight held the exclusion order applicable, one demanded the importer to show evidence that the products have been licensed and refurbished using the permissible steps. (HQ 474182 (Nov. 6, 2003), *available at* 2003 WL 22794084).

16. HQ 474939 (Jan. 6, 2004), *available at* 2004 WL 254590.

International Trade Commission exclusion orders, and dismissed the defendant's motion for summary judgment.[17]

The preceding rulings relate to prospective transactions—those in which the importation has not yet occurred. If imported goods are excluded from entry by Customs pursuant to a Commission exclusion order, the importer may contest Customs' action by filing a protest under 19 U.S.C. § 1514 within 180 days of notice of the action protested.

Importers may appeal adverse Customs decisions (whether by administrative ruling or by denial of a protest) to the U.S. Court of International Trade.[18]

D. CUSTOMS PENALTIES

Section 337 does not provide for penalties (other than seizure of the imported goods) for violating exclusion orders issued by the Commission. Nevertheless, persons violating an exclusion order could potentially be subject to penalties imposed by Customs. In practice, however, Customs has rarely sought to impose such penalties.

Customs' primary penalty statute is 19 U.S.C. § 1592. Under this statute, any person who, by fraud, gross negligence, or negligence, enters or introduces, or attempts to enter or introduce, any merchandise into the commerce of the United States by means of data, information, written or oral statement, or act that is material and false, or any omission that is material, is subject to varying degrees of penalties.[19] For fraud, the maximum penalty may not exceed the domestic value of the imported merchandise. For gross negligence, the maximum penalty may not exceed the lesser of the domestic value of the merchandise or four times the duties, taxes, and fees of which the United States is deprived. And, for negligence, the maximum penalty may not exceed the lesser of the domestic value of the merchandise or two times the duties, taxes, and fees of which the United States is deprived. In the case of gross negligence and negligence, if the violation does not affect the assessment of

---

17. Funai Elec. Co. v. United States, 645 F. Supp. 2d 1351, 1354–58 (Ct. Int'l Trade 2009).

18. 28 U.S.C. § 1581(a) (2011); *see also* Fuji Photo Film Co. v. Benun, 463 F.3d 1252, 1255 (Fed. Cir. 2006) (noting that the Court of International Trade has exclusive jurisdiction over denials of protests arising under 19 U.S.C. § 1515).

19. 19 U.S.C. § 1592 (2006).

duties, the maximum penalties are, respectively, 20 and 40 percent of the dutiable value of the imported merchandise. For purposes of 19 U.S.C. § 1592, fraud encompasses situations in which the action of the person subject to the penalty is voluntary and intentional. Gross negligence encompasses situations in which the action of the person subject to the penalty is with actual knowledge or wanton disregard. Negligence is the failure of the person subject to the penalty to exercise reasonable care.

Customs has indicated that it believes Section 1592 could be applicable to an importer of merchandise subject to an exclusion order who cannot establish that it used reasonable care to ensure compliance with the exclusion order.[20] However, it does not appear that Customs has ever initiated a penalty action under 19 U.S.C. § 1592 that related to enforcement of a Commission exclusion order. Instead, Customs has issued a penalty determination in regard to merchandise subject to a Section 337 exclusion order under another Customs penalty statute, 19 U.S.C. § 1595(a). Pursuant to Section 1595(a), persons who direct, assist, or are in any way concerned with the introduction or attempted introduction into the United States of an article contrary to law are subject to penalties up to the value of the merchandise introduced or attempted to be introduced. Section 1595(a) also provides for seizure and forfeiture of merchandise introduced or attempted to be introduced into the United States if certain conditions are present.

In HQ 655205, Customs applied this statute to the importation of certain lamps subject to the exclusion order in *Multi-Level Touch Control Lighting Switches*, Investigation Number 337-TA-225.[21] Customs denied any mitigation of the penalty, noting that penalties under 19 U.S.C. § 1595(a) do not require a finding of culpability and that publication in the *Federal Register* of exclusion orders is public notice to the importer. Customs limited the penalty amount to the deposit made by the importer at the time of entry to obtain release of the merchandise.

E. ADVISORY OPINIONS

Pursuant to Commission Rule 210.79(a),[22] any person can request the ITC to institute an advisory opinion proceeding to provide guidance on

---

20. 19 C.F.R. § 171 app. B, Customs Regulations, Guidelines for the Imposition and Mitigation of Penalties for Violations of 19 U.S.C. § 1592, at (D)(6), (E)(1)(b)(ii) (2012).

21. HQ 655205 (Aug. 5, 1988).

22. 19 C.F.R § 210.79(a).

whether a proposed course of action, e.g., importation of a design-around product, would violate an ITC exclusion order, cease and desist order, or consent order.[23] In practice, this request would most likely come from the importer who believes the importation of a particular product or other conduct does not violate an order. When considering a request for an advisory opinion, the ITC looks to the following factors:

(1) whether the issuance of an advisory opinion would facilitate the enforcement of Section 337;
(2) whether the issuance of an advisory opinion would be in the public interest;
(3) whether an advisory opinion would benefit consumers and competitive conditions in the U.S.; and
(4) whether the person making the request has a compelling business need for the advice and has framed its request as fully and accurately as possible.[24]

Advisory opinions are not explicitly addressed in Section 337, and there are no statutory or regulatory deadlines for issuing an advisory opinion. When the Commission initiates an advisory opinion proceeding, however, it sometimes sets a deadline for the ALJ. In one proceeding, for example, the Commission established a deadline of nine months.[25] The Commission's authority to issue advisory opinions has been recognized by the U.S. Court of Appeals for the Federal Circuit.[26] The court acknowledged that advisory opinions are not subject to appeal.[27]

---

23. *See, e.g., Certain GPS Devices & Prods. Containing Same*, Inv. No. 337-TA-602, Advisory Op. (Apr. 20, 2010) (concluding, upon a third-party request for an advisory opinion, that the third party's products would not violate the limited exclusion order); *see also Certain Laser Bar Code Scanners & Scan Engines, Components Thereof & Prods. Containing Same (Laser Bar Code Scanners)*, Inv. No. 337-TA-551, Advisory Op. (Oct. 4, 2007) (holding that respondents' redesigned products were not covered by the Commission's remedial orders issued in the underlying investigation).

24. 19 C.F.R. § 210.79(a); *see also Laser Bar Code Scanners*, Advisory Op., at 5 (Oct. 4, 2007).

25. *See Certain Hardware Logic Emulation Sys. & Components Thereof (Hardware Logic)*, Inv. No. 337-TA-383, Notice of Institution of an Advisory Opinion Proceeding, at 2 (Nov. 10, 1999).

26. Allied Corp. v. U.S. Int'l Trade Comm'n, 850 F.2d 1573, 1578 (Fed. Cir. 1988).

27. *Id.*

F. DESIGN-AROUNDS

Developing a non-infringing variation of an accused product can be an effective method to avoid being barred from participating in the U.S. marketplace (in the event the complainant prevails in the investigation). Such a design-around is normally developed in consultation with patent counsel to ensure non-infringement of the patents raised in the investigation.

The design-around, or "work-around," option should be implemented at the earliest opportunity during the proceeding to facilitate a non-infringement finding, first by the ALJ and then by the ITC. Such early action is the safest and surest means of having the design-around addressed with respect to the ITC's remedy determination.[28] The design-around must fall within the scope of the investigation, which is governed by the ITC's Notice of Investigation published in the *Federal Register*, not by the complaint.[29] For example, the ITC has issued infringement determinations regarding products that were not specified in the complaint (and were merely under development at the time of filing), but nevertheless fell within the scope of the Notice of Investigation.[30] In *Flash Memory Circuits*, the ITC found that the ALJ erred in declining to determine whether the respondent's newly designed products infringed the patent-in-suit. The ALJ found that the documentation provided by one of the respondents in the investigation was inadequate for the complainant to determine whether the new designs were capable of infringing the patent-in-suit.[31] The ALJ further found that the respondent's new designs were not part of the investigation and that the respondent had not

---

28. Vizio, Inc. v. U.S. Int'l Trade Comm'n, 605 F. 3d 1330, 1345 (Fed. Cir. 2010) (*rev'g Certain Digital Televisions & Certain Prods. Containing Same and Methods of Using Same*, Inv. No. 337-TA-617) (Clevenger, J., dissenting-in-part) (issue of whether respondent-appellants' "work-around products" infringe was untimely raised and therefore not appealed).

29. *Hardware Logic,* Order No. 57, at 7 n.9 (Dec. 9, 1996).

30. *See Certain Flash Memory Circuits & Prods. Containing Same (Flash Memory Circuits)*, Inv. No. 337-TA-382, Comm'n Op., at 19–25 (July 1997); *see also Certain Voltage Regulators, Components Thereof, & Prods. Containing Same*, Inv. No. 337-TA-564, Enforcement Initial Determination, at 43 (Mar. 18, 2010) (finding no modification of limited exclusion order necessary because order "would encompass the accused products at issue in this enforcement proceeding (i.e., the design-around products)").

31. It is not expressly stated in the opinion whether Samsung had already deployed the newly designed products. Based on the discussion set forth in the opinion, however, it appears that the new products were still in the development stage.

provided any documentary evidence that it was importing flash memory products using the new designs. The ALJ, therefore, declined to determine whether the respondent's newly designed products infringed the patent-in-suit. The Commission reversed the ALJ's holding, stating that "questions regarding the importation or development stage of [the respondent's] new designs did not offer any appropriate basis for the ALJ to decline to make a determination of infringement."[32] The ITC went on to note:

> Questions regarding importation and the developmental stage of the devices go not only to jurisdiction but also to the merits of the case itself. Where the jurisdictional requirements of section 337 mesh with the factual requirements necessary to prevail on the merits, the appropriate course of action is to assume jurisdiction and resolve the complaint on its merits.[33]

While the complainant had the opportunity at the hearing to address the new designs that fell within the scope of the notice of investigation, it failed to do so. As a result, the new designs were found not to infringe "due to a failure of proof."[34]

A corollary of the Commission's authority to rule on products not yet in existence at the time of filing of the complaint is that discovery may be allowed into such products. The requirement that developmental products be commercially available has been rejected.[35] In general, discovery of "new products under development that fall within the scope of the investigation where such products are likely to be made or imported

---

32. *Flash Memory Circuits*, Comm'n Op., at 12.

33. *Id.* at 12–13 (citing Amgen, Inc. v. U.S. Int'l Trade Comm'n, 902 F.2d 1532, 1536 (Fed. Cir. 1990)). It should be noted, however, that "the importation and development of the new designs were only minor considerations in the ALJ's analysis. The primary reason why he declined to determine whether [the respondent's] new designs infringe[d] the [patent-at-issue] was that [the respondent's] document production has allegedly been inaccurate, inadequate, and untimely."

34. *Id.* at 16.

35. *See Certain Plastic Encapsulated Integrated Circuits (Integrated Circuits)*, Inv. No. 337-TA-315, Order No. 15 (Dec. 11, 1990); *see also Certain Static Random Access Memories & Integrated Circuit Devices Containing Same, Processes for Making Same, Components Thereof & Prods. Containing Same*, Inv. No. 337-TA-325, Order No. 12 (July 9, 1991).

into the United States prior to the close of the evidentiary record" has been permitted.[36]

Following this line of decisions, a motion in limine to limit evidence and argument to products that were commercially available and imported into the United States was denied in *Abrasive Products*. In the motion in limine, the respondent asserted that "the Commission cannot have jurisdiction over a claimed threat of infringement by devices to be produced in the future that have not yet entered the United States."[37] Rejecting this assertion, the ALJ noted that the prototype products were being marketed in the United States, and therefore, "[u]nder these circumstances, the scope of this investigation includes [the respondent's] prototype products because they may enter the stream of commerce in the United States during the course of this investigation."[38]

Although no clearly identifiable standard has been expressly articulated by the ITC for determining whether a product has reached a sufficient stage of development to be considered in a Section 337 investigation, decisions by various ALJs, primarily in the context of discovery, provide some guidance. If the design of a product in development is at or near completion, or such a product is likely to be made or imported into the United States during the course of the investigation, an infringement determination should be made by the ALJ. This is particularly true if the product is actually being marketed in the United States. Making such an infringement determination adheres to the ITC admonition in *Flash Memory*

---

36. *Certain Network Interface Cards*, Inv. No. 337-TA-455, Order No. 34, at 5 (Aug. 30. 2001) (citing *SDRAMS*, Inv. No. 337-TA-325, Order No. 12 (Sept. 23, 1991)); *see also Integrated Circuits*, Order No. 15; *Certain Hardware Logic Emulation Sys.*, Inv. No. 337-TA-383, Order No. 57, at 7 (discovery regarding products within the scope of the investigation that are in development, and that are likely to be imported into the United States, has been permitted in Section 337 investigations); *Certain Audio Processing Integrated Circuits, & Prods. Containing Same*, Inv. No. 337-TA-538, Order No. 7, at 2–3 (July 18, 2005) (the products under development had already "advanced to the 'beta' test stage," thus "[i]t appears more than plausible that the [products under development] will enter the marketplace during the pendency of this investigation").

37. *Certain Abrasive Prods.*, Inv. No. 337-TA-449, Order No. 37, at 2 (Oct. 10, 2001).

38. *Id.* (citing *Certain Safety Eyewear & Components Thereof*, Inv. No. 337-TA-433, Order No. 15 (Aug. 11, 2000)).

Circuits that, under such circumstances, "the appropriate course of action is to assume jurisdiction and resolve the complaint on its merits."[39]

A design-around strategy depends, of course, on the ability to develop a variation of the accused product that can be persuasively demonstrated to fall outside the scope of the asserted patents. There are also several practical considerations with respect to a design-around strategy. First, and most important, the design-around product has to be commercially feasible. There is no point in offering the marketplace something it does not want.

Second, the design-around product must be capable of being brought to market rapidly because of the expedited time frame of Section 337 investigations. The goal is to make the facts regarding the new product available as early as possible during the discovery period, which normally lasts five to eight months from the time the investigation commences. It is critical for the respondent to introduce its design-around product early enough to give the complainant the opportunity to take discovery of the product and related information.[40] Meanwhile, the respondent can develop its own expert testimony regarding the design-around in time for the evidence to be introduced at the evidentiary hearing.[41]

A third consideration, closely tied to the second, is that the design-around product must be procedurally positioned for consideration by the ALJ as part of the case. To ensure that this occurs, the design-around product should be as close as possible to commercial realization in the U.S. market before the case goes to trial. While it is not clear how "close" is close enough, simply having the product on the drawing boards is probably not enough. Similarly, any prototypes of a new product should be representative.[42] The entire purpose of the design-around product is to

39. *Certain Flash Memory Circuits*, Inv. No. 337-TA-382, Comm'n Op., at 19 (June 26, 1997).

40. Respondents may also seek modification or rescission of any remedial orders pursuant to 19 C.F.R. § 210.76 by citing "changed conditions of fact or law."

41. Merritt R. Blakeslee & Christopher V. Meservy, *Seeking Adjudication of a Design-Around in Section 337 Patent Infringement Investigations: Procedural Context and Strategic Considerations*, AIPLA Q. J. (Fall 2007).

42. *See, e.g., Certain Plastic Encapsulated Integrated Circuits*, Inv. No. 337-TA-315, Order No. 15, 1990 WL 710761, at *2 (Dec. 11, 1990) ("The question is not whether an individual exemplar is commercially available, but whether it is representative of circuits encapsulated by a respondent and thus reasonably calculated to lead to admissible evidence[.]"); *cf.* Sierra Applied

give the ITC jurisdiction over the new product so as to obtain a hoped-for non-infringement decision. Such a decision will avoid future difficulties with Customs or the need to seek an advisory opinion after an exclusion order has issued. By the time an advisory opinion can issue, it is often too late to reenter the U.S. market because key customers have been lost.

Sci., Inc. v. Advanced Energy Indus., Inc., 363 F.3d 1361, 1379 (Fed. Cir. 2004) (noting that infringement finding based on products in a "relatively early stage of development" is not desirable because "[t]he greater the variability of the [product], particularly as to its potentially infringing features, the greater the chance that the court's judgment will be purely advisory, detached from the eventual, actual content of that subject—in short, detached from eventual reality.").

CHAPTER 16

Frontiers of Section 337

Though primarily used in recent years for protection of intellectual property rights, particularly patents, Section 337 was drafted as a trade statute that encompassed a broad range of "unfair acts" within its scope. This chapter addresses the "frontiers" of Section 337—places where the statute has rarely traveled but nevertheless might reach. For example, though not generally thought of as an antitrust forum, the Commission has used Section 337 to investigate violations of U.S. antitrust laws.[1] Furthermore, practitioners have credibly suggested that the Commission could adjudicate Section 337 complaints alleging an "unfair method of competition," such as the violation of labor laws, breach of environmental standards, and the importation of unsafe consumer products, though no such cases have yet been brought.

This chapter also discusses the extraterritorial reach of Section 337, as highlighted in a recent trade secret-based investigation. The potential for an increase in pharmaceutical patent litigation, where the Commission might provide an alternative to the Hatch-Waxman Act's district court litigation framework, is also discussed. The chapter concludes with a discussion of the effect of the America Invents Act on the ITC.

---

1. *See Certain Airtight Cast-Iron Stoves*, Inv. No. 337-TA-69, Comm'n Op., at 5–6 (Jan. 1981); Tom M. Schaumberg, *Section 337 of the Tariff Act of 1930 as an Antitrust Remedy*, 27 J. Am. & Foreign Antitrust & Trade Reg. 51 (1982).

A. NON-IP CAUSES OF ACTION AS UNFAIR METHODS OF COMPETITION

Section 337 was enacted first as Section 316 of the Tariff Act of 1922[2] and subsequently was renumbered as Section 337 by the Tariff Act of 1930, also known as the Smoot-Hawley Tariff Act.[3] Its original purpose was to provide relief to U.S. industries against unfair competition from importers in light of the inability to obtain jurisdiction over foreign manufacturers in U.S. courts and the absence of effective remedies under the laws of the countries where the importers were located. The statute was intended to cover a broad range of unfair acts and was not confined to, or even primarily focused on, the protection of intellectual property. Because the jurisdiction of the Commission in Section 337 investigations is nationwide and in rem,[4] the statute is, potentially, a very powerful tool in matters involving a wide range of causes of action, notwithstanding the forum's reputation for focusing on infringement of intellectual property rights.[5]

Subsection 337(a)(1)(A) prohibits, in relevant part, "[u]nfair methods of competition and unfair acts in the importation of articles" into the United States.[6] The terms "unfair methods of competition" and "unfair acts" are not defined in subsection 337(a)(1)(A), effectively giving the Commission broad discretion in construing the scope of the statute.[7] The Commission has construed these terms to include, inter alia, false designation of origin, misappropriation of trade secrets, false labeling, false

---

2. Tariff Act of 1922, Pub. L. No. 67-318, § 316, 42 Stat. 858, 943 (1922) (current version at 19 U.S.C. § 1337 (2006)).

3. Tariff Act of 1930, Pub. L. No. 71-361, § 337, 46 Stat. 590, 703 (1930) (codified as amended at 19 U.S.C. § 1337 (2006)).

4. *See* Sealed Air Corp. v. U.S. Int'l Trade Comm'n, 645 F.2d 976, 985–86 (C.C.P.A. 1981).

5. *See, e.g., Certain Nut Jewelry & Parts Thereof,* Inv. No. 337-TA-229, Initial Determination, at 10 (Nov. 1986) (assuming jurisdiction though no intellectual property right was at issue in the case, because the failure to mark the proper country of origin was an "unfair act" under Section 337).

6. 19 U.S.C. § 1337(a)(1)(A) (2006). The statute also extends to the sale of such articles by the owner, importer, or consignee.

7. *In re* Von Clemm, 229 F.2d 441, 443–44 (C.C.P.A. 1955) ("Congress intended to allow [the Commission] wide discretion in determining what practices are to be regarded as unfair.").

advertising, violations of the Digital Millennium Copyright Act, and antitrust violations.[8]

As long as the other statutory requirements are satisfied, including importation, domestic industry, and injury,[9] the universe of "unfair methods of competition" potentially within the scope of Section 337 is limited only by the complainant's imagination. The following discussion addresses causes of action that have rarely, if ever, been asserted at the ITC but could take on increasing importance in the future.

1. Antitrust

There is little dispute that antitrust violations can constitute an "unfair method of competition" under Section 337.[10] Nevertheless, for many years Section 337 was considered unsuitable for antitrust claims because the only available remedy in the event the Commission found a violation was an exclusion order, which restrained trade rather than encouraged trade.[11] As a result, prior to amendment of the statute in 1974, the Commission instituted only two Section 337 investigations based on antitrust causes of action and in both cases found no antitrust-based violation.[12]

---

8. *See, e.g., Certain Universal Transmitters for Garage Door Openers*, Inv. No. 337-TA-497, Initial Determination, at 8-10 (Nov. 4, 2003) (Notice of Commission Determination to Affirm Initial Determination Denying Temporary Relief issued Nov. 24, 2003) (DMCA); *Certain Electronic Audio & Related Equip.*, Inv. No. 337-TA-7, Opinion of Comm'rs, at 2–3 (Apr. 1976) (predatory pricing); *Certain Alkaline Batteries*, Inv. No. 337-TA-165, Views of Comm'rs, at 1 (Nov. 1984) (false labeling and false designation of origin); *Certain Floppy Disk Drives & Components Thereof*, Inv. No. 337-TA-203, Comm'n Op., at 2 (Sept. 1985) (breach of contract).

9. Injury is not a required element in investigations based on statutory intellectual property, but remains a requirement in all other types of investigations into "unfair methods of competition." *See, e.g., Certain Digital Multimeters, & Prods. With Multimeter Functionality*, Inv. No. 337-TA-588, Order No. 22 (Initial Determination), at 16–18 (Jan. 14, 2008) (discussing the "broad range of indicia" considered in injury determination as it pertains to trade dress) (unreviewed); *see also infra* Chapter 3, "Types of Investigations."

10. *See, e.g.*, Ting-Ting Kao, *Reexamining Antitrust Claims Under Section 337*, 337 REPORTER VOL. XXIII, Summer 2007, at 4.

11. *See, e.g.*, Will E. Leonard & F. David Foster, *The Metamorphosis of the U.S. International Trade Commission Under the Trade Act of 1974*, 16 VA. J. INT'L L. 719, 754 (1976) (an exclusion order has always seemed to be an "inappropriate remedy" for antitrust violations because it is anticompetitive).

12. *Certain Watches, Watch Movements & Watch Parts*, USITC Pub. 177 (1966); *Certain Tractor Parts*, USITC Pub. 443 (1971).

The 1974 amendments to the statute gave the Commission the power to issue cease and desist orders for violations of Section 337, a potentially more appealing and appropriate remedy for addressing antitrust violations.[13] Commentators subsequently predicted an increase in the number of antitrust-based Section 337 complaints.[14] Nevertheless, complaints alleging antitrust causes of action remain infrequent. Most of the more recent Section 337 antitrust investigations ended with a finding of no violation,[15] and in the one case where the Commission found a violation, the Commission's cease and desist order was overturned by the President on public policy grounds.[16]

Although antitrust claims are not often raised, this should not be interpreted to mean that Section 337 does not cover or provide sufficient relief to these claims. The language of the statute covers any "unfair methods of competition and unfair acts," which would include antitrust violations; the ITC website lists "antitrust claims relating to imported goods" as a type of claim that may be asserted under Section 337;[17] and the statute states that the Commission must consult with the Federal Trade Commission when appropriate, which suggests that Congress intended

---

13. *See Certain Elec. Audio & Related Equip. (Electronic Audio)*, Inv. No. 337-TA-7, USITC Pub. 768, at 30 (Apr. 1976) (Section 337 is "clearly a type of antitrust regulation," and application of Section 337 as an antitrust regulation "has been further substantiated" in light of the statute's authorization to the Commission of the power to issue cease and desist orders.). Section 337 was subsequently amended in 1988 and 1994, but these amendments had no effect on limiting the statute's scope.

14. *See* L. Peter Farkas, *Litigating Antitrust Claims and Defenses Before the International Trade Commission*, 2 A.B.A. ANTITRUST 26 (1987); Schaumberg, *supra* note 1.

15. *See Certain Electrically Resistive Monocomponent Toner & "Black Powder" Preparations Therefor*, Inv. No. 337-TA-253, Comm'n Action & Order, at 1–2 (Mar. 1988); *Certain Airtight Cast-Iron Stoves*, Inv. No. 337-TA-69, Comm'n Op., at 5–8 (Jan. 1981); *Electronic Audio*, USITC Pub. 768; *Certain Tractor Parts*, USITC Pub. 443, at 1–3 (1971); *Certain Watches, Watch Movements & Watch Parts*, USITC Pub. 177 (1966).

16. *Certain Welded Steel Pipe & Tube*, Inv. No. 337-TA-29, Comm'n Determination & Action, at 1–4 (Feb. 1978) (finding predatory pricing by Japanese producers and issuing a cease and desist order); Presidential Determination of April 22, 1978: Welded Stainless Steel Pipe & Tube Industry, 43 Fed. Reg. 17,789 (Apr. 26, 1978) (citing "the need to avoid duplication and conflicts in the administration of the unfair trade practice laws of the United States").

17. www.usitc.gob/intellectual_property/ (last visited April 13, 2012).

antitrust claims to be brought at the Commission and aimed to provide a solution for the agencies' jurisdictional overlap.[18]

The potential of Section 337 as an antitrust enforcement statute has clearly not been reached.

2. Uncharted Waters: Unfair Labor Practices, Sustainable Environmental Practices, and Unsafe Consumer Products

Congress, by declining to define restrictively the terms "unfair methods of competition" and "unfair acts," intended to enact a statute effective against "every type and form of unfair practice."[19] Significantly, the statute was enacted to protect domestic labor as well as industry, as illustrated by legislative history expressing approval of the bill that became Section 337 due to its "honest protection of American labor and industry and agriculture."[20] Thus, notwithstanding the forum's predominant focus on intellectual property–based allegations, Section 337 could reach a wide variety of "unfair acts" that have yet to be the subject of an investigation at the Commission.

Commentators have proposed, for example, the use of Section 337 to redress unfair competition based on unfair labor practices, including the use of child labor.[21] Similarly, although no such complaint has yet been filed at the Commission, a Section 337 investigation could conceivably be based on unfair competition arising from the use of unsustainable practices in manufacturing, agriculture, or fishing. Such practices have been a long-standing source of contention between major trading nations at the World Trade Organization, but the ITC could become an appropriate forum for the resolution of such disputes. Yet another potential area for use of Section 337 is to exclude the importation of unsafe consumer products. Although no such complaint has been filed at the Commission,

---

18. Ting-Ting Kao, *Reexamining Antitrust Claims under Section 337*, ITCTLA 337 Reporter Summer Associate Edition, 2007, at 4.

19. *See Certain Welded Steel Pipe & Tube*, Inv. No. 337-TA-29, Comm'n Determination & Action, at 1–4 (Feb. 1978); *see also* 67 S. Rep. No. 595, at 3 (1922) (legislative intent regarding Section 316 of the Tariff Act of 1922, the predecessor to The Tariff Act of 1930).

20. 71 Cong. Rec. 1566 (1929) (statement of Reps. Kelly and Goodwin).

21. *See* Tom M. Schaumberg, *A Revitalized Section 337 to Prohibit Unfairly Traded Imports*, 77 J. Pat. & Trademark Off. Soc'y 259 (1995); *see also* Bryan A. Edens, *An Expanded Perspective: Child Labor Claims Under Section 337*, 337 Reporter Vol. XXIII, Summer 2007, at 13.

at least one practitioner speculates that imports that violate federal or state safety standards could be excluded under Section 337.[22]

B. EXTRATERRITORIAL APPLICATION OF THE STATUTE

The extent to which Section 337 can reach "unfair methods of competition" or "unfair acts" that take place overseas has not always been clear. The Federal Circuit's recent decision in *TianRui Group v. U.S. International Trade Commission*[23] responds to these concerns and clarifies and arguably expands the scope of Section 337's extraterritorial application.

In *TianRui*, the Federal Circuit examined whether the Commission could exercise jurisdiction over imported products manufactured using trade secrets misappropriated in China.[24] The complainant, Amsted Industries, a manufacturer of cast steel railway wheels in the United States, had licensed a Chinese company to manufacture wheels using Amsted's technology. The respondent, TianRui, had attempted to license the technology, but when negotiations between the two companies failed, TianRui hired employees from the Chinese licensee, resulting in a finding of misappropriation of Amsted's trade secrets.

In defending against Amsted's Section 337 complaint, TianRui argued, inter alia, that the statute did not give the Commission authority to investigate the alleged misappropriation because it occurred in China.[25] The Commission, and on appeal, the Federal Circuit, disagreed.[26] While the Federal Circuit acknowledged that U.S. statutes are typically presumed to "apply only within the jurisdiction of the United States,"[27] it determined that the presumption does not apply to Section 337 for three reasons.[28]

---

22. *See* Gary M. Hnath, *The Use of Section 337 in Non-Patent Matters*, 998 PRACTICING LAW INST./PAT. 137, at 142 (2010).

23. 661 F.3d 1322 (Fed. Cir. 2011).

24. *Id.* at 1324.

25. *Id.* at 1325.

26. As a threshold matter, the Federal Circuit held that the Commission had erred by applying the trade secret law of Illinois, rather than a "uniform federal standard." *Id.* at 1327. The Federal Circuit held this error to be harmless, concluding that the same result would have been reached under the "uniform federal standard." *Id.* at 1328. The Federal Circuit did not further expound upon the content of the applicable federal standard.

27. *Id.* at 1328 (quoting EEOC v. Arabian Am. Oil Co., 499 U.S. 244, 248 (1991)).

28. *Id.* at 1329.

First, because Section 337 governs importation, it is an "inherently international transaction."[29] Second, Section 337 had not been applied to sanction "purely extraterritorial conduct, because the foreign activity resulted in the importation of goods into the United States."[30] Third, the legislative history of Section 337 supported the Commission's interpretation that the statute permits the Commission to consider conduct that occurs abroad.[31]

TianRui arguably vests the Commission with broad authority over almost any "unfair methods of competition and unfair acts" so long as they are connected to a product imported into the United States and injure a domestic industry.

C. STANDARD-ESSENTIAL PATENTS AND FRAND AGREEMENTS

The increasing popularity and complexity of electronic devices has led to a corresponding increase in standard-setting organizations (SSOs), which allow industry participants to decide on technology standards for devices in a given field. Because standards are often covered by patents owned by various members of the organization, SSOs typically require that the owners of patents essential to adherence to a particular standard license those patents according to fair, reasonable, and non-discriminatory (FRAND) terms.[32] Many involved in standard-heavy industries are concerned that the ability to seek exclusionary relief at the ITC will jeopardize the SSO system, with negative effects on competition and consumer welfare.[33]

Respondents in Section 337 actions involving SSOs have asserted affirmative defenses that standard-essential patents are unenforceable, asserting theories of equitable estoppel, contract, implied license, and waiver.[34] The fact that a complainant is a member of an SSO and its

---

29. *Id.*
30. *Id.*
31. *Id.* at 1330.
32. Also referred to as "RAND" (reasonable and non-discriminatory) terms.
33. *See* Paul M. Bartkowski and Evan H. Langdon, *Standard-Essential Patents: An Increasingly Contentious Issue at the U.S. International Trade Commission,* WASHINGTON LEGAL FOUNDATION, Contemporary Legal Note Series No. 71 (July 2012).
34. *See, e.g., Certain Gaming & Entertainment Consoles, Related Software, & Components Thereof* (Contemporary Legal Note Series No. 71) (July 2012), Inv. No. 337-TA-752, Initial Determination, at 282 (May 10, 2012) (rejecting respondent's affirmative defenses of implied license and equitable

asserted patent is subject to FRAND obligations is not dispositive on the issue of whether a respondent has violated Section 337 with respect to that patent. In investigations involving such patents, the Commission is required to investigate whether a violation has occurred under Section 337, which is informed by principles of patent law. If the Commission determines that a violation has occurred, as in all cases, the Commission must then consider the statutorily contemplated remedies in light of the public-interest factors set forth in Section 337.

The Commission has not squarely addressed whether an LEO or CDO is appropriate in such cases; however, recent cases present the Commission with opportunities to do so.[35] These recent cases may be the first opportunity for the Commission, as opposed to an ALJ, to determine whether to issue an exclusion order where the patent-in-suit is subject to a FRAND commitment.

Pending resolution of this issue, some light can be shed on how FRAND issues at the Commission might be handled in the near future. In *Dynamic Random Access Memories*, the ITC indicated that it was not the appropriate forum for patent litigation involving a contractual commitment to renegotiate an expired license in good faith.[36] There, the ALJ

---

estoppel where four of the five patents complainant asserted against respondent were subject to commitments by complainant to license patents according FRAND terms) (Commission Determination to Review a Final Initial Determination Finding a Violation of Section 337: Remand of the Investigation to the Administrative Law Judge issued June 29, 2012).

35. *Id.*; *see also Certain Wireless Commc'n Devices, Portable Music & Data Processing Devices, Computers & Components Thereof (Portable Music & Data Processing Devices)*, Inv. No. 337-TA-745, Notice of Comm'n Decision to Review in Part a Final Initial Determination Finding a Violation of Section 337; Request for Written Submissions (June 25, 2012) (requesting briefing specific to RAND-based defenses and whether exclusionary relief is appropriate in cases involving patents subject to RAND commitments); *Certain Elect. Devices, Including Wireless Commc'n Devices, Portable Music & Data Processing Devices, & Tablet Computers (Portable Music & Data Devices)*, Inv. No. 337-TA-794, Order No. 47, at 35–38 (Mar. 30, 2012) (denying respondent's motion for summary determination terminating the investigation as to two patents based on complainant's agreements with chip suppliers and FRAND commitments, noting that the ITC was not the "appropriate tribunal" to address whether complainant had breached its FRAND obligations to the relevant SSO).

36. *Certain Dynamic Random Access Memories, Components Thereof & Prods. Containing Same*, Inv. No. 337-TA-242, Initial Determination (May 21, 1987).

concluded that the complainant's promises to negotiate a license renewal were "inconsistent with a suit against [the respondent] for an injunction" and thus, the complainant was barred "from recourse to the equity power of the Commission."[37] The complainant's agreement to negotiate a license renewal is arguably analogous to an SSO member's agreement to negotiate a license on FRAND terms. In particular, SSOs seek to prevent members from advocating the use of their patents as an industry standard, only to try to enjoin competitors from practicing that standard. Indeed, issuing an exclusion order or cease and desist order on a patent subject to a FRAND commitment is arguably inconsistent with SSOs' general policy requiring members to make FRAND commitments.[38] However, if the SSO member has met its obligation and the infringer has refused a license, exclusion may well be appropriate.

The Commission is limited by statute in its discretion to decide upon and issue relief. Of note in the FRAND context, Section 337 mandates that the Commission investigate violations of Section 337 upon complaint and determine whether or not a violation has occurred in each investigation unless one of two statutory exceptions applies.[39] These exceptions provide that the Commission may terminate an investigation without making such a determination only by (1) issuing a consent order or (2) on the basis of an agreement between the private parties to the investigation, including an agreement to present the matter for arbitration.[40] Therefore, as long as a complaint has been filed, the Commission appears bound by Section 337 to institute an investigation and determine whether a violation has occurred—regardless of whether a patent subject to a FRAND commitment is implicated.[41] Notably, however, even if the Commission finds that a violation has occurred with respect to a patent subject to FRAND commitment, the Commission must still consider the

---

37. *Id.*

38. *Cf.* Apple, Inc. v. Motorola, Inc., No. 1:11-cv-08540, slip op. at 18–19 (N.D. Ill. June 22, 2012) ("I don't see how, given FRAND, I would be justified in enjoining Apple . . . unless Apple refuses to pay a royalty that meets the FRAND requirement.").

39. *See* 19 U.S.C. § 1337(c) (2006).

40. *Id.*

41. Spansion v. U.S. Int'l Trade Comm'n, 629 F.3d 1331, 1358 (Fed. Cir. 2010) (noting the Commission's limited discretion in determining whether to issue the statutorily provided relief; "[b]y statute, the Commission is required to issue an exclusion order upon the finding of a Section 337 violation absent a finding that the effects of one of the statutorily-enumerated public interest factors counsel otherwise").

statutory public interest factors set forth in Section 337(d)(1) when considering whether to issue remedial orders. The determination whether to grant relief will, therefore, depend on the Commission's public interest analysis in each FRAND-based investigation.[42]

D. PHARMACEUTICAL COMPANIES AND LITIGATION BEYOND THE HATCH-WAXMAN ACT

The ITC has recently encountered a modest uptick in Section 337 pharmaceutical patent litigation.[43] Traditionally, patent-holding pharmaceutical companies have infrequently filed Section 337 complaints because of regulations promulgated under the Hatch-Waxman Act.[44] The Hatch-Waxman Act was created in 1984 in response to some negative results of the 1962 Federal Food, Drug, and Cosmetic Act,[45] such as higher costs for product development and longer drug approval periods. The Hatch-Waxman Act requires drug creators to list the patents covering their drugs in the Food and Drug Administration's *Approved Drug Products with Therapeutic Equivalence Evaluations*, more commonly known as the "Orange Book."[46] While almost all of the relevant patents related to the drug must be listed in the Orange Book, there are a few exceptions to this requirement, one of which is process patents.[47] The Act also created an

---

42. The recent determination to review in *Portable Music & Data Devices* provides the Commission with its first opportunity to address FRAND-related issues. *Certain Wireless Commc'n Devices, Portable Music & Data Processing Devices, Computers & Components Thereof*, Inv. No. 337-TA-745, Notice of Comm'n Decision to Review in Part a Final Initial Determination Finding a Violation of Section 337; Request for Written Submissions (June 25, 2012); *see also* Bartkowski & Langdon, *supra* note 31.

43. *See, e.g., Certain Gemcitabine & Prods. Containing Same*, Inv. No. 337-TA-766; *Certain Vaginal Ring Birth Control Devices*, Inv. No. 337-TA-768; *Certain Coenzyme Q10 Prods. & Methods of Making Same*, Inv. No. 337-TA-790.

44. Drug Price Competition and Patent Term Restoration Act of 1984, Pub. L. No. 98-417, 98 Stat. 1585 (1984).

45. Kefauver-Harris Drug Amendments of 1962, Pub. L. No. 87-781, 76 Stat. 780 (1962).

46. 21 C.F.R. §§ 314.3(b), 314.53(e).

47. 21 C.F.R. § 314.53(b) ("Process patents, patent claiming packaging, patents claiming metabolites, and patents claiming intermediates are not covered by this section, and information on these patents must not be submitted to the FDA.").

exclusivity period for new drugs, during which time generic versions may not be made.

If a generic drug maker wishes to begin manufacturing a drug in the Orange Book within the exclusivity period, it must file an Abbreviated New Drug Application (ANDA) with the FDA and notify the original drug creator that it believes the related brand-name drug patent(s) are invalid or that the generic drug will infringe the patent(s). Once the drug creator receives such a notice, it may choose to file suit against the generic manufacturer for patent infringement in a federal district court.[48] Process and other non-Orange Book-listed patents need not be litigated in district court, however, and can form the basis of a Section 337 complaint at the ITC.

In *Gemcitabine*, Eli Lilly filed a Section 337 complaint against several generic drug makers for infringement of a process patent covering the manufacture of one of its cancer drugs.[49] Prior to bringing its Section 337 complaint, Eli Lilly had litigated two patents covering the chemical composition of the cancer drugs in U.S. district court under the procedures set forth in the Hatch-Waxman Act. Both patents covering the cancer drug's composition were found invalid by the district court, thereby allowing generic drug makers to immediately sell the drug pending approval of its ANDA. However, Eli Lilly also owned an unexpired process patent for manufacturing the cancer drug that had not been subject to the prior patent litigation brought under the Hatch-Waxman Act. The case was later terminated based on a settlement agreement.

It remains unclear whether other pharmaceutical companies will follow Eli Lilly's lead in asserting drug patents at the ITC. At least one other pharmaceutical process patent has since been asserted at the Commission.[50] Insofar that asserting a process patent provides an additional means for maintaining market exclusivity, the Commission provides a potentially favorable forum. In particular, the accelerated schedule of ITC investigations may allow process patent holders to obtain a judgment before generic manufacturers can design around the process patent.

---

48. 21 U.S.C. § 355(j)(5)(B) (2006).

49. *Certain Gemcitabine & Prods. Containing Same*, Inv. No. 337-TA-766, Complaint, at 1 (Jan. 20, 2011).

50. *See Certain Coenzyme Q10 Products & Methods of Making Same*, Inv. No. 337-TA-790, Complaint, at 7 (Feb. 2, 2012).

E. THE AMERICA INVENTS ACT PATENT REFORMS AND POSSIBLE EFFECT ON ITC LITIGATION

The Leahy-Smith America Invents Act (AIA)[51] has recently altered the patent law landscape. Two particular AIA provisions stand to impact Section 337 patent investigations at the ITC: (1) heightened joinder requirements for joining multiple defendants in patent infringement civil actions brought before U.S. district courts, and (2) new USPTO postgrant review proceedings.

1. Strengthened Joinder Requirements in U.S. District Courts under AIA § 19

Prior to the AIA, some circuits interpreted broadly the joinder rules of Rule 20 of the Federal Rules of Civil Procedure with respect to patent infringement actions. Essentially, the sole requirement in those circuits for joining multiple defendants was merely that the defendants all allegedly infringed the patent(s)-in-suit.[52] The AIA amends 35 U.S.C. § 299 to explicitly reject this broad interpretation of the joinder rule. To join multiple defendants in a single patent civil action, the revised statute requires that (1) the same transaction or occurrence relating to infringement give rise to the cause of action against each defendant and (2) there be "questions of fact common to all defendants or counterclaim defendants."[53] Furthermore, the amended Section 299 states that "accused infringers may not be joined in one action as defendants or counterclaim defendants, or have their actions consolidated for trial, based solely on allegations that they each have infringed the patent or patents in suit."[54] Thus, allegations that multiple defendants infringe the patents in suit are insufficient for joining multiple defendants in a patent civil action. Bringing multi-defendant patent lawsuits in U.S. district courts is now undoubtedly more difficult than prior to the AIA.

---

51. Leahy-Smith America Invents Act, Pub. L. 112-29, 125 Stat. 284 (2011).

52. The Eastern District of Texas, for example, was a district that applied this broad interpretation of joinder under the Federal Rules prior to the AIA. Since the passage of the AIA, that district has preliminarily encountered a decrease in the number of patent suits brought before it. *See AIA Changes the Role of the Eastern District of Texas,* PATENTLY-O (Mar. 20, 2012), *available at* http://www.patentlyo.com/patent/2012/03/aia-changes-the-role-of-the-eastern-district-of-texas.html.

53. Leahy-Smith America Invents Act § 19(d)(1), 125 Stat. at 332–33 (2011) (amending 35 U.S.C. § 299(a)(1)–(2)).

54. *Id.* (amending 35 U.S.C. § 299(b)).

Because Section 299's heightened joinder requirements only apply to "civil actions"[55]—patent lawsuits brought in U.S. district courts— Section 299 does not affect the Commission's conduct of Section 337 investigations. Therefore, the Commission's practice of joining multiple respondents in a single investigation remains unaltered by the AIA. In fact, joining multiple respondents is effectively required when a complainant seeks a limited exclusion order covering "downstream products."[56] Consequently, the number of Section 337 patent investigations could increase due to complaints filed by patent owners who seek to reduce net litigation expenses by asserting their patents in a single investigation against several accused infringers rather than in separate district court litigations. In this vein, non-practicing entities, insofar that they are able to meet the Commission's domestic industry requirements, may increasingly turn to the Commission as a preferred patent litigation forum.

2. New Post-Grant and Inter Partes Review Procedures

Due to its statutory obligation to conduct investigations in an expeditious fashion, the Commission rarely grants stays of Section 337 investigations in light of a pending PTO reexamination proceeding.[57] Under the AIA, however, a new system of "inter partes" and "post-grant" review at the PTO has been established to cancel recently issued patents on grounds of invalidity.[58] Under the system, after a patent issues, a nine-month window initiates in which any party other than the patentee may petition the PTO to find the patent invalid. The PTO must fully adjudicate the proceedings within twelve to eighteen months[59]—a speedier resolution than

---

55. *Id.* (amending 35 U.S.C. § 299(a)).
56. *See, e.g.*, Kyocera v. U.S. Int'l Trade Comm'n, 545 F.3d 1310 (Fed. Cir. 2008) (holding that manufacturers of downstream products should be named as respondents in order to obtain a limited exclusion order against them).
57. *See infra* Chapter 6, Section H, "Stays of the Procedural Schedule."
58. *See generally* Leahy-Smith America Invents Act § 6, 125 Stat. at 299–313 (2011). The inter partes review procedures will take effect September 16, 2012 and will be available for any patent. Leahy-Smith America Invents Act § 6(c)(2), 125 Stat. at 304. Post-grant review procedures will also take effect September 16, 2012, but will only apply to patents with an effective filing date of March 16, 2013, or later. *Id.* § 6(f)(2)(A), 125 Stat. at 311.
59. *Id.* § 6a (amending 35 U.S.C. § 316(a)(11)), § 6(d) (amending 35 U.S.C. § 326(a)(11)).

typically occurs in existing reexamination proceedings.[60] Additionally, after completion of the PTO's post-grant review or inter partes review, the private party that initiated the review proceeding is precluded from raising in subsequent litigation any of the invalidity arguments it raised or could have raised at the PTO.[61] This issue preclusion rule applies not only to U.S. district courts, but also to Section 337 investigations before the Commission.[62]

After inter partes or post-grant review proceedings are filed at the PTO, any subsequent district court action challenging the validity of the patent must be stayed pending resolution of the PTO proceeding.[63] This mandatory stay requirement, however, does not apply to Section 337 investigations at the Commission.[64] Parties that cannot afford to wait may choose to enforce their patent rights at the Commission rather than in district court. However, in light of the potential preclusive effect of inter partes or post-grant review under the AIA, as well as the speedier resolution of such review compared to traditional reexamination, it is possible that the Commission may be more inclined to grant stays depending on the progress of pending inter partes or post-grant review.

How the Commission responds to the AIA's post-grant and inter partes review procedures will be a development worth following in the coming years.

---

60. During the first three quarters of fiscal year 2010, the average time from filing to Notice of Intent to Issue a Reexamination Certificate ranged from 28 to 32 months. U.S. Patent and Trademark Office, *Reexaminations – FY 2010* (June 30, 2010), *available at* http://reexamcenter.com/wp-content/uploads/2009/09/2010-06-30-Operations.pdf.

61. Leahy-Smith America Invents Act § 6a (amending 35 U.S.C. § 315(e)), § 6(b) (amending 35 U.S.C. § 325(e)) (outlining the estoppels effects of inter partes review and post grant review respectively).

62. *Id.* at § 6a (amending 35 U.S.C. § 315(e)(2)).

63. *Id.* at § 6(a) (amending 35 U.S.C. § 315(a)(2)), § 6(d) (amending 35 U.S.C. § 325(a)(2).

64. *Id.* (mentions only civil actions before the court).

Index

P

Rejoinder requirements impacting Section 337 investigations, 276–77
Relief, types of, 183–204
Remedial orders, 184
Remedy, 183–204
  adversely affected parties filling an appeal, 224–25
  and downstream relief, 199–202
  bond, 195–99
  Commission enforcement of, 251–63
  preclusion of due to public interest factors, 214–16
  Presidential review of Commission remedial orders, 219–22
  temporary rescission of, 202–04
  types
    cease and desist order (CDO), 191–93
    general exclusion order, 186–90
    limited exclusion order, 184–86
    temporary exclusion order, 193–95
Reply post-hearing briefs, 180
Requests for admission in discovery process, 124–26
Res judicata effect, 19, 245
Respondent in Section 337 investigation, 49–52
  from foreign countries, 6, 51–52
Revenue-driven licensing, 76
Ride-On Toy Vehicles, 68
Rotary Wheel Printing Systems, 69, 86

S

Safe harbor provision, 62, 148, 233
Sale for importation provision, 57
Sale in the United States after importation provision, 57

Sanctions in discovery process, 147–52
Seagate Technologies, Inc. v. U.S. International Trade Commission, 226
Section 337
  advantages of, 13–20
  applications of
    extraterritorial, 270–71
    redressing child labor, 269
    standard-essential patents and FRAND agreements, 271–74
    sustainable environmental practices, 269
    unfair methods of competition, 266–70
    unsafe consumer products, 269–70
    with antitrust violations, 267–69
  as a trade statute, 10–11
  interpretation of statute, 231–35
  jurisdiction over the accused products, 13–14
Section 337 decisions, review by Federal Circuit, 223–37
Section 337 investigation, 89–110
  affirmation of determinations by higher courts, 15
  and approval of violation and remedy by the President, 12–13
  complainant, 48–49
  consideration of the public interest mandate, 11–12
  consolidation of investigations, 103–06
  contrasted with infringement action in federal court, 3–4, 9
  copyright infringement, 25–27
  designation of "more complicated" investigation, 110

About the ABA Section of Intellectual Property Law

From its strength within the American Bar Association, the ABA Section of Intellectual Property Law (ABA-IPL) advances the development and improvement of intellectual property laws and their fair and just administration. The Section furthers the goals of its members by sharing knowledge and balanced insight on the full spectrum of intellectual property law and practice, including patents, trademarks, copyright, industrial design, literary and artistic works, scientific works, and innovation. Providing a forum for rich perspectives and reasoned commentary, ABA-IPL serves as the ABA voice of intellectual property law within the profession, before policy makers, and with the public.

ABA Section of Intellectual Property Law
Order today! Call 1-800-285-2221
Monday-Friday, 7:30 a.m. – 5:30 p.m., Central Time
or Visit the ABA Web Store: www.ShopABA.org

Qty	Title	Regular Price	ABA Member Price	ABA-IPL Member Price	Total
_____	ADR Advocacy, Strategies, and Practice in Intellectual Property Cases (5370195)	$139.95	$129.95	$114.95	$_____
_____	ANDA Litigation (5370199)	$299.00	$299.00	$249.00	$_____
_____	Annual Review of Intellectual Property Law Developments 2011 (5370196)	$169.95	$149.95	$134.95	$_____
_____	Annual Review of Intellectual Property Law Developments 2010 (5370191)	$149.95	$127.95	$119.95	$_____
_____	Annual Review of Intellectual Property Law Developments 2009 (5370169)	$149.95	$127.95	$119.95	$_____
_____	Annual Review of Intellectual Property Law Developments 2006-2008 (5370164)	$149.95	$139.95	$129.95	$_____
_____	Computer Games and Virtual Worlds (5370172)	$69.95	$59.95	$55.95	$_____
_____	Distance Learning and Copyright (5370163)	$89.95	$89.95	$79.95	$_____
_____	Fundamentals of Intellectual Property Valuation (5370143)	$69.95	$59.95	$49.95	$_____
_____	The Intellectual Property Handbook (5620116)	$110.00	$100.00	$90.00	$_____
_____	IP Attorney's Handbook for Insurance Coverage in Intellectual Property Disputes (5370168)	$129.95	$110.95	$103.95	$_____
_____	A Lawyer's Guide to Section 337 Investigations before the U.S. International Trade Commission (5370171)	$89.95	$76.95	$71.95	$_____
_____	A Legal Strategist's Guide to Trademark Trial and Appeal Board Practice (5370190)	$129.95	$110.95	$103.95	$_____
_____	New Practitioner's Guide to Intellectual Property (5370198)	$89.95	$89.95	$69.95	$_____
_____	The Patent Infringement Litigation Handbook (1620416)	$149.95	$129.95	$129.95	$_____
_____	Patent Obviousness in the Wake of *KSR International Co. v. Teleflex Inc.* (5370189)	$129.95	$110.95	$103.95	$_____
_____	Preliminary Relief in Patent Infringement Disputes (5370194)	$119.95	$109.95	$94.95	$_____
_____	Settlement of Patent Litigation and Disputes (5370192)	$179.95	$159.95	$144.95	$_____
_____	The Tech Contracts Handbook (5370188)	$89.95	$76.95	$71.95	$_____
_____	Trademark and Deceptive Advertising Surveys (5370197)	$179.95	$179.95	$134.95	$_____

* Tax
DC residents add 6%
IL residents add 9.50%

Payment
❏ Check enclosed payable to the ABA
❏ VISA ❏ Mastercard ❏ American Express

* Tax $_____
** Shipping/Handling $_____
TOTAL $_____

**Shipping/Handling
Up to $49.99	$5.95
$50 to $99.99	$7.95
$100 to $199.99	$9.95
$200 to $499.99	$12.95
$500 to $999.99	$15.95
$1,000 and above	$18.95

Please allow 5 to 7 business days for UPS delivery. Need it sooner? Ask about overnight delivery. Call the ABA Service Center at 1-800-285-2221 for more information.

Guarantee: If – for any reason – you are not satisfied with your purchase, you may return it within 30 days of receipt for a complete refund of the price of the book(s). No questions asked!

Name_____

Firm/Organization_____

Address_____

City_____ State_____ Zipcode_____

Phone_____ E-mail_____
(in case of questions about your order)

Please mail your order to:
ABA Publication Orders, P.O. Box 10892, Chicago, Illinois 60610-0892
Phone: 1-800-285-2221 or 312-988-5522 • Fax: 312-988-5568
E-mail: orders@abanet.org

Thank you for your order!

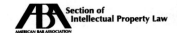

Section of Intellectual Property Law
AMERICAN BAR ASSOCIATION